The Art of Wen Cheng-ming (1470–1559)

The University of Michigan
Museum of Art, Ann Arbor
January 25 through February 29, 1976

Asia House Gallery, New York City
April 7 through June 7, 1976

Scholar Fishing (no. **XXXII**), detail

The Art of Wen Cheng-ming (1470-1559)

Richard Edwards

With an essay by
Anne De Coursey Clapp

And special contributions by
Ling-yün Shih Liu
Steven D. Owyoung
James Robinson
and other seminar members,
1974–1975

The University of Michigan,
Ann Arbor

Seminar members, 1974 and 1975:
  Bruce Darling
  Stephen Goldberg
  Ling-yün Shih Liu
  Steven D. Owyoung
  James Robinson
  Marsha Weidner

Published with the assistance of a grant from The JDR
3rd Fund and of a publications grant from the Horace
H. Rackham School of Graduate Studies, The University
of Michigan

Designed by University Publications, Doug Hesseltine,
  Supervisor of Graphic Arts
Composed in Garamond #3 by Central Trade Plant, Grand
  Rapids, Michigan
Printed by the John Henry Company, Lansing

Contents

Foreword

This exhibition continues a tradition of close cooperation between scholars in the field of Asian art and the staff of The University of Michigan Museum of Art. Earlier exhibitions and their accompanying catalogues, *The Painting of Tao-chi* and *The Poet Painters: Buson and His Followers,* have been recognized as having made significant contributions to their fields. It is our hope and belief that the present exhibition and its catalogue are worthy exemplars of this tradition.

Professor Richard Edwards, the exhibition's organizer, has recognized in his acknowledgments the assistance of many lenders, colleagues, and other scholars. I add my thanks to his on behalf of the Museum.

I wish to express, in addition, our gratitude to several individuals and organizations for their help in meeting the costs of this project: The Asia Society and Mr. Allen Wardwell, Director of Asia House Gallery, where the exhibition will be held following its Michigan showing; The JDR 3rd Fund and Mr. Richard Lanier, Director, Asian Cultural Program; the Horace H. Rackham School of Graduate Studies and Associate Dean Ralph B. Lewis; The University of Michigan Center for Chinese Studies and its director, Prof. Rhoads Murphey.

Finally, I am pleased to acknowledge the valuable contributions of several members of The University of Michigan staff: Mr. Hiram W. Woodward, Jr., Assistant Curator of the Museum of Art, on whom numerous editorial tasks have fallen; Mr. John E. Holmes, Assistant Director of the Museum, who has had primary responsibility for the installation of the exhibition; Jacquelynn R. Slee, Museum Registrar, Melissa Herrick, student assistant, and Andrew Jendrzejewski, Museum Technician, all of whom have shared the responsibility for the handling and care of the objects included; Mr. Douglas H. Hesseltine, Supervisor of Graphic Arts, University Publications Office, to whom all credit is due for the design of the catalogue, and Mr. John R. Hamilton, Senior Editor of the same office, who assisted in editorial and production phases of the catalogue. To these individuals and to the many other persons who have helped in various ways I extend my thanks on behalf of the Museum of Art.

Bret Waller
Director

Acknowledgments

An exhibition and catalogue of this nature is an undertaking both in time and space. As such one must acknowledge a wide range of assistance from various sources.

Grants from the Center for Chinese Studies and from the Rackham Graduate School of the University of Michigan allowed me a term of leave in 1973 and the opportunity to travel both to the People's Republic of China and to Hongkong, Japan, and Taiwan. As a result my knowledge of Wen Cheng-ming was increased immeasurably not only from actually being able to visit the city of Suchou itself, but from studying a wide range of paintings, including a few glimpses in Shanghai and Peking.

I owe a special debt to Dr. Chiang Fu-tsung, Director of the National Palace Museum in Taipei, for the kindness which he and his staff afforded me during a visit there in November of 1973. That was on the occasion of the incomparable exhibition of Ninety Years of Wu School Painting. That exhibition was organized by the Curator of Painting and Calligraphy, Chiang Chao-shen, whose knowledge and scholarship opened a whole new understanding of Suchou painting. I am particularly grateful to Chiang Chao-shen not only for that exhibition but for friendship and his studies on Wen Cheng-ming, without which neither an exhibition nor a catalogue of this scope would have been possible. In many ways this exhibition—admittedly on a less exalted level—is a counterpart of the great Palace Museum display. It is hoped that, in placing together paintings which ordinarily must be viewed separately in scattered geographical locations, a similarly coherent view of Wen Cheng-ming may be obtained to supplement what the Palace Museum has already offered. In connection with that exhibition I must also thank Louise Yuhas for supplying me with her translations of the comprehensive labels that were used.

In western scholarship my most especial debt is to Anne De Coursey Clapp, who in respect to Wen Cheng-ming, it must be admitted, arrived there first, but who has been both generous in sharing her knowledge and enthusiastic in support of this undertaking. Both her scholarship and her pen have accordingly enriched this catalogue.

The way an academician usually fosters both his research and teaching is to organize a seminar. There have been two such seminars at the University of Michigan—the first in the winter of 1974 dealing more generally with the painting of Wen Cheng-ming, the second in the winter of 1975 turning specifically to the exhibition itself and problems of selecting paintings and putting together a catalogue. While the names of seminar members are listed at the beginning of this publication, I can here extend my personal thanks to them and to Stephen Addiss who often joined in enthusiastic discussion and provided many a study photograph from his wide-ranging travels.

Because of the cooperative nature of the undertaking it has not always been possible to pinpoint individual contributions. While I must assume responsibility for the writing of the entries themselves, students have done most of the basic groundwork in assembling information on seals and colophons, often contributing important translations. Some have been able to carry out more specific tasks than others. In this connection particularly to be mentioned are the sections on seals and the index by Steven Owyoung, the designing of maps by James Robinson, and the identification of countless difficult seals, clarification in matters of translation, and the writing of Chinese characters by Ling-yün Shih Liu. James Robinson carried on important research during the summer of 1974 with the partial assistance of the Center for Chinese Studies at the University of Michigan. The carefully researched knowledge of Professor Ellen Laing has been often used and I wish to thank her particularly for her writing in entry XXXI. I am indebted to Elizabeth Bennett for supplying me with a copy of her Princeton undergraduate thesis on three Wen Cheng-ming scrolls. Two of her translations have been the basis for those printed here.

In the task of bringing sixty-odd works together from Asia, Europe, and America one has most to thank the collectors and museums themselves who have been so willing to cooperate. Friends are too many to acknowledge individually and I hope they will understand. In Japan, I must thank Kozo Sazaki for helping to show me Wen Cheng-ming. And I am especially indebted to Chozo Yamanouchi, both for guidance to Wen Cheng-ming and in his handling of negotiations in connection with vitally important loans. Bo Gyllensvärd and the staff of The Museum of Far Eastern Antiquities, Stockholm are thanked for making possible the loan from the Erickson collection.

Always at hand has been the enthusiasm and encouragement of Bret Waller, Director of the University of Michigan Museum of Art. In matters of installation I am in the debt of John E. Holmes and for countless hidden behind-the-scenes tasks, the museum's registrar, Jacquelynn Slee. Seemingly endless correspondence would not have been possible without the willing efficient skills of Jo W. Lau.

At the end is the vital task of actually putting the catalogue together and thereby giving the exhibition lasting tangible form. Alita J. Mitchell is to be thanked for mastering my own unstandard "calligraphy" and thus being able to do most of the preliminary typing of the manuscript. In her capacity as Archivist she has also been most helpful in obtaining photographs for many of the illustrations. Thanks for final typing must go to Chitra Muliyil, Rob J. Nuismer, and Elinor Pearlstein, who with her growing knowledge of things Chinese and her care in detail has added editorial skills to that of typist. For many hours of hard proofreading I am in further debt to Louise Yuhas, who returned from Taipei just in time.

At the last it is to my friend and colleague, Hiram W. Woodward, Jr., who has seen the catalogue through the intricacies of editing and printing, that final gratitude is due.

Lenders to the Exhibition

Edwin Binney, 3rd
British Museum, London
Mr. and Mrs. Jackson Burke, New York
T. Y. Chao, Hong Kong
The Art Institute of Chicago
The Cleveland Museum of Art
John M. Crawford, Jr., New York
Hellen and Joe Darion, New York
Charles A. Drenowatz, Zurich
Jean-Pierre Dubosc, Paris and Tokyo
Mr. and Mrs. Richard Edwards, Ann Arbor
Ernest Erickson, New York
James Freeman, Kyoto
Hashimoto Collection
Honolulu Academy of Arts
Hwa's Hou Chen Shang Chai
Indianapolis Museum of Art
Los Angeles County Museum of Art
The Metropolitan Museum of Art, New York
The University of Michigan Museum of Art,
Ann Arbor
Mr. and Mrs. Earl Morse, New York
Nelson-Atkins Gallery, Kansas City, Missouri
Osaka Municipal Museum of Fine Arts
Mrs. A. Dean Perry, Cleveland
The Arthur M. Sackler Foundation
Mr. and Mrs. David Spelman, Great Neck,
New York
Hsien-ch'i Tseng, Peterborough, New
Hampshire
Vannotti Collection, Muzzano, Switzerland
Mr. and Mrs. Wan-go H. C. Weng, New York
Worcester Art Museum
Two anonymous lenders

Principal Dates in the Life of Wen Cheng-ming

1470 Born, eleventh month, sixth day
T'ang Yin born

1478 Receives instruction in the classics from Wu K'uan

1488 Is studying calligraphy with Li Ying-chen

1489 Is studying painting with Shen Chou

1494 Ch'iu Ying born (probable date)

1495 Takes official examinations in Nanking; fails

1497 Eldest son, Wen P'eng, is born
Wu K'uan leaves for Peking; he never returns to Suchou

1499 Wen Lin, Wen's father, dies in Wen-chou, sixth month, seventh day

1501 Second son, Wen Chia, is born

1502 Nephew, Wen Po-jen, is born, son of Wen's elder brother Wen K'uei (T. Cheng-ching)

1509 Shen Chou dies

1514 Refuses to serve Ch'en Hao, Prince of Ning

1516 Takes official examination in Nanking, seventh time; fails
Mid-summer in Nanking

1520 Wen P'eng marries

1522 In Nanking, last of ten examination failures
Li Ch'ung-ssu, inspector of Kiangsu, recommends Wen for employment at one of the National Academies

1523 Goes to Peking with Ts'ai Yü as one recommended from the provinces; sails second month, twenty-fourth day; arrives fourth month, nineteenth day; appointed attendant of Han-lin academy, intercalary fourth month, sixth day
T'ang Yin dies, twelfth month, second day

1526 Withdraws from government service

1527 Returns with Huang T'ai-ch'üan to Suchou, spring
Builds retreat, Yü-ch'ing shan-fang (the name, however, occurs much earlier in Wen's work)
From now on "events" in life most clearly indicated in his paintings

1530 Paints Yüan Piao's studio, Wen-te chai; Yüan family close to Wen at this time

1533 Wang Ch'ung dies

1536 Wen K'uei dies

1541 Ts'ai Yü dies

1542 Wife dies

1552 Ch'iu Ying dies

1559 Dies, second month, twentieth day

Introduction

Within the Chinese tradition—and by extension within the general history of art of the world—the claim of Wen Cheng-ming (1470–1559) to greatness must rest on the foundation that he was an artist's artist. This does not mean that he had no message for the rest of the world, but rather that his was an art based on art. He knew, revered, and interpreted the work of artists who had preceded him. He lived in wealthy and highly cultured Suchou—the Athens, or Florence, or Paris, or New York of its day—surrounded by artists, and because of the intensity of his vision, aided by a near ninety-year life-span (one thinks of his younger contemporary, Titian, ca. 1486–1576) painting in the Suchou that followed him never escaped his influence.

Later, at the end of the Ming dynasty and further into the seventeenth and eighteenth centuries the focus of creative painting was to shift to Sung-chiang, near the present Shanghai and to Yangchou, northwest of Suchou. But within the highest scholar-culture traditions of China, Suchou was in the fifteenth and sixteenth centuries the painting capital of China. If because of a temporal analogy to European history one is tempted to suggest that this must indeed have been the heart of the Renaissance of China, one is correct insofar as in Suchou one may find wealth, a love of the arts and a devotion to "classical" truth which at the same time fostered individual creativity. China, however, did not need a rebirth. Her "classical" traditions, despite seventy years of Mongol rule from 1279 to 1368, never died, but were in the very nature of Chinese culture constantly being recalled to life. A love of nature linked to a broad humanism was an integral part of these traditions. The present was essentially inconceivable without knowledge of the past and the past lived on only through its constant creative application to the present. Wen Cheng-ming, the painter, was this process of constant rebirth. His individuality realized through the tradition was no less "individual." One cannot, in the paintings attributed to Wen Cheng-ming in this exhibition, consider any as the work of another "individual" except insofar as in quality or perhaps motif or sensitivity of brush they may to knowledgeable eyes reveal someone trying to be *like* the individual, Wen Cheng-ming. No matter, the individuality of Wen Cheng-ming—in the most comprehensive sense—is what we are seeking to explore. It is this individuality that marks a high point in the art of sixteenth-century China.

As we seek a further understanding of it, one is perhaps first of all impressed by the fact that we have entered a world of general thematic consistency. Subjects are from nature. There may be people or architecture. The scene may be viewed from very close or from a distance. But it is the Chinese scene in which the basic referents are rocks and trees, flowers and grasses, mountains and water. Humans somehow must "fit" this rather than the other way around. But once this kind of constant view is accepted, one must, I think, be then struck by Wen's variety.

In the next section Anne Clapp will explore more fully the rather special factors that helped form the complexities of this art that is an interweaving of free individuality and precise tradition—its patronage, its subject-matter, the weight as well as the inspiration of the past, Wen's dealing with this, and his ultimate emergence as his own great master. She will also generally outline steps in the progress of Wen's own style. From there the viewer can go on to a more detailed critical analysis of each work of art in the exhibition.

Here in introduction, one can, as a kind of general framework, a structure into which to place the varied individual experiences of sixty-odd works of art, suggest that despite first appearances, variety is not the open door to confusion. Inevitably an exhibition such as this involves a random selection. It is random because it is limited to what happens to be outside of China; or is prey to the whims or ability of a collector to lend; or, finally, to the fallibility of selection in a process whereby we are still exploring and attempting to affirm what is worthy of consideration. But when all is said and done, enough has been included to affirm the variety and range of Wen's art.

In reviewing this art, one must remember that it is always closely allied to the *person* of the artist, and the very fact of its variety reflects not only wide-ranging interests, but his mood and personal feelings at a given time. How else are we to explain the fact that apparently no important masterpiece has emerged from Wen's unhappy Peking years? Judgments on individual paintings must be made, where possible, in the conscious light of the circumstances under which they were created. Hopefully through the varied experiences of many paintings the viewer will be led to sense the nature of the artist himself. Yet in a more abstract sense, the exhibition does reveal a pattern.

Historical patterns are the result of the play of

time. Of this Wen himself was much aware. On occasion he saw paintings that he had done years before, and he recognized change in his own work. As he affirms, "I cannot recreate interests of former times" (no. IX). "I doubt that I could do this again" (no. XIII). Or, "I sink into old age—no longer to return is the spirit of those days" (no. XXIV).

Accepting time as the major catalyst in the process of artistic change, the exhibition begins with Wen's involvement with his teacher, Shen Chou. There are works they have done together. There are works by Shen Chou alone that have special relevance to what Wen Cheng-ming was later to create. Wen's art is here divided into periods, marked by the broad time of "development" before his trip to Peking and then by three somewhat separate decades of work after his return. Although Wen went to Peking when he was over fifty, he matured slowly and the periods up to that time can justly be called "early." The Peking years produced little artistically, although certainly as a painter-calligrapher there were strong official demands on Wen's talent and some traces remain. His return south in 1527, as we shall see, resulted essentially in a new artistic life. The 1530s were a decade marked by artistic brilliance. The qualities of his craft often emerge to reveal a special tense skill. With the 1540s his art matures in the direction of combining this with spatial recession so that his painting is often embraced by, or at least related to, a feeling for depth. And in his final decade he is involved not so much with discovery as acceptance, particularly toward the decade's close. Brilliant tensions may often be there, but in redoing themes of the past his brush-work is often briefer, his sense of space calmer. He does again what he has done before—in poetry, in calligraphy and in painting. He is essentially at one with tradition, with nature, with himself.

It is recorded that at 89, Wen Cheng-ming greeted the new year with a poem, and on the twentieth day of the next month, after writing the epitaph of another, he laid aside his brush and died.

The Sources of Wen Cheng-ming's Style

by Anne De Coursey Clapp

A generation ago Western writers on Chinese painting either ignored the middle Ming period, the later fifteenth and sixteenth centuries, or defined it in such dark phrases as "traditional," "archaistic," or most pernicious of all, "eclectic." The Ming before Tung Ch'i-ch'ang (1555–1636), they felt, had little historical validity because it was mired in its own regard for antiquity and knew no method but an eclectic picking at the bones of the past. The reasons for their suspicious attitude toward the Ming lay in part with the Ming itself, which deliberately sought a perilously close balance between the artist's task of invention and his reverence for history; and in part with twentieth century Western thought which places an inordinately high priority on novelty and a rapid pace of change as signs of cultural vitality.

Especially disconcerting to the Western mind was the sheer number and diversity of painting styles, which flourished concurrently, particularly in the sixteenth century, and sometimes in the oeuvre of the same artist. The peculiar features of historicism and variety of style, which proved such a stumbling block to early students of the field, are the very ones which should give Ming painting the right to a place in the history books. They are a unique phenomenon, special to China without exact parallels elsewhere, which offers a humanistic definition of art, closer to methods and attitudes of scholarship than anything in our own past. This scholarly ideal might seem to us likely to dampen the ardor of creative activity, but in fact it had a quite opposite effect and stimulated one of the richest outpourings of pictorial art in Chinese history.

The Ming (1368–1644) was a post-classical age which looked back not only to the classical achievements of the T'ang (618–907) and Sung (960–1126) dynasties, but also to the Yüan (1279–1368), a phase which has no parallel in the West but in Chinese art history at once gained an authority equal to that of the classical. Thus the inheritance of the Ming artist was compounded of two great traditions joined in unbroken progress over seven centuries. Otto Brendel, speaking of the Roman artist's relation to classical Greece, states the dilemma of the heir to a great tradition in all ages and cultures: "The classical examples and conceptions can be accepted or declined as standards of artistic creation, but they are not easily forgotten. In this circumstance alone lies a source of possible choices and conflicts not present in any pre-classical art."[1]

The Chinese artist, brought up in a traditionalistic society, which was at its strictest in the Ming, was even less likely to forget than the Roman. He accepted the challenge in the conviction that it was a benefit and set himself to the task of reconciling history with innovation. He did not see himself as threatened by repetition and decadence because he had before him the example of the

Yüan, a moment of supreme creative energy which also coincided with a concerted study of the past. He undertook to imitate not only the Yüan masters' pictorial forms, but also their elastic relationship to antiquity and their freedom to accept or decline it.

Among Ming painters the outstanding instance of the antiquarian artist, devoted to history and wholly unwilling to decline its lessons, was the artist of this exhibition, Wen Cheng-ming. He carried on throughout his life a systematic research into the art of the old masters, collected and copied their works, and discovered in them the touchstone for his own painting. Because he ranged so widely in his pursuit of the past, his painting reveals no obvious unity of approach and lacks the inner coherence which the art historian assumes when he accepts the notion of personal style. Both Wen's oeuvre as a whole and the fraction of it included in the present exhibition are conglomerate and do not appear as closed stylistic groups. His art resists the effort to force upon it a tidy integrity of style, and demands instead to be accepted as diverse, originating in different sources and motivated by different formal aims; and to be appreciated for its historical as well as its aesthetic meaning.

The Learned Painter

Wen Cheng-ming was born to happy circumstances in Suchou, a southern city of great beauty and prosperity, and since Yüan times a lively center of intellectual and artistic life. The scholars of Suchou were celebrated for their long tradition of learning, and for centuries the district had sent more than its share of candidates to fill the ranks of government officials in the capital. It was an aristocratic world, jealous of its prerogatives, which accepted the authority of the landed gentry in social as in government affairs. Its bulwark was Confucianism and, though many of the intelligentsia dabbled in Taoism and the occult sciences and most had a certain sympathy for Ch'an Buddhism, they all without question followed in their daily lives and professional careers the tenets of conservative Confucianist thought.

Wen Cheng-ming was perhaps a stricter Confucianist than most and by nature deeply concerned with the problems and practice of ethical philosophy, sometimes so much so that he was made the butt of jokes by less strait-laced friends. He was introduced early to the brilliant circle of the intelligentsia and, though slow-spoken and reserved, he strove to live up to their example. He worked relentlessly at his academic pursuits and, though he never became an articulate or expressive speaker, his studies prospered and it became apparent early in his life that he was born to the scholar's robe and the academic career.

Among the Confucianist gentry it was accepted that the noblest task of man is leadership and this was to be attained only in statecraft after overcoming the long course of obstacles set by the civil service examinations. Wen pursued the prescribed course of liberal arts leading to the examinations. He began by concentrating on the writing of modern prose, a special skill essential for success in the examinations; but he fell increasingly under the spell of classical literature and history and the time-honored Confucianist ideal of the universal personality. He became entranced with the image of the liberally educated man versed in all periods of history, master of the ancient styles of prose-writing, poet, painter, art historian, and calligrapher. He became also a confirmed idealist and antiquarian, more at home in the past than in the ambience of pragmatism and expedience in which government is actually conducted.

He was appalled when he failed the examination and deeply wounded when this failure was repeated in nine successive efforts. He protested against the examination system in letters ringing with polemical heat, and continued to labor stubbornly for official advancement.[2]

In 1523, when he was still without the benefit of a higher degree, he at last received provincial recommendation and went to Peking to take examinations. However, before having to take them, he was appointed to a vacancy in the Han-lin Academy. He had departed for the capital in the expectation that government administration was to be his life's work. He had served little more than a year when he experienced an extreme revulsion from the sphere of practical politics, and submitted several letters of resignation, finally escaping from office and returning to Suchou in 1527 after a bare three years in Peking. This action was both a resignation in protest against the dictatorial methods of the Ming court and an implicit admission that his temperament was unfitted to political life. After retirement he withdrew into the relative seclusion of Suchou's literary and artistic society and refused further contact with court functions and government affairs.

The Suchou artists formed an exclusive and even elite group, which assembled at first around Wen's master in painting, Shen Chou (1427–1509), and after his death around Wen himself. Its members were all men of letters, calligraphers, or painters, strongly antiquarian in their interests and sensitive about their closely guarded liberty. Some were government officials and some came from the merchant class, or even lower origins, but all acknowledged a desire for seclusion from the world at large and the right of the scholar to freedom from commercial enterprise. In most cases they supported their claim to independence on income derived from inherited property or from minor provincial posts, and they were as a result a leisured and protected class. In spite of some differences in social and economic standing, they all shared the same educational and cultural background, and enjoyed among themselves a social harmony and integrity of belief which created a fertile ground for the fine arts. Thus their painting was a private activity, isolated both from political pressure and from the lower social orders, and even in straitened circumstances they remained jealous of their independence.

The styles which arose under such conditions were markedly aristocratic, intellectualized, and more refined and high-bred than any that had been seen before. All of these styles take root from the great masters of antiquity, and art history was the tool with which they approached the problems of the studio, just as political and social history were the tools with which they undertook to govern. Universality and humanism extended to the study and practice of art as to other disciplines, and they aspired to fuse their learning into the very substance of the painting.

The Deferential Patron

Western art history acknowledges that the requirements of the patron—the commissioner, buyer, or ultimate consumer of the work of art—frequently have a direct formative effect on both subject and style. In Chinese literature information on patronage is conspicuously absent from the comments of critics, and written records of commissions, specifications, payments for paintings have been destroyed, if indeed they ever existed. In discussions of literati art we find instead repeated insistence that money was never exchanged for a painting, that art was a gift freely given with no expectation of return. Many are the tales of the unfortunate merchant, or even prince, who was vulgar enough to offer cash or attempt to cajole an artist with promises of material reward in return for his handiwork.

Wen Cheng-ming defined the proper consumer of the literati painting in the lofty phrase "the right kind of man," by which he meant not necessarily someone of the same social status as himself, but someone with the same tastes and education.[3] A survey of the records of Wen's and Shen Chou's works shows that they were presented to a relatively small circle of men, who were bound to the artist by close ties of family or friendship. The largest group of recipients consisted undoubtedly of colleagues and students who, if the artist were in a receptive mood, had only to present him with a fine piece of silk or mulberry paper and await the result, which was duly inscribed and presented to them (nos. XI, XXXIV). A painting often changed hands as a return for hospitality extended to the artist on travels with a friend, or during a sojourn with a generous host (no. XLVII), while certain social events demanded an honorific presentation of poem or painting. Commentators report that Wen was especially inclined to give paintings to his poorer friends and relations, and that these works soon found their way to the marketplace.[4]

Where art functioned as a currency of social interchange and family loyalty, and where many of the recipients were in no position to pay a fair figure for it, its absolute value was of small importance to the artist and his high-minded claim to commercial disinterest is justified. But this was not always the case.

Some scattered and delicately phrased remarks indicate that the gift of a painting did convey a certain obligation and that a return was in order, though it was probably of a different kind; and, conversely, that such a gift could dissolve a debt.[5] Shen Chou occasionally apologizes for being dilatory with a painting or an autograph as if it were a bread-and-butter note, and the literature contains at least one dark hint that Wen allowed another hand to execute pictures under his name to fulfill his social debts.[6] Several paintings by Shen Chou, T'ang Yin, and Wen have survived which were presented to doctors, apparently in payment for professional services.

The monetary value of a painting is never mentioned, but we know that the works of the literati were extremely valuable even in their own lifetimes, because these works were copied almost immediately by professional forgers for commercial sale. Wang Shih-chen (1526–1590) says such copies were scattered everywhere, a hundred spurious pieces for every genuine one.[7] Prices rose rapidly and competition for authentic works was keen.

The wealthiest collectors came from the successful merchant families of Suchou, an enterprising class of men, sometimes but one generation removed from the shop, who aspired to higher things. They enjoyed the benefits of a classical education, sometimes rose to influential government positions, and tended increasingly to leave behind the merchant ranks (at the low end of the social ladder) and to join the literati and the hereditary landed gentry in their mores and their intellectual pleasures. There does not seem to have been any stricture against admitting merchants and the sons of merchants to the literati society, provided they came with native taste and talent and were able to meet the standard of "the right kind of man."[8] Together with the gentry they formed a moneyed class of enthusiastic collectors,

who pursued contemporary paintings as well as antiquities and courted the famous artists and poets of the time. During his long friendship with Wen the prodigiously wealthy Wang Hsien-ch'en (chin-shih 1493) allowed him the use of a studio in his famous Cho-cheng Garden (no. LI), and the artist responded with both paintings and literary works.[9] Wen seems to have performed gladly and freely for these devoted admirers, and also to have given liberally to them of advice and expertise on ancient masterworks.[10]

Shen Chou enjoyed a handsome income from his estates and from a hereditary position as tax collector, but Wen's financial position in the wide spectrum of Suchou wealth was relatively modest, and he held no official position or emolument after his retirement from government service. In point of income he did not approach the vast wealth of the great collectors who so ardently desired to own his paintings and to benefit from his critical acumen. Some of his gifted colleagues were exceedingly poor: Ch'iu Ying (ca. 1494–1552) remained a professional artist dependent on commission all his life; T'ang Yin (1470–1523) frankly confessed to painting for money;[11] and Lu Chih (1496–1576), though he continued to follow his own tastes, drifted into increasingly difficult circumstances.

Although there is no shred of written evidence that Wen, Shen Chou, and Lu Chih accepted cash, it is virtually certain, where the paintings were highly valued and the artists often needy, that there was some form of remuneration for them. Given the strong and universally accepted social convention proscribing the actual sale of literati works, it is not to be expected that the fact or means of remuneration would be recorded, but there can be little doubt that the balance was kept even.

The initial reason for the ban on the sale of literati paintings was to raise painting from the level of a craft to that of a fine art equal to literature, and thus sanction it as an occupation for gentlemen and intellectuals. The appreciation of painting to this protected rank had been accomplished centuries earlier, but the distinction between craftsman and scholar carried perhaps even greater weight in the Ming than before, and the Ming literatus still considered that his art was founded on an intellectual and psychological basis denied to the professional painter.

What this basis was may be glimpsed in colophons by Shen Chou and Wen, where the artist repeatedly insists that in the act of painting he reached a state of nervous excitation and heightened awareness so intense that he lost consciousness of self and poured forth the painting in a surge of natural energy and spontaneity.[12] Because the work was produced thus, from the depths of his being without effort or premeditation, it bore naturally the mark of his mind and temperament and could not appear labored, perfunctory, or superficial—all qualities which he associated with the level of the professional craftsman. The implication is that what he valued was his freedom to paint when he was "in the mood," to choose a style that would stimulate that essential psychic energy, and to feel that the fundamental motivation of the painting was the aggrandizement of his own spirit. None of these cherished aims, he felt, could be attained if the work were commissioned, ordered for a certain date, detailed in exact specifications, and dealt with a subject matter and style dictated by the patron.

In fact, the ambitious collector came by a painting by quite different and more tactful means, which allowed the artist to preserve a full measure of control over its actual execution. He asked for it, if he dared, or acquired it on the market only after it was finished, but contributed nothing directly to its inception, even though he might be present when it was painted. Numerous colophons by Wen show him making decisions about subject, format, style, color, or brush technique, but nowhere is there a hint that the final recipient of the finished work intruded his opinions on the artist. Sometimes we may feel the ghostly presence in the studio of Chao Meng-fu or some other old master, but other guests attended as passive spectators.

We may conclude that, though the exchange of a painting probably implied some reward for the artist, the "patron" had no right to specify style and only rarely to suggest a topic. These decisions rested with the artist, and the only way he insured that the patron would not be disappointed was by limiting his public to men of his own persuasion. In the relationship between maker and consumer the limitations were all placed on the patron, who awaited deferentially what the painter elected to bestow on him.

Thus the cultural value system, which of old protected the literati's independence, continued to outweigh the payment of reward, and the patron never acquired the right to dictate. What made the artist the arbiter of standards rather than the rich, was the fact of his education, his intellectual discipline, and his expertise in ancient art. No independent critics handed down decisions from an omnipotent press and no academic art historians issued theories from an ivory tower. The artist served himself as critic and connoisseur by right of learning, as well as artistic talent, and enjoyed the privilege of choosing the aesthetic problem.

The Ostensible Theme

The range of subject matter admitted to Chinese painting grew steadily narrower after the Sung dynasty. The subjects acceptable to the literatus had always been sharply restricted, and the Ming literati obeyed these limits. Regarding choice of subject matter as a sign of social and intellectual status, they rejected outright topics from popular life and the lower classes. Wen Chia (1501–1583) speaks for an elitist point of view, when he says of Chang Tse-tuan's *Ch'ing-ming Festival on the River:* "It is a common-place painting of Sung times and lacks the spirit of remote antiquity."[13] Figure paintings by the Suchou literati are scarcely known, except in a few instances where they are infused with "the spirit of remote antiquity" by following such recognized literati forebears as Li Kung-lin (Lung-mien), or such genuinely archaic styles as the Six Dynasties (222–589). Portraits are so rare as to prove the rule that they were not recognized as a legitimate genre for scholars, and figure paintings in Sung style of the kind practiced by T'ang Yin and Ch'iu Ying caused these painters to be censured as popular and plebeian. Ch'an Buddhist subjects and most history themes were also deprecated, and bird and flower paintings fell to a small minority of the whole.

The steady attrition of subject matter after Sung was such that the iconography of literati painting by middle Ming was virtually reduced to landscape and such components of it as trees and plants. The literati did not regard this situation as an impoverishment of their tradition, but rather as a proper safeguard against the trivial and materialistic. They devoted themselves to the vast genre of landscape, introducing a few new themes, frequently subdividing and refining old ones more suited to convey their aristocratic views.

In one large and important class of themes the style responds in part to the subject, which imposes certain requirements of form and mood, so that the thing represented colors the way in which it is represented. This class was the topographical picture, which depicted in the extended format of handscroll or the multiple format of album leaves a series of views of famous sites in Wu (Suchou). This type together with the garden scene was still immediately tied to the physical world and the daily experience of the artist, for he was a confirmed traveler in his own land and deeply proud of and sensitive to the scenic beauty of the southeast.

The paintings made to commemorate his journeys were, in a certain sense of the word, illustrations, because it was their purpose to describe real places, intimately known to artist and patron, with sufficient immediacy and attention to fact to arouse in their audience the pleasure of recognition. The artist, however, did not observe any strict obligation to visual realism in the Western sense, nor did he concern himself with the actual sequence of geographical localities. His knowledge of the country was cumulative, based on a lifetime of wandering rather than any particular journey, and no more limited in time than in space. Laborious description and illusionist devices would have dragged his work down to a mundane level. It was intended to arouse memory and mood, not merely to record facts.

This subtype of the genus landscape had been inherited from the Yüan dynasty, chiefly from Wu Chen, but had been practiced by other masters as well.[14] It reached a rare degree of perfection in the hands of Shen Chou, whose pithy, synoptic style was ideally suited to presenting its vast panoramas without relapsing into the particular or adventitious. An example of it, begun by Shen Chou and finished by Wen, is no. III, which exhibits the stringent abstraction and abstention from illusionism which marked Shen's work even when he confronted this most concrete and familiar of all his subjects.

Belonging to this same category, and posing the same problem of relationship to the material world, are the garden scenes, a subject of great antiquity which was vastly enlarged by Shen Chou and rose to the height of fashion under Wen and Ch'iu Ying (nos. XXVI, XLI).[15] Some of these scenes were actually imaginary images of famous gardens of the past (no. LXI), roughly grounded on literary descriptions with detail and mood supplied by the artist's fancy. In every case the imagined scene was connected with some illustrious historical personage, who symbolized the literati ideal and with whom the Ming man, painter and patron both, desired to identify himself. Ch'iu Ying's *Chao Meng-fu Writing the Heart Sutra* (no. XXXIX) is such an imaginary recreation, where Chao appears as the mirror of his age, initiating a style of calligraphy accepted by the sixteenth century as a paradigm.

The garden itself became in middle Ming a visual symbol of a mode of life which combined high thinking and a patrician standard of conduct and manners (no. XXXVII). It also signified the ultimate refinement of human pleasure, compounded of the sensual enjoyment of natural beauty and the rational satisfactions of the mind. Its potency as a cultural symbol, combined with pride of ownership, fired Suchou's great landowners with ambition for portraits and literary records of their estates. The artists responded with a new genre of landscape, probably the only one in which the patron may, by sheer proprietary feeling, have influenced the production of art.

These paintings could not be imaginary if they were to serve their chief purpose of lending lustre to the owner's reputation as scholar and gentleman.

We can see in *The Cho-cheng Garden* (no. LI), which represents a real site in Suchou, how objectively Wen deals with the landscaping and architecture of each specific locale, pointing up the special features for which the garden was renowned, but restraining movement and detail lest they destroy the sense of permanence essential to the meaning.

Of quite different origin from subjects of travel and gardens are the literary themes drawn from poetry and stories, exemplified in the exhibition by four versions of *The Red Cliff* (nos. XXV, LII, LVIII, and LXII). These tales were known and acceptable to every educated person. They usually carry with them a moralizing overtone, but a larger attraction was the fact that many earlier painters had illustrated them and the Ming artist accepted the theme, as he accepted the old style, as a challenge.[16] In treating poetic narrative the Wu school painters tended to abbreviate rather than expand, and to avoid exposition of events in favor of evocation of sentiment, an attitude carried over from their writing of poetry, where they considered mood the quintessential aim. Narrative, like realism in painting, was suspect and its role underplayed in both the literary and visual arts.

A large component of the Suchou artist's oeuvre is made up of paintings couched in the style of an old master, and in these works where the ancient style is preserved more or less intact, the subject matter formed by a typical combination of motifs is retained exactly as in the model. Wen automatically and unconsciously, it seems, accepts the old master's preferred motifs as indivisible from his style. His handscrolls in the style of Ni Tsan (nos. XIII, XIV) and Mi Fei (no. XI) are patent examples of subject and motif riding the coattails of style, and signify a devaluation of objects having meaning in their own right. With the exception of the themes mentioned above and in by far the majority of his pictures Wen tended to strip meaning from the material subject and confer it upon style.

This shift stimulated the different use of an old iconography in the art-historical and special theme albums, types which first appeared in Yüan and early Ming, but were not widely practiced until the Suchou masters adopted them. The art-historical album presented the painter playing a series of roles as the great masters of the past and assumed a knowledgeable audience who could appreciate his versatility and expertise. Such an exercise may seem to the western mind to compromise the painter's individuality, but was seen by the Chinese artist as a contest demanding a subtle blend of the contemporary style with the old.

The special theme album offered a similar trial and display of technical prowess, in which the artist performed variations on the treatment of bamboo, flowers, or landscape, limiting himself to a narrow subject the better to display his ingenuity (nos.

II A–E, LIII, LIX).[17] In tests of this kind it is the very absence of iconography, or the utter sameness of it, which is of positive value. The proliferation of these albums, which grew even more popular in the seventeenth century, is a sure indication that subject matter was never to regain its primacy.

From Yüan times on, the single most common subject of literati art was the mountainscape, for reasons which are not far to seek. No matter how firmly he might reject naturalism, the later Chinese painter was never willing to reject nature itself in preference for non-objective art (a position in any case already preempted by calligraphy). But he increasingly sought a natural material without rigid laws or inflexible character of its own, which could assume many shapes and textures on many levels of abstraction. This fictile material must lend itself to countless configurations and unlimited metamorphosis. He discovered it in the mountain facade with its rocks, cliffs, and plateaus, natural objects which have their own structural laws, but in such numberless kind that there seems no restriction on their formal possibilities.

The mountain became the supreme icon of Ming painting, chosen not for its literary symbolism of power and independence, but for its tractability to a formalistic program of art. It fitted so well with Wen's aims that it developed into a specialized and narrowly limited stylistic problem which he followed throughout his career, arriving eventually at a new iconographical subtype. The *Mountain Landscape* belonging to The University of Michigan (no. XV) illustrates this type fully realized and unadulterated by any vestige of literary meaning. The type stands at the opposite pole from the garden scenes, which served as the conventionally accepted vehicle of a philosophy, and owes its dominant position in later painting to aesthetic considerations alone.

The genre of flowers, plants, and trees, which embraced the broad and varied realm of growing things in the Sung dynasty, yielded to the literati repertory in the eleventh and twelfth centuries certain plants endowed with a moral symbolism deemed especially suited to the gentleman painter: the bamboo, plum, chrysanthemum, and pine and cypress trees. Most of this symbolism, too, succumbed to time and the impulse of the sixteenth century to turn all themes towards pure design. Wen's *Bamboo* and *Chrysanthemums* (nos. XXXIII, XXXV) and Shen Chou's *Chrysanthemums and Elegant Bird* (no. VII) show how the plants, once the microcosmic symbol of nature, have become chastened and regulated by the laws of brush and ink.

Only one subject from this group, the pine, cypress, and juniper trees, maintained its original meaning in Wen's art. These species, evergreen and enduring, appear repeatedly in his pictures, sometimes as the sole subject (no. XXX), sometimes as the central component of a landscape (no.

LVII), but always as a focal point of the composition, radiating a special meaning which is inherent in the visual form. Both their suggestive shapes and the poems which occasionally accompany them imply that the trees are metaphors of the artist's own experience, embodying his apprehension of the perpetual struggle of the human will. Invested with a terrible intensity of feeling, they are rarely, like his bamboo and flower subjects, a mere pretext for the brilliant display of art.

All of the themes discussed here are private ones, though some, like the trees, are so subjective that their full personal meaning to the artist is hidden and can probably never be known. Topics suited to public presentation in large format with a general appeal are not found in either Shen Chou's or Wen's oeuvres. They rarely undertook the large decorative scrolls which were hung in groups in reception halls to mark the seasons or celebrate festivals, and no screen paintings are attributed to them.[18] So far as subject matter is concerned, their claim to have painted for a small and discriminating audience is borne out, and supports what we know of their attitude toward patronage.

The Historical Canons

Wen Cheng-ming's predisposition to the study of history and antiquities led him into a long and arduous apprenticeship in the ancient styles of painting, an apprenticeship which he began under Shen Chou and continued afterwards under his own guidance. Though separated by forty-three years of age, Shen Chou and Wen were extremely congenial and worked in the closest social and artistic communion from about 1489 to Shen Chou's death in 1509. Wen mastered Shen Chou's style with such facility that he could perform creditably in it at an early age (no. II F), and at seventy-five, without significantly altering the style, completed a handscroll which Shen Chou had left unfinished at his death (no. III). His best work in this vein is seen in the late landscape (no. LIV), where he gives a freer rein to his own volatile and fluent brushwork, allowing a new buoyancy to the forms and an acceleration of the rhythmic line. He never abandoned this style, but we may note that he used it most frequently in works of small format, especially fans and album leaves, and that it prompted few personal innovations on his part.

Wen and Shen Chou, though very similar in their philosophy and mode of life, were actually of quite different artistic temperaments. Shen Chou's painting speaks of a deep conviction of harmony between man and the world, and his visual forms preserve a consistent agreement and equilibrium with the content. His technique is simplistic and unstrained, attaining in the late works a kind of serene and cultivated primitivism. This is directly contrary to some of Wen's most original styles, which press to the verge of mannerism, seeking an elaboration of form and stressed feeling, and which often place subject and expression in opposition to each other. Shen Chou's most valuable gift to him was not so much his style, but a thorough grounding in the art of the major Yüan masters, from whom Shen had drawn all his own most fertile ideas, and the view of himself as Shen Chou's successor in the Yüan tradition.

Up until the late fifteenth century the accumulated authority of the Yüan dominated the practice of the literati to the virtual exclusion of the Sung and earlier styles. Shen Chou's predecessors followed undeviatingly in this path, and Shen Chou himself, though he occasionally ventured into older styles (he experimented with the blue-green technique and is known to have copied classical Sung works), never admitted them to a definitive role in his major style. The Yüan line of descent was continuous, never revived because it had never been broken, and thus never subjected to critical examination. The Suchou artist assimilated it almost unconsciously and without the exercise of the objectivity required by the art of "high antiquity," three centuries or more removed from him.

Wen acquired the distinctive manners of Huang Kung-wang (nos. VIII, X), Wu Chen, Ni Tsan, and Wang Meng in the first decade of the 1500s and continued to work in all of them thereafter, sometimes keeping the style fairly pure, more often as he matured, selecting and combining certain features in ways that eventually obliterated the source. Though he was competent in all four manners, he soon found Wang Meng's, which was dynamic, technically intricate, and sensuously rich, the most compatible. From 1515 on there issued from his studio an extended and close-linked series of mountainscapes based on Wang (no. XV), which included both copies of his original works and also bold and imaginative extrapolations from a generalized norm of the style. From Huang Kung-wang he learned a method of structuring rocks and mountains, which enabled him to infuse a greater clarity and tautness into his own compositions (fig. c); and from Ni Tsan an idiosyncratic brushwork, later to become one of the standard idioms of the Wu school (no. XIII). Wu Chen contributed also to Wen's repertory of brush techniques (nos. LV, LVI), but his relaxed and painterly touch was less congenial to Wen, who preferred a more linear articulation of form and a clear-cut integrating rhythm.

Wen's studies in the classical styles of Sung and T'ang began very early under Shen Chou's tutelage in the private picture collections in which Suchou was extremely rich. That the most ancient styles were of intense interest to him, we know from a conversation held with his brilliant contemporary, T'ang Yin, in 1496, which Wen later recorded, quoting himself: "In painting we should take the Six Dynasties (third to sixth centuries) as our teacher, but such ancient works are no longer to be seen; that old style, indeed, has not survived. Even in the excitement of laying on color and spreading ink, simplicity and unassertiveness should be most highly valued."[19] From this we may surmise that they were ambitious to push their art-historical researches back to the fountainhead of painting, but found themselves blocked for lack of originals; and that they admired the simplicity and unpretentiousness of the archaic style, even though they presumably knew it only in copies.

Only a few T'ang paintings are mentioned in the literature as existing in Suchou collections in the sixteenth century, and probably in most cases this style was transmitted to them through the agency of later Sung and Yüan practitioners. The earliest classical landscapes available to them, dating to the tenth and eleventh centuries, were more numerous and included several paintings known by name to have been in contemporary Suchou collections. Wen studied and reproduced a miniaturist style treating panoramic landscape, which is termed "Ching-Kuan" in sixteenth century records, meaning a generic type fusing the manners of the ninth and early tenth century painters, Ching Hao and Kuan T'ung. The compound term is a fairly sure indication that the two styles were not well enough known in middle Ming to be distinguished.

Wen was especially taken with the art of Li Ch'eng (died 967), which had fallen out of favor since the fourteenth century, when the last vestiges of the Li Ch'eng inheritance had finally succumbed to the rising vitality of literati art. Wen's reconstruction of this style contrasts so dramatically with his works based on the Yüan masters that it can only be explained by the adoption of a completely new set of spatial principles (nos. XL, XLIV).

He also imitated Li Kung-lin, Mi Fei (no. XI) and other Sung literati, though none of their styles stirred him deeply and he carried none to any new position. His copies and his insistent claims to follow in their wake may be taken as his personal confirmation of the literati creed and as an expression of his admiration for them as its originators. Of more value to his own maturation than their actual styles was their antiquarianism and their position in history as the first artists to make a systematic and creative use of archaism. Li Kung-lin was the leader in this new movement to restore the past, soon followed in the twelfth century by the brothers Chao Po-chü and Chao Po-su, who were active in reviving T'ang blue-green landscape. Wen mastered the technical canons of their styles, and blue-green landscape proved a particularly rich and provocative experience to him, eventually yielding in his hands some of the most urbane and sophisticated paintings of the sixteenth century (fig. d).

It is interesting to observe from the extant colophons and paintings that these investigations extended through the twelfth century painters, Liu Sung-nien and Li T'ang, and then fell off about the middle of the century. With the exception of three references to Ma Yüan and Hsia Kuei the Southern Sung is passed over in silence.[20] We may infer that the depreciation of this school, which became outspoken in Tung Ch'i-ch'ang's theory of the Northern and Southern traditions, was already presaged in the middle Ming. There seems to have been a consensus that the Northern Sung and early twelfth century ranked as the classical period and were worthy of emulation, whereas the later twelfth and thirteenth centuries represented a decline which offered no lessons for the Ming literatus.

Among the patriarchs of art history none exercised a more direct and pervasive influence on Wen than Chao Meng-fu, who held in his eyes an oracular authority on all matters related to the practice and criticism of calligraphy and painting. Chao, whose career bridged the gap between the end of academic painting and the radical inventions of the Yüan dynasty, was both a preserver and an innovator, aspiring to revive and maintain the classical sources, while simultaneously seeking in them a stimulus to fresh concepts. He followed many lines often unrelated to each other—figure subjects and blue-green landscapes of the T'ang, the classical Northern Sung academic style, ink bamboo and flower painting after the Sung literati—and, not least of his accomplishments, gave the first impetus to a new abstract and linear landscape, which under the four Yüan masters finally broke decisively with naturalism.

A statistical survey of the surviving records and paintings indicates that Wen resorted to Chao as model far more often than any other old master, and that his copies, revisions, and interpretations of Chao's works date over a very long span of time from his earliest years as a painter to his death. All of Chao's leading styles except figural subjects contributed importantly to his own repertory, particularly the T'ang and Northern Sung styles, which from the thirteenth through the fifteenth centuries had been ignored by virtually all the literati except Chao and Ch'ien Hsüan. The reopening of these currents in the early sixteenth century was accomplished chiefly by Wen, and was of sufficient importance that even Tung Ch'i-ch'ang took note of it: "His fine brushwork and antique elegance derive from the styles of the T'ang and Sung masters. Painters of the last dynasty (Yüan) did not think them worth following."[21] The restoration of these older orthodox styles, almost diametrically opposed to the four Yüan "houses," was to make a deep impression on some of Wen's younger contemporaries and eventually on the Ming as a whole. He employed it mainly in garden scenes, to which its descriptive detail and decorative color were suited, and it launched a new trend toward refinement of scale, freer use of color, and more exact depiction of form.

Wen's commentaries on Chao Meng-fu tell us something of his views on eclectic methods in art and on his own position in the history of painting. He regarded Chao as a mediator between himself and "high antiquity" and gained from him a more intellectualized and liberal outlook on the past. He came to expect of art a necessary historical as well as aesthetic content, and eventually saw himself serving the sixteenth century in the same capacity of guardian and expositor of the classical heritage in which Chao had served his age.

An important question presents itself as to what sources Wen employed in his investigations of ancient art. Did he always draw upon original masterworks, or sometimes upon later copies or even free interpretations of them? The question is complicated by the fact that some of his most admired models, Li Kung-lin, Chao Meng-fu and Chao Po-chü, were themselves revivers of earlier traditions, and he must sometimes have studied material like blue-green landscape, which had already undergone a first reincarnation in the twelfth century and a second in the fourteenth. Such material came to him twice removed from its source, bearing already the impress of two other epigoni.

Added to this was the immediate influence of Shen Chou's revisions of the Yüan masters, works which were not in any sense copies, but inventive, exegetical reconstructions of the original styles, often as in the case of his "Ni Tsans" and "Wu Chens," as powerful and moving as the originals. A certain family likeness can be observed in these middle Ming treatments of the Yüan styles, in which the Ming period style has imprinted itself over the Yüan features, effecting a distinct if subtle change.

How much objectivity could Shen Chou's student preserve, confronted with contemporary works which matched the revered canons in quality, but considerably compromised their initial character? Was he aware of these fine distinctions? The answer is almost certainly that he was. His standing as a critic and connoisseur was unrivaled in his lifetime and was soundly based on a knowledge of genuine works in the great Suchou collections. He had access to these private holdings, and was probably one of the first to be called on to view a new acquisition. The contents of these collections are known in part from contemporary catalogues, so we can point to the actual masterworks he studied.[22] Two of his letters appraising antiquities have survived, as have many of his colophons about or actually inscribed on ancient paintings.[23] There can be no serious doubt that he was familiar with the original paintings, and that these included an ample number from the Yüan, somewhat fewer from the Sung, and only a handful from the T'ang.

The situation regarding the sources of his own painting, then, was very complex. He had the opportunity to work from the originals which had survived, and we are assured by many colophons that he took advantage of it; but he also knew, and may well have used, later versions and revisions, particularly if the intervening master had already initiated a trend towards change that coincided with his own aims. From his notes on the paintings he saw it is clear that he knew when a style was pure, and when it had been reformed, debased, or otherwise modified by the hand of either a copyist or an imaginative follower.

We have used the term 'style' for the historical canons which Wen so assiduously excavated from the layers of the past, but they are styles only in a narrow and limited sense. More exactly, each canon was a set of rules governing the forms and motifs created by a single great master, in his lifetime a fluid, changing continuum, but with the master's passing hardened into a permanent set of characteristic qualities. This kind of style, once crystallized into a classic or standard form in the minds of those who inherit it, does not change. It is a norm, static and permanent, which tells no "story."[24] It constitutes a visual language rather than a history and, because it has been conventionalized, can be taught and learned. In the process of reduction to conventions it gains simplicity and integrity, but loses clarity, life, and motivation, all of which must be restored by the later artist in the course of reviving it.

This function of style first appeared in the late eleventh century with the learned archaism of the Sung literati, and reappeared in Chao Meng-fu's art. From Chao it passed to the masters of the Wu school, who accepted it unanimously as a primary tenet of painting, and vied with each other in propagating the canons in ever more ingenious and subtle colorings. Collectors and critics joined the contest with equal enthusiasm, esteeming a painting more highly in proportion to the depths of its historical layers.

What effect did this mode of thought have on the art of Wen Cheng-ming, with his ingrained habit and long experience as connoisseur? It posed an intimidating psychological challenge: the ancients had achieved the pinnacle of excellence; how could the Ming artist match himself against perfection? Wen's position vis-à-vis his inheritance was the same as the later sixteenth century in the West vis-à-vis the High Renaissance. He was profoundly aware of having to compete against an almost invincible authority. He accepted the essential necessity of invention and change, but clung in his youth to the lifeline anchoring him to the established canons. Only slowly did he free himself

of these bonds and in his middle and late works finally reveal a power of invention equal to the idols of the past.

The T'ing-yün Studio

If the historical canons represent a secondary level of style, which is distinguished by its permanence and its independence of time, Wen Cheng-ming's personal styles represent the primary level. At this primary level his special individual traits in distinctive combinations separate him from his contemporaries and from the derived canons. This concept of style is bound to the sixteenth century and to Suchou, and cannot repeat itself. It is one-directional, shifting in a sequence of events which forms the structure of Wen's oeuvre, as the canons supply the substance on which it operates. It is marked not only by continuous change but also by growth, emerging slowly and often untidily from the impersonal mass of borrowed material and shifting in aesthetic quality.

The oeuvre presently attributed to Wen is one of the largest in the Ming period, amounting to over four hundred paintings, and is much adulterated and confused by copies, derivations, and forgeries. It extended over a span of seven decades from 1491, when his first painting is recorded, to his death in 1559 at the great age of eighty-nine. Before 1523 he gave only part of his time to painting, but nevertheless initiated in these years all of the old canons discussed above. Throughout his long career recurrent archaizing studies, more or less faithful to their models, are found interspersed with paintings which appear quite novel and independent. Most of the earliest surviving designs, dating to the vicinity of 1497 to 1523, show him treading cautiously in the paths of a variety of old masters, conscientiously and methodically reproducing the correct motifs, type-forms and brushwork for the given model. He returned repeatedly to certain favored models, chiefly Chao Meng-fu, Wang Meng, Li Ch'eng, and the tradition of blue-green landscape, implying by his choices a preference for specialized kinds of formal problems. By the late 1510s and early 1520s he had begun to lay the groundwork for the personal styles which were to figure most importantly in his later work.

His first paintings show a method of composition which is quite consistent in the use of a steeply slanted ground plane and in piling mountainous forms to the upper limits of the frame (no. VIII, after Huang Kung-wang). This formula was widely used by the fifteenth century literati painters and must have been the first he learned. It led him into experiments with a flatter and more compacted three-dimensional space and a greater stress on richly worked surfaces. A predilection for miniaturism is noticeable in many instances: he leaned toward old styles of complex brushwork and reduced them in scale (no. IX, after Tung Yüan and Chü-jan). The brushwork is light, elegant, restless, working in opposition to plastic values and virtually banishing solid substances from the painted image.

Although the early works are heterogeneous in style, certain collective features separate them from what came after. Most owe a heavy debt to the past, and even those which seem most freely conceived are often flawed by a too ambitious program not yet within the artist's grasp. The control of composition is uneven and we are always aware of an intense striving with technical problems of brush and ink.

These youthful efforts do, however, proclaim unmistakably a fresh and original talent, descended from Shen Chou, but already beginning to diverge from him in quest of a reduced space and small maze-like patterns inseparable from structure. According to the tenets of literati painting the scholar-artist was supposed to abhor minutiae and all sensuously appealing qualities, and to avoid laboring over the execution of a painting. But Wen's native gifts drew him in exactly this direction. His challenge in 1523 was to discover a means of integrating a complex design and of investing it with a quality of astringency to counteract the rich, highly wrought patterns and textures. His advance to the rank of master was a long and arduous process of stripping his art of the superfluities which still clung to it in the early twenties.

When he resumed painting in 1527, after his return from Peking, he took up a concentrated program consisting of the same problems that had occupied him four years previously. His unflagging discipline in matters of composition and technique bore fruit in the works of the thirties, which show a new mastery and ease. His advance in these middle years was recognized by collectors. Chang Ch'ou, after he had bought a handscroll of the master's maturity for a very steep price, compared it to an early work and pronounced the difference like that "between high heaven and a deep abyss."[25] The weight of the past lies less oppressively on this phase, even when the painting in question is explicitly identified as being in the manner of an old master. Wen had grown bolder in exploring new transformations of his sources, combining ideas more freely, and occasionally forcing such radical changes that the model cannot always be identified.

With his vision of a closed compacted space reinforced by further studies of Wang Meng, he set out to construct a frieze-like design, obstructing and contradicting recession so that depth all but vanishes in the stirring, scintillating movements of the surface (no. XV; fig. a). He revels in elaborate figures of the brush, searching for an epicurean elegance and high finish. The abstraction of the image is achieved by complication and elaboration,

rather than by simplification and resort to semi-geometric form, as in Shen Chou's painting. Where the intricacy and fineness of the patterns threaten to overwhelm the whole, he introduces blank areas, prunes out motifs, and sharpens the silhouettes (nos. XXVI, XXVII). In a few years he has learned the virtues of abstemiousness, as well as luxuriance, and has begun to exercise an economy which will keep pace with the most complex designs. In this middle phase he moved decisively away from the Yüan masters to discover a new Ming concept of space, which was to have a far-reaching effect on the later sixteenth century.

Wen's most powerful instrument of expression was his gift for dynamic motion and linear rhythm. It is allowed little outlet in his early years and only comes into full play in the 1530s, where it appears in purest form in the motif of the juniper tree (no.

a. Wen Cheng-ming, *Luxuriant Pines and Clear Streams*, 1542. National Palace Museum, Taipei

XXX). Here he concentrates on a narrow aesthetic issue, consciously seeking dramatic spectacle and nervous excitement. The trees are subjected to extreme torsion in a restricted space. The bark and branches are made into figurative forms and persuaded into disturbing shapes and postures, as if to suggest organic pain. For the first time a note of fantasy and eccentricity appears, born partly of expressionism and partly of the artist's extemporizing play with line. Wen and T'ang Yin are the first members of the Wu school to admit the irrational element into painting. It is not seen in the fifteenth century literati masters, but is increasingly common in the generation after Wen.

In the last two decades of his life Wen introduced no new styles to his repertory. The distinction between his middle and late work is largely one of quality and greater freedom in interpretation. The transition occurred slowly by drift around the mid-1540s, and seems to have been part of a naturally continuous development toward a more succinct and potent image in all styles.

One group of late works brings to a climax the search for surcharged tension built up by prodigious movement within a limited volume of space (no. LVII; fig. b). Spiraling and thrusting forms lock together in a close-knit, centralized composition, and energy is generated by structure itself. In this last phase the central theme of Wen's painting is rhythmic motion, a non-descriptive movement which belongs to art rather than nature and subsumes all other formal qualities. There is an increase in scale and breadth of handling over the restrained and delicate paintings of his youth. Where he uses the "rough brush," the line is harsh, rapid, and moves ceaselessly in a caustic, twisting line. The rhythm is enlarged, evolving in one direction, while the forms roll and turn in the constricting frame with a new sculptural force (no. XLVIII).

Many of these same late characteristics can be seen in the superb *Old Trees by a Wintry Brook* of 1551 (no. L), except that here Wen introduces an unusual spatial system which was little practiced by other Ming masters. The striking novelty is the unexpected appearance in the sixteenth century of the device of level-distance perspective, which sprang from his earlier studies of Li Ch'eng (no. XL). Wen seized on this device as if its very difference from the flat frieze-form space gave it special significance. He reiterates the recessional formula of the winding stream to drive a perspective vista into the center of the picture. This kind of space is atypical of the Ming and brings to the landscape an atypical air of naturalism. The style should more correctly be termed pseudo-naturalism, for it is not based on any new experience of nature, but on a revival of classical Sung glossed over with the Ming taste for exaggerated movement.

A restlessness and unease invade the trees, mountains, and streams of the forties and fifties

b. Wen Cheng-ming,
A Thousand Cliffs Vying in Splendor,
1551. National Palace Museum, Taipei

15

and break into a new region of spiritual crisis and conflict, more personal and deeply felt than anything before. These discordant, morbid emotions are objectified most often through the medium of trees and seem to grow more intense in the late period. In such works Wen arrives at a new vision of a dark and convulsive beauty, which looks beyond his time to the end of the sixteenth century.

Exactly contemporary with these mordant and perturbed images is a class of landscapes which typically treats broad and spacious views of lake scenes in a spirit of deep tranquility. *Grass Hut on the T'iao River* presents the style honed at the last to a fine edge of perfection (fig. c). The style works with few and rarified motifs, lightly massed in open space so they seem to float like islands on a limitless sea. The parts are oriented along the horizontals and verticals and have acquired a stability, which gives the paintings an air of almost classic repose. Everything is immaculate, fastidious, cleansed of all excess. The exasperated sensibility and foreboding of the tree paintings are calmed, and the world materializes before us in unearthly stillness and serenity. The recherché mood and loveliness of this style seem to speak for an experience exactly opposite to the tree paintings, as if the artist had set out to capture two poles of feeling. In both it is the Ming temper which impels him to press the symptomatic expression to a final extreme.

Wen was a leader in the resurgence of the archaic T'ang blue-green landscape which was transmitted to the sixteenth century by Chao Po-chü and Chao Po-su. Fascinated by the simplistic, archaic forms, he added yet another level of primitivism to those already established in this tradition, and in time evolved a sixteenth century recension of the type (fig. d). He reduces the T'ang mountains to a transparent thinness of fabric and, making a virtue of repetition, works them into semi-geometrical shapes which captivate by their bizzare inventiveness and sheer craftsmanship. The type-forms of rocks and trees are allowed to remain naive and uncouth—unpromising material to mould —but the variety of configurations they assume and the brisk staccato rhythm they obey are the fruit of a long experience in pure design.

In archaizing of this kind, elements of the primitive style are deliberately preserved, and then dislocated by shifting the motivation of the work from representation to decoration. The ancient style intervenes between the artist and nature and again, as in the tree paintings, opens the way to fantasy. These pictures, on the surface so toy-like and ingenuous, actually represent a quite extreme position in mannerism (possible only at a fairly late stage of cultural history), in which the author affects the limitations of a phase in art history before the appearance of a fully naturalistic landscape art. They reveal, as few other works do, the Ming artist's awareness of his position in the stream of time and his pride in the sophisticated historicism of his age.

The view of Wen's oeuvre we have seen certainly does not support the supposition of a unitary set of stylistic conventions. It presents rather an array of stylistic options, which were continuously before the artist because he himself researched and exposed their precedents in ancient art. However, this array of styles does not mean that his age had no character of its own and that anything could be expected of it. A common denominator can be discovered in the conjunction of certain traits and in a formalistic approach to all artistic problems.

Wen's art declares almost from the beginning the formalist's impulse to elaborate on special visual and expressive features and urge them to extreme positions. This is most notable in the manipulation of rhythmic forces, which are sometimes so violent and strained they dominate the whole picture. An opposite extremity reigns in other designs, which appear as if under a spell of silence and immobility—shifted to a state of arrested being, which allows no implication of movement or time. His two most original spatial inventions, the flat frieze-form type and the receding space derived from Northern Sung, also seem to be the products of a conscious and purposeful quest for visual systems exaggerated until they approach a kind of theoretical purity. A similar contrast occurs in the scale of the paintings, which shifts unpredictably from the miniature to the monumental; and in the contrasting modes of fine and rough brushwork,

c. Wen Cheng-ming, *Grass Hut on the T'iao River,* 1551. Shanghai Museum

which Chinese writers long ago singled out as peculiar to him. Some of his most innovative works, especially in the last two decades, are complicated with ambivalent or contradictory images and distortions pushed well beyond the norm.

This preoccupation with the structure of design, with the assertion and denial of dynamic power, with space and its negation, with fine-spun pattern and absolute void, with extremes of delicacy and boldness, leads to a premeditated formalism, which takes precedence over literary and illustrative meaning and defies natural subject matter. All the pictorial conventions he borrows succumb in the end to a relentless intellectual curiosity to know the limits of their potential. The very different expressions generated by these contradictory qualities should be seen both as revelations of the artist's subjective feelings and also, more significantly for the history of painting, as the outcome of willfully contrived experiments forcing these visual forms to their limits.

NOTES:

1. Otto Brendel, "Prolegomena to a Book on Roman Art," *American Academy in Rome Memoir,* XXI (1953), p. 73.
2. *Wen Cheng-ming ch'üan-chi,* II, ch. 10/pp. 2, 4.
3. Sirén, *Chinese Painting* (1956–58), IV, p. 119.
4. *P'ei-wen chai* (1708 ed.), ch. 56/p. 36; *Wen Cheng-ming ch'üan-chi,* Wang Shih-chen, "Biography," p. 3.
5. In 1499 Wen wrote to Wu K'uan, his teacher and his father's close friend, asking him to compose an epitaph for his father. Wu agreed, but stipulated that Wen must not offer to pay for it. The incident plainly implies that some sort of payment was usual. *Wen Cheng-ming hui-kao,* ch. 9/pp. 107–108.
6. The other hand was Chu Lang. *Wen Cheng-ming hui-kao* (1929), ch. 9/p. 107.
7. *Wang Yen-chou* (1577), ch. 155/p. 17.
8. Some of Wen's teachers and closest friends, like Wu K'uan, Wang Ao, T'ang Yin, and Wang Ch'ung, rose from the merchant class by sheer talent to become leaders of the intelligentsia.
9. Another version of *The Cho-cheng Garden,* dated 1533, is published in Wen, *Cho-cheng yüan* (1929), and recorded in Pien, *Shih-ku t'ang* (1929 ed.), III, p. 285. Literary works for Wang Hsien-ch'en: *Wen Cheng-ming ch'üan-chi,* II, ch. 1/p. 3; II, ch. 3/p. 8.
10. For a discussion of the Suchou collectors and their society see Wilson and Wong, *Friends* (1974), pp. 16–36.
11. Chiang Chao-shen has definitely established that T'ang Yin wrote and painted for money: "T'ang Liu-ju chü-shih," *Ku-kung chi-k'an,* II, 4, pp. 28–29; III, 1, pp. 43–44; III, 3, pp. 71, 74–76 passim.
12. Clapp, *Wen Cheng-ming* (1975), pp. 32–33. In his colophons Shen Chou repeatedly stresses his excitement and the suspension of self-consciousness while painting, e.g., Yü, *Yü-shih shu-hua* (1634), ch. 10/p. 5.
13. Wen Chia, *Ch'ien-shan t'ang* (1569), p. 51.
14. See Wu Chen's "Eight Scenic Spots at Chia-ho" (*I-yüan i-chen,* Hongkong, 1967, II, no. 17) which was in Wen's collection; and Ch'en Ju-yen's *View of the Ching River (Ku-kung shu-hua chi,* Peking, 1929–35, XVII).
15. See Weng, *Gardens* (1968).
16. One of Wen's rare narrative subjects was *Yüan An Sleeping During the Snow,* which he painted twice, in 1531 and 1542 (Clapp, *Wen Cheng-ming* [1975], p. 47, fig. 10). The attraction of *Yüan An* was not so much the subject, which glorifies the Confucian virtues, as the fact that it had been treated by Huang Ch'üan, Tung Yüan, Li Kung-lin, Fan K'uan, Li T'ang, and Chao Meng-fu, and embodied in itself a good part of the history of classical painting.
17. James Cahill in an unpublished manuscript, which he kindly made available to me, points out that Wang Li's *Hua-shan* is one of the earliest albums known to treat a specialized theme.
18. A well-known story tells how Shen Chou was forced by a high official to decorate a wall in a yamen, Sirén, *Chinese Painting,* (1956–58), IV, p. 150. Whether it is apocryphal or not, the story demonstrates that such an incident was considered unusual and shocking in the career of a scholar-artist.
19. *Kuo-yün lou shu-hua chi,* ch. 4/pp. 27–28.
20. Clapp, *Wen Cheng-ming* (1975), p. 18.
21. Colophon by Tung Ch'i-ch'ang on Wen's "copy" of Chao Meng-fu's *Autumn Colors on the Ch'iao and Hua Mountains (Wen Cheng-ming hui-kao,* ch. 8/p. 95).
22. The major collections are recorded in: *Shan-hu-wang hua-lu,* ch. 23; *Ch'ien-shan t'ang shu-hua chi;* and *P'ei-wen chai shu-hua p'u,* ch. 98, 99.
23. Wen's letter on antiquities: *Wen Cheng-ming hui-kao,* ch. 9/p. 108.
24. James Ackerman, "A Theory of Style," *The Journal of Aesthetics and Art Criticism,* XX, 3 (Spring, 1962), p. 227.
25. *Wen Cheng-ming hui-kao* (1929), ch. 8/p. 98.

d. Wen Cheng-ming, *After Chao Po-su's 'Red Cliff,'* 1548. National Palace Museum, Taipei

Catalogue and Plates

I. SHEN CHOU/WEN CHENG-MING PORTRAIT ALBUM

Album consisting of eight leaves; ink on paper, ink and light color on paper, and ink on silk; each leaf 15⅜″ high and 12½″ wide (39.0 x 31.5 cm.)
Hwa's Hou Chen Shang Chai

Anonymous
I C. PORTRAIT OF WEN CHENG-MING

(Wen Tai-chao hsiao-hsiang)
No date
The third leaf of the eight-leaf album, ink and light color on paper

INSCRIPTION: the title is inscribed in clerical script by Chou T'ien-ch'iu (1514–1595)

SEALS: *(The code that follows each seal is the excellent one used for location by Wilson and Wong,* Friends of Wen Cheng-ming. *Roman numerals refer to columns of seals from right to left; arabic numerals refer to the vertical position of a seal within the column. Where the identification of an individual is found in standard biographical or seal dictionaries these have not been specified since scholars will know of their sources. Only when such identification appears to come from a more obscure origin has there been an attempt to guide the reader to that source.)*
Chou T'ien-ch'iu (1514–1595), from Suchou; painter, follower of Wen Cheng-ming
   Ch'ün-yü chü-shih   [painting: I/1]
Unidentified
   Pai-tsao   [painting: II/1]
   Lan-ling Wen-tzu shou-ts'ang   [painting: II/2]
   ——— ———*t'ang yin* (half seal)   [painting: I/2]
   Hsüan-shan ——— ——— (half seal)   [painting: II/3]

REMARKS: If the writer of the inscription, as indicated by the seal beneath it, can accurately be identified as Wen's pupil, Chou T'ien-ch'iu, we can be sure that the portrait itself dates from close to Wen's own lifetime.

Hsüeh I (b. 1563, copyist)
I D–H. WANG SHIH-CHEN'S BIOGRAPHY OF WEN CHENG-MING

(Wen hsien-sheng chuan)
Dated 1634
The fourth, fifth, sixth, seventh, and eighth leaves of the eight-leaf album; ink on paper

SEALS:
Hsüeh I (1563–after 1634)
   Hsüeh I   [calligraphy: I/1]
   Yü-ch'ing   [calligraphy: I/2]

REMARKS: Hsüeh I wrote this biography by Wang Shih-chen (1526–1590) when he was seventy-two *sui;* thus Hsüeh's year of birth can be figured as 1563. According to Hsüeh's inscription, he identified himself as the great-grandnephew of Wen Cheng-ming. His mother was the daughter of Wen Po-jen (nephew of Wen Cheng-ming). She married into the Hsüeh family.

文待詔小像

Yu-ch'i (copyist)
I A. PORTRAIT OF SHEN CHOU AT THE AGE OF EIGHTY

(Shen Shih-t'ien pa-shih sui hsiao-hsiang)
No date
The first leaf of the eight-leaf album; ink on silk

COLOPHON AND SEALS:
Wen Chia (1501–1583), writer of poem by Shen Chou:
> There are those who think
> My eyes are rather small
> Or my jaw too narrow;
> As for me
> I wouldn't know
> This, nor what is lacking.
> Of what use my face and eye,
> My only fear, loss of character—
> Improper these eighty years!
> Now is death
> Only a wall away.

The poem is by Shen Chou. I happened to see this copy of Shen's portrait by Yu-ch'i. So I wrote the poem on it. 1562, twelfth month, eighth day. The later student, Wen Chia.

Wen Chia yin	[painting: II/1]
Wen Hsiu-ch'eng yin	[painting: II/2]

Hsiang Yüan-pien (1525–1590)

Hsiang Yüan-pien yin	[painting: III/1]
Mo-lin sheng	[painting: III/2]
Shen-yu hsin-shang	[painting: III/3]
Hsiang Tzu-ching chia chen-ts'ang	[painting: III/6]

Sung Lo (1634–1713)

Ch'ing-li lü-so chai ts'ang	[painting: I/1]

Unidentified

Hsieh shih Lin-ts'un	[painting: III/4]
—— *Ch'ang* —— *wa*	[painting: III/5]

REMARKS: The original portrait, by an unknown artist, is now in Peking. On it is Shen Chou's poem, as written above, brushed in his own hand. Above this portrait is also a second poem, written by Shen early in the next year. It gives further insight into the artist's view of himself:
> Like or not like
> True or not true
> High and low, shadows outside myself
> For man, life death—a dream—
> Heaven and earth a stream of dust
> Happily I contemplate myself!

BIBLIOGRAPHY:
Edwards, *The Field of Stones* (1962), frontispiece.
Fourcade, *Art Treasures* (n.d.), pp. 70-71. Here is reproduced the original portrait.

Ch'en Yüan-su
I B. BIOGRAPHY OF SHEN CHOU

Dated 1620
The second leaf of the eight-leaf album; ink on paper

SEALS:
Ch'en Yüan-su, a Ming poet, painter, and calligrapher

Yüan-su	[calligraphy: I/1]

I A

The Debt to Shen Chou

Aside from their own in-born skills—talent—it is teachers with whom artists start. In the preceding section Anne Clapp has shown the importance of the past, the significance of "style," in the art of Wen Cheng-ming. In one sense, it could be maintained that all the artists of the past were Wen's teachers. But clearly he had one important contemporary teacher, the great Suchou master Shen Chou (1427–1509). Chiang Chao-shen claims that Wen began studying with Shen Chou in the late 1480s[1] when, by Chinese count, Wen was approaching the age of twenty.

The fact that we can begin the artistic association of Wen Cheng-ming and Shen Chou with this time makes it clear that they enjoyed two decades of important relationship. Yet from that time there are only bits and pieces of evidence to suggest just what that relation was. Under Shen's guidance Wen was certainly involved with studying old masters. On one famous occasion in 1497, he felt inadequate to copy a painting by Chao Meng-fu, the artist of the past he would grow to admire most, and refused to do so despite Shen Chou's urging.[2] On the other hand when in the same year he visited a nearby temple with Shen's great friend, Wu K'uan, he had no difficulty in quickly imitating a Huang Kung-wang landscape that was brought out for viewing (see no. VIII). As we shall see shortly, Shen Chou once evaluated his pupil's treatment of the tenth-century artists Ching Hao and Kuan T'ung.

Relations between the two had little to do with structured academic learning. Much more accurately they could be defined as a matter of easy friendship between an older and a younger man, a revered master and a younger painter-scholar of great promise, the son of a friend, socially and intellectually from the same familiar world. Friendship must have grown as their association continued. In 1500 we can sense their closeness when Wen wrote a colophon after a painting by the Yüan artist Chou Chih that Shen Chou, for a time, owned.

He wrote that the painting was worthy of Shen Chou's praise. Since Shen's poem-colophon follows, it is perhaps not too much to suggest that Shen first asked Wen to write, and then the pupil in turn insisted on the need for Shen's own comment.[3] Further, in 1502 they collaborated on a scroll for a mutual acquaintance, Shen T'ao-chu, on the occasion of his fiftieth birthday.[4] In 1507 Shen Chou painted a landscape to add to a scroll of Chao Meng-fu's calligraphy of a Su Shih poem. Early in 1508 Wen added his painting to the same scroll.[5] In 1507, Shen Chou also gave Wen Cheng-ming a poem he had written for him.[6] There is a brief undated reference stating that Shen painted a scroll, *The Great Peaks of Fu-ch'un,* for his pupil.[7] And in 1508 Wen is found closely connected with a famous series of poems on *Falling Flowers* that had originated with Shen Chou four years previously. Shen Chou painted one of his very beautiful still extant late masterpieces and to it are attached both Shen's and Wen's poems, the latter dated 1508.[8] Shen Chou gave Wen Cheng-ming's two sons their names, born as they were in 1497 and 1501.[9] The poems that Wen wrote on Shen Chou's death in 1509 still survive.[10]

All this, however, does relatively little to tell us what in fact Shen Chou taught his gifted pupil. We need to look further. A major piece of evidence for their earliest association comes from the important inscription that follows a long landscape handscroll in this exhibition—a scroll that was begun by Shen Chou but never finished (no. III). Years later, in 1546, when Wen was seventy-six, the then owner, Wang Yü-ch'ing, asked Wen to complete the painting. With proper expressions of reluctance, Wen did so and took the occasion of its completion to reminisce:

I remember back in 1489 visiting the master (Shen Chou) at the hut of the priest Shuang-wo and watching him paint the *Endless Miles of the Long River.* I was full of admiration. The master

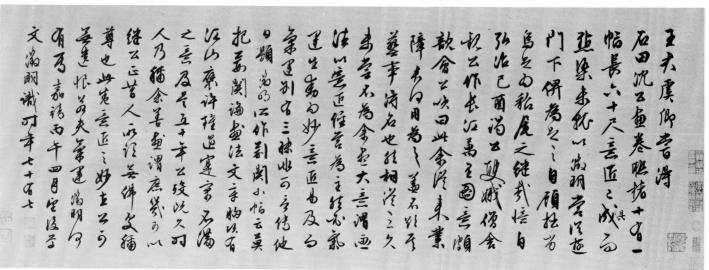

III, inscription by Wen Cheng-ming

laughed and said, "This is retribution for past sins; how can you consider it anything at all?" He never thought of his art as something to give him a name. But I was with him a long time; I could not help but understand his real meaning. He believed:

"Basic to the style of painting is the realization of the design (i-chiang), yet it is spirit-rhythm life-movement (ch'i-yün sheng-tung) that must give a sense of wonder. Design is readily attained, but spirit-rhythm is a different perfection. That is nothing one can teach."

On another occasion, writing on my small painting after Ching Hao and Kuan T'ung, he said, "You can't just take Ching Hao and Kuan T'ung and say you have a painting style; when art comes from within (the breast) you have rivers and mountains."

This is perhaps the clearest single surviving statement by Wen about his teacher and his teacher's attitude toward painting. From it we know that something called "design" (i-chiang), layout, or the external appearance of a past style, can be taught and repeated by a pupil, but that this has very little to do with the core of what makes great painting.

On another occasion, in the writing of a colophon following a painting by the Yüan master Wu Chen, now in the Cleveland Museum, Shen Chou himself looked back on the historical process as it related to two great old masters:

I love the Old Man of the Plum-blossom (Wu Chen),
Who inherited the secrets of Chü-jan from heart to heart.[11]

This essentially undefinable "heart transmission" (ch'uan hsin) describes what Shen Chou considered important to understand in the past and realize in the present. Whatever else it may mean, it most certainly directs importance toward an inner truth rather than superficial external appearance. And we have the testimony of Wen Cheng-ming's son, Wen Chia, that his father did, indeed, carry on such ideals, for faced by old masterpieces, he "perceived the basic meaning and with his heart as master, he realized it."[12] Wen Chia continued to stress this attitude in his father's work. In regard to a painting done in 1543 after Chao Meng-fu's famous *Water Village* he insisted that his father "did not reproduce Chao's actual forms."[13]

Such a view, stressing the intangibles, is reinforced by what Shen Chou also said after the long handscroll *Autumn Colors among Streams and Mountains* (no. VI). The painting is dateable to the early 1490s, clearly during the time when Wen was Shen's student. Shen Chou wrote:

This scroll was made to imitate Ni Yün-lin's (Ni Tsan's) conception. Yün-lin's methods were sparing, mine are cluttered. Yet though he was sparing, his meaning was ample. This is that which is known as the unlearnable.[14]

Here the lesson seems to be that one cannot simply repeat the accomplishments of a great master.

Close to this same time—in 1492—Shen Chou, on a very personal level, was recording his experience of the importance of an inner truth gained through one's own self-realization. He wrote of this on a well-known hanging scroll, *Night Vigil,* now in the National Palace Museum in Taipei. Here he described the problem of dealing with "sounds and shapes" and in this solitary vigil being able to reach a realization of "an understanding of things."[15] (Years later Wen Cheng-ming was to have similar musings while listening to bamboo: see no. XXXIII.) Again we are speaking of a truth reached on a personal intuitive level. This was of vital importance to Shen Chou and translated into terms of art and teaching tells again of things that just could not be taught—indeed the most important things. Truth is intuitively sensed; its manifestations realized through self-discovery. How, indeed, then, can we define a meaningful teacher-pupil relationship between Shen Chou and Wen Cheng-ming?

Perhaps we cannot completely do so, but in this exhibition the best opportunity from the evidence of actual early painting is afforded by the album, now mounted as a handscroll, that comes from the Nelson-Atkins Gallery in Kansas City.

NOTES:
1. Chiang, "Life" (1971–1972), I, p. 66.
2. Sickman, ed., *Chinese Calligraphy and Painting* (1962), p. 135.
3. Tomita and Tseng, *Portfolio* (1961), p. 4 and pls. 16–17.
4. Chiang, "Life" (1971–1972), II, p. 37.
5. *Liao-ning* (1962), II, pls. 22–29.
6. Chiang, "Life" (1971–1972), II, p. 49.
7. An, *Mo-yüan* (1908 ed.), painting, ch. 2/p. 74b (supplementary section).
8. *Ku-kung shu-hua lu* (1965), ch. 4/p. 159.
9. Chiang, "Life" (1971–1972), II, p. 51.
10. Chiang, "Life" (1971–1972), II, p. 55.
11. Lee and Ho, *Chinese Art under the Mongols* (1968), no. 252.
12. From *Wen Chia hsing-lüeh* (sixteenth century) as found in Lu, *Sung Yüan i-lai* (1829), ch. 8/2a–b. I essentially have followed Sirén's translation of this passage: *Chinese Painting* (1956), IV, p. 175.
13. *Shih-ch'ü pao-chi ch'u p'ien,* ch. 6/p. 51b. Both of Wen Chia's comments are cited by Clapp, *Wen Cheng-ming* (1975), pp. 23 and 31.
14. Whitfield, *In Pursuit* (1969), p. 50.
15. Edwards, *The Field of Stones* (1962), p. 57.

II. SHEN CHOU/WEN CHENG-MING JOINT ALBUM

(Shen Wen shan-shui ho-chüan)
Six album leaves mounted as a handscroll with five leaves by Shen Chou and one leaf by Wen Cheng-ming; ink and light color on paper, each leaf 15¼" high and 23¾" wide (38.6 x 60.5 cm.)
Nelson-Atkins Gallery, Kansas City, Missouri (Nelson Fund)

II F. STORM OVER THE RIVER

(Feng-yü ku-chou)
By Wen Cheng-ming
Dated before 1504
Inscription and seals of the artist

Wen Cheng-ming's single surviving painting in this important series of album leaves appropriately follows those of his master. In the album's present state there are five leaves by Shen Chou and one by Wen Cheng-ming. Wen's colophon, written later in 1516, explains the circumstances. Shen Chou had done six album leaves for his great friend Wu K'uan. There was some paper left over, and Wu K'uan asked Wen Cheng-ming to finish the album for him. With proper protestations of inadequacy and the embarrassment that it really brought upon a pupil, Wen took four T'ang couplets and with them as a basis added his paintings—that is, four paintings. Now he is writing later (1516) at the request of Wu K'uan's nephew, Wu I (Wu Ssu-yeh). Both Wu K'uan and Shen Chou have died.

Wu K'uan died in 1504; Shen Chou in 1509. The painting then was done before 1504. One suspects it may date to the late nineties. We know that Wu K'uan was in Suchou in 1497 when he left the city to return to the capital, and according to Chiang Chao-shen, this was the last time that Shen Chou and Wu K'uan were together.[1] This fact is further corroborated by the Ch'ing scholar Weng Fang-kang (see no. VIII). Shen Chou, of course, might later have sent paintings to his friend, but Wen's account seems to tell of a request from Wu K'uan in person:

Wu K'uan asked me to finish the extra paper. I declined with thanks as being inadequate, but I could not brush off his requests.

If, then, Wen's painting was done close to 1497 it becomes one of his very early works. The Shen Chou album leaves stylistically could have been done around the late 1480s, but their unquestioned maturity—a combination of their ease and strength—makes it completely reasonable for them to have been done ten or twelve years later. However, it must be noted that we are working with an incomplete album. It lacks one leaf by Shen Chou and three by Wen Cheng-ming. But with Wen's single extant leaf we clearly see his art when he was very

much his master's pupil. Here, since he is "finishing" his master's work—in the full consciousness of Shen Chou's concrete example—one has a special opportunity to compare the art of master and pupil.

In the first place, Wen Cheng-ming adopts the same point of view as Shen Chou. For all of the scenes (no. II A–E) the viewer is generally raised above the ground and usually looks down upon the landscape. Shen Chou's leaf C, *Scholar and Crane Returning Home,* with its basic elements of foreground trees in the lower right, boat toward the middle left and distance beyond, at first seems to offer the closest analogies to Wen's *Storm on the River.* But actually it is Shen's first leaf, *Gardeners,* which is most rewarding as a comparison.

Each of these two paintings is a rather exact and specific view. With Shen Chou we are looking over the fence, into the fields. We see the momentarily half-open gate, crouching gardeners, glancing at each other, caught in a particular momentary pose. The man with the hoe is about to plunge it into the earth. That the viewer is located at a particular spot and not allowed to wander timelessly over a generalized scene is established by the receding grove of trees, their trunks deliberately angled toward a central point in the top distance, and holding our vision accordingly. It is this importance of capturing a specific scene that is also at the heart of Wen's view. Given the concreteness of an exact imagery from the T'ang poet Wei Ying-wu, he wants us to feel the immediacy of his view of a swollen river in Anhui province:

The spring flood carries the rain,
    swifter by evening.
And at the wild ford, no one—
    only the empty, angled boat.[2]

While the upper part of Shen Chou's painting may appear to be more specifically filled, Wen's is by no means empty. Lined clouds and slanting rain make its atmosphere exact. This direct, even impressionistic rendering of a rainstorm comes ultimately from Southern Sung painting (and of course was made much of among Wen's contemporaries in the so-called Che school of painting).

But to return to Shen Chou, it is in the lower right-hand corner of each painting that the closest specific comparisons can be made. Land slanting modestly from the right edge becomes an outcropping of tumbled moss-dot rocks, a somewhat precarious foundation for a selected group of trees that create a half-open foreground screen of trunk and leaf and twig (combined with some architecture). Given these general similarities, however, it does not take long to realize that Wen is not really following his master's style. He certainly has learned from Shen Chou the importance of a blunt, thick stroke combined with touches of rich ink. One thus sees parallels in outline of rock and tree, in the fusing of texture-strokes, in thin tree-twigs,

春湘帶雨晩來急
野渡無人舟自橫

II F

in the black rich massing of leaves or moss-dots. But Wen has handled all of these in an individual manner. Thus, if one carefully compares his treatment with that of Shen Chou, it is clear that Wen's individual strokes are flatter; rock outlines are more angular; moss dots *(tien)* more easily fly away from the surfaces of the rocks; leaves mingle readily together and are not so sharply differentiated.

Another way of defining this is to indicate that the type of brush-stroke is different. Wen's so-called "slanted tip" comes from the side or an angle, *ts'e-feng,* whereas Shen Chou's brush usually meets the paper straight on, the brush held perpendicular to the paper, *chung-feng.* The result in Shen Chou is to create a deliberately stable line, whether dry or wet—a series of strokes, differentiated by their shape and strength, carefully knit together. The forms are more static, more solid. Shen Chou is almost a kind of careful sculptor in paint. In contrast, the flatness, the angularity, the freedom of dotting, the blending of ink-touches create in Wen a feeling for irregular movement, perhaps a kind of elegant virtuosity. The individual stroke, less contained within itself, jumps more readily to the next, and whereas Shen Chou's "moment" in the garden is static, Wen's "moment" is filled with action. Nowhere is this more clearly symbolized than in the contrasting treatment of the fronds of the willow tree (or trees) that in the lower center of each painting is a key motif.

Aside from telling us the circumstances of the painting of the scroll, Wen's colophon of 1516 sums up a view of his teacher. He tells us that Shen Chou was a man of the highest integrity, out of which his painting emerged as a kind of play that is not to be compared with the activity of ordinary craftsmen-artists. Then he concludes, "The more he created, the deeper he went. There is no telling where it starts or finishes." The term for "starts or finishes," *tuan-ni,* comes directly from the great Taoist of the fourth century B.C., Chuang-tzu, appropriately in his chapter, "The Great and Venerable Teacher." It only serves to emphasize the significance of that which cannot be defined in ordinary terms, and by inference something that cannot be transferred. If the unlearnable is to be realized one must discover it within oneself.

NOTES:
1. Chiang, "Life" (1971–1972), I, p. 82.
2. The poem is a well-known one included in the anthology *T'ang-shih san-pai shou* [Three Hundred Poems from the T'ang Dynasty] (Shanghai, 1948 ed.), p. 147. There is an alternate and not very exact translation in Witter Bynner, *The Jade Mountain* (New York, 1960), p. 206 and an accurate one in Burton Watson, *Chinese Lyricism* (New York, 1971), p. 118.

SEALS OF THE ARTIST:

T'ing-yün sheng	[painting: II/1]
Wen Pi yin	[painting: II/2]
Wen Cheng-ming yin	[colophon: I/1]
Wu-yen shih yin	[colophon: I/2]
Heng-shan	[colophon: I/3]

INSCRIPTION BY THE ARTIST: translated above in text

COLOPHON BY THE ARTIST: [four poems and explanation]

Venerable Shih (Shen Chou) was lofty in spirit when wielding the brush;
The calmness in his bosom is reflected in the slow-drifting white clouds.
He had no need to follow the style of Yüan-hui (Mi Yu-jen)
In painting the mountains around Suchou, after the rain.

Around Suchou which part is most wet with ink?
It is West Mountain, most wonderful after rain.
Who is it that can attain even one part of this unique feeling?
Only Mo-ch'i's (Wang Wei's) painting in his poetry, a thousand years ago.

Years ago he (Shen Chou) achieved excellence in his poetry;
In later years greatness in painting all but obscured this earlier fame.
Life's affairs are many and vast, who knows what he will gain?
Your white-haired student is still unaccomplished and ashamed.

The superior man has left and his creation has ceased.
The fisherman spends many sunsets on the beach.
Looking, through tears, at the broken ink and remnants of his work.
A thousand peaks of green mountains melt into the sad clouds.

(tr. James Robinson)

Shen Chou was a man of the highest integrity. His writings were full of wisdom. His scholarship was deep. In his leisure he played (at painting), not something that ordinary craftsmen-artists could attain. In his early years he followed Wang Meng and Huang Kung-wang and through them entered the halls of Tung Yüan and Chü-jan. The more he created, the deeper he went. There is no telling where it starts or finishes. These six leaves were done for Wu K'uan. The use of the brush and the arrangement of the landscapes go far beyond the usual. Wu K'uan asked me to finish the extra paper. I declined with thanks as being inadequate, but I could not brush off his (persistent) requests.

And so I decided to take four T'ang couplets and sketched some paintings. But with my inferior skill how could they be added to such a famous brush. The pupil was embarrassed. Wu K'uan has left us, for several years now, and Shen Chou has also gone. His (Wu's) nephew, Ssu-yeh, brought the album to show me; one cannot help sighing. The man and his lute are both dead. I composed four poems and added these remarks. Autumn, the eighth month of 1516. Wen Cheng-ming, the pupil, wrote in the Yü-ch'ing shan-fang (Jade-chime Mountain House).

COLOPHONS AND SEALS:
Hsieh Lan-sheng (1760–1831), poet and calligrapher from Nan-hai, Kuangtung. Dated 1824, first month, twenty-sixth day; at this time Hsieh points out that the full complement of leaves already was missing.

Hsieh Lan-sheng yin	[colophon: I/1]
Li-p'u	[colophon: I/2]

P'an Cheng-wei (1791–1850), Cantonese collector

P'an shih Chi-t'ung chen-ts'ang	[painting: II/3]

Unidentified

Shih-ch'üan hsin-shang	[painting: I/1]

REMARKS:
Yü-ch'ing shan-fang, a hall built by Wen Cheng-ming. Wen Chia, in his father's biography, claimed that it was built after his father's return from Peking. The occurrence of its name here casts doubt on that fact. This can be explained only by Wen's using the term early, perhaps for some minor room, and later constructing a new *Yü-ch'ing shang-fang.* See Wen, *Fu-t'ien chi* (1968 ed.), ch. 36/p. 4a (p. 899).

West Mountain is West Tung-t'ing Mountain in Lake T'ai (see map).

BIBLIOGRAPHY:
P'an, *T'ing-fan lou* (1947 ed.), ch. 2/pp. 567–568.
Lee, *Chinese Landscape* (1962), no. 54a.
Wilson and Wong, *Friends* (1974), p. 27, fig. 3.

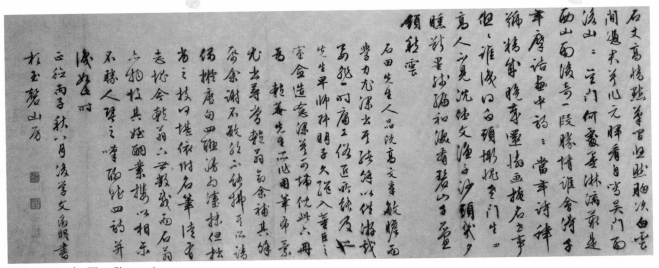

II, inscription by Wen Cheng-ming

Shen Chou (1427–1509)
II A–E. FIVE-LEAF ALBUM

No date
Album mounted as a handscroll with one leaf by Wen Cheng-ming
  (see II F), ink and light color on paper, each leaf 15¼" high and
  23¾" wide (38.6 x 60.5 cm.)
Inscriptions, signatures, and seals of the artist
Nelson-Atkins Gallery, Kansas City, Missouri (Nelson Fund)

Although the specific relation of Shen Chou to
Wen Cheng-ming has just been analyzed with
particular reference to the first of the Shen Chou
album leaves, a view of the remaining four helps
fix in our minds the essential uniqueness and
nobility of the art of Wen Cheng-ming's teacher.

The album as a whole was described some years
ago.[1] Here it is well to remind ourselves that in
settings that range from the close familiar garden
to the far mountaintop or the distant reaches of
river or lake, there is general thematic unity. Both
poetry and painting relate to man's wandering and
his longing for home.

The views have about them a very special sense
of directness and stability. This is perhaps first seen
in their compositions, in the positioning of the key
elements in each painting. A cliff, a plateau, a cloud,
a tree, a boat—each form is realized, both in its
definition and placement, with consummate
selectivity and authority. Although distance may be
part of the theme, there is even here no room for
misty vagueness, as the flat, limiting washes of
distant mountains declare. It is, as already suggested
above, a kind of sculpture in paint. But however
sure the brush that realizes that sculpture, it does so
with a subtle spontaneity and variety so that
inevitably there is a vitality and tension to each
part and to each detail that breathes life. Washes,
free strokes, thick even lines, colors, all work
together to create a varied "classic" statement about
the world. Wen's greater elegance, a sense of
outward brilliance, a fine correctness, which in
seeming contradiction often revealed the tensions
of great struggle, never ultimately could be at home
in this blunt harmony. Yet, as the next painting
will show, he could come close. . . .

II A, *Gardeners*

白雲如帶東山腰石
磴飛空細路遙攔倚
杖藜舒眺望欲因鳴
澗落吹簫　沈周

II B, *Poet on a Mountain Top*

載鶴攜琴湖
上歸白雲紅葉
互交飛儂家
正在山深處竹
裡書聲半檻
廎　沈周

II C, *Scholar and Crane Returning Home*

浦樹生秋
紅山烟凝暮
禁可是尊
鱸人歸來
自千里
沈周

II D, *Return from a Thousand Li*

碧樹沉〻綠
本齋釣舟閑
倚雲川西行
人岸上空田
肯各自車輪
與馬歸
沈周

II E, *Mountain Travelers*

NOTE:
1. Edwards, *The Field of Stones* (1962), pp. 38–41.

INSCRIPTIONS BY THE ARTIST:
[A. *Gardeners (Liu-wai ch'un-keng)*. Has signature only:]
Shen Chou. [The same signature follows the poems on leaves B–E.]
[B. *Poet on a Mountain Top (Chang-li yüan-t'iao):*]
    White clouds like a belt
        encircle the mountain's waist
    A stone ledge flying in space
        and the far thin road.
    I lean on my bramble staff
        and gazing into space
    Make the note of my flute
        an answer to the sounding torrent.
[C. *Scholar and Crane Returning Home (Tai-ho fan-hu):*]
    Carrying a crane and my *ch'in*
        homeward bound on the lake
    White clouds and red leaves
        flying together
    My home right in the very
        depths of mountains
    The sound of reading within bamboo,
        a tiny couch, a humble gate.
[D. *Return from a Thousand Li (Yang-fan ch'iu-p'u):*]
    The red of autumn comes to river trees
    The mountain smokes freeze fast the purple evening.
    Those who long for home
    Return from a thousand *li.*
[E. *Mountain Travelers (K'uang-yeh ch'i-lü):*]
    Still and heavy the trees of jade
        and not an even green.
    A fishing boat resting
        at the western edge of the Cha.
    Travelers on the bank
        turn back an empty head
    Each having left his carriage wheel
        for a horse's hoof.

SEALS OF THE ARTIST:

Ch'i-nan	[A: II/1]
	[B: II/1]
	[D: I/1]
	[E: II/1]
Shih-t'ien	[A: II/2]
	[C: I/1]
	[E: I/1]
Pai-shih-weng	[B: I/1]

SEALS:
P'an Cheng-wei (1791–1850), a Cantonese collector

T'ing-fan lou ts'ang	[B: III/1]
Chi-t'ung p'ing-sheng chen-shang	[C: II/1]
Chi-t'ung pi-wan	[D: II/]1
P'an Chi-t'ung chien-shang chang	[E: III/1]

Unidentified

Shih-ch'üan hsin-shang	[A: III/1]
———— ———— ———— ————	[A: I/1]
Indecipherable	[A; I/2]

Fragmentary part of a seal in the lower left corner of each leaf

BIBLIOGRAPHY:
P'an, *T'ing-fan lou* (1947 ed.), supplement, ch. 2/pp. 565–566.
Arts of the Ming (1952), p. 9, nos. 12–17.
Munsterberg, *Landscape Painting* (1955), pls. 54–55, no. 2
Edwards, *The Field of Stones* (1962), no. XXIV, pls. 14B, 17A,
    18A, 18B, 19A.
Lee, *Chinese Landscape* (1962), no. 54.
Sickman and Soper, *Art and Architecture of China* (1968), pls. 132–133.

III. SHEN-CHOU/WEN CHENG-MING JOINT HANDSCROLL

(*Shen Wen liang hsien-sheng ho-tso ch'ang-chüan*)
Date completed: 1546
Handscroll, ink on paper, 14½" high and 680⁵⁄₁₆" long (37.0 x 1708.8 cm.)
Inscription, signature, and seals of the artist
Mr. and Mrs. Wan-go H. C. Weng, New York

Wen's inscription from this important long land-scape has already been cited. It affords the earliest clear original reference to Wen's relationship to Shen Chou. The painting itself confirms their closeness long after Shen Chou's death. That Wen could so exactly "complete" the work of his master, years after Wen had become his own master, stands as a moving tribute to a kind of immortality of art, the harmony of the dead and the living in the greater life of Chinese civilization itself.

For those who have viewed the authority and mastery in Shen Chou's *Five-leaf Album,* his mature approach to the landscape will be known and certainly recognized in this seemingly endless unfolding of natural forms. The lay-out is all Shen Chou. This is most noticeable in the bold selectivity of large forms, their careful, ordered placing in a space which is distinctly limited, often, as in the Kansas City album, by sheets of far mountain wash, flat curtains on the paper.

Another factor, not always so evident in the album "views," is the sharp cutting of forms top and bottom by the edge of the scroll. This stresses their size and power (they cannot be contained in what is already a large format), and it has the effect of thrusting the viewer into close association with the physical reality of objects themselves (we are not allowed to stand back and from a distance see them whole).

In this strong, close view one will recognize shapes familiar from the album: the slant of a hill with its free but essentially parallel texture strokes; the rounded form of a hillock or rock edged by the rhythmic accents of dark dots; expanses of water rimmed by shadowed shoals; the wet-ink forms of a tree-grove, white-trunked, a flat uneven screen along a land-crest; in it perhaps the accents of bare, black twigs; firm cliff-top plateaus, seemingly carved, enduring changeless platforms for the contemplation of real or imagined scholars; figures who are themselves reduced to es-sential silhouettes, quiet and sure as the nature they inhabit.

Drawn close, one will follow, too, the rhythm and direction of wash and brush-stroke whether it defines a leaf or a tree-trunk, a mountain-texture or a rock edge, a bridge or a house. But as one moves along from right to left in this inevitable experience in time, one will perhaps remember and retain the basic compositional order. There is a tripartite division. First is an area of prominent land formations varied by shallow tight pockets of space. This is followed by a complete gap creating an angle of paper untouched from top to bottom. Water and sky are the same emptiness. From here we move to a second section, a major area of land at the central point of which a triangular grotto—like a peaked roof—reveals a half-hidden waterfall within. This section ends in another untouched area of paper-water-sky, at the upper edge of which is a single bit of land, a kind of answering note in the emptiness to the land we have just traversed (and incidentally the kind of compositional device that might have been drawn from the tenth century). Now a few stable water-reeds and seven silent skiff-seated fishermen accent the quiet paper—the fishermen as much a part of the land-scape as the firm, bent willows that begin the final section. Here is both form and space, a single unit which has its own tripartite division but one which never breaks completely into emptiness, or, conversely, into strong massing of solids. It serves as a kind of balanced summation of what has gone before, ending with as firm a definition as was in the beginning, this time, however, picking up again the motif of the grotto-waterfall.

This is not a composition that fades into misty distance, as it might in the mature Sung. It is far closer to classical T'ang ideas of form. It is a painting that Ming eyes would certainly see as perpetuating the great post-T'ang tenth-century tradition of Tung Yüan and Chü-jan, but certainly also in its moist, often free treatment of ink, it would reveal those masters filtered through the intermediary of the Yüan master Wu Chen, generally accepted as a major influence in Shen Chou's late work. Such, for a Ming artist, were the traditional strata of style.

All this applies accurately to Shen Chou. Where then is Wen Cheng-ming, now forty years later? Basically, as is demanded, he conforms to his master. But what did, or could, he add to, as he says, this "sable tail"? Essentially he tells us what was needed: details, or, literally, *tien-jan,* "dotting and washes." In searching for Wen Cheng-ming, he can, I think, be taken literally. It becomes a kind of fascinating game. Where are the traces of Wen's brush? However, it is more than just a game, for in defining the difference one learns to understand both artists.

In a brief catalogue entry one cannot touch on every point. Each will want to examine and dis-cover for himself. As a general principle, Wen's touch is seen in a greater play—a more varied, perhaps broken line, a tendency toward angularity, sharp spikes of cliff-side grass or loose surface dotting. It is possible to imagine certain areas as originally incomplete, then filled by Wen—for

III

example, the first bridge with its thin-legged wood-gatherers and the lines of water beneath completing a gap, the "flying-white" plateau edge (detail a); the addition of the empty pavilion that follows the first water-sky space and at least the broken outline at the far edge of its plateau (detail b). Again Wen might be seen in the texturing of the pine-trunks and the grass-hut beneath them that peeks out from behind the rocky shore (detail c) when we come to the next wide open areas. Here the reeds could be by either, the island of rocks basically Shen Chou (possibly embellished with a later dot or a touch of wash). The silent fishermen exactly fit Shen Chou, as do the strong quiet willows beyond them. On the other hand much of the detail in the village scene that follows must be attributed to Wen, including some of the washes on the far hills. Later, the meditating plateau-seated figure is precisely Shen Chou, as are the strong dark rock forms that frame him (detail d). But much of the detail in the final waterfall-grotto, including the figures gazing at the fall, seems to betray Wen's sharper brush.

SEALS OF THE ARTIST:

Wen Cheng-ming yin   [colophon: III/1]
T'ing-yün kuan   [colophon: III/2]

COLOPHON BY THE ARTIST:

Mr. Wang Yü-ch'ing has obtained a scroll by Shen Chou consisting of eleven sections of paper joined together to make a single painting of sixty feet. The design, *i-chiang,* was all laid out, but the dotting and washing, *tien-jan,* had not been completed. Since (Wen) Cheng-ming was his student, he was the one to finish it. But consider his clumsy effort, how could he add to this "sable tail"! I remember back in 1489 visiting the master (Shen Chou) at the hut of the priest Shuang Wo and watching him paint the *Endless Miles of the Long River.* I was full of admiration. The master laughed and said, "This is retribution for past sins; how can you consider it anything at all?" He never thought of his art as something to give him a name. But I was with him a long time; I could not help but understand his real meaning. He believed:

Basic to the style of a painting is the realization of the design (*i-chiang*), yet it is spirit-rhythm life-movement (*ch'i-yün sheng-tung*) that must give a sense of wonder. Design is readily attained, but spirit-rhythm is a different perfection. That is nothing one can teach.

On another occasion, in writing a colophon on (Wen) Cheng-ming's small painting after Ching Hao and Kuan T'ung, he said, "You can't just take Ching Hao and Kuan T'ung and say you have a painting style; when art comes from within (the breast) you have rivers and mountains." The praise was rather excessive and really suggested inadequacy.

It has been some fifty years. Shen Chou has already been gone for a long time. Now people consider that I am a good painter; they think that somehow I can continue as the master. This is indeed as in the old days when respect was asked where there was no Buddha. The wonder in the design of this scroll is all the master's. As for spirit-rhythm, how can Cheng-ming supply this!
Written at the age of seventy-seven *sui.*

COLOPHONS AND SEALS:

Teng Fu (1507 *chü-jen*), landscape painter from Ch'ang-shu; dated 1546
Teng Fu Wen-tu fu   [colophon: II/1]
Weng T'ung-ho (1830–1904), H. Shu-p'ing, official, calligrapher, writer from Ch'ang-shu (Hummel, *Eminent Chinese* [1943–1944], pp. 860–861). Dated 1878; second colophon dated 1880, apparently written by Weng to record a gathering of his contemporaries who also viewed the scroll; frontispiece dated 1901.

Sung-ch'an chü-shih	[frontispiece: I/1]
Weng T'ung-ho ch'i-shih sui-hou shu	[frontispiece: I/2]
Weng P'ing-sheng	[frontispiece: II/1]
Shu-p'ing hua-chien	[painting: II/1]
	[mounting: I/2]
Ch'ang-shu Weng T'ung-ho mo-so shen-ting	[painting: II/2]
	[mounting: I/3]
Weng T'ung-ho yin	[painting: XIV/1]
T'ung-ho yin	[colophon: I/1]
Shu-p'ing	[colophon: I/2]
Chün chai pi-chi	[mounting: I/1]

Ts'ai Ch'i (ca. 1662– ca. 1722), T. Wei-kung; calligrapher from Manchuria

Wei-kung chen-shang	
[painting: III/1]	[painting: VIII/1]
[painting: IV/1]	[painting: IX/1]
[painting: V/1]	[painting: X/1]
[painting: VI/1]	[painting: XI/1]
[painting: VII/2]	[painting: XII/1]
San-han Ts'ai Ch'i shu-hua chih chang	[painting: I/3]
	[Wen colophon: I/1]
Ts'ai shih Wei-kung shu-hua chih chang	[painting: XIV/2]

Sun Fan (Ch'ing Dynasty), T. Hsiao-wei; landscape painter from Ch'ang-shu

Yü-shan Sun shih Ts'e-feng ——— – t'u-shu	[painting: I/4]
Yü-shan Sun Fan yen-yü shih chih yin	[painting: IX/3]
[painting: III/4]	[painting: X/4]
[painting: V/3]	[painting: XII/3]
[painting: VI/3]	[painting: XIV/5]
[painting: VIII/4]	[Wen colophon: I/4]
Yü-shan Ts'e-feng Sun shih ch'uan ching ssu-chi	[painting: XIV/3]

III, section

Ts'e-feng ping-she
  [painting: III/2]
  [painting: V/2]
  [painting: VI/2]
  [painting: VIII/2]
  [painting: IX/2]
Sun erh ch'ih

Hsiao-wei

[Wen colophon: I/2]
[painting: X/2]
[painting: XII/2]
[Teng colophon: I/1]
[Teng colophon: II/2]
[painting: XIV/4]
[Wen colophon: I/3]
[painting: XIV/6]
[Wen colophon: I/5]

Wang Ming-sheng (1722–1797), T. Hsi-chih; calligrapher from Chia-ting
  I-ts'ao t'ing   [painting: I/1]
Ch'en T'ing-ching (1639–1710), T. Tzu-tuan, H. Wu-t'ing shan-jen, 1658 *chin-shih;* calligrapher from Chin-ch'eng, Shansi
  Tsun-wen chai t'u-shu chi   [Wen colophon: II/1]
Unidentified
  Wu Mei-ch'i shih chien-ting   [painting: I/2]
  Wu K'ai-chih yin   [Wen colophon: IV/1]

Mei-ch'i   [Wen colophon: IV/2]

Han-yang Wu shih ts'ang shu-hua yin chi   [painting: XIII/1]
Ts'ai yao chen-shang   [painting: IV/2]
                              [painting: VII/1]
                              [painting: XI/2]

K'uei-chi t'ai-shih sun
  [painting: III/3]
  [painting: V/4]
  [painting: VI/4]
  [painting: VI/4]
Chu Ssu-hsiang chiu-chia

[painting: VIII/3]
[painting: IX/4]
[painting: X/3]
[painting: XII/4]
[Teng colophon: II/3]

REMARKS:
Teng Fu, from Ch'ang-shu, was a painter of landscapes.
Wang Yü-ch'ing, who was also from Ch'ang-shu and for whom Wen finished the scroll, asked Teng for his colophon. Apparently the scroll stayed in Ch'ang-shu from the time it was finished to the time of Weng T'ung-ho, who was also from that district.

III, detail a

III, detail b

III, detail c

III, detail d

Shen Chou (1427–1509)
IV. CATALPA TREES

(San tzu t'u)
No date
Hanging scroll, ink on paper, 43¹³/₁₆″ high and 16¹/₁₆″ wide (100.7 x 40.8 cm.)
Inscription, signature, and seals of the artist
Indianapolis Museum of Art, gift of Mr. and Mrs. Eli Lilly

Fan Kung's hand planted objects of a thousand years,
Fitting for descendants' nurturing care.
Over and over leaves fall returning to the ages;
Again and again good spring rises from the earth.
Watch them as Chi Cha guarded the auspicious trees.
From Chuang-tzu I know the beauty of their timber;
So for you I take the brush and paint their likeness—
Bright sun, the wind, the rain awe lesser plants.

Thus the artist links his painting to poetry; poetry, to his painting. This is the first of four scrolls by Shen Chou which have been selected for inclusion in this exhibition, because, well-known to students of Chinese painting, they illuminate with great clarity certain key aspects of the art of Wen's master. Each in its own way expresses—beyond the album and handscroll already discussed—something of the essential Shen Chou. They all represent Shen Chou's art in its full maturity. All but this scroll can be dated exactly to the time when Wen Chengming was his pupil. However, this meeting of two scholars under three catalpa trees has the special importance of relating closely to a theme or themes that play a key role in Wen's art.

Since Chou Ting, whose poem also appears at the top of the scroll, died in 1487 we cannot project the painting into a period when we are sure of Wen's apprenticeship, but the maturity of the style relates it to what Wen certainly would have known and admired in his teacher. The painting is a second version. From another source we know that Liu Hsien-chih, for whom Shen two years earlier did the first, was in Suchou in 1479.[1] A date close to 1481 is surely a safe assumption.

As often with Wen himself, this for Shen Chou, then, is a second brushing of an earlier painting. In Suchou a "copy" could often be brushed by the master himself, and this applies both to the writing of poems and the painting of paintings.

But our main interest is to point out how Shen handles this theme. Again it is a limited, essential view. Three trees are exactly positioned on a brief stage. The central one is darker. More forward, it is

IV

at the apex of a gentle triangle. The two flanking catalpas fall modestly behind it. There is enough of rock and dot and sparse texturing of the land to define the brief plain which supports the trees and the two scholar-friends. Lesser tree-growth at the right acts as a counter-weight to the two scholars and helps ensure, within the notion of variety, an essential stability. Characteristically there is no far distance. There is nothing to compete with the play of branch and twig and leaf and hanging moss against the sky. The notion of placing the trees forward, the figure behind, is a constant aspect of the way Wen Cheng-ming handled this theme, or often the variant of it, the tree-grove combined with the scholarly retreat. It is not too much to add that this is an exact "impression." No violence is done to what the eye might see. Objects fall into place, some forward, some back. It is such sure, if limited, spatial recession that marks the view of the garden in Shen Chou's *Five-leaf Album* (no. II A–E). After all, his poem on the catalpas says they are exact, a kind of portrait: "I . . . paint their likeness."

This is not only a scholarly meeting, it is also a portrait of old trees. Both play a major part in Wen's art. Emphasis may be on one or the other of these two ideas or perhaps, as was done by Wen very late in life, the two can be linked exactly: tree and scholar are essentially one. Earlier, consider Wen's *Farewell at T'ing-yün* (no. XXVI). Late is *Two Scholars, Old Cypress, and Mountain Waterfall* (no. LVII). Always the tree forward, at the apex of a triangle, the scholars behind.

However, if paintings such as this are an immediate source of Wen's art, even more striking is the difference. For Shen Chou the old tree never became the excuse, as with Wen, for intense and brilliant virtuosity. Although they were known to him, Wen seems never to have painted these catalpas. They grew by the shrine of the famous Sung dynasty figure Fan Kung or Fan Chung-yen (989–1052) at nearby T'ien-p'ing Mountain. Wen made a well-recorded trip there in 1508 (no. X). Clearly for him they lacked the dramatic implications that would have attracted his brush—exactly what he was to discover in the junipers at more distant Ch'ang-shu (no. XXX). Shen Chou also painted those trees, but there and here he will not force the subject.

NOTE:
1. Chiang, "Life" (1971–1972), I, p. 52.

SEALS OF THE ARTIST:

Yu-chu chü	[painting: I/1]
Ch'i-nan	[painting: II/1]
Shih-t'ien	[painting: II/2]

INSCRIPTION BY THE ARTIST: [poem, translated above; signed] Ch'ang-chou Shen Chou

COLOPHONS AND SEALS:
Chou Ting (1401–1487); undated:
Shen Chou once climbed to the Fan ancestral temple with Liu Hsien-chih of Liao-yang and looked on the three catalpa trees by the outer wall. Later he did a painting of them for Liu as a going-away present. I wrote three *fu* (prose-poems) in T'ang dynasty form. After two years, Ming-chi called and asked me to copy these old phrases as a request to Shen Chou to do the painting again.
[A poem follows.]

Jung-hsi hsüan	[painting: III/1]
Chou Ting	[painting: IV/1]
Unidentified	
Ch'i-tsung chen-shang	[painting: V/1]
Ch'ang-ch'i Shen shih t'u shih chih chang	[painting: V/2]

REMARKS:
Chi Cha (Shen's poem) in the sixth century B.C. had a sword much desired by the ruler of Hsü. After returning from a diplomatic mission for him, Chi Cha found his lord had died. So he took the sword and hung it as a votive offering on a tree at the prince's grave.
Chuang-tzu. Richard Barnhart calls attention to the sage's significance in Shen's poem. Chuang-tzu characterized the catalpa as an unfortunate tree because with such valuable wood it is usually cut down early for utilitarian purposes.
Liu Hsien-chih. Unidentified.

BIBLIOGRAPHY:
1000 Jahre (1959), no. 53.
Edwards, *The Field of Stones* (1962), pp. 33-34, no. XXVI, pl. 20C.
Goepper, *The Essence* (1963), pls. 56-57.
Barnhart, *Wintry Forests* (1972), p. 49, no. 13. I am indebted to Professor Barnhart's translation of Shen's poem, which helped me correct my own.

Shen Chou (1427–1509)
V. PINE AND HIBISCUS

(Sung-hsia fu-jung)
Dated 1489
Handscroll, ink and color on paper, 9¼″ high and 32¾″ long (23.5 x 82.7 cm.)
Inscription, signature, and seals of the artist
The University of Michigan Museum of Art, Margaret Watson Parker Art Collection

If the last scroll presented an exact tree-portrait joined to the idea of specific friendship, here is an even more essential reduction of the meaning of nature to man's life. In an almost heraldic statement the dark section of a pine partially embraces the fragile fresh color of a single slanting stem of hibiscus. It was painted in the very year, 1489, when we are sure that Wen was beginning his studies with Shen Chou.

As often later with Wen Cheng-ming's works (cf. nos. XXIV, XXXIV), this is a case where calligraphy or a previous writing precedes the painting. Actually twelve years earlier, in 1477, T'ang Hsia-min had written of his problems,

I was unsuccessful in the examination halls— seven times—and so in the autumn of 1477 I returned home.

His explanation follows two poems, one on the theme of the pine, the other on the hibiscus. The evergreen pine told of qualities of solitary endurance; the hibiscus blooms late, for China in her autumn season, and thus stood for late fulfillment. Of them T'ang wrote:

Peach blossoms and plum, spring is thick,
The music of the pipes following day on day;
For this full beauty men eagerly contend—
Who then is to love the torrent-bank pine?

The west wind blowing cold fills heaven out—
Old autumn it is, and hibiscus first flowers;
So may the recluse look toward evening,
Let peach let plum possess the spring.

Ultimately friends, eleven of them, were to write in sympathetic harmony poems that followed the rhyme and subject of T'ang's two poems. Among the writers were the well-known painters Yao Shou and Tu Chin. Shen Chou did not write a poem; he painted a picture.

The scroll has been published and explained in some detail. Here we are most concerned with its relation to Wen Cheng-ming. There is the incidental fact, already mentioned, of its being painted when Wen was beginning his apprenticeship with Shen Chou. It expresses a situation that Wen himself would experience. Wen was to encounter the same difficulties as T'ang Hsia-min, only instead of seven examination failures, it would be ten. This kind of consolation piece, for which the handscroll was the most convenient format, was popular in Suchou. It clearly expresses solidarity of class, and one of Wen Cheng-ming's most famous paintings would be part of just such a scroll, *Cypress and Old Rock* (no. XLVIII), painted to speed the recovery from illness of a young scholar.

More important, however, at this stage of our exploration is the significance of Shen's own style within a genre—the partial tree, the blossoms of a flower—that also had their attractions for his pupil. As I have previously written:

The symbol . . . is exact; but more important is Shen Chou's realization of that symbol. There is no confusion of setting, only the background of white aging paper. A single rose blossom is centered between the "parentheses" of a dark pine and two dark exact lines of calligraphy. As with the collection of paired poems, the painting is a dialogue between two different subjects that speak with equal assurance of a single goal: the monochrome hard dark of pine against the light looseness of cool green and gentle rose; the "boned" structure of ink against "boneless" *(mo-ku)* color wash; the tight spiked knot of pine needles against free wetness of plant-leaf; that which is vertical, and thus only visible in fragmented facets on a narrow handscroll, against the completeness of a full stem which we see to the very end; that which is permanent against that which is seasonal; endurance against passing beauty.[1]

V

The importance of nature as close and essential—
a fragment treated with special care because it was a
living part of civilization itself—was a lesson not
lost on Wen Cheng-ming. He, too, was to present
this kind of narrow window on the world, as a
pine-tree (no. XVII), as a flower (no. XLVII)—but
in his own style, not Shen Chou's.

NOTE:
1. Edwards, "Pine, Hibiscus," p. 21.

INSCRIPTION BY THE ARTIST:
Summer, 1489. Shen Chou of Ch'ang-chou (Suchou).

SEAL OF THE ARTIST:
Shen shih Ch'i-nan   [painting: II/1]

CALLIGRAPHY: by T'ang Hsia-min, dated 1477; ink on "calendered
flower paper" *(ya-hua-chih)*, 9⅜" high and 33¾" long (23.8 x 85.7 cm.).
Two poems, translated above. Followed by:
   I was unsuccessful in the examination halls—seven times—and so
in the autumn of 1477 I returned home, and as before, I lived hidden
from ridicule. I was ashamed of my scholastic failure, and yet perhaps
it was Creation's doing. Thus a former poet declared:

   Man's fate bestows its quick, its slow;
   Pure clouds are hard to reach.

   From my lonely mountaintop I offered a toast in self-amusement
and riding on wine learned to chant two poems. My hope was that
among others who shared these longings some would continue the
tune. The result has been pearls and jade, filling my poetry sack. Among
contributors are even those of the older generation. And so I have
mounted all as a handscroll. When I have leisure I may ask my children
to unroll it and intone (the poetry). Is this not better than excelling at
flute or strings? And then my feelings will be turned to joy (through
their fulfillment).
   If at some other time I do succeed, even so I should keep this scroll in
order to look upon the depth of all you poets' comfort and understanding. But if this aging worthlessness is not up to it, then, that is the
difficulty of the examination.
1477, during the first day of the first month of winter. Written by
T'ang Hsia-min.

SEALS:
Chu Chih-ch'ih (Ming dynasty), T. Wo-an
   Wo-an so ts'ang   [painting: I/2]
Chang Jo-ai (1713-1746), T. Ch'ing-lan, painter from T'ung-ch'eng,
Anhui
   Ch'ing-lan chien-ting   [painting: III/1]
   Yün-chen ko t'u-shu chi   [painting: III/2]
Unidentified
   Ch'ien-ch'iu li-jen   [painting: I/1]

WRITERS OF MATCHING POEMS (for a more complete listing, see
Edwards, "Pine, Hibiscus"): P'u Ying-hsiang (fifteenth century), Ch'en
Hu-chüeh (fifteenth century), Sun Lin (Hsi-yüeh) (fifteenth century),
Yao Shou (1423–1495), Tu Chin (active 1465–1510), Ch'en Yü
(fifteenth century), Chou Chao (fifteenth century), Ch'en Huang
(fifteenth century), Tsou Luan (fifteenth century), Pien Hsün (fifteenth
century), Weng T'ung-ho (1830–1904).

BIBLIOGRAPHY:
Chu, *Chu Wo-an* (1928 ed.), p. 1a (possible reference to this scroll).
Edwards, *The Field of Stones* (1962), pp. 74–75, no. XXXI, pl. 45B.
Edwards, "Pine, Hibiscus" (1965-1966), pp. 15–28.

Shen Chou (1427–1509)
VI. AUTUMN COLORS AMONG STREAMS AND MOUNTAINS

(Ch'i-shan ch'iu-se)
No date
Handscroll, ink on paper (five joined sheets, including inscription), 7⅞" high and 252¹³⁄₁₆" long (20.0 x 642.8 cm.)
Frontispiece, inscription, signature, and seals of the artist
Anonymous loan

The title of this painting is Shen Chou's own as is shown by the artist's strong calligraphy that precedes it. Yet in the whole scroll there is no color as such. Thus the autumn colors on these streams and mountains must be found in tones of ink or, perhaps more importantly, in the whole abstraction of the meaning of the season—its sparseness, its openness, the chance for the far view through clear, cool air.

The artist discovers such meaning in following one of the most spare and selective of Yüan painters —Ni Tsan. Part of Shen Chou's inscription on the scroll has already been quoted (in "The Debt to Shen Chou") as an example of the difficulties inherent in the process of learning. Actually, by this time Shen Chou was far beyond the learning stage. The presence of an old master in the work of a mature new master has little to do with early learning and more with the conjunction of the greatness of the past with the creativity of the present.

Although the painting is undated, its time is secure. A colophon by the well-known painter Yao Shou—whose calligraphy is also connected with the last painting—is intimately connected with it, and Yao Shou died in 1495. Further its complete maturity in execution precludes an early date in Shen Chou's career. A date close to 1490 is virtually assured. Wen Cheng-ming is now working closely with his teacher.

Having described the plan of one long landscape by Shen Chou (no. III) as having essentially a tripartite division, one might consider the compo-

sition of this scroll in similar terms. The proportions, however, are rather different. Thus here the opening section is merely a brief platform of foreground land. Then comes a slanting break of sky and water. This is followed by a build-up of mountain area—in plan a broad triangle with its apex at the lower front edge. After a second angled gap of water and sky is the final section, where there is a continuous play of foreground and mid-distance land forms and which in actuality extends for well over half of the total scroll-length. Uneven as it is, the sense of pattern in terms of "three" is perpetuated. The scheme is a variant but affirms, in compositional order, the clarity that lies at the core of Shen Chou's art. There is also a precise harmony at beginning and end, not—as in the long landscape handscroll already described—the result of a filled beginning and end, but rather of an analogous sparse, open quality: a few touches of land and much open paper.

The brief introductory passage is in its iconography all Ni Tsan. Its very brevity should not be confused with a lack of importance—a low land-contour, an empty open pavilion, a thin small grove of trees, wide reaches of empty space. More would do damage to the precision with which the referent, this particular Yüan master, is evoked. With this beginning and with what follows Shen seems literally to be painting the poem that he brushed at the end of the landscape:

> It is more than a hundred years since Yün-lin
> (Ni Tsan) looked on the world and painted it;
> What remain are only sparse trees, that look like
> old sparse ones.
> What are left for this fellow to continue
> Are the long ranges piled up, with level wastes
> between them.
>
> (tr. Roderick Whitfield)

So it is that after a sparse beginning—the exact Ni Tsan—Shen Chou presents a compact, flat triangle of "long ranges piled up." The final major area combines both solid areas and spaces.

Without ever losing sight of Ni Tsan, or the development of Ni Tsan, Shen Chou, as his poem

VI, opening section

VI, mountain area

suggests, moves on to further, more complex ideas. The colophon commentary written on the scroll by Lo Chen-yü in 1915 refers to all four of the great Yüan masters as well as the more ancient tenth-century artists, Tung Yüan and Chü-jan.[1] We have already picked up such a tenth-century, Yüan sequence in the Shen-Wen joint handscroll. Thus, further historical references are present, and any later critic is bound to see them. There are rich Mi-style dots (an artist mentioned by Yao Shou). There is Huang Kung-wang's notion of mountain structure and space, with, at a few scattered points, the Y-shaped convention on a rock that is symbolic of Huang's rock of three faces. There is Wu Chen in simple direct passages contrasting dark and light, and even the restless texturing of Wang Meng on some of the rocks. As a general rule it is safe to affirm that any Ming artist working in the manner of a specific Yüan master more often than not would include suggestions of other great masters of that time. The goal was broad understanding, not narrow antiquarianism.

This bland scroll, seemingly colorless, even dull, is actually marvelously alive. As Yao Shou praised the mode:

VI, final section, land forms

Not much ink but more than enough *hsing.*

Hsing is "delight," "excitement," a key aesthetic ideal. One must have more than many-faceted traditions. Unless traditions are brought to life in a vital present, they are worthless. For that, one can affirm that this painting is all Shen Chou. Yao Shou is the better critic:

> Because the trees are sparse many rocks appear;
> As the water is shallow it hides few of its pebbles.
> Among men wine from Wu-ch'eng
> Or a plain board door in Chiang-nan.
>   (tr. Roderick Whitfield)

Yao Shou's further declaration here that he loved the mountains of Shen Chou is exactly the same "love," *ai,* that Shen Chou declared for Wu Chen (see "The Debt to Shen Chou"), and here in painting is expressed for Ni Tsan. But Shen Chou will not compromise himself. He is always there: his blunt brush, his condensed forms, his clear order.

One can compare Shen's *Autumn Colors among Streams and Mountains* with Wen Cheng-ming's treatment of the Ni Tsan mode—the balancing of spaces and solids in *Summer Retreat in the Eastern Grove* (no. XIII), the "ranges piled up" in *Autumn*

Mountains (no. XIV). In *Summer Retreat,* with its sense of an exactly controlled structure, a movement across precise islands of form, Wen seems to have learned a lesson in order that parallels what Shen Chou realized in *Autumn Colors among Streams and Mountains.* In *Autumn Mountains,* the whole notion of a mountain landscape seems to rely, as we shall see, on the master's prior realization.

NOTE:
1. Whitfield, *In Pursuit* (1969), p. 52.

INSCRIPTION BY THE ARTIST: [poem translated above in text; followed by]
This scroll was made to imitate Ni Yün-lin's (Ni Tsan's) conception. Yün-lin's methods were sparing, mine are cluttered. Yet though he was sparing, his meaning was ample. This is that which is known as the unlearnable. Shen Chou.
                    (tr. Roderick Whitfield)

SEALS OF THE ARTIST:
Shen	[on each of three joints where paper sections are connected]
Chu-shih t'ing	[frontispiece: I/1]
Shen Ch'i-nan	[frontispiece: I/2]
Shih-t'ien	[frontispiece: II/1]
Shen shih Ch'i-nan	[colophon: I/1]

COLOPHONS AND SEALS:

Yao Shou (1423–1495), painter and poet from Chia-shan, Chekiang:

> Not much ink but more than enough excitement *(hsing)*:
> (That is) old Ni's brushwork; his trees are plain and sparse.
> He only keeps a broken-down house, under the tall trees.
> Ridiculing the wastes of shattered tile among men.
>
> Hsien-ch'ih, Yao Tzu-ho (Yao Shou)

I like paintings of mountains by Shen Shih-t'ien (Shen Chou) of Ch'ang-chou (Suchou). Nowhere does he talk about their value, nor yet does he boast that his brush is as good as Old Ni's; instead he lets himself go with an elegant poem, keeping close to Madman Mi (Mi Fu, 1051–1107). In appreciation of Shih-t'ien. Ch'ih (Yao Shou).

[Yao Shou's second poem is translated above in text.]

I asked Shih-t'ien for an inscription. In using ink he doesn't care if it is too pale; in pale (ink) the meaning is deep. Why are Tao-ning's (Shen Yeh-yün, a Taoist practitioner, active ca. 1405–1425) paintings so black, and not aloof like this? I-shih (Yao Shou).

(tr. Roderick Whitfield)

Kung-shou	[colophon: I/1]
Yün-tung i-shih	[colophon: II/1]
Chia-ho Yao-shih	[colophon: II/2]
T'ao Keng (unidentified)	
T'ao Keng chih yin	[colophon: I/1]
Hsiang Hung-tso (1798–1835)	
Lien-sheng shen-ting	[Yao colophon: V/1]
Sun Yü-wen (active ca. 1856)	
Lai-shan chen-shang	[painting: IV/1]
	[Yao colophon: III/1]
Wen	[Yao colophon: IV/1]
Pan-ch'an san-su	[Yao colophon: IV/2]
Lo Chen-yü (1866–1940)	
Lo Chen-yü yin	[colophon: I/1]
Lo Shu-yen	[colophon: I/2]
Yamamoto Teijirō (1870–1937)	
Tz'u Yüeh-chih yüan-t'ing shu-wu chien-ts'ang chen-chi	[frontispiece: III/1]
Chia-wu	[frontispiece: III/2]
Kuei-yü Ch'ih-an	[frontispiece: III/3]
Ch'ih-an	[mounting seam: I/1]
Ch'ih-an shu-hua	[Yao colophon: IV/3]
Erh-feng ch'ing-shang	[label: I/1]
Shan-pen shih Hsiang-hsüeh shu-wu ping-ch'en hou chih yin	[wrapper]
Kuan-ts'e chen-chi shih chüeh wei-che shen k'o-hsiao yeh	[wrapper]

REMARKS: For a more detailed account of these writers and collectors, see Whitfield, *In Pursuit*. Translations and description of seals on this scroll are all taken from Dr. Whitfield's full publication.

BIBLIOGRAPHY:
Yonezawa, "Autumnal Landscape" (1966), no. 894.
Whitfield, *In Pursuit* (1969), pp. 25–27, 50–52.

Shen Chou (1427–1509)
VII. CHRYSANTHEMUM AND ELEGANT BIRD

(Chü-hua wen-ch'in t'u)
Dated 1509
Hanging scroll, ink on paper, 41″ high and 11½″ wide (104.0 x 29.3 cm.)
Inscription, signature, and seals of the artist
Osaka Municipal Museum of Fine Arts

This scroll is a very late work by Shen Chou. Painted in the last year of his life, it tells us that the artist's strength and abilities continued to the very end. In some ways it is a very simple painting. A flower, a bird, and an insect are brought together in a study of free-ink expression. In it is only the shallowest suggestion of space. The concern—within a clear recognition of natural objects—is for the play of ink on the paper. With this, the block of Shen Chou's calligraphy is in complete harmony.

But the emphasis on ink and pattern never do violence to our belief in the natural source of what we see. It is precisely what might be visible in an exact garden. Thus the almost impossibly long, thin stem of chrysanthemum with its drooping leaves and heavy flowers is held vertical not merely by our faith in ink, brush, and the tenseness of a paper surface but by the support of a bamboo stake which at once assures us of a physical ability to remain upright and offers in its white outlined form a contrast to the ink of the flower-stem. We can imagine Shen Chou both seeing these objects in nature and delighting in the personal arrangement of what he saw.

Poetry continues as a persistent part of Shen Chou's painting, here precisely so. In reading it remember that Shun was a great emperor in early Chinese history-myth:

Elegant bird, five colors full,
Stands, hopes before chrysanthemum;
How like it was on Shun's robes—
Brilliant the cloud, the dragon!

By now the relation of Shen Chou and Wen Cheng-ming had been sealed by long association, and although we cannot find an example of Wen's painting of the chrysanthemum during Shen's lifetime, his brushing of it in 1535 (no. XXXV) offers a meaningful comparison. The subject differs in that Wen's flowers are accompanied, not by bird and insect, but by bamboo and rock. However, it is the same kind of close-up scene, and the chrysanthemum is a product of the same ink-conventions, beginning with the slight ink-stem just visible at the foot of the rock, and extending to veined leaves and thickly massed rays of petals. In contrast, the pupil's touch is lighter, and it displays a conscious elegance in manipulating varied passages of the brush. The result is a knitting together of form into a series of tight, exact relationships: the

precise angle of the land, the repeated curve of the grasses, bamboo spears, rock textures, dots, soft leaves and tense flower-petals. Thus meaning for the chrysanthemum is found not as some independently growing form but as an explosive climax to a cluster of varied shapes. The flowers come not from the ground but from the top of the rock. Like the dancing shapes of the junipers done three years before (no. XXX), the flowers exist as forms separated from the earth and have their own independent life on the paper itself.

The contrast with Shen Chou must be apparent. All we have said about Wen's master is somehow here: the freedom of his brush which yet reveals the certainty of exact structure; the ability to condense and define a precise image; the limitation, but not elimination, of the spatial ambient that, thus, forces us to concentrate on the form he has chosen to reveal; the quality of understatement that paradoxically contains great richness; the unmistakable personal style that still respects the objective facts of nature itself. But above all in this painting is a quality of joy. Here is something of pure delight—*hsing*—and marvelous whimsy.

Shen Chou was the great painter of the ordinary. He painted what everybody knew. The style-subject equation with which he worked was not hidden from other eyes. He simply monumentalized it. But withal, grandeur was suspect. Shen Chou's basic modesty prevented the kind of unquestioned brilliance that at times could be the boast of Wen Cheng-ming. Nor did it lead to Wen's sense of struggle. What, at the very edge of a long life, is Suchou's then greatest painter telling us? A young awkward garden chicken, large-footed, scrawny-winged, aiming impossibly at the dancing beauty of two butterflies, niched by the uncertain arch of a fragile blossom, is somehow beauty and a fact linked to hope that is worth passing on. From the content it must have been painted for a younger friend. But only Shen Chou would claim that a young chicken and almost fading flowers equal in splendor and significance the most remote and sacred ancient myths, the dazzling cosmic pattern of Shun's robe.

This is as appropriate a final image for Shen Chou as was to be the late old cypress in his pupil's final decade. When Wen was over eighty, he painted *Old Trees by a Wintry Brook* (no. L). Shen Chou in the truest sense believed in his own garden. As in the late poem about himself (no. I A), death now was something just over that garden's wall.

INSCRIPTION BY THE ARTIST: [poem, translated above; followed by]
Sketched by an eighty-three-year-old man for Ch'u-chai to enjoy its elegant pattern. 1509. Shen Chou.

SEALS OF THE ARTIST:
Shih-t'ien [painting: I/2]
Ch'i-nan [painting: II/1]

SEALS:
Liu Shu (1759–1816), from Suchou
Jung-feng pi-wan [painting: I/1]

BIBLIOGRAPHY:
Sōraikan (1930–1939), vol. 5, pl. 49.
Min Shin (1964), p. 10, no. 24.
Chūgoku bijutsu (1966), p. 49.
Osaka (1970), p. 54, no. 21.

The Developing Years

VIII. HUANG KUNG-WANG'S LEISURELY LIVING AT THE STREAM PAVILION

(Ch'i-ko hsien-chü t'u)
No date
Hanging scroll, ink on paper, 35⅝″ high and 16⁹⁄₃₂″ wide (90.5 x 41.4 cm.)
Inscription, signature, and seals of the artist
Edwin Binney, 3rd

This painting may well be one of the earliest surviving scrolls by Wen Cheng-ming. According to the artist's inscription it is a direct copy *(mo)* of a scroll by Huang Kung-wang, *Leisurely Living at the Stream Pavilion.* The artist claims he brushed this without hesitation upon being shown Huang's scroll by the "mountain man," Lu Tzu-ching, when Wen and Wu K'uan were visiting him at Chih-hsing (Grindstone) Mountain, one of those hill-retreats just outside of Suchou.

Certainly the whole aura of the painting is one that breathes rather swift, free creation. It makes use of bold touches of the brush, and areas of flat wet wash that as a general stereotype at this time also suggest the art of Huang's contemporary, Wu Chen. But in both motifs and composition it is an exact reflection of Huang Kung-wang, and among surviving works by or attributed to that great Yüan figure it seems closest to a painting now in the Palace Museum entitled *The Nine Pearl Peaks* (fig. 1).[1] At the same time Wen's landscape is a painting which, while rather freshly expressive and certainly generally true to the model, has its passages of uncertainty, and we are justified in affirming it as student work.

There are, nevertheless, problems. First of all there is no date on the scroll. Wen's inscription, rather uniquely written from left to right, lists only the general circumstances and adds a poem. However, surrounding the painting, like a wide textured frame, are written on the mounting full commentaries by the great Ch'ing scholar Weng Fang-kang (1733–1818) and his immediate circle. These include a poem by the well-known eighteenth century artist Lo P'ing, actually written down in the calligraphy of Weng's follower, Feng Min-ch'ang. From the fact that Wen was with Wu K'uan at the time, Weng Fang-kang deduces that the painting must have been done when Wu K'uan was in Suchou in 1496 or 1497. Thus, affirms Weng, the artist was "only twenty-seven or twenty-eight" *sui.*

Modern opinion agrees with Weng's statement of Wu K'uan's Suchou stay (see no. II F). Indeed, this is thought to be the last time that Wu K'uan was in Suchou. He died in Peking in 1504. The modern viewer, however, may raise further questions about the certainty of a 1496–1497 date. Wen's inscription is signed with his later name, Cheng-ming, rather than his earlier one, Pi. He made the change sometime after 1512 (cf. no. XIII). It is also doubtful that the calligraphy style is consistent with his early writing. Its manner is rather more properly two or three decades later. If that is so, we can only logically interpret the inscription as a kind of informal later addition by Wen—a note to himself reminding him of what the painting was about and adding a poem that was in his head—and that is all. Certainly, if as a young student he had done the painting for presentation to either Wu K'uan or Lu Tzu-ching, he would have been more formal and polite about what he wrote. Similarly if it had been a later presentation or a painting rediscovered in a friend's collection he would have been much more historically specific. A final possibility that cannot be discounted would make the scroll an informal personal memory-sketch executed, perhaps, sometime around 1515.

With all these uncertainties, however, the painting itself leaves little doubt but that it is a fresh, informal landscape to be placed somewhere within the early work of Wen Cheng-ming. From what one can tell it rather exactly follows the model. When compared to *The Nine Pearl Peaks* (fig. 1) it shows a similar view of space: a zigzag passage of water between alternating land-spits, shadowed by ink-shoals, retreating to a wall of mountain cliffs. There rise peaks with their

1. Huang Kung-wang (1269–1354), *The Nine Pearl Peaks.* National Palace Museum, Taipei

VIII

hazed valley pockets, the farthest mountains a grey sheet of wash. In detail one can find repeated Huang Kung-wang conventions: the spare lines of foreground trees, their blunt wet twigs and even wetter leaves, a flat sketchy bridge, simple blocks of architecture, the curving shapes of rocks or hills whose surface textures are defined by both long straight strokes and the overlay of shorter, more irregular daubs of ink. Add to this the convention of distant trees usually lining the hill-crest, and a free range of moss-dots that may be round, may be horizontal, or may be vertical in basic shape. It is a soft, sensitive style which from the irregularities of spontaneous personal touches of the brush builds assurances of real space and believable form—nature's variety anchored in an ideal, certain structure. In imitating

the Yüan artist, this is what Wen sought.

The basic source in Huang Kung-wang is thus clear, but the bold, moist treatment of ink rather goes beyond an exact duplication of the Yüan master. For Suchou painters, such freedoms, however, were often linked to Huang Kung-wang. This is true of an early Shen Chou painting done for his friend Liu Chüeh around 1470, a painting also associated with Mi Fu.[2] That Shen Chou could create a free ink sketch closer to the time of Wen Cheng-ming's apprenticeship is attested by a landscape, *Rain,* in the National Palace Museum, Taipei, which is dated 1487 (fig. 2). Here is a wonderfully moist hanging of curtains of semi-transparent ink on a basically firm Shen Chou composition.

Huang Kung-wang was noted for painting a so-called "three-sided rock." This became conventionalized in later landscapes to a Y-shape brushed on the face of a rock (i.e., the view of a rock from the top and two sides). We have already noted its presence in a Shen Chou handscroll (no. VI). In Shen Chou's *Rain* such a form is lightly suggested on the moist central foreground rock. In Wen's painting it is on two of the foreground rocks and on a lesser central peak in the mid-distance.

The style of Mi Fu might also be linked with *Rain,* and there is a similar suggestion of "Mi-dots" on the peaks of Wen Cheng-ming's painting. But mostly, such a landscape as *Rain* would have afforded a precedent for ghostly transparent areas of ephemeral land and tree and mist, like those in the left middle-distance in Wen's early landscape. In 1508 we will see him working solely in a Mi manner (no. XI). In that latter scroll is not only the light wash but also the motif of vertical, wet, pointed strokes that rim a hill—a free version of the so-called "nails-drawn-from-mud" *(ni-li pa-ting ts'un)* convention. These, found modestly in Huang Kung-wang, appear in this painting along the crest of the foreground land masses.

With all its noble pedigree, Wen's landscape lacks sure coherence. Its motifs are too varied, their sketchiness often too loose. They are all there, but the relationships are not secure. Its freshness offers tremendous appeal, and lessons have been well-learned. But they are not properly digested. Thus the whole area at the base and to the left of the waterfall—a rectangle of ephemeral shadowy form, a kind of dream—is taken from too utterly different a world from that of the firm rounded land areas and of the certain spaces that precede and to some extent surround it. In its over-ambitious effort to combine free brush and bold forms into a monumental statement of nature this painting reminds us of the Palace Museum's early *Listening to the Waterfall under Pines* (fig. 3).[3] This latter shares much with the scroll exhibited here—the flat-grey tonalities, and despite a different stylistic source, some of the same motifs. Above all, it too is the

2. Shen Chou, *Rain,* 1487. National Palace Museum, Taipei

work of a painter who has not yet mastered the presentation of convincing unities.

This landscape after Huang Kung-wang, *Leisurely Living at the Stream Pavilion,* appealing in its

3. Wen Cheng-ming, *Listening to the Waterfall Under Pines.* National Palace Museum, Taipei

freshness, appears to be a clear and rather rare instance of an extant painting by a Chinese master that truly shows an artist who has not yet reached the necessary goal for greatness, "a style of his own."

NOTES:
1. The painting has been discussed as a genuine Huang Kung-wang by Li, "Huang Kung-wang's 'Chiu-chu feng-ts'ui' " (1973), pp. 1–9.
2. Edwards, *The Field of Stones* (1962), pl. 7B.
3. It is signed Wen Pi. At least one seal is repeated in 1508 (on the Shanghai Museum *Traveling to T'ien-p'ing Mountain,* fig. 6). Chiang Chao-shen has recently exhibited fig. 3, which is undated, in Taipei as one of Wen's early works, placing it, however, as late as 1510. If the Binney scroll is stylistically to be pushed into that time, it makes it more possible for the inscription to have been done at the same time as the painting.

INSCRIPTION AND SEALS OF THE ARTIST:
I accompanied my teacher, Wu Pao-weng (Wu K'uan), on a visit to Chih-hsing Mountain. The Mountain-man, Lu Tzu-ching, is a man of sincerity and refinement, attached to what is pure. He opened a path, cut the grasses, and boils clouds in a stone tripod. He brought out to show us a painting by Huang Kung-wang, *Leisurely Living at the Stream Pavilion,* and told me to copy it. So without hesitation (?) I took up the brush and painted this, adding a short poem:

A hermit enjoys his solitude, sits quiet and chants long songs.
The sun sets, purpling tumbled mountains; rain's aftermath cools scattered trees.
Idleness disperses worldly matters; the wilderness brings on its autumn glow.
We know the immortal's home is near; a narrow track winds round the lofty hill.

Cheng-ming

Cheng-ming	[painting: III/1]
Cheng-chung-fu yin	[painting: III/2]
Cheng-chung	[painting: I/2]

COLOPHONS AND SEALS:
Weng Fang-kang (1733-1818), T. Cheng-san, Chung-hsü, H. T'an-ch'i, Su-chai, from Ta-hsing, Peking

T'an-ch'i shen-ting	[painting: I/3]
T'an-ch'i chien-ts'ang	[painting: II/1]

Colophon on the right side on the mounting, dated 1795, first month, seventeenth day:

Ta-ya	[colophon: I/1]
T'an-ch'i	[colophon: I/2]

Colophon on the top left side of the mounting:

Weng Fang-kang	[colophon: I/1]

Colophon on the bottom left side of the mounting, dated beginning of the second month:

Su-chai	[colophon: I/1]
Tzu Cheng-san hao Su-chai	[colophon: I/2]

Colophon across the top of the mounting, dated the second quarter of the second month:

Weng Fang-kang	[colophon: I/1]

Colophon on the top right corner of the mounting, dated 1807, tenth month, twenty-first day.
Yüeh Kung-p'u (1801 *chü-jen*), T. Lien-shang, from Lin-ch'uan, Kiangsi; a student of Weng Fang-kang. Colophon on the left side across the bottom of the mounting, dated 1795, second month.

Yüeh Kung-p'u	[colophon: I/1]
Lien-shang	[colophon: I/2]

Wu Hsi-ch'i (1746–1818), T. Sheng-cheng, H. Ku-jen, from Ch'ien-t'ang, Chekiang; colophon on the right side across the bottom of the mounting, undated:

Wu Hsi-ch'i yin	[colophon: I/1]

Feng Min-ch'ang (1747–1806), T. Po-ch'iu, H. Yü-shan, from Ch'in-hsien, Kuangtung; a student of Weng Fang-kang. He writes a poem by Lo P'ing and a poem of his own, both following the rhyme-scheme of Wen Cheng-ming's poem. Center bottom of the mounting, undated:

Min-ch'ang	[colophon: I/1]

Unidentified

Feng	[painting: I/1]
T'ien-shui chün shou-ts'ang shu-hua yin chi	[painting: IV/1]

BIBLIOGRAPHY:
Clapp, *Wen Cheng-ming* (1975), fig. 1.

IX. LANDSCAPE

(Shan-shui t'u)
Dated 1502
Handscroll, ink on silk, 7³⁄₄″ high and 66⁷⁄₁₆″ long (19.7 x 168.8 cm.)
Inscription, signature, and seals of the artist
Hashimoto Collection

While there may be some uncertainty as to the exact year when Wen painted *Storm over the River* (no. II F) or the landscape just discussed (no. VIII), there can be no doubt about the 1502 date of this unusual handscroll. In its fine meticulous style—miniature ink-forms brushed on silk—the handscroll would seem to have nothing to do with Shen Chou. It helps prove that Wen's formative years were involved with far more than imitating a revered contemporary master.

The painting received considerable attention in Suchou, and close younger contemporaries of Wen have added their comments. Among these colophons, his son Wen Chia, often interested in the exact history of his father's works, records it precisely:

> The former Tai-chao brushed this painting when he was thirty-three *sui*. His colophon comes from the time when he had been back from the Han-lin (i.e., Peking) some seven years. He was sixty-four. Now it is 1577, another forty-five years later. . . .

Wen's own colophon is a similar looking back on time past:

> I painted this handscroll in 1502. The painting was not finished when a boy stole it. That was some thirty years ago. Now a guest has brought it to show me. Suddenly it is like something from another existence. It is not only that these old eyes are dim that I cannot repeat this, or that my mental powers are in decay, but I cannot recreate interests of former times.
> Once (in the T'ang dynasty) the Censor Chao and Han Yü meeting together were examining a horse-and-figure painting and recognized it as a youthful work (of Chao's). Gone for twenty years it had kept coming back in his thoughts. So Han Yü had the presence of mind to return it, and then wrote it all down. Today we cannot see the painting, yet Han's writing preserves it for us. Now, as to this scroll, an enthusiast has acquired it. I hardly dare ask its return, but how can we find another Han Yü to record it and relieve my disturbed longings (for it)?
> The fourth day of the tenth month, 1533, at the Yü-ch'ing shan-fang.

This somewhat whimsical approach to his early art does, however, give us insight into Wen's own view of himself in his youth. As will be clear later on, by 1533 he has been long practicing his art: he has been to Peking, he has returned to become the center of a rather close group of like-minded colleagues, and famous in his highly cultured city. Thus a painting of 1502, when he was still in the shadow of Shen Chou, was indeed as though from another existence. He recognized not only a personal change in physical powers, but an interest, ideas—a style—to which he was no longer attuned. Our lives, thus, are many lives; and this is particularly true of an artist who lived as long as Wen Cheng-ming.

The reference to Han Yü (768–824) is to his *Hua-chi,* and the painting recorded in that essay is particularly appropriate. It is not only a matter of the disappearance of a painting that rather miraculously returns years later; the parallel extends to style itself. Censor Chao's painting was done in his youth, a careful imitation of something else. Thus the concept of learning is important. Above all Han Yü was impressed by meticulous detail packed into the small format, and he describes this with obvious delight: "Eighty-three horses, large and small, and not one the same . . . eleven heads of cattle, three camels, etc. . . ." The whole was a veritable array of horses, riders, and accoutrements.[1]

Wen felt that his own painting was unfinished. This is, perhaps, affirmed by a certain quality of rawness—sharp ink on the empty silk—but Wen's

IX

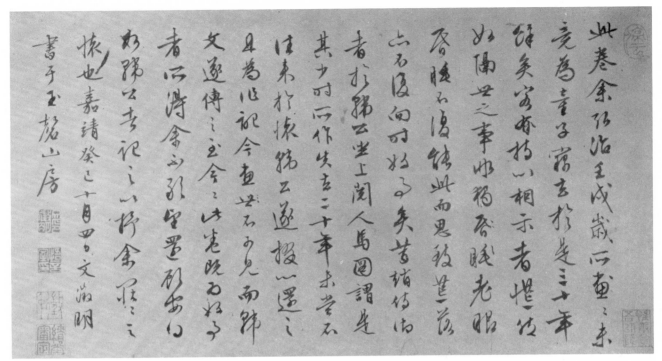

IX, detail. Colophon by Wen Cheng-ming, 1533

seals are on the painting (does one add them before finishing?), and it is a painting packed with such complete detail that one wonders what is to be added. Looking at it thirty years later it may well have seemed incomplete—too much of an early painstaking sketch—and it may be that a few touches would have smoothed it out—color for example, or ink dots (*tien*) to enliven the surface or help move the viewer across the landscape.

On first appearance, there is very little in Shen Chou's mature style that parallels such a careful, meticulous scroll and would serve to affirm his position as Wen's teacher. The scroll is rather a combination of the meticulous care of a gifted student with traditions that go far back in Chinese history. Here the referent is at least the Northern Sung. Before tight-packed, piled-up rocks and mountains tiny hair-like figures must inevitably stand in awe. So filled is the scroll with the structure of nature that in all but the very end distance is blocked off. Figures, unable to penetrate this great wall, are forced to move across a foreground plane or at best find only a slightly higher perch or path or promontory hemmed in by the towering strength of mountains. This sense of the power of nature is a feature of Chinese painting in the tenth and eleventh centuries. One of the colophon-comments that follow the scroll indicates more exactly how this painting appeared to Wen's contemporaries. This was written by Yüan Chih (1502–1547), one of the six famous Yüan brothers and cousins with all of whom Wen was particularly close during the 1530s (see no. XXII). Inevitably appreciation of the painting is, by Yüan Chih, generalized to the level of high excellence: *Hsing-i kao-shen*— "the sense of delight is both lofty and deep." From this Yüan praises the rich density of the entire composition, the fine workmanship, the rare mood of antiquity, finally coming to a concrete historical source: "generally speaking, Tung Yüan and Chü-jan." For Yüan Chih, therefore, the painting slips into what was increasingly being accepted as

57

IX, section

IX, section

the orthodox view of the art. These two great names of Southern painting in the tenth century, given varied personal revivals by the four great masters of the Yüan, were passed on to the great Ming painters. Shen Chou was seen squarely within this tradition. The logic of Wen continuing it inevitably follows. It is, in this scroll, possible to see at least a general relation to this venerable source, in particular in the end, with its open passages, its landspits, the curving contours of the distant hills, the spare horizontal line of trees.

Moreover, throughout the meticulous detail it is clear that the brush is used with a sensitivity to the creating of varied textures—hence that personal feel, as one brings form to life, that was so much a part of the great Yüan painters. Once again Wen's early work is revealed as lying within a complex framework of sources. It is not inconsistent to have embraced a variety. Here is the personal skill of a young artist developing his style. In a tight and careful manner he can be his own master. But he embraces many things, rather exactly—which is the nature of conscious learning.

NOTE:
1. Han Yü, *T'ang fa-chia Han Wen-kung Wen-ch'ao* (Collected works of Han Yü), 1628, ch. 8/9a–10b.

COLOPHON BY THE ARTIST: translated above in text

SEALS OF THE ARTIST:

T'ing-yün sheng	[painting: I/4]
Wen Pi Cheng-ming	[painting: III/1]
Heng-shan	[painting: III/2]
T'ing-yün	[colophon: I/1]
Wei keng-yin wu i chiang	[colophon; I/2]
Wen Cheng-ming yin	[colophon: II/1]
Wu-yen-shih yin	[colophon: II/2]
Cheng-chung	[colophon: II/3]

COLOPHONS AND SEALS:
Wang Ku-hsiang (1501–1568), T. Lu-chih, from Suchou; dated 1534, second month, twelfth day

Yu-shih	[colophon: I/1]
Ku-hsiang	[colophon: I/2]
Wang Lu-chih yin	[colophon: II/1]
Chien-pai chai	[colophon: II/2]

Yüan Chih (1502–1547), T. Shang-chih, from Suchou; undated

Ju-nan	[colophon: I/1]
Yüan Yung-chih shih	[colophon: II/1]
Hu-ch'iu pieh-shu	[colophon: II/2]

Wen Chia (1501–1583), T. Hsiu-ch'eng, second son of Wen Cheng-ming; dated 1577

Wen Chia Hsiu-ch'eng	[colophon: I/1]

Tung Ch'i-ch'ang (1555–1636), T. Hsüan-tsai, from Hua-t'ing, Sung-chiang, Kiangsu; undated

Chih chih kao jih chiang kuan	[colophon: I/1]
Tung Ch'i-ch'ang yin	[colophon: I/2]

Unidentified

Chi t'ang hsin-shang	[mounting after painting: I/1]
Chi t'ang shen-ting	[Wen's colophon: II/4]
Hsüeh-yu t'ang Ts'ao shih ———— ts' ang t'u chi	[mounting after painting: I/2]
a half round seal	[painting: I/1]
P'ing-ling Yen En-yün hao Yao-t'ang chih chang	[painting: I/2]
Ch'eng-wu nan chia-ch'eng	[painting: I/3]
Kao ———— shan ———— (half seal)	[painting: II/1]

BIBLIOGRAPHY:
Hashimoto, *Hashimoto Shuzo* (1972), pl. 11.

X. TRAVELING TO T'IEN-P'ING MOUNTAIN

(T'ien-p'ing chi-yu t'u)
Dated 1508, second month, fifteenth day
Hanging scroll, ink on paper, 18¹¹/₃₂″ high and 10⁵/₈″
  wide (47.0 x 27.0 cm.)
Inscriptions, signature, and seals of the artist
Hsien-ch'i Tseng, Peterborough, New Hampshire

Six years later, in 1508, Wen made an early spring trip to the site where Shen Chou had enjoyed the Catalpa Trees (no. IV): T'ien-p'ing Mountain, which lies to the west of Suchou in the rich green hills that there rise sharply out of the flat plain:

> In 1508 on the sixteenth of the second month, with Wu Tz'u-ming and Ch'en Tao-fu, taking a boat we left Chiang-ts'un ch'iao (River-Village Bridge) and arriving at Shang-sha (Upper Sands) unexpectedly met Ch'ien K'ung-chou and Chu Yao-min. Together we climbed T'ien-p'ing Mountain and drank at Pai-yün t'ing (White-cloud Pavilion), and I consecutively wrote four poems.

Like the French Impressionists of the nineteenth century, the pleasure of an outing—leaving the city for the country—was a key to art. But, unlike the Impressionists', Chinese vision was not caged in an exact moment of time and by exact and momentary light. Long before Cézanne—clearly by the four-teenth century—the experience of nature had been made permanent by calling upon the old masters. In this case, Wen's experience of nature claimed geographical accuracy, and his calling upon the old masters led him to turn to the fourteenth-century master Huang Kung-wang, who himself was a kind of early impressionist. Later critics described Huang as one who "wandered about with paper and brush in his sleeves and when he came to some beautiful scenery took down a record of it. . . ."[1]

The painting itself is known in at least three other versions.[2] While this raises problems of authen-ticity, they are all from the same mold. Of particular interest is the contrast between Wen's approach to recording a famous place and that of his master, Shen Chou.

In a well-known album now in the Shanghai Museum, Shen Chou, in his mature manner, painted views of Wu. Among them is T'ien-p'ing Mountain (fig. 4). Shen's blunt brush, outlining for us exact symbol-like forms, is despite all brevities a direct view of the scene—the wall, the mountain, the trees, the temple of the famous Sung figure Fan Chung-yen. It is not too far from a condensed version of what a modern photograph can reveal (fig. 5). The mountain was noted especially for its cluster of rocks, and these, as in nature, are grouped at the top and signal the uniqueness of the famous site.

Turning to Wen's version—or to the variants seen here and in Shanghai (fig. 6) and Paris (fig. 7) —on the basis of Shen Chou's view one can recog-nize a temple roof, a pavilion near the top, and clusters of rocks. But the whole concept of the scene is so generalized as to be immediately trans-formed from a perception of nature into nature seen as past style, which here is Huang Kung-wang: the angled composition with its water-approach receding to a wash of distant mountain, the sensitive shapes of a few carefully isolated foreground trees, the further patterning of clusters of a single distant tree-type, and the sensitive touches of the brush that gradually build up form and create cliff and hill and rock. Through this runs the emptiness of bits of pathways—now open, now hidden—that suggest how we may wander there.

How narrowly we can affirm the individuality of Wen within this framework of old-master art must depend on careful judgements as to the certain authenticity of the extant versions. The painting is part of the same tradition as the handscroll of 1502.

4. Shen Chou, *T'ien-p'ing Mountain*. From the album *Famous Views of Two Rivers*. Shanghai Museum

戊辰二月望日與次明道復
汎舟出江邨橋拒上沙解后
錢孔周茶庄民間登天平飲
於雲亭次第課詩四首
村江橋畔小海佃
帆掦一鴻桃花偏入意江
影春衫薄對畫溪陰翠
好山無賴上眉頭風掃鬢
為一笑謀新水巴塘浮舴子
不教塵負蹣青進出卻娜
舟行欲盡有人家記課橫
橋是上沙南望風烟隨島
沒西來墟落帶山斜堰催
新緑初歸柳水映紅忽
見花錢酒來醒春困劇波溪
卿試雨前茶
十里扶興渡野塘縱穿松
嶠入蒼二風麥平疇亂日
衰草花村路香春色釀晴
洪樂事巖光搖翠落飛
艦清帆劉被山雲笑卻笑
掃夫為庭帆
松根小徑入天平兴舍䲱
與入翆屏陝嶺試宿千
里目勺泉懸半山亭后凌蒼
露相離立對巵晴烟不斷
青落日英賢嘩不誤荒祠
古木有儀刑
　　　衡山文壁

Behind them both lies, at least traditionally, the soft southern landscape of Tung Yüan and Chü-jan. And the ending of the 1502 scroll (no. IX) is consistent with Wen's perception of T'ien-p'ing, considering the latter's vertical format and its softer relation of ink to paper, not silk. Thus the angled recession across flat water and over thin land-spits to a screen of distant mountains, the thin, fragile-branched pine, the groves of mid-distance trees, and even, too, the pile-up of sharp cliffs interspersed with clusters of smaller rocks can be found in both scrolls.

NOTES:
1. Sirén, *Chinese Painting* (1956–1958), IV, p. 60. There it is drawn from the painter-critic, Li Jih-hua (1565–1635).
2. Aside from those illustrated here there is a copy-version in *Chung-kuo ming-hua* (1925), vol. 18.

INSCRIPTION BY THE ARTIST:
[The first section translated above in text. Followed by:]
Laying aside the dust of the world, we travel in spring;
Leaving the suburbs, it is for the sake of a laugh.
The fresh water is now high enough for floating our boat;
The good mountains are easily seen in the distance.
The wind's in our hair, spring gowns are thin,
Trees cover the stream with shadow, the green tent is dense.
The village peach-blossoms happen to enter my thoughts;
Beside Chiang-ts'un-ch'iao we linger for a while.

(tr. Ling-yün Shih Liu)
[There follow three more poems—four in all—that successively relate the progress of the journey. The fourth poem takes the travelers to the foot of T'ien-p'ing Mountain, up the mountain for the view, and ends with a reference to Fan's temple:]
In the setting sun we call the hero in vain—
Only the shapes of the desolate shrine, the ancient trees.

SEALS OF THE ARTIST:
Yü-lan t'ang [painting: I/1]
Cheng-ming [painting: II/1]

COLOPHONS AND SEALS:
Wu Hu-fan (1894?–1965), Shanghai collector
Tung-chuang chü-shih [colophon: I/1]
Unidentified
Ming-chai chen-wan [painting: II/1]

REMARKS:
The poems are recorded in *Wen Cheng-ming hui-kao* (1929), ch. 4/pp. 30a-b. Here the date of 1544 is indicated. It must have been taken from another writing of the earlier poems.

Wu Tz'u-ming is Wu Kuan, poet, calligrapher and collector (Chiang, "Life" [1971–1972], II, p. 52).

Ch'en Tao-fu (1483–1544) is Ch'en Shun, famous painter from

5. T'ien-p'ing Mountain, spring, 1973

Suchou and follower of Wen (cf. nos. XII, XXX).

Ch'ien K'ung-chou, T. T'ung-ai (1475–1549), connoisseur, collector, and friend of Wen. His daughter was to marry Wen's son (cf. no. XIII).

T'ien-p'ing shan, a hill-mountain about ten miles by water, southwest of the city. Its forests were rich, and many extraordinary rocks have strange and weird configurations. Among its noted features are a flat top which is called the Lake Viewing Terrace (Wang-hu t'ai), for one can see the "Great Lake" (T'ai-hu) from it and the White Cloud Temple (Pai-yün ssu) at its southern foot. There is located the ancestral grave of Fan Chung-yen (989–1052). (Edwards, *The Field of Stones* [1962], p. 43.)

6. *Traveling to T'ien-p'ing Mountain,* signed Heng-shan Wen Pi (Wen Cheng-ming). Shanghai Museum

7. *Traveling to T'ien-p'ing Mountain,* signed Heng-shan Wen Pi (Wen Cheng-ming). Musée Guimet, Paris

XI. CLOUDY MOUNTAINS

(Yün shan t'u)
Dated by inscription to 1508, fifth month
Handscroll, ink and light color on gold-flecked paper, 11¾″ high and
331⁹/₁₆″ long (30.0 x 843.0 cm.)
Inscriptions, signature, and seals of the artist
Hwa's Hou Chen Shang Chai

Three months after his experience at T'ien-p'ing Mountain Wen is painting this unusual landscape. Different as it may first appear, the style can be placed within a similar aesthetic orthodoxy as the last two scrolls. A handscroll, it is brushed on paper touched with flecks of gold. As the earlier Hashimoto handscroll (no. IX) was clear and precise, this is sombre and seemingly unstructured in its broad spread of flat, light and dark washes. Mi Fu and his son, Mi Yu-jen, were twelfth-century revivers of the soft low-level landscapes of the same tenth-century Tung Yüan and Chü-jan, whose names keep recurring in discussions of Ming literati painting. The extremely different look of this scroll is the result of the Mi emphasis on unlined daubs and washes of ink for mountains and trees, which was the source of a continually repeated mannerism in later paintings. In respect to this mannerism the imitators tended to be far more "Mi" than its originators—affirmation of an idea we have already encountered: that outward appearance is easier to come by than inner meaning. Wen, the developing painter, is no exception, and *Cloudy Mountains* captures these "mannerisms" precisely. His fondness for the mode at this particular time is supported by several published scrolls, two of them claiming close connection with Shen Chou.[1]

Indeed, because the painting is so full of the Mi *style* it is worth citing Wang Shih-chen's (1526–1590) colophon after the scroll, which claims that in respect to this Mi manner Wen is the equal of Kao K'o-kung (1248–1310), the most famous imitator of Mi in the Yüan dynasty. Very subtly this painting is far closer to a Yüan style than it is to a Sung style. It lacks the assurance of both logically receding deep space and solid forms within that space that marks the classic Sung mode.

Except for the blunt thick outlines of architecture and bridge, it is possible to stress that there is really not a single line as such in the painting. It would seem to be the precise opposite of the handscroll of 1502. But there is the same intensity in pursuing a learned manner. In the 1502 handscroll this takes the form of almost infinite patterns of linear detail. In the handscroll of 1508 it is ink wash and flat daubs of the brush.

It must be admitted that the foundation for the result was established from the beginning by the "patron." The painting was done for a scholar-official from nearby K'un-shan, Huang Yün, who seems to have had close association with Suchou scholars in the early sixteenth century.[2] Huang brought to Wen a blank scroll of paper and Wen responded by writing poems and painting this painting. The paper itself was rather elegant—smoothly finished and flecked with gold. Thus, the ink lies flat on the surface and serves even further to emphasize Wen's interest in that surface—a rather persistent aspect of his art. The smooth monochrome, however, is subtly enlivened by the play of warm and cool color, ochre and *hua-ch'ing* (light blue). Beyond a sufficiency for the painting, Huang Yün's paper was in good supply, and thus the poem colophons after the painting—twenty in all—seem to go on almost forever.

To return to the landscape, however, it is possible to over-exaggerate its flatness. Washes and the ink daubs that give the washes further definition are clearly layered. Light foundations in almost exact steps of deepening value come forward into dark black and thus, despite the curtains of ink, despite the glitter of gold on an elegant piece of paper, the

XI

XI, section

total sense of space is real. Thus, through the Yüan Wen was searching to catch something of the spatial realities of the Sung. We start in pale mists, come forward to a promontory of form which we reach by a bridge, and then pass through to the goal of a temple roof and the far peaks beyond. Detail again falls off at the very end of the scroll.

Painted, as Wang Shih-chen declares, when Wen was a *hsiu-ts'ai* (first degree candidate), we should still think of him as close to his student days as a scholar-painter. Shen Chou did not die until 1509. As a good "student" Wen is evaluating a landscape type created in the Sung along earlier traditional lines and transformed by the Yüan.

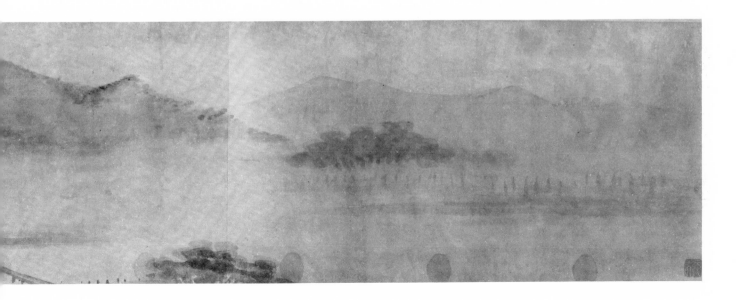

NOTES:

1. The finest, a handscroll of 1508 in the Liaoning Museum as already mentioned, follows a Shen Chou painting of 1507 *(Liao-ning* [1962], II, pls. 25–29). A hanging scroll, undated, has both Shen Chou's and T'ang Yin's calligraphy *(Chiao-yü-pu* [1943], pl. 107). A third, also of 1508, in Osaka, appears at least to be a faithful copy *(Sōraikan* [1930–1939], VI, pl. 53).
2. Chiang, "Life" (1971–1972), II, p. 39, under 1503, for example, lists a meeting with several of them in which he is viewing a painting by Hui-tsung.

INSCRIPTION BY THE ARTIST (following twenty poems by the artist):

Doctor *(po-shih)* Tan-yen (Huang Yün) asked me to inscribe a blank roll of paper with my work. My poetry is not very good and my calligraphy is lacking in style *(fa).* I am deeply ashamed to demean his intention. Perhaps by doing it I can solicit his opinion. That is why I show my poor work. 1508, fifth month. Heng-shan Wen Pi records.

(tr. James Robinson)

SEALS OF THE ARTIST:

Cheng-ming	[painting: II/1]
Wu-yen-shih yin	[painting: II/2]
Wen Cheng-ming yin	[colophon: II/1]
Wen Pi yin	[colophon: II/2]

COLOPHONS AND SEALS:

Huang Yün (active late fifteenth–early sixteenth century), H. Tan-yen, T. Ying-lung; from K'un-shan; dated 1508, fifth month, twenty-sixth day. Apparently close to Wen at this time, he was according to one source the writer of a prose-poem about the Seven Junipers of Ch'ang-shu (cf. no. XXX).

Huang	[painting: I/1]
Huang	[colophon: I/1]
Ying-lung ssu-yin	[colophon: II/1]

Wang Wen (1497–1576), T. Tzu-yü, from Wu-hsi, Kiangsu; well-known artist; writer of the two characters of the frontispiece: *Ch'ing-wan* ("Elegant Pleasure")

T'ai-hsien chih chang	[frontispiece: I/1]
Wang shih Tzu-yü	[frontispiece: I/2]

Wang Shih-chen (1526–1590), from T'ai-ts'ang, Kiangsu; dated 1570, third month

Chen-yüan	[Wen colophon: I/1]
Yu-ming Wang shih t'u-shu chih yin	[Wen colophon: II/3]
Wang Yüan-mei shih	[colophon: I/1]
T'ien-t'ao chü-shih	[colophon: I/2]
Yüan-mei	[painting: I/2]
T'ai-p'u ssu yin	[colophon: II/1]
Fu chih yün-yang teng ch'u kuan-fang	[colophon: II/2]

[The last two are official seals used by Wang Shih-chen. See *Signatures and Seals* (1964), II, p. 154; Na, *Hsi-yin* (1970), p. 103.]

Pi Mao-k'ang (1598 *chin shih),* T. Tung-chiao, from She-hsien, Anhui; dated 1633

Pi Mao-k'ang yin	[colophon: I/1]
Wu-hsü chin-shih	[colophon: I/2]
Ta-na-yen chang	[colophon: I/3]

Sun Ch'en; colophon dated 1634

Sun Ch'en	[colophon: I/1]
Po-hsiang shih	[colophon: I/2]

REMARKS:

Fu-t'ien chi (1968 ed.), vol. I. Poems 1, ch. 1/p. 14a (p. 97); 3, ch. 2/p. 7a (p. 115); 6, ch. 2/pp. 4a-4b (pp. 109-110); 7, ch. 2/p. 5a (p. 111); 8, ch. 2/p. 6b (p. 114); 15, 2/p. 8a (p. 117); 16, ch. 2/p. 9a (p. 119); 18, ch. 2/p. 10a (p. 121); and 19, ch. 2/p. 10a (p. 121), are recorded in the *Fu-t'ien chi;* all except poems 1, 3, 8, 15, 18, and 19 are recorded with the same title.

Wen-shih wu-chia chi (1934–1935 ed.), ch. 3. Poems 2 (p. 7a), 3 (pp. 6a-6b), 4 (pp. 4a-4b), 5 (pp. 5a-5b), 6 (p. 6a), 16 (p. 7b), 18 (p. 7b), and 20 (p. 8a) are recorded in the *Wen-shih wu-chia chi;* all except poems 4 and 5 are recorded with the same title.

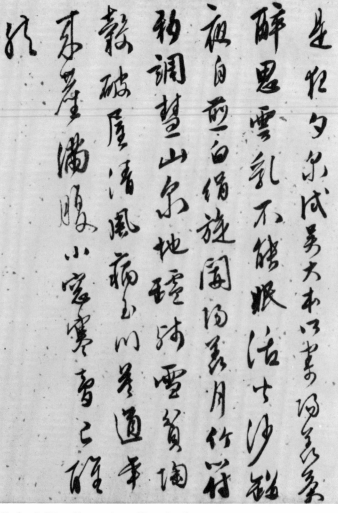

XI, detail. Wen Cheng-ming calligraphy, from poem ten

XII. CHRYSANTHEMUM, BAMBOO, AND ROCK

(Huang-hua yu-shih)
Dated 1512, ninth month, ninth day
Hanging scroll, ink on paper, 51¹⁵/₁₆″ high and 17¹⁵/₁₆″ wide
   (131.9 x 45.5 cm.)
Inscription, signature, and seals of the artist
Osaka Municipal Museum of Fine Arts

In this exhibition the close-up of chrysanthemum, bamboo, and rock is the first clearly dated scroll painted after Shen Chou's death. Wen is still signing his name "Wen Pi." Despite its presence in a famous Japanese collection, the painting has never received much serious attention from Japanese scholars. One can doubtless attribute this to its generally loose construction. It lacks coherent conviction. However, in recent years, other scholars involved with the range of Wen Cheng-ming's work have indicated its importance as an early example of a subject-type, drawn from the Yüan, which interested Wen throughout his life. Marilyn and Shen Fu have stressed the scroll's relationship to *Rock and Chrysanthemums* of 1535 (no. XXXV):

A similar centralized composition. . . . The rock shape, also tapering at its base . . . built up with slanting brushstrokes . . . forming long concavities . . . bamboo executed in the same tripartite *ko*-character form . . . .

They also note, however, that "Wen Cheng-ming was not in full command of a 'free' style and tended to force his effects."[1] Speaking generally, the same comment could also be made of the "free" Huang Kung-wang landscape we have already discussed (no. VIII).

Without contradicting the similarities suggested in the above description it is appropriate to indicate another major difference with the painting of 1535. The outline and consequently the contour-shape of the rock differ, particularly the tendency to create a concavity in the edge as it moves from point to point in shallow loops. This, to look ahead, is rather like some of the rock-shapes in the next painting (no. XIII), also to be dated 1512 and also of Yüan-dynasty inspiration. There, in addition to similar contour-shapes, the texturing with slanting brush and an occasional free interior line indicate a convincingly consistent touch for this time.

Chrysanthemum, Bamboo, and Rock, following its inscription, is a reminder of an experience of beauty and friendship on the ninth day of the ninth month, when chrysanthemums were particularly to be enjoyed and when one traditionally climbed high places for the view. For it Wen has turned directly to the Yüan dynasty, when this kind of nature "still-life" was a constant subject. It was particularly important for Chao Meng-fu, and we cannot escape the significance of that artist in this theme or, as we will see later, the theme related to it—the old cypress

XII

tree (nos. XXX, XLVIII). The repeated dark curves of the grasses or the partially broken outline ("flying white") of the rock are aspects of brushwork that relate directly to Chao. It is, however, a painting not so much concerned with the skills of an exact "style" as it is with the rather free rendering of the appearance of a Yüan painting. The presence of the two birds, wagtails, behind the screen of grasses at the lower left is particularly significant in this respect. For Yüan artists the intrusion of feathered life was a kind of hold-over from the mature Sung, when direct realism in this genre was a major concern. Wen, himself, was never seriously interested in birds, and only on the rarest of occasions do they appear in his works (cf. nos. XVI, LIX). There is an important philosophical reason for this. Birds never lend themselves to personal interpretation. Their integrity is destroyed if they are placed in the cage of individual style. Birds fly. Birds sing. They live in a different realm from man. Birds serve man as metaphor, but to live they must be left where they are.

Wen Cheng-ming's fundamental interest in rocks and trees is also, thus, a statement of his concern for personally expressive style. These stable but endlessly varied facts of nature did, indeed, lend themselves to the play of his brush. Shen Chou, by contrast, for the very reasons of consistent objectivity we have suggested in analyzing his painting, could and did draw on the bird-metaphor (no. VII). If birds occur in Wen, it is a kind of clue to his directly *seeing* something.

NOTE:
1. Fu, *Studies in Connoisseurship* (1973), p. 82.

INSCRIPTION BY THE ARTIST:
> In the eastern suburbs there is a famous winding river.
> Living happily these three years I have come twice to this place.
> It's just as before, this old setting, with the walls shading the trees.
> People have long ceased coming, the stone path is covered with moss.
> With the setting of the sun I long for you as the waters flow into the distance.
> The chrysanthemum blossoms with the caress of the autumn breeze.
> This beautiful moment before my eyes, I shan't let it slip away.
> Facing the mountain priest I drink a cup of wine.

This is a record of my trip with Tzu-chung (T'ang Chen) to Tung-ch'an Temple, on the ninth day of the ninth month in 1512. On this day Tao-fu (Ch'en Shun) and others failed to arrive for our appointment, so while sitting and thinking of them I wished to bring these associations together. Wen Pi.

(tr. Stephen Goldberg)

SEALS OF THE ARTIST:

T'ing-yün	[painting: I/1]
Wen Pi yin	[painting: II/1]
Wu-yen shih yin	[painting: II/2]

SEAL:
Liu Shu (1759–1816), from Wu-hsien, Kiangsu

Jung-feng Liu Shu pi-ts'ang	[painting: I/2]

REMARKS:
T'ang Chen (sixteenth century), from Suchou, studied for fifteen years with Wang Ch'ung (1494–1533) at the Chih-p'ing Temple at Stone Lake.
Ch'en Shun (1483–1544): see no. X.

BIBLIOGRAPHY:
Min shitaika (1924), p. 55.
Sōraikan (1930–1939), II, p. 30.
Sirén, *Chinese Painting* (1956), VI, pl. 200.
Fu-t'ien (1968 ed.), ch. 4/p. 159.
Fu, *Studies in Connoisseurship* (1973), p. 82.

XIII. SUMMER RETREAT IN THE EASTERN GROVE

(Tung-lin pi-shu)
Dated by inscription ca. 1512
Handscroll, ink on paper, 12½" high and 42½" long (31.8 x 107.8 cm.)
Inscription, signatures, and seals of the artist
John M. Crawford, Jr., New York

A second work by Wen to be dated in or close to 1512 is the beautifully ordered handscroll *Summer Retreat in the Eastern Grove.* Although the year 1515 is recorded in the colophon, Wen then recognized the calligraphy—and presumably also the painting—as having been written three years before, in the Western Garden of the connoisseur-collector Ch'ien K'ung-chou. He was among the friends with whom Wen had traveled to T'ien-p'ing Mountain in 1508 (no. X). Later, around 1520, Ch'ien's daughter married Wen Cheng-ming's son, Wen P'eng.

The painting encompasses the great scholarly arts of poetry, calligraphy, and painting and adds further elements that accrued to paintings in scholarly circles. There is often such a life that goes beyond the specific creation and inevitably becomes a continuation of that original moment. Thus, the title *Tung-lin pi-shu (Summer Retreat in the Eastern Grove),* in bold seal script, was brushed after the painting had left Wen's hands. It was written by Wu I, who was Wu K'uan's nephew (cf. no. II). When Wu I wrote, *Summer Retreat* was owned by a priest, Nan-chou.

Wen alludes to all this in his colophon of 1515 and also to that inevitable swift passage of time that has always been a standard lament for Chinese poets. Wen's calligraphy of 1512 is beautifully bold and strong—and moves with the poem series from a clear, almost block-like standard script into a running script which then becomes extremely free in the most obvious "grass" manner.

The third poem then reverts back to a thick standard style with Wen's brief explanation again in a free manner. Since, as with painting, it was common to identify calligraphy styles with great masters of the past, the modern colophon by P'an Po-ying does just that. Thus the three manners are connected with Huang T'ing-chien (1045–1105), the monk Huai-su (eighth century), and Su Shih (1037–1101).

The additional calligraphy of 1515 continues the running script. But the characters are smaller, and there is more of a sharp staccato effect, although the style is similar, as can be seen in the free writing of the character *shu* second from the bottom of the second line of the early writing, and in the first line of the later.

Wen's colophons never specifically mention the painting by name. It could have been painted on a separate occasion. But we can be sure that it was joined early—possibly in 1512, no later than 1515 —to the writing since the split halves of Wen's seal are on the now-divided left edge of the painting and right edge of the calligraphy. The painting thus once moved readily into the calligraphy sections —a close, single work of art.

As for the inevitable old-master connection, the guiding mode—and mood—comes from Ni Tsan (1301–1374), who as we have seen in discussing Shen Chou (no. VI) had set high standards. The debt to Shen Chou is revealed here in Wen's creation of an exact compositional order. Each unit is clear in itself, and relationships between them are established with precision. Wen has assured psychological distance by not allowing any part of the landscape to touch the front edge of the scroll. Nor does he enliven his form with any use of *tien* or the strokes of distracting grasses. Trees never obscure our understanding of land-form. They are few and placed in thin, numerical lines; and in turn the bare twigs, the few symbolic leaves allow us readily to grasp their clear if varied shapes.

As has been previously written, the importance of the painting rests in its fresh, cool remoteness:

XIII, detail. Wen Cheng-ming calligraphy in the manner of Huang T'ing-chien

澤國春深霧雨收
蘸城橋畔
水爭流斷
烟西去浮
蒼靄嶼

雁門文壁寫

XIII

XIII, detail

We admire it . . . not because of a ready pictorialism or an open emotional content but because of a kind of careful skilled reserve—the order, the sense of propriety that made Wen Cheng-ming revered both for his learning and his high moral conduct. He moves from rock to rock, from separate tree to separate tree, along a carefully planned course and in the end our summer's reward is the vertical drop and the sure arcs of a waterfall, the vibrant surface of a cliff and the remote cool of the empty paper from which to enjoy it.[1]

NOTE:
1. Sickman, ed., *Chinese Calligraphy and Painting* (1962), p. 135.

INSCRIPTION BY THE ARTIST:
Sketched by Yen-men Wen Pi

FIRST COLOPHON BY THE ARTIST:

[Done in a Boat on Stone Lake During the Cold Food Festival:]
In the Marsh Country it is deep spring and the foggy rains have ended;
By the Yüeh-ch'eng Bridge bank, the turbulent waters flow on.
Wisps of clouds going westward are floating among green isles;
The setting sun shines in mid-river on rising white gulls.

Village shops are lonely and still—it's the "Cold Food Festival";
The traveler is far away upon a magnolia boat.
The fragrance fills the day while the east wind flurries;
Though I would like to gather shore flowers, I cannot do so.

[Remembrance While Walking Alone in the Morning by a Stream:]
Outside the city in the green mist the willow leaves are tender,
Going westward over (Lake) Tung-t'ing the waters are vast and gentle.
I do not see my old friend by the crabapple oar,
Swallows fly evenly over the islands of *tu-jo* flowers.
As the sun falls the evening wind blows my night wine,
The sky is cool and the river grasses call forth new sadness.
Good time is loneliness—spring is like this.
Ungrateful for the mountain flowers, I put them in my hair.

[Drinking During a Late Rain in Mr. T'ang's Garden Pavilion:]
In a lofty studio while the sun was setting, we casually did what others have done:
With wine-cups we lingered, with laughter.
Fragrant grasses filled the yard and swallows were on the wing.
In the evening cool a gentle rain fell on the *wu-t'ung* trees.
River fish plump as cooked jade—circling chopsticks.
The green trees had stored springtime—a reddish glow.
Relaxing, no doubts, and return was all the slower,
I was at home in that lake lodge of the "Mountain-loving Gentleman."
Wen Pi, Cheng-ming, has just written this at a place deep within the verdant green bamboo area of Mr. Ch'ien's Western Garden.

(tr. James Robinson)

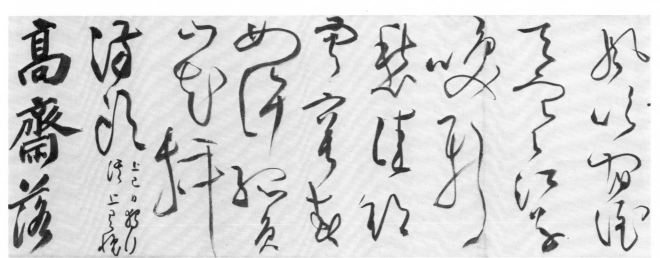

XIII, detail. Wen Cheng-ming calligraphy in the manner of Huai-su and (lefthand column) Su Shih

SECOND COLOPHON BY THE ARTIST:

Previously I wrote this at (Ch'ien) K'ung-chou's place, and did not know that this was (since) acquired by Nan-chou. On the twenty fourth day of the ninth month of 1515 I happened to pass by th T'ien-wang Temple. Examining it, there welled up feelings of sadness. It has been three years since I wrote it. Each day my powers fail. I doubt that I could do this again. Cheng-ming again inscribed.

(tr. James Robinson)

SEALS OF THE ARTIST:

Wen Cheng-ming yin	[painting: IX/1]
Heng (-shan)	[painting, half seal: X/1]
(Heng)-shan	[colophon, half seal: I/1]
Heng-shan	[colophon, three seals on seams]
Wen Cheng-ming yin	[colophon: VII/1]
Heng-shan	[colophon: VII/2]

COLOPHONS AND SEALS:

Wu I (1472-1519), frontispiece:
Summer Retreat in the Eastern Grove. Written by Wu I for the venerable Abbot Nan-chou.
[no seals]

Ch'ien-lung emperor (r. 1736-1795)

Ch'ien-lung yü-lan chih pao	[painting: I/1]
Shih-ch'ü pao-chi	[painting: I/2]
Pao-chi san-pien	[painting: I/3]
San-hsi t'ang ching-chien hsi	[painting: VII/1]
I tzu-sun	[painting: VII/2]

Chia-ch'ing emperor (r. 1796-1820)

Chia-ch'ing yü-lan chih pao	[painting: IV/1]
Chia-ch'ing chien-shang	[painting: VI/1]

Hsüan-t'ung emperor (r. 1908-1911)

Hsüan-t'ung yü-lan chih pao	[painting: V/1]

P'an Po-ying (twentieth century)

P'an Po-ying so-chien chin-shih shu-hua	[frontispiece: I/1]
Po-ying shen-ting	[mounting seam: I/1]
	[Wen colophon: II/1]
P'an Po-ying yin	[Wen colophon: VI/1]
Mo ———	[colophon: I/1]
P'an Po-ying	[colophon: I/2]

John M. Crawford, Jr. (present owner)

Ku Lo-fu	[painting: II/1]
Han-kuang ko	[painting: III/1]
Han-kuang ko chu Ku Lo-fu chien ts'ang	
Chung-kuo ku-tai shu-hua chih chang	[painting: VIII/1]

Unidentified:

Fan Yang	[painting: I/4]
Hsing-yüan	[painting: I/5]

REMARKS:

The *Marsh Country (che-kuo)* refers to the area around Suchou (*Suchou fu-chih,* ch. 8/p. 1a [p. 223]).

The *Yüeh-ch'eng Bridge* is outside the city near Wu-men Bridge.

Mr. T'ang is T'ang Chen, T. Tzu-chung, from Suchou.

Ch'ien K'ung-chou (1475–1549), T. T'ung-ai, was to be related to the Wen family by the marriage of his daughter to Wen P'eng. He was an avid collector. His family was famous for the practice of medicine. (Wilson and Wong, *Friends* [1974], pp. 23, 31–32, 108.)

Nan-chou was the abbot of the Buddhist T'ien-wang ssu (Temple of the Kings of Heaven) on West Tung-t'ing Mountain (Wilson and Wong, *Friends* [1974], p. 79.)

Wu I was the nephew of Wu K'uan (1435–1504) (Wilson and Wong, *Friends* [1974], pp. 95–97).

The first poem (with title) is recorded in *Wen-shih wu-chia chi,* ch. 6/p. 14a, and *Fu-t'ien chi,* ch. 4/p. 2a (p. 153), where it is entitled "Returning from Heng-chin afloat on Stone Lake during the Cold Food Festival." In the next to last line *Fu-t'ien chi* has *jih* 'day', not *mu* 'eyes'.

The *Cold Food Festival* occurs from the 105th to the 107th day after the winter solstice and commemorates Chieh Tzu-t'ui of the Spring and Autumn Period.

The second poem (with title) is recorded in *Wen-shih wu-chia chi,* ch. 6/p. 14a, and *Fu-t'ien chi,* ch. 4/p. 2a (p. 153), where it is entitled "Thinking of Chiu-k'uei (Ts'ai Yü) while walking alone in the morning by a stream."

The third poem (with title) is recorded in *Fu-t'ien chi,* ch. 4/p. 3a (p. 155). In the sixth line *Fu-t'ien chi* has "wild" not "green." In the seventh line *Fu-t'ien chi* has "none spoke" not "no doubts."

BIBLIOGRAPHY:

Fu-t'ien chi (1968 ed.), I, pp. 153 and 155.
Wen-shih (1934–1935 ed.), ch. 6/p. 14a.
Sickman, ed., *Chinese Calligraphy and Painting* (1962), no. 60.
Shih-ch'ü san (1969 ed.), pp. 1908–1909.
Wilson and Wong, *Friends* (1974), pp. 79–81.

XIV. AUTUMN MOUNTAINS

(Ch'iu-shan t'u)
No date
Handscroll, ink on gold-flecked paper, 12½" high and 47½" long
 (31.8 x 120.8 cm.)
Inscription, signature, and seals of the artist
The Art Institute of Chicago, Kate S. Buckingham Collection

Wen Cheng-ming did not always date his paintings. It is style itself that must tell us where such paintings are to be considered in the pattern of the history of the artist. Since Wen was himself so concerned with style—or more accurately, styles—and brought so many style-patterns from various historical times into the one time of his own time, it might be claimed that history is sufficiently challenged so as to deny its basic importance. But at least on one occasion—the scroll of 1502 (no. IX)—we have seen Wen, himself, indicate that his interests (and capabilities) changed. He was, within the convention of modesty, aware of the transformation of the years; and thus, despite his own skill in transforming times past into the timelessness of a living present, he was not able (or willing) to deny the reality of his own "historical development."

In this exhibition, several undated paintings may, on grounds of style, be considered "early." One of these is *Autumn Mountains.* It has much the same proportions as the last scroll. Also its seal-script title and poem-colophon are by well-known contemporaries and must have been written close to the time the scroll was painted. As with the Crawford painting, there is no addition of color, and one is

surely facing the cool manner of Ni Tsan. But now the play of grey forms with their thin lines of tree-groves presents a kind of positive to the negative of *Summer Retreat* (no. XIII). Where the latter is essentially empty with a few sparse bits of definition leading to a firm block of form in the upper left, *Autumn Mountains* is all form with a few sparse pockets of space. Rather like the painting of 1502, it is filled except for a release into the distance at the very end. One can also occasionally catch touches of detail which are in line with what we have already seen. Thus the paper is flecked with gold, as in the Mi-style handscroll of 1508 (no. XI); the first tree motif is that of crossed trees, as in *Summer Retreat;* figure scale—the mid-point single figure—is of an exaggerated tininess in relation to architecture and tree, as are the minute hair-like human forms in the painting of 1502.

There is also external evidence for a relatively early date. The poem-colophon that follows the painting was written by the important scholar-official from Wu-hsi, Shao Pao. Shao Pao died in 1527. Further, one of the artist's seals, *Yen-men shih chia,* is rare and when it is used appears to be early. Wen used the term *Yen-men* in his signature on the last scroll, apparently in 1512. However, the *Autumn Mountains* signature, *Cheng-ming,* pushes us toward the later 'teens, a logical historical niche.

A major difference from the *Summer Retreat* rests in the fact that *Autumn Mountains* is more exactly conforming to an established type. In this connection there is something a bit impersonal about the inscription: ". . . done (or made) for Tzu-yang," an as-yet unidentified patron. The type called for modification in the direction of a more exact,

traditional notion of what lay behind Ni Tsan, namely the inevitable tenth-century master Tung Yüan. For this Shen Chou had established the pattern—his "long ranges piled up" in *Autumn Colors* (no. VI). Now Wen's *Autumn Mountains* carries on with his own more elegant, vibrant, angular touch many of the same conventions. Noteworthy are the repeated curving shapes of hills, shadowed at their base; behind the hills loom far dark washes of mountain peaks; hill-contours are paralleled by sparse texture-strokes; there is a use of unique dark horizontal ink-dots; spare ranks of stick-like trees never conceal the land-structure; and even Wen's single central symbolic figure has its parallel in the solitary man that begins Shen's scroll.

The Shen Chou idea of Ni Tsan was so firmly established in his work that it is known in a whole series of his paintings.[1] How surely the mode became an inescapable part of Suchou painting is indicated not only by Wen's *Autumn Mountains,* but also by a similar handscroll in Taipei from the 1535 brush of his student, Lu Chih (fig. 8).

NOTE:
1. Edwards, *The Field of Stones* (1962), pls. 23A, 24, 25B, 40A, 41A, 41B.

INSCRIPTION BY THE ARTIST:
Painting of Autumn Mountains, done for Tzu-yang. Cheng-ming.

SEALS OF THE ARTIST:
Yen-men shih chia	[painting: I/4]
T'ing-yün sheng	[painting: III/2]
Wen Cheng-ming yin	[painting: III/3]

FRONTISPIECE, COLOPHONS, AND SEALS:
Hsü Lin (1490–1548), T. Tzu-jen, Tzu-yüan, Jan-hsien, etc. He was a painter, calligrapher, and seal-carver. He was noted for his seal script. An example of his running-style calligraphy is in the Crawford Collection (Ecke, *Chinese Calligraphy* [1971], no. 53).
Hsü shih Tzu-jen	[frontispiece: II/1]

Shao Pao (1460–1527), T. Kuo-hsien, Erh-ch'üan; important scholar-official from Wu-hsi, noted for his calligraphy in the running and grass styles. His poem-colophon is on gold-flecked paper and in it he mentions specifically "autumn mountains."
Erh-ch'üan	[colophon: II/1]
Kuo-hsien	[colophon: III/1]
Shao-ssu-t'u chih chang	[colophon: III/2]

(seal of the Vice-President of the Board of Revenue)
Wang Sui-an (Ming dynasty, unidentified)
Wang Sui-an ts'eng kuan	[painting: III/7]

Shen Han (second half of seventeenth century, calligrapher)
Chi-an chien-ting	[painting: I/2]

Liu Shu (1759–1816)
Jung-feng chih yin	[frontispiece: I/3]
Liu shih Han-pi chuang yin	[frontispiece: III/1]
	[painting: III/1]
Jung-feng chien-shang	[painting: I/1]
Wu-i Liu Shu sheng-ting	[painting: I/3]
Jung-feng shen-ting	[painting: III/5]
Jung-feng chen-shang	[colophon: I/3]

Wang Hsiang-shu (Ch'ing dynasty), from Hsü-i, Anhwei
Lu-yün lou shu-hua chi	[frontispiece: I/1]

Weng T'ung-ho (1830–1904)
Weng Shu-p'ing sheng ch'ang-wu	[painting: II/1]

Wang Tsu-hsi (1858–1908), T. Erh-lang, from Chia-hsing
Tseng-ts'ang Wang shih Lou-hsiang ko	[frontispiece: III/2]
T'i-an so te ming-chi	[painting: III/4]
T'i-an chen-ts'ang	[colophon: I/2]

Unidentified
Ho Ch'ang-keng so ts'ang	[frontispiece: I/2]
Ho Ch'ang-keng chien-shang shu-hua chih chang	[painting: II/2]
T'ing-yü chen-ts'ang	[painting: III/6]
Shih-yüan	[colophon: I/1]

BIBLIOGRAPHY:
Dubosc, *Mostra d'arte* (1954), no. 808.
Giuganino, *La pittura* (1959), II, p. 327.
Art Institute of Chicago, *Ming-Ch'ing* (1964), no pagination.

8. Lu Chih (1496–1576), *Landscape* (in the manner of Ni Tsan), section. From a scroll of *Calligraphy and Painting.* National Palace Museum, Taipei

XV. MOUNTAIN LANDSCAPE

No date
Hanging scroll, ink on paper, 36¾″ high and 8³/₁₆″ wide (93.2 x
  21.3 cm.)
Seals of the artist
The University of Michigan Museum of Art, Ann Arbor

To the early handscroll essays in the ink tradition
of one Yüan master, Ni Tsan (nos. XIII, XIV), may
now, in a different format, be added another—after
another master of that time: Wang Meng (ca. 1309–
1385). The painting is a tall, thin hanging scroll,
even more crowded with shapes than the Chicago
handscroll.

Certain early features are present—the packed
format with only a small vision of space at one end,
the delight in the miniature. It is a mountainscape,
as Max Loehr has pointed out, that is not dominated
by a single mountain. It is thus hardly a view in the
Western impressionist sense, or even according to
the modified objectivity of Chinese vision during
the Sung period. Because of the wonderfully delicate powdery ink-detail, we are inevitably drawn
close to the slightly rough brown-grey paper where
the dry, cool rock—only occasionally accented by
the dark, flat forms of tree leaves or a stronger
ink outline—"unshaded and transparent, appears
like congealed froth. . . ."[1] Since it is a painting
not to be comprehended in a glance, we follow
a close zigzag course, introduced by a bent bridge-
standing scholar, the counterpart of the single
figure in *Autumn Mountains* (no. XIV) or in the
landscape after Huang Kung-wang (no. VIII).
Across a void, two companions sit on a precarious
upward-soaring plateau. We then move back and
forth either side of a thread of space which is
paper, or a stream, or a tight mountain path, and
eventually reach a flat, thin fall of water suddenly
emerging from the mysterious turbulence of the far,
far heights, where man can wander only in the mind.

It is like a handscroll turned on end, and because we can never lose sight of "format" we are
always aware of the landscape as "art"—paper, ink,
line that is always dissolving into texture. The denial
of open, easy spaces is nowhere more evident than
at the top, where the even grey washes of the last
mountains can be only a symbol for distance and
prepare us for the flat paper beyond. There the thin
inscription by the artist's son, although not part of
the original conception, is, accordingly, completely
acceptable.

If we are to liken this mountainscape to a tipped-
up handscroll, the handscroll that immediately
comes to mind is that of 1502 (no. IX). But this
is no thinned, tight-lined affirmation of graduate-
student seriousness and exactly learned potential.
Here is creative expression, a personal sensitivity
of touch, the inevitable manipulation of a special
format that became the basis of what was to be

XV, detail

painted in later, more mature years, and continued beyond that by his followers. While originating in the Yüan, Wen was the great exploiter of its possibilities. For him the work was historically the first of a series. His pupils were to continue to use the idea.

In the pattern of Wen's own history, how early can we place this sensitive, inventive work? Wen Chia, again with his consciousness of history, recognized it, almost two decades after his father's death, as an early work. Loehr, who at the time of his writing did not have access to works before 1507, was not willing to place it before that date. Now that we know of some very early painting, his caution seems justified. Within the variety of his early painting, Wen has clearly found a new and uniquely expressive vision. Although, as we have seen, Wen was never tied to Shen Chou in a literal sense, this mountainscape is sufficiently inventive to affirm a special power. It is logical to think of it as coming from the second decade of the century (after the death of Shen Chou in 1509), early, but maturely individual.

A painting of detail, in which no single part assumes a separate uniqueness, it is still worth pointing out something of the nature of its individual forms. Many are part of an already established vocabulary. Clustering of rocks, undercut cliffs, tight channels of space are all found in the more linear conceptions of them in the scroll of 1502. The flat wash of far-mountain peaks is also an accepted convention. Certainly there is a basic general adherence to the modes of Wang Meng. However, the individual texture strokes, the manner of feeling one's way through form, the sensitive overlay of interlocking shapes, in defiance of specific antiquarianism, suggests a broader allegiance. Loehr has mentioned Huang Kung-wang. The left-hand tree in the grove by the pavilion with its flat, grey wash areas of leaves is a Wang Meng feature, but further back it is found in the Northern Sung artist Kuo Hsi.

The leaning cypress tree—light textured trunk, white vine, dark clustered dots of leaves, a few un-leafed, bare-twig branches—is the first example in this exhibition of an ever-recurring motif in Wen's later work: the old tree and particularly the enduring symbols of it that mark the end of Wen's long life. Here, too, as in later landscapes (no. LVII), the tree is related to the converse of two scholars. But unless we make it so, this painting is not a close-up of any one thing. It is a complete landscape. Despite its varied shapes there is no lasting sense of conflicting parts. In the understatement of gentle tones, brushed with jewel-like care, we find not juxtaposition, but interweaving. As one withdraws a little, dry ink and aging paper become, in harmonious relationships, transformed into a single ideal vision.

NOTE:
1. Loehr, "A Landscape" (1959), p. 150.

SEALS OF THE ARTIST:

Wu-yen shih yin	[painting: I/2]
Wen Cheng-ming yin	[painting: I/3]

COLOPHON AND SEALS:
Wen Chia (1501–1583); colophon:
This was painted by the *tai-chao* (Wen Cheng-ming) in his early years. 1576, third month, sixteenth day.

Hsiu-ch'eng	[painting: II/1]

Ch'ien-lung emperor (r. 1736–1795)

Shih-ch'ü pao-chi	[painting seam: I/1]
Ch'ien-lung yü-lan chih pao	[painting: 1/1]
Ch'ien-lung chien-shang	[painting seam: II/1]
San-hsi t'ang ching-chien hsi	[painting seam: II/2]
I tzu-sun	[painting seam: II/3]

Yeh Ch'ang-ch'un, T. Fang-lin, a Ch'ing painter from Chia-ting

Fang-lin chu-jen chien-shang	[painting seam: I/2]

Teng Shih (twentieth century)

Teng Shih	[painting seam: II/4]

Unidentified:

Ch'en Ch'ing ssu-yin	[painting seam: II/5]
(possibly Ku Ho-ch'ing, b. 1766)	
Li shih chen-pi	[painting seam: II/6]
Tan-ju chai chen-wan	[painting seam: II/7]

REMARKS: Teng Shih was the editor of *Fu-chai chi-chin lu* Catalogue of the Collection of Ch'en Chieh-ch'i, 1813–1844). Teng's preface is dated 1918. He was also the compiler of Chin Nung's (1687–1764) collected colophons under the title *Tung-hsin hsien-sheng tsa-hua t'i chi* (Yü Shao-sung, *Shu-hua shu-lu chieh-t'i*, Peking National Library, 1932, ch. 5/p. 15b).

BIBLIOGRAPHY:
Loehr, "A Landscape" (1959), pp. 143–152.

XVI. MAGPIES AND JUNIPERS

No date
Hanging scroll, ink on paper, 21¼″ high and 12⅞″ wide (54.0 x 32.7 cm.)
Seal of the artist
Nelson-Atkins Gallery, Kansas City, Missouri (Nelson Fund)

As one examines detail in the lower left-hand corner of the last painting, one perhaps finds an entry into the understanding of an otherwise puzzling painting attributed to Wen Cheng-ming—*Magpies and Junipers,* from the Nelson Gallery in Kansas City. Like the Michigan mountainscape this small close-up of rocks and trees is not inscribed by the artist, and its connection with Wen is verbally affirmed by only a small seal—*Heng-shan*—in the lower left-hand corner. Given the lower section of the Michigan painting for comparison there are general similarities: the introduction of a flat horizontal piece of land, the then dramatically rising undercut escarpments that offer somewhat restless foundation for selective tree-groves. In the Kansas City picture the four cypress trees and the bare-twigged grove at the left suggest a season either very late or very early. The rock contours are analogous not only in their undercut profiles but also in their basic angularity of outline. Broken by sharp points, no line continues in a single direction for long. Its thin restless definition is supplemented by texture-strokes leaving layers of form light at the outer edges, dark in the shadowy folds. The cypresses are a play of the white, forked forms of trunk and brush against the crowded varied-toned dots of leaf-clusters. It is a feature of Wen's studied approach to the technical detail of these leaf dots that he creates them carefully, in bunches, each bunch a circular unit clustered around an implied central core. Such "wheel-like" groups are here. The stream can be thought of as a more precisely linear version of the shifting parallel lines and dancing foam that in the center of the Michigan picture Wen has hidden in the ravine above the empty pavilion.

Still the differences remain, and no amount of study can dispel them. The works can only be accepted as from the brush of a single master if we accede to Wen's versatility. Yüan ideals in the mountainscape have given way to those of the Sung in *Magpies and Junipers.* Richard Barnhart tells of its poetic vision, quoting the T'ang poet Wang Wei:

Mountains deserted after fresh rain,
Autumn weather comes late in the day.
Pines in the bright moon shining.
Rocks under clear water flowing.

(tr. John Hay, Jr.)

He further points out the auspiciousness of the theme—the magpies of happiness, the juniper as the tree of sages, hallowed as such by Confucius.

Thus the close-up scene could be a simple modest auspicious gift by a developing painter. It is in a style and of a theme that, like the early album-leaf *Storm over the River* (no. II F), may recall T'ang poetry in a vision whose directness is of the Sung. Indeed, the feeling for atmosphere behind the *Magpies and*

9. Wen Cheng-ming, *Deep Snow Over Streams and Mountains,* 1517. National Palace Museum, Taipei

XVI

Junipers, where cloud has condensed to mist that conceals the sharp wall of background rock, is similar to the mist and slanting rain that curtain the background of *Storm over the River.* Like the boat at evening in the latter, here the trees—however enduring the symbol—are seen as in many late Sung paintings at a moment in time. Anchored in the lower left corner, we look directly at them. We go into the shallow distance not because the artist has conveniently tipped up the background for us to explore but simply by standing where we are and looking past trunk and foliage or into a pocket from which the stream flows toward us. As in the late Sung, the momentary is reinforced not only by the point-of-view but also by the actions of the sole inhabitants of the scene—the magpies. They are precariously perched at the very tip of the junipers, with one seemingly at an instant of just establishing his perch, another stopped at a point in mid-flight.

Wen might well have had in mind the late Sung approach found in a monumental hanging scroll, *Wintry Trees,* a painting now in Taipei.[1] The Taipei painting is attributed to the tenth-century painter Li Ch'eng, as is inevitable of all hoary tree-groves in the Sung manner. But powerful as it is, surely it cannot be dated earlier than the twelfth century. However, with this clear referent, *Magpies and Junipers* becomes the earliest example of the Li Ch'eng mode—a manner of deep and lasting concern throughout Wen's later career.

Aside from viewing *Magpies and Junipers* beside the lower section of the Michigan hanging scroll,

it is most instructive to compare it to the elegant, restrained *Deep Snow over Streams and Mountains,* a painting in Taipei that was painted for Wen's great friend Ts'ai Yü in 1517 (fig. 9). It was with Ts'ai Yü that Wen was to travel north in 1523 (no. XVIII). The fact that this winter landscape is on silk accounts for a different quality in the way ink relates to the painting's surface. But in form and structure there are striking parallels with the Kansas City picture: the filled bottom edge of the scroll just above which is a space-gap; the shapes of the plateaus; their undercut sides; the shadowing within the rock-layers; the long drawn-out shapes of the tree-trunks; their outlining by a changing varied brush, the trunks themselves often similarly knotted and textured. But particularly it is the sharp contending juxtaposition of cliff and rock-forms creating irregular gateways to narrow pockets of space that confirms a similar formal intent in the two landscapes.

The inscribed time of 1517 on the snowscape helps to anchor the date of both the uninscribed Kansas City and Michigan scrolls.

NOTE:
1. Li, "Pine and Rock" (1970), p. 3.

SEAL OF THE ARTIST:
Heng-shan   [painting: I/1]

BIBLIOGRAPHY:
Sullivan, *Introduction to Chinese Art* (1961), pl. 119.
Speiser, *Chinese Art* (1964), III, pl. 59.
Barnhart, *Wintry Forests* (1972), pp. 51-52, pl. 14.

XVII. OLD PINE TREE

(Ch'iu-jan t'u)
No date
Handscroll, ink on paper, 10¾″ high and 54⅝″ long (27.2 x 136.0 cm.)
Inscription, signature, and seals of the artist
The Cleveland Museum of Art, Andrew R. and Martha Holden
   Jennings Fund

This dramatic close-up of an old pine tree is inevitably linked to the truth that joins age and beauty in the creation of forms whose complexity extends quite literally to suggestion of even greater mysteries. Particularly in China, it has been the magic power of dragons—their writhing shapes, their claw-like reaching into voids—that has been evoked by the old tree. Wen's explanatory title sums up his condensed complex vision:

> Transformations with power difficult to bind,
> Dragon-whiskers like a forest of lances.

Possibly because of the rather wet, free treatment of ink, certainly because of Wen's fondness for the old-tree theme in his late years, this undated painting has often been considered a late work. However, on careful study, there is little to support the assumption. One cannot find closely parallel expression from the 1540s and 1550s, when Wen's

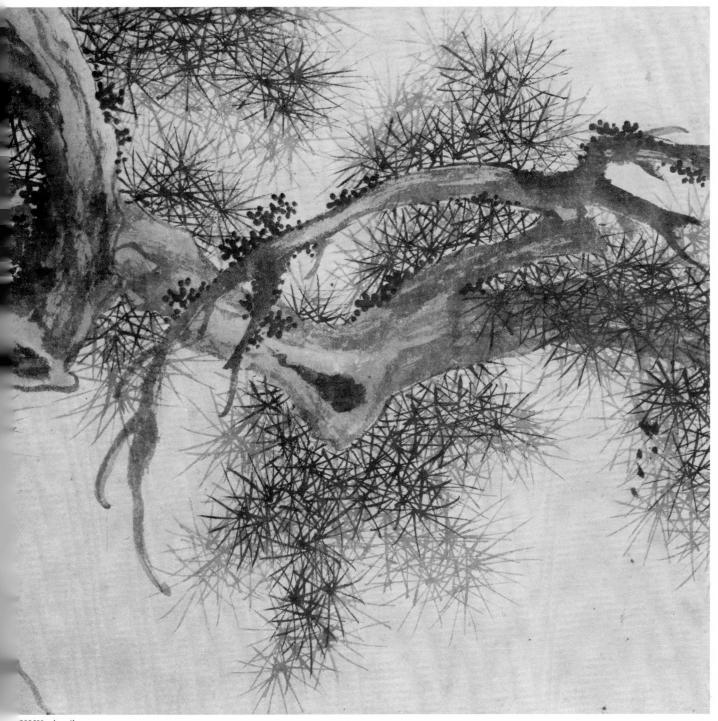

XVII, detail

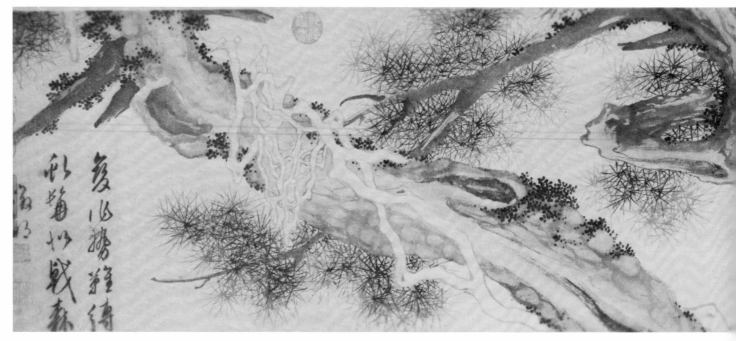

XVII

style, like the dragon trees, had itself undergone transformations. Consider the nature of Wen's approach to his theme.

The branch-end at the right is the beginning. We trace our way back along this branch to find the source which is the trunk, sharply leaning to the left, framing, as it were, the free calligraphy of title and signature. But still we have not truly found that source, for connection between claw-like branch and solid trunk is only apparent. The branch is actually suspended in space. If, indeed, it is connected with a physical trunk at all, the union is somewhere far above what the picture-plane allows us to see. Even more dragon-like then is this self-supported form, the gestures of its dance moving out in directions counter to and independent from the statelier movement of the vine-bound trunk.

Dramatic tensions certainly are part of Wen's late and mature art, but we already have implications of them in his early work, in for example the contending forms of mountain shapes that rise in the tall thin landscape, likewise undated, from The University of Michigan Museum of Art (no. XV). The mountainscape is a thin vertical "window" rather as the pine is a similarly proportioned horizontal one. But more important, just as with the old tree, the towering landscape was a theme picked up again and further elaborated in Wen's more mature years.

The key to a possible early date for the *Old Pine* inevitably rests in its style. It simply does not reflect the maturity of an artist whose vision has been absorbed into the confident unified expression of his brush. The more one looks, the more one realizes that the painting depends on its separate individual elements, the care with which each is rendered, and the way each is placed.

They can be listed, and each is different: the outlined, pale untextured vine; the loosely textured ink that describes trunk and branch with its wet, often indeterminate greys; the dark exact clusters of moss-dots; the rayed sharpness of repeated pine-needles ("dragon-whiskers"); the easy-flowing calligraphy; the undefined paper.

Furthermore, these elements are held together not by the uniformities of the personal brushwork of a personal style but rather by the fact of their believable physical juxtaposition. The vine is over and appears to surround the trunk. The trunk is behind the vine. The moss-dots are clustered on the bark. The dragon-like branch claws outward into space along the surface of the paper, but it never really breaks forward. It twists and turns back on itself (writhes, if you will) as an alive, three-dimensional organism. We do not question the space in which it exists. Parts are sometimes in front, sometimes behind. And if you look closely at those tense rays of needles, the juxtaposition of dark and light, of grey and black, builds them into clusters of separate mass and depth.

It is a painting which holds the proper "look" of the subject. However much varied devices are used —the cutting-off of forms, the different uses of ink, the precision of the line of a pine needle—the painting is a direct transcription of what nature is. Its unities are not those of an artist's will, but the unities of nature itself. However imaginative, this is the way the segment of a growing tree might appear to the eye.

If it fits with a direct interpretation of nature, within the Chinese tradition this means that it fits with the Sung. Broadly speaking its treatment is in line with the portrayal of an old-tree idea that was generally associated with Li Ch'eng (919–967) and Kuo Hsi (ca. 1020–1075), the Li-Kuo manner. In the form of a handscroll that sharply cuts off

the tree in mid-section, so that neither base nor top is visible, the best known surviving example comes from the twelfth-century Chin artist, Wang T'ing-yün (1151–1202), whose *Old Tree and Bamboo* in Kyoto's Fujii Yurinkan, while not a pine, certainly gives precedent for the rather free touches of ink that in turn suggest the texture of Wen Cheng-ming's pine-trunk and limbs.[1] Earlier, Su Shih (1036–1101) had apparently dealt with this kind of subject in a rather flamboyant way. For this we have the description of his contemporary, Mi Fu, "Branches like dragons turning, no limits; hard stone-textures—very strange, very strange."[2]

In the Yüan, Kuo Pi (1280–1335) has given us a similar handscroll section of *Lonely Bamboo and Bare Tree*.[3] The use of the old tree as a vehicle for free touches of ink might by the fifteenth century best be seen in the Wu-hsing artist Yao Shou (1423–1495), himself a direct heir of the famous Yüan artist Wu Chen. His vine-wrapped *Pine* in Chicago is a version of the theme painted near the end of his life. And in this exhibition Shen Chou's brief suggestion of pine in his *Pine and Hibiscus* of 1487 (no. V) shows the same mid-section view. Here, again, is Wen's allegiance to the web of tradition and at the same time his rejection of Shen Chou's blunt view of a well-known theme. Wen's pine is marked by a sure exactness in rendering its differing elements and certainly by a unique infusion of dramatic power.

Finally, the style of calligraphy cannot be matched with late calligraphy by Wen. The gently elongated shape of each character and the easy flow of the movement of the brush come closest in this exhibition to the writing that is found after the landscape in no. XI, the 1508 *Cloudy Mountains* in the style of Mi Fu. The tendency toward curves and the elongation of a slanted line are mannerisms that can be particulary noted. However, Wen signs the painting with the name Cheng-ming, rather than the earlier name, Pi. Apparently as we have seen, the transition occurred somewhere around 1515 (no. XIII). Following this logic, the painting should be dated sometime in the late 'teens.

To put it another way, this is not an old tree seen from the experience of age, but rather age seen in the freshness of relative youth. It is the wonder of age that we can see. Later we will understand what it is to know that age.

NOTES:
1. Cahill, *Chinese Painting* (1960), p. 96.
2. *Wen wu* (1965), no. 8, pp. 24–25. The Mi Fu quotation is found in his *Hua shih*.
3. Lee and Ho, *Chinese Art under the Mongols* (1968), no. 226.

INSCRIPTION BY THE ARTIST: [translated above in text; signed] Cheng-ming.

SEALS OF THE ARTIST:
Wen Cheng-ming yin	[painting: VI/1]
Heng-shan	[painting: VI/2]

SEALS:
Ch'ien Shih-sheng (1575–1652)
Wei-t'ang kuei chu	[painting: VII/1]
Wei-t'ang Ch'ien shih tz'u	[painting: VII/2]

Ch'ien-lung emperor (r. 1735–1796)
San-hsi t'ang ching-chien hsi	[painting: I/1]
I tzu-sun	[painting: I/2]
Ch'ien-lung yü-lan chih pao	[painting: II/1]
Shih-ch'ü pao-chi	[painting: II/2]
Yang-hsin tien chien-shang pao	[painting: II/3]
Ch'ien-lung chien-shang	[painting: V/1]

Chia-ch'ing emperor (r. 1796–1821)
Chia-ch'ing yü-lan chih pao	[painting: III/1]

Hsüan-t'ung emperor (r. 1909–1912)
Hsüan-t'ung yü-lan chih pao	[painting: IV/1]

BIBLIOGRAPHY:
Dubosc, *Mostra d'arte* (1954), p. 225, pl. 811.
"Oriental Art Recently Acquired" (1965), p. 76, fig. 7.
Lee, "Literati and Professionals" (1966), pp. 7–8, fig. 2.
———, *Colors* (1974), p. 74, no. 28.

Peking
1523–1527

XVIII. LETTERS HOME FROM PEKING: CALLIGRAPHY

Dated third month–sixth month (1523)
Handscroll, ink on paper, 9¼″ high and 195¼″ long (23.5 x 496.0 cm.)
Signature and seals of the artist
Mr. and Mrs. Wan-go H. C. Weng, New York

Wen Cheng-ming is as concerned and involved in his letter-writing as often as in his painting. In these letters the beginning of his time away from home comes to life. There is no pretense in what he tells his family. The letters speak for themselves. Students of calligraphy will want to examine his free, spontaneous, informal hand and compare it with other examples of calligraphy in this exhibition. Still, letters are written essentially for what they communicate.

ONE:
I left home on the twenty-fourth of the second month, arriving at Lü-ch'eng only by the twenty-seventh. Since Wen P'eng returned home, you probably already know what happened up to the time he left. On that evening (the twenty-seventh), we left Lü-ch'eng and arrived at Tan-yang during the night. We set out early in the morning on the twenty-eighth, later arriving at Chen-chiang, where we boarded the ferry right away, soon arriving at Kua-chou, then bought a boat and moved to the embankment.

Before noon on the twenty-ninth we arrived at Yang chou. Since the watergate was not open, we had to wait until afternoon before continuing. We stayed overnight at the head of the lake. On the thirtieth we took advantage of a following wind to go past Kao-yu and stayed overnight at Chang-chia-kou. During the night, there was a strong wind; our two boats were shaking; I was also worried about thieves; I could not sleep the whole night.

On the first (of the third month), there was a contrary wind; we could not go, so we stayed at Chang-chia-kou the whole day. The wind was gone by evening, so we moved for the night to Ho-k'ou. On the morning of the second, we passed by Chieh-shou-i. Taking advantage of a favorable wind, we crossed Pao-ying Lake and arrived at Pao-ying hsien that night. There I met Chu Kung-chih and learned that Ku Hua-yü had arrived at Pao-ying on the nineteenth and had waited for me until the twenty-fifth. Then he took a boat to Huai-an where he waited another three days. He did not get my letter, so on the twenty-eighth went on the long section of the journey by himself. He left a letter for Chu explaining why he could not wait any longer and also asked Chu Sheng-chih's brothers to hire a boat (for me). That evening (the second) I went to Chu Sheng-chih's home. His father, the district magistrate, insisted that I stay at their place. But I did not and returned to spend the night on the boat. It started raining that night, and on the third it was raining much harder. Also there was a contrary wind, and so I was asked to stay another day by the Chus. On the fourth, Chu Kung-chih and his nephew prepared a boat and accompanied us to Huai-an and asked his friend Ma(?) to hire a boat (for us). On the fifth it was arranged

and that evening we moved into a large boat. It was more spacious than the one on which we had come. We are free to sit down and stand up. Tomorrow we will start on the long part of our journey. From Suchou to here, we have already traveled eight hundred *li*. We still have twenty-eight hundred *li* to go. It is difficult to estimate the number of traveling days. I do not know when we will arrive.

Although travel is hard, I fortunately am in good health and the food is fine. Also I have Chiu-k'uei (Ts'ai Yü) to keep me company. I don't think there should be any problems on the journey ahead. You can take care of affairs at home very well, so I do not have to worry. But you must save your energy, and not work too hard, please! please! Above all take care of your health. Since setting out I find I am able to adjust to changing conditions. Don't worry about me. Wen Wang (a servant) is leaving for home, so I simply write this to let you know. Take care of all the many things at home. No need for me to mention them. The third month, fifth day, Cheng-ming, writing on the boat while staying in Huai-an. For the third *hsiao-chieh* (Wen's wife)[1] to read.

TWO:
On the sixth, I sent Wen Wang back home with a letter; by now you must have a rather good idea of how the trip has gone.

We left Huai-an on the seventh and stayed overnight at Ch'ing-ho (Ch'ing-chiang) hsien. On the eighth we took advantage of a favorable wind to cross the Huai River. But in the afternoon, the wind was against us, so we only got to T'ao-yüan. On the ninth, after traveling thirty *li* against a contrary wind, suddenly the wind changed, so we arrived at Su-ch'ien without stopping. On the tenth we passed P'i-chou without stopping and arrived that night at Hsin-an. We traveled in all 180 *li* that day. On the eleventh, we arrived at Lü-liang and soon crossed the Hung. In the morning of the twelfth we arrived at Hsü-chou. Li *chu-shih,* who was in charge of the Hung (canal), came to see us. He sent men to open the Hung. Since leaving Huai-an on the seventh, up to now, we have traveled a total of six days covering 560 *li*. Fortunately, everything has gone smoothly. I am in good health. All the servants are also fine. Since a fellow villager of Chiu-k'uei (Ts'ai Yü) is leaving for home, I am sending this letter to you by him.

Take special care of everything at home. Especially look out for your mother. Finish the things I instructed you to do. Do not put them off. The twelfth day of the third month, Cheng-ming. Personal letter to P'eng and Chia. After reading, give this to your mother to read.

THREE:
When we arrived at Hsü-chou on the twelfth of this month we met a relative of Chiu-k'uei (Ts'ai Yü) on his way home, so I asked him to bring a letter. It was enclosed in Chiu-k'uei's letter home. I wonder if it has arrived. If not, send Ming-yü to ask for it. From this you will have learned what has happened up to now.

On the thirteenth, because it was the Ch'ing-ming festival, the boatmen would not travel. Early on the fourteenth, we left Hsü-chou, traveling all night 110 *li*, and arrived at Hsin-hsing-cha. On the fifteenth, we covered sixty *li*, arriving at P'ei-hsien. On the sixteenth, we sailed 120 *li* to Nan-yang-cha. We happened to meet boats loaded with pigment from Nanking. Since the

XVIII, one

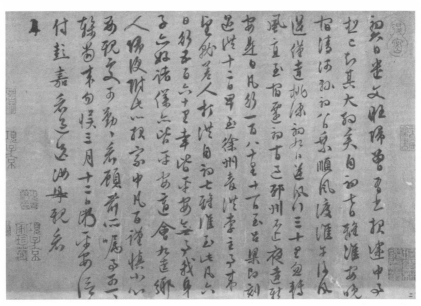

XVIII, two

XVIII, three

eunuch (in charge) refused to open the watergate, we sat for two days. On the eighteenth we left Nan-yang, rode only a few tens of *li*, and got to Lu-ch'iao. Then we were stopped by him again; we had no choice but to send a boatman to the control station at Wan-ning to tell P'iao(?) *chu-shih*. Since Governor Yang of Yü-yao saw my name, he especially sent a courier to come and meet me and show us a detour. Unfortunately, the water was clogged with many boats. From the nineteenth to the twentieth we only went through three watergates covering twenty *li*, reaching Hsin-cha and stopping. On the twenty-first we arrived at Shih-fo-cha. On the twenty-second, we arrived at Chao-ts'un, by evening reaching Wan-ning.

From Nan-yang to here, in six days, we traveled only a little over seventy *li*. On the twenty-fourth we arrived at Liu-ch'eng. Today while still waiting for the opening of the watergate, I happened to meet Fang Ssu-tao, who was promoted to Intendant of Hunan and Kuangtung provinces, on his way back (south). So I asked him about our route ahead. He told me that it was very difficult, that we would have to spend at least half a month to get to Lin-ch'ing. Along the route there has been a severe drought. It is dreadful . . . What can we do! What can we do!

While Mr. Fang was waiting with his horse, I quickly wrote this letter. Take good care of everything at home. You both must study hard and strive to improve. If there is nothing important, do not go out. Remember this! Remember! Take special care of your mother. The new bride[2] should help with the house. Your mother is already[3] getting old and has been sick; you must pick up some of her work. Although there are less than ten *li* from-here to Nan-wang, with the water drying up and being unable to fly there—what can we do! What can we do! The third month, twenty-fifth day, at Liu-lin-cha. Personal letter, Cheng-ming. For P'eng and Chia to read and then tell their mother.

FOUR:

On the twenty-fifth of the third month while at Nan-wang-cha, I met Fang Ssu-tao *ch'ien-shu* (intendant) and asked him to bring a letter to you. I am not sure when it will arrive.

I left Nan-wang on the twenty-eighth. Unexpectedly I met Ch'ai Te-mei *kuang-lu* (imperial entertainer) and Li *chin-shih* of Sung-chiang. Also I met Cha *shu-fu* of Hai-ning and Wang *lang-chung* (bureau director) of Ning-po. Traveling together, they helped us and for several days the boats did not encounter any great delays. On the third day of the fourth month, we went through Tung-ch'ang. On the fourth day at Wei-chia-wan we unexpectedly met Wang Lü-yüeh (Wang Shou). The boats were moving so fast I did not get to send a letter through him. But I asked him to bring the message that we were all right. I wonder when he will arrive (in Suchou).

On the fifth day, we reached Lin-ch'ing; since the boatmen were paying money to get bricks we were delayed for two days. On the eighth, we got to Wu-ch'eng. There was a headwind and rain, so we stopped for one day. On the tenth we arrived at Cheng-chia-k'ou; on the eleventh we passed Te-chou. On the fourteenth we passed Liu-ho-i (Hopei province). On the boat, because of wind-chill, I was a bit sick, but I soon recovered. On the fifteenth, we arrived at Ho-hsi-wu. Ts'ai Chiu-

k'uei (Ts'ai Yü) left us to travel by carriage. I stayed with the boat. On the seventeenth we arrived at the harbor (Chang-chia-wan). Since there was no carriage available, I could not get to the capital until the nineteenth.

I am temporarily staying at Wang Sheng-wu's home. The Board has not yet started the examination. On the twentieth I went to present my papers. On the twenty-fourth I received my examination forms, and the examination date is set for the beginning of the intercalary fourth month.

I plan to leave after taking the examination and receiving the certificate; however, the authorities seem to want me to stay. But if I receive the certificate and do not beg the favor of an official rank, there is no reason to stay. So I will wait to attend the imperial court and see what the situation is; then I will make a decision.

Since I am staying at Sheng-wu's home, I cannot have my own kitchen. I feel badly about bothering him. Anyway, I shall wait until after the examination and then if I do not go home I will have to find another place to live. While I am here, to avoid trouble, I do not want to pay visits to the authorities. However, Chien-su visited me twice, so I cannot help but pay one return visit. Pai-yen sent an invitation to dinner, and to avoid trouble I asked Chien-su to decline for me.

There are so many social affairs going on here that I cannot cope with them. Fortunately I am in good health. Take special care of everything at home. You should study diligently and try to improve. If there is nothing special, do not go out. Take care of your mother. Since I am far away, I can't take care of things. You and others can take over more responsibility. Wen T'ai[3] should study diligently. I do not have time to write to second uncle, third uncle and elder brother; please send my regards to them. I will write to them when I have time. The twenty-fifth of the fourth month, a personal letter written under the lamp. Cheng-ming to P'eng and Chia.

FIVE:

This month on the twenty-fourth, Hsi *liang-chang* of K'un-shan returned and I asked him to bring a letter. I do not know when it will arrive.

I entered the capital on the nineteenth, and went to Wang Sheng-wu's home. It is peaceful and convenient, but I cannot have my own kitchen. Also there is a great deal of coming and going of guests. If I do not leave after the examination, I must move. Sheng-wu expects to receive a commission from Prince Feng(?) and he wants to return home this fall.

High ranking officials of the various Boards, the Censorate, and the Grand Court of Revision (Supreme Court), forgetting their important positions, came to pay formal calls and asked my opinions—the honorable Ch'iao, Ho, and Chin, three of them who don't usually visit people. Indeed, who am I to receive such honor. Such embarrassment! Such embarrassment! The President of the Board of Punishments recommended me generously. But I am afraid that my destiny is thin; my knowledge, shallow; and my conduct, unpolished. I don't deserve this.

Next month, after the final court examination, if I receive the certificate there is no reason for me to stay. I do not know how they will treat me. Since I was (only) recommended by the provincial governor, I want to avoid trouble and suspicion (of excessive politicking), so I don't dare pay return visits. Because of this, one of

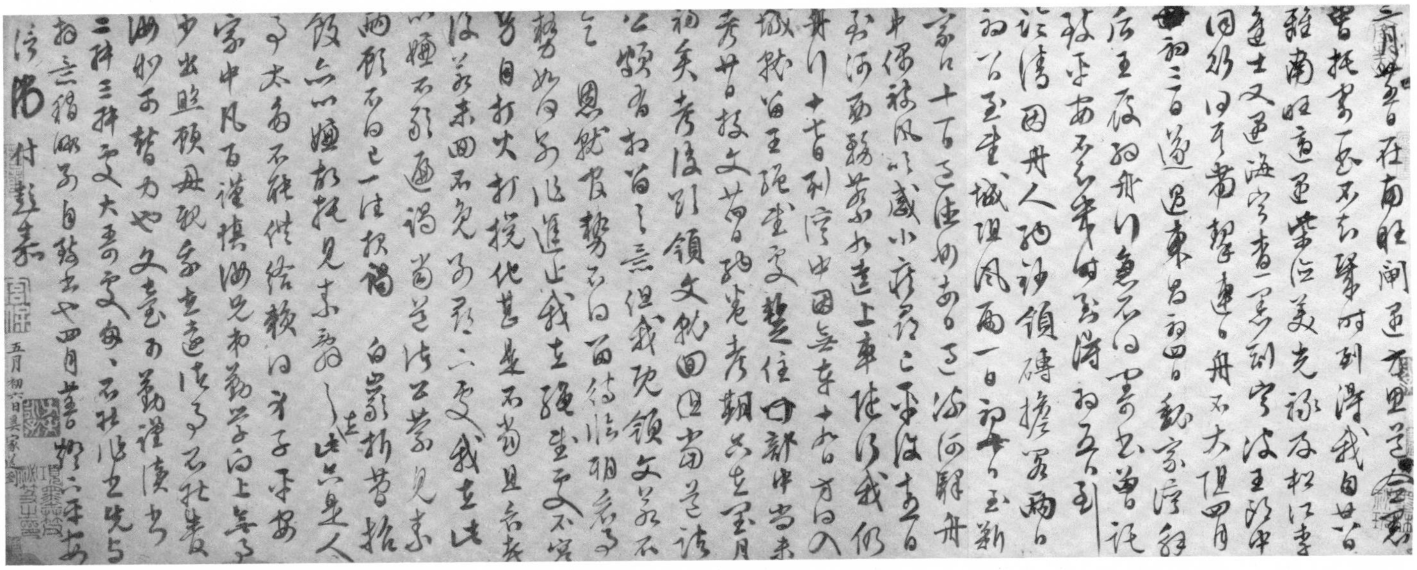

XVIII, four

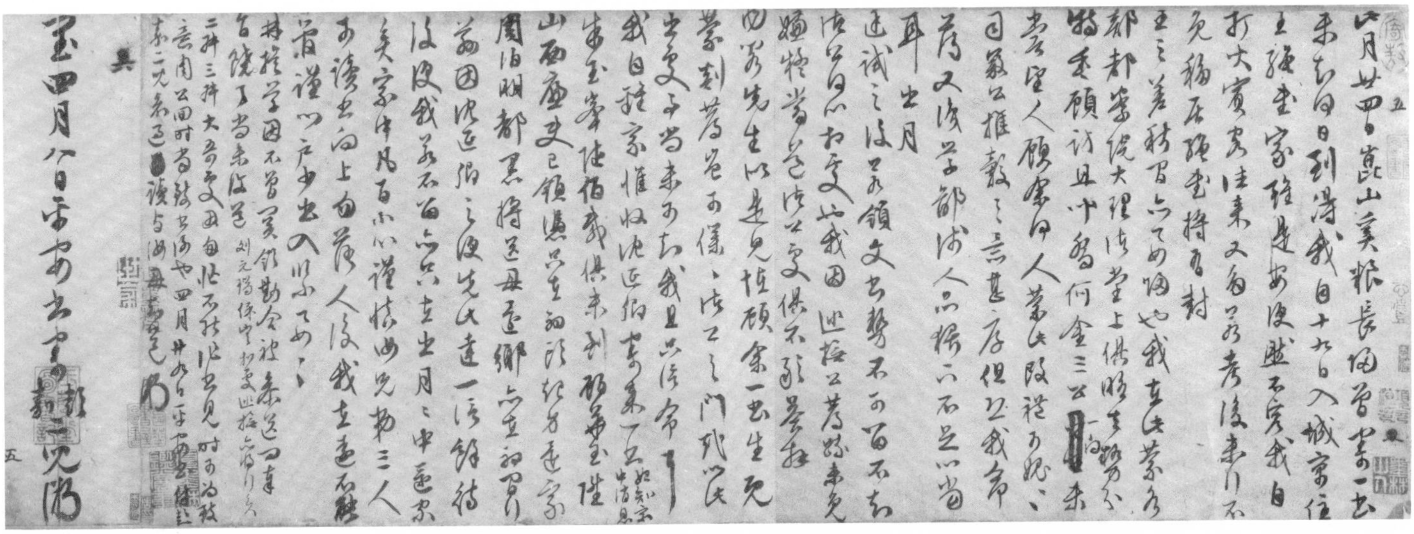

XVIII, five

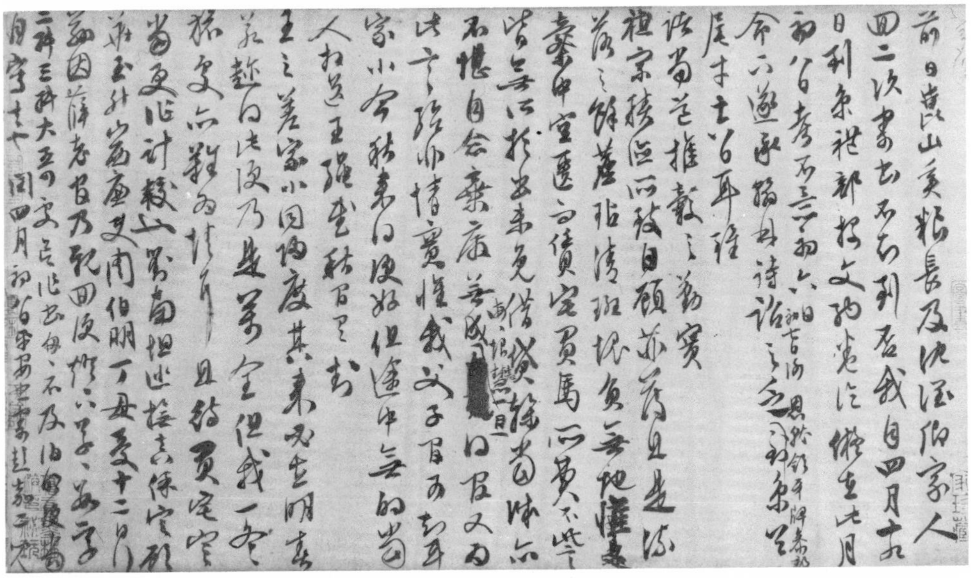

XVIII, six

the members of the Grand Secretariat was offended. But I am just a student who has been recommended, how could I be busy at the doors of such authorities! Because of this I don't know what will happen; I can only follow my destiny.

Since leaving home, I have received only the one letter brought by Shen Yen-ch'ing—and so had my first news from home. Chu Yü-feng coming with Po-tsai has not arrived yet. Ku Hua-yü has been promoted to be *lien-shih* of Shansi. He already has received his certificate and will leave for home at the beginning of next month. Chou Po-ming *tu-shu* is going to take his mother home, also at the beginning of next month. Before they leave, since Shen Yen-ch'ing is going I will ask him to bring this letter; more news will be sent later.

If I am not going to stay, I will be returning the middle of next month. Take special care of everything at home. You three should study hard and improve. Do not fall behind others. Since I am far away I cannot help; take care not to go out too often. It's important! very important! Since Lin *t'i-hsüeh* (literary chancellor) never obtained the *kuan-ling* tally, he has been impeached and sent home but was pardoned by Imperial decree. Liu Yüan-jui, *hsün-fu* (governor) of the Pao-ting pacified district, is going.

Since I am so rushed, I cannot write to second uncle, third uncle and the elder brother. Please give them my regards whenever you see them. When Mr. Chou leaves for home, I will write to thank them. The twenty-ninth of the fourth month, personal letter to two sons P'eng and Chia. After reading, read it to your mother so that she will know.

SIX:

Not long ago Hsi *liang-chang* of K'un-shan and a relative of Shen Jun-ch'ing left for home; I sent letters twice. I wonder if they have arrived.

When on the nineteenth of the fourth month I arrived at the capital, I went to the Board of Rites to present and submit my papers and receive examination forms. I was to take the examination on the eighth. Unexpectedly, Imperial notification arrived on the sixth, telling of my appointment to fill a vacancy as an Attendant of the Han-lin Academy. On the seventh I presented my thanks. Now I am waiting to receive my credentials ("ivory tablet") from the proper ministry. From beginning to end it has been only sixteen days since I reached the capital.

Although important authorities enthusiastically recommend me, actually it is all due to the merit our ancestors have accumulated. Looking at myself I see what is meagre and thin. Moreover I have been drifting without employment, just soiling the pure ranks. I feel my extreme unworthiness.

Right now, my purse is empty. Renting a house and buying a horse need a great deal of money. I don't have a source of funds, so I must borrow. It is very embarrassing.

I worry that I have not accomplished anything. I am frustrated. Now I have received an official position, but I talk this way! If it weren't the true situation—but it must be only between us: father and sons.

It would be fine if my wife could come up here this fall, but there is no dependable person to escort her on the trip. Wang Sheng-wu will have a commission from Prince Feng(?). His family will return with him. I guess they will be coming here in the spring. If my wife can take advantage of this opportunity, that would be perfect. However, I will have a hard time by myself in the capital this winter. Anyway, I will wait until I have bought a house and then see what the situation is.

Liu Nan-t'an (Liu Lin; see no. XLI) *hsün-fu* is going to Pao-ting, Ku Hua-yü is promoted to *lien-shih* of Shansi, and Chou Po-ming, in mourning for his mother, will be leaving on the twelfth. But now since Hsüeh *lao-kuan's* parents are going home, I have very hastily written a few words under the lamp. I do not have time to write to second uncle, third uncle, and elder brother. Give my regards. I will write them when Po-ming leaves. The eighth of the intercalary fourth month, personal letter to two sons, P'eng and Chia.

SEVEN:

Since leaving home on the twenty-fourth of the second month, I have spent fifty-four days on the trip, arriving at the capital on the twentieth of the fourth month. On the sixth of the intercalary month I was appointed *Han-lin tai-chao*. On the seventh, I went to offer thanks for the favor. I was busy paying visits to the authorities for several days. I am really exhausted—more than I can say.

Since arriving I have been staying at Wang Sheng-wu's house. I feel badly bothering him. Also (my servant) Ti Ch'ien lost one of Wang's horses. And so I have been renting a horse, going and coming. I have no choice. What can I do! On the seventeenth, I bought a horse for twelve ounces of silver. Also I bought a saddle for 2.3 ounces. The money in my purse is just about gone. And now I have to lease a house. The current price of a house is very high. The smallest requires an amount of a hundred ounces. So I must rent and pay a rent of two ounces of silver a month. Since my official position is low, my salary is small; how can I make out?

This fall I want to bring my wife, but I am afraid that there is no one dependable to accompany and take care of her on the way. Although Wang Sheng-wu will return home on an official mission, I am not sure if he will come back next year. That is why I cannot make a decision now. You should, in the meantime, be ready at home in case I have a place and send for her to move up here.

Chiu-k'uei (Ts'ai Yü), fortunately, received a first in the *kung-sheng* examination. It was announced on the thirteenth, saying, "Under the empire *kung-sheng* Ts'ai Yü and the others . . . twelve hundred in all. . . ." It is quite an honor. I am very unhappy here. You brothers should take care of yourselves and the hundreds of things at home. I cannot do anything. Since Chang Ying(?) is going home, I report all this in a hurry. Chiu-k'uei (Ts'ai Yü) is coming home soon. The eighteenth of the intercalary month under the lamp. Personal letter to two sons, P'eng and Chia. After reading it, read it to your mother and let her know.

P.S. Since I left home, I have only received one letter brought by Shen Yen-ch'ing and another by Chu Yü-feng. Jen Chün'ch'iu has not yet arrived; I wonder if you have sent letters and things with him. Hsieh *she-jen* came yesterday, saying that he repeatedly went to the house to see if there were letters and did not get them. I am far away and letters from home are as gold. Why are you so heartless? Things which I have mentioned in the previous letter are not being done. What can I do!

EIGHT:

Recently Chang Ying(?) has gone. I asked him to bring a letter. I wonder if it has arrived.

XVIII, seven

XVIII, eight

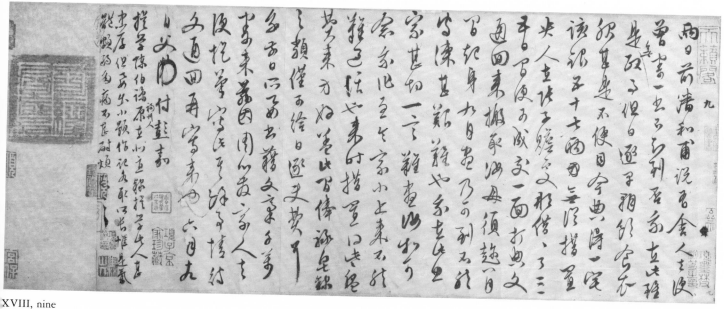

XVIII, nine

On the twenty-second, I moved to the Ch'ing-shou Temple to the extreme north end of the west verandah, where the priest Yüan-chü is staying.

Unfortunately, Ti Ch'ien (the servant) in losing his horse fell and was injured, becoming ill. I told him to stay temporarily at Wang Sheng-wu's to recover. On the twenty-fourth, Wen T'ung also became ill. I have to go to court early each day. Only Yung Fu is here to take care of the horse and do the cooking. Hardships are endless. Life is too much! What can I do about it! Also because I was impolite, the honorable Wen-hsüan is upset.

I begin to feel that this business of being an official is hardly a good thing. There is still no decision on buying a house. I will probably borrow money from Chiu-k'uei (Ts'ai Yü). I am not sure about this.

Recently Mr. Chien-su, since matters in the Board were in opposition to the eunuchs, received an Imperial decree calling him to account. He is all the more eager to return home.

Conditions in the capital are not what they were. My official position is low; my salary is small. I cannot support myself. I am afraid I cannot stay very long.

For two days now I have wanted to write to second uncle, third uncle and elder brother. However, I am in a bad state of mind—and without a single vacant day writing poems and compositions for social occasions, so I have put off writing the letter. When you see them be sure to tell them how difficult it is and apologize; allow me to write to them later when it is more convenient. Otherwise take special care of the hundreds of things at home. Pay particular attention to your mother. The twenty-fifth, intercalary fourth month, personal letter to the two sons, P'eng and Chia. Cheng-ming.

NINE:

Two days ago, when P'an Ho-fu told me that one of his household was going (south) I sent a letter. I wonder if it has arrived.

Although I do not have much work to do in my office, I have to be in Court early every day. Food and drink and clothing are matters of great inconvenience. I arranged a mortgage on a house today which costs fifty-seven ounces of silver. I do not have the money. So I sent to Chang Tzu-shan to borrow some. It will take three to five days to complete this, largely because of the mortgage. I am sending Wen T'ung home to bring back your mother. She should leave here by the middle of the eighth month in order to arrive here by the end of the ninth month. Otherwise it (the water) will all be frozen, and she will have great difficulty. Here I am very homesick; it is hard to describe how I feel. You can all imagine why I made the decision to ask my wife to come up here; otherwise life is too difficult for me. Before departure, you had better arrange to get some money; since here what I receive in salary is like that of a servant. It is just enough to meet my daily expenses.

The books and manuscripts that I asked for earlier—be absolutely sure to send them. Since a relative of Chou I-fa is going, I have raised the brush to write this. Other matters can wait until I write again for Wen T'ung's return. The nineteenth of the sixth month, your father Cheng-ming to P'eng and Chia.

P.S. Ch'en Po-liang, t'i-hsüeh to Chih-li (Hopei province), is a very solid person, but he makes a lot of small matters. Look for his good points. His health is poor and being often sick, he is not a patient person. You should know this.

NOTES:
1. Before she was married, Wen's wife would have been called this, indicating she was the third daughter in her house. Wen continued to use this term after marriage.
2. This must be Wen P'eng's wife, the daughter of Ch'ien K'ung-chou (no. XIII).
3. Wen's third and youngest son. See *Wen shih tsu-p'u* (1929), pp. 8 and 14.

SIGNATURES OF THE ARTIST:
Cheng-ming [each letter except letters 6 and 7].

SEALS OF THE ARTIST:

Yü-lan t'ang t'u-shu chi	[letter 6, seam: II/1]
Wen Cheng-ming Chung-fu	[letter 8, seam: II/1]

COLOPHONS AND SEALS:
Hsiang Yüan-pien (1525–1590)
seventy-five seals (including half-seals)
Yao Hsi-meng (1579–1636); colophons dated 1636

Yao Hsi-meng yin	[colophon: I/1]
Yao Meng-ch'ang shih	[colophon: I/2]

Wen Chen-meng (1574–1636)

Ch'ang-chih	[colophon: II/1]
Wen Chen-meng yin	[colophon: II/2]
Shih-ching t'ang yin	[letter 1, seam: I/2]
Shih-ching ——— yin	
[mounting before letter 1, seam: I/2]	[initial mounting,
[mounting after letter 9: I/1]	seam: II/1]

Wang Wan (1624–1690); two colophons, dated 1673 and 1690

Wang Wan chih yin	[initial mounting, seam: I/2 (half-seal)]
	[colophon: III/1]
	[colophon: IV/1]
Shan-kuang t'a-ying lou	[initial mounting, seam: I/1 (half-seal)]
	[colophon: III/2]
	[colophon: IV/2]
Tun-weng	
T'iao-hua shu-wu t'u-shu	
[letter 2, seam: I/1]	[letter 7, seam: I/1]
[letter 3, seam: I/1]	[letter 8, seam: I/3, seam: III/2]
[letter 4, seam: I/2]	
[letter 5, seam: I/1]	[letter 9, seam: I/2]
[letter 6, seam: I/3, seam: II/2]	

Yang Pin (seventeenth–eighteenth century); colophon dated 1715

Hsiang-ssu lou	[colophon: V/1]
Yang Pin	[colophon: VI/1]
Ta-p'iao	[colophon: VI/2]
Shan-yin pu-i	[colophon: VI/3]

Ch'iu Yüeh-hsiu (1712–1773); colophon dated 1751

Yüeh	[colophon: VII/1]
Hsiu	[colophon: VII/2]

Hsü Yü-chuan (unidentified); colophon dated 1888
Weng T'ung-ho (1830–1904)

Chün-chai shou-ts'ang	[mounting: I/1]
Yü-shan Weng T'ung-ho yin	[mounting: I/2]

Chou Shu-te (unidentified, probably Ming dynasty)

Chou Shu-te yin	[letter 5, seam: I/3 (half-seal)]
[initial mounting, seam: II/2]	
[letter 2, seam: I/3]	[letter 6, seam: I/3 (two half-seals)]
[letter 3, seam: I/3]	
[letter 4, seam: I/3, I/6 (both half-seals)]	[letter 7, seam: I/3 (half-seal)]
[letter 4, seam: II/2]	

Unidentified

undecipherable (impressed over seal)	[mounting, seam: III/3]
undecipherable (impressed over seal)	[mounting: II/1]

REMARKS: The translation has been something of a collaborative effort in which Ling-yün Shih Liu laid the principal groundwork and Professor Emeritus Li Ch'i helped with many difficult passages, as did Professor Chang Ch'un-shu. There are still some problems, for which Wen himself in the fifth letter has supplied the only answer: ". . . my destiny is thin; my knowledge, shallow. . . ."

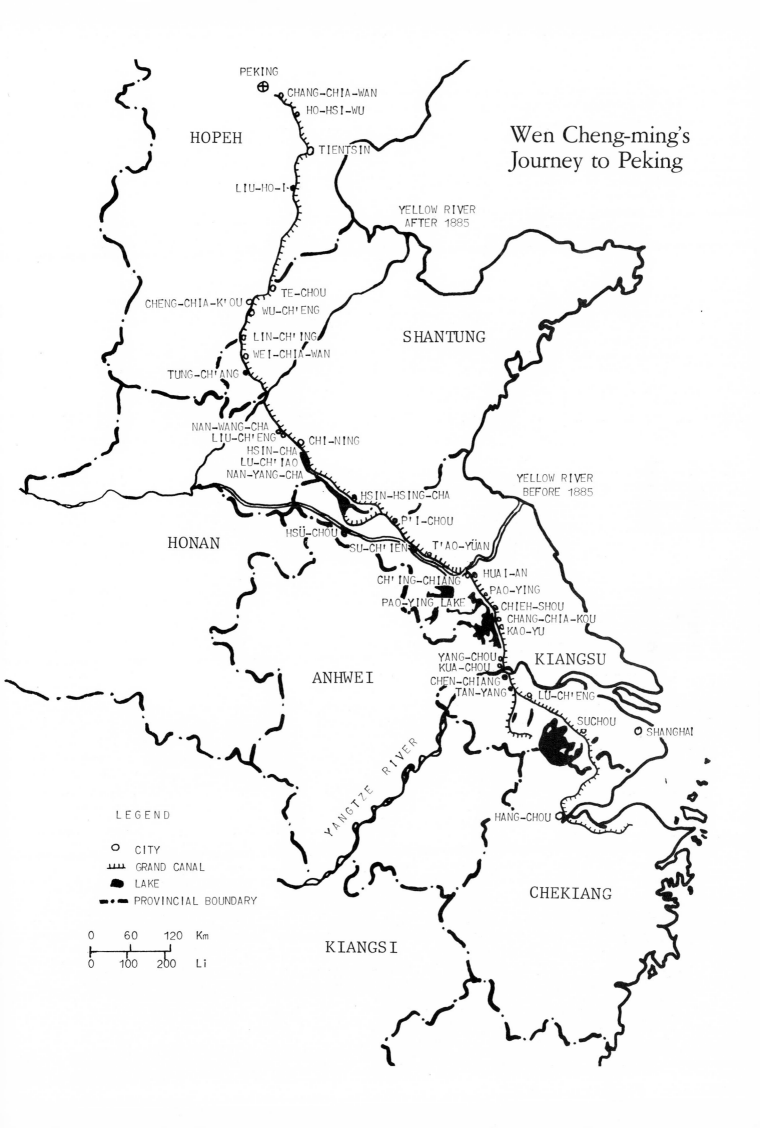

Wen Cheng-ming's
Journey to Peking

PEKING
CHANG-CHIA-WAN
HO-HSI-WU
HOPEH
TIENTSIN
LIU-HO-I
YELLOW RIVER
AFTER 1885
TE-CHOU
CHENG-CHIA-K'OU
WU-CH'ENG
SHANTUNG
LIN-CH'ING
WEI-CHIA-WAN
TUNG-CH'ANG
NAN-WANG-CHA
LIU-CH'ENG
CHI-NING
HSIN-CHA
LU-CH'IAO
NAN-YANG-CHA
YELLOW RIVER
BEFORE 1885
HSIN-HSING-CHA
HONAN
P'I-CHOU
HSÜ-CHOU
SU-CH'IEN
T'AO-YÜAN
CH'ING-CHIANG
HUAI-AN
PAO-YING
PAO-YING LAKE
CHIEH-SHOU
CHANG-CHIA-KOU
KAO-YU
YANG-CHOU
KIANGSU
KUA-CHOU
CHEN-CHIANG
TAN-YANG
LÜ-CH'ENG
ANHWEI
SUCHOU
SHANGHAI
YANGTZE RIVER
HANG-CHOU

LEGEND
○ CITY
⊥⊥⊥ GRAND CANAL
◆ LAKE
‒‥‒ PROVINCIAL BOUNDARY

0   60   120   Km
0   100   200   Li

CHEKIANG

KIANGSI

XIX. WAITING UPON THE EMPEROR'S RETURN FROM THE SOUTHERN SUBURBS: CALLIGRAPHY

SEALS:
Probably Hu Tien (Ch'ing dynasty)
Yen-chen Hu Tien? chia ts'ang t'u chi [calligraphy: II/1]

REMARKS: This poem is recorded in *Wen shih* (1934–1935 ed.), ch. 6/p. 19a and *Fu-t'ien* (1968 ed.), ch. 10/p. 2a (pp. 255-256). Not only the subject matter, but also the position of the poem in *chüan* 10 of *Fu-t'ien* suggests a date early in Wen's stay in Peking.

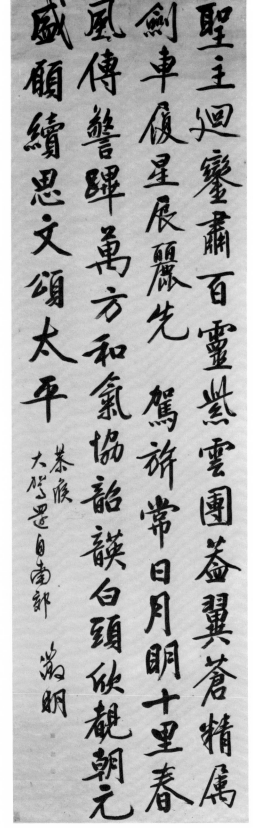

(Kung-hou ta-chia huan tzu nan-chiao)
Running-standard or semi-standard script
No date
Hanging scroll, ink on paper, 136″ high and 39¼″ wide (345.4 x 99.7 cm.)
Signature and seals of the artist
The Metropolitan Museum of Art, New York; Anonymous Gift, in memory of Mrs. Muriel Morris Stokes, 1950

> The bell on the Imperial Lord's returning chariot calms the singing of the lark;
> Purplish clouds, gathering above, shelter the powerful essence.
> Officials' carriages — swords and shoes — surround like brilliant constellations.
> Outriders and imperial banners are the brightness of sun and moon.
> For ten miles the spring wind comes to stir the Emperor;
> Ten thousand places harmonize with peaceful music.
> The white-haired, happily seeing the grand occasion of an Emperor's appearance,
> Promises continued writing in praise of this great peace.

> (tr. Ling-yün Shih Liu)

Such grand and to our ears excessive, awkward formal praise can only be for the majesty of Peking's official life. The National Palace Museum in Taipei, at heart the old Ch'ing imperial collection, has a large hanging calligraphy scroll by Wen of similar dimensions. That too has a seven-character line poem, and it is brushed in a similar style.[1] Place such scrolls as these against Wen's easily brushed letters (no. XVIII) and the public-private conflict—both in conduct and calligraphy form—can only be too apparent. Recall, in contrast to the last line above, Wen's personal confession to his family (no. XVIII, eight):

> I am in a bad state of mind—and without a single vacant day writing poems and compositions for social occasions. . . .

Still, one admires the scale. One understands the majesty of Imperial presence—these strong blocks of formal words fit the public purposes for which they were brushed, the strength of a hand essentially serving Imperial command.

NOTE:
1. *Ku-kung shu-hua lu* (1965), ch. 2/p. 10.

SEALS OF THE ARTIST:
  Wen Cheng-ming yin [calligraphy: I/1]
  Heng-shan [calligraphy: I/2]
  T'ing-yün [calligraphy: I/3]

XIX

XX. GREAT LIQUID LAKE: CALLIGRAPHY

(T'ai-yeh ch'ih)
Running-standard script
No date
Hanging scroll, ink on paper, 135¼" high and 48¼" wide
  (343.5 x 122.5 cm.)
Signature and seals of the artist
Anonymous loan

As with the last, this second large scroll of calligraphy is also part of the Peking environment. Once again its size suggests official purposes. The poem written here is actually the second in a series of ten composed by Wen about the Western Gardens that lay outside the inner city. The lake, whose name was used in earlier important imperial gardens, is seen mysteriously, a focus for the wonder of traditional magic and elaborate allusion:

> The water's expanse, the vast pond merging with heaven;
> Ten *li* of lotus, a smooth embroidered cloud.
> I have heard that Yüeh-fu[1] caused the yellow crane[2] to sing
> And seen that Ch'iu-feng[3] moved a stone whale[4] to swim.
> The curved jade rainbow descends across the blue sky;
> The silver mountains rise from the world through the mist.
> Following those places where the phoenix chariot passed,
> The wild geese wheel round the air, never startled.

(tr. Ling-yün Shih Liu)

Wen often wrote out this and the other nine poems in handscroll form. One such scroll is dated as late as 1555.[5] The poems are also recorded in Wen's collected works. There, in a preface, Wen tells us that the Great Liquid Lake is surrounded by several *li* of forests and pavilions, that a stone bridge runs east and west, and that there are flower islands within it.

The original writing occurred as the result of a trip by Wen to the gardens in the spring of 1525. On that occasion he was with three government friends: Ch'en I (1469–1539), T. Lu-nan, from Nanking, who was himself known as a painter and calligrapher; Ma Ju-chi (1493–1543), T. Chung-fang; and his friend from K'un-shan, Wang T'ung-tsu (1497–1551), T. Sheng-wu, who is importantly mentioned in Wen's letters (no. XVIII) as the friend with whom he first stayed on arriving at the capital. Ch'en I knew the official in charge of the garden and so they were able to visit all the famous spots of this imperially restricted area.

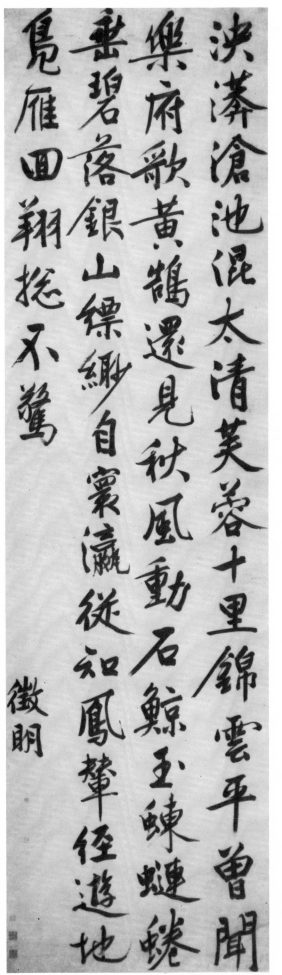

XX

Once again we are impressed by the bold strength of these large blocks of form. The style is substantially, but not exactly, the same as in *The Emperor's Return*. Historically the style of this and the last scroll (see also no. XIII) relates to the great Sung calligrapher Huang T'ing-chien. In following the manner Wen is continuing the interests of his master Shen Chou, who was famous for his writing in such a style, often said to be characterized by the diagonal "oar stroke" (first line: second, third, sixth, eighth, and ninth characters). Tseng Yu-ho, in publishing the scroll, has indicated as well that the kind of elaborate poetry written here is related to the Hsi-k'un school of poets. It is a school of which Huang T'ing-chien was an active member.

NOTES:
1. *Yüeh-fu,* songs collected by the music office *(yüeh-fu)* during the Han dynasty (206 B.C.–220 A.D.).
2. Yellow crane, a huge bird ridden by immortals.
3. Ch'iu-feng, a music tune from the Wu dynasty (222 A.D.–277 A.D.).
4. A carved stone whale thirty feet long, in K'un-ming, Yunnan province.
5. *The Grand Tradition* (1975), no. 10. The scroll is owned by Mr. and Mrs. Wai-kam Ho in Cleveland.

SEALS OF THE ARTIST:
Wen Cheng-ming yin	[calligraphy: II/1]
Heng-shan	[calligraphy: II/2]

SEALS:
Lü Ch'ien (1643 *chin-shih),* painter, calligrapher
Lü K'ung-chao	[calligraphy: III/3]

Kao Weng-ying (seventeenth century), calligrapher
Kao Weng-ying yin	[calligraphy: III/2]

Unidentified
Ssu-hsüeh chai	[calligraphy: I/1]
Nan-t'ung Wu shih shou-ts'ang	
shu-hua yin	[calligraphy: III/1]

REMARKS: This poem is recorded in *Wen shih* (1934–1935 ed.), ch. 6/p. 23b and *Fu-t'ien* (1968 ed.), ch. 10/pp. 5b-6a (pp. 262–263). In the latter book it is listed as the second poem of the ten verses of the Western Gardens *(Hsi-yüan)*, which are dated to the spring of 1525.

BIBLIOGRAPHY:
Ecke, *Chinese Calligraphy* (1971), no. 49.

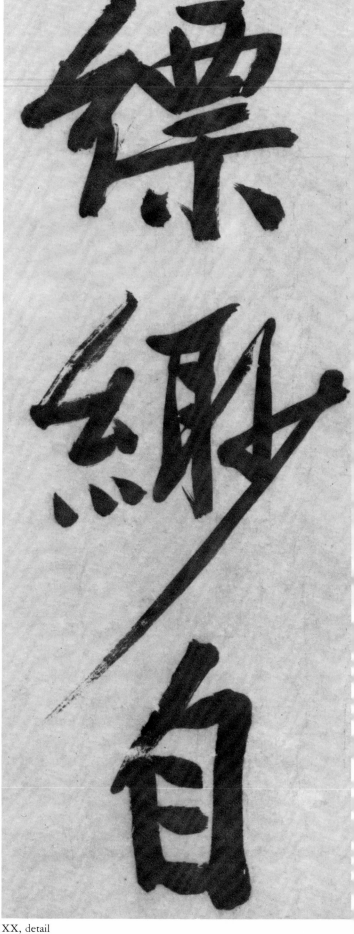

XX, detail

XXI. PLAYING THE CH'IN IN THE SHADE OF PINES

(Sung-yin lung-ch'in)
No date
Hanging scroll, ink on paper, 138″ high and 40¾″ wide (351.0 x 103.5 cm.)
Inscription, signature, and seals of the artist
Anonymous loan

This towering landscape in size alone belongs with the giants of calligraphy we have just examined. Generally speaking, Wen was not at home in such a large scale, but on occasion he turned to it. For example, although the proportions are different, he painted on a rather large format as early as 1519 a hanging scroll, *Scholar's Leisure at Valley's End,* now in Taipei.[1]

Such commissions must be thought of in terms of necessity—a request by some important person that must be met. They are historically significant in relaying to us the great scale of palaces and villas that they must have been designed to embellish. They are inevitably symbols of the grandeur of Ming China. They are portable wall-paintings.

Everything we know about Wen indicates discomfort with ostentatious display. He is at his best in a more intimate world, both as a person and an artist. As we know from his letters (no. XVIII), he found out all too soon—a matter of days—how poorly suited he was to the demands and pretensions of an official world.

Playing the Ch'in in the Shade of Pines is a strong painting. But it is the strength of outward show. Its very boldness destroys the sense of intimacy—either as a personal "awkward" scholar-painter or a more conscious craftsman—that lay at the core of Wen's greatest art.

One can understand this difference by comparing the scroll to the refined, imaginative *Cascading Falls in the Pine Ravine,* 1527–1531 (fig. 10). It is the difference between careful, painstaking creation involving experience with a close friend, Wang Ch'ung, over a period of years, and the swift, bold brushing of the same basic idea on a very impersonal level. The composition is extremely close—introductory forms (a slant of land, plateau, stream and rock) leading to a grove of pines (eight in one, nine in the other), the white path of falling water just above them, and the leaning mountain peaks reaching close to the top of the scroll. It is the peculiar hunch-backed mountain form, leaning to the left as it towers upward, that is a special mark of both paintings. In the mountains both paintings are interested in restless, turning shapes. Both support the larger masses of mountain with round bouldery-shapes—so-called "alum-head" rocks. As Benjamin March describes them: "The effect

is of numerous round white heads, suggesting eroded or exfoliated granite much rounded at the joints."[2]

Such motifs immediately bring us into the range of the tenth-century paragons, Tung Yüan and Chü-jan. And any detailed section of the rocks shows us how he has exploited this manner, with its many parallel texture-strokes, for strong expressive purposes. That such bold treatment of ink on paper may be part of his interpretation of the tenth-century masters at about this time finds support in a somewhat curious "experiment" of 1536, *Quiet Fishing by Trees and Stream,* where he states he is imitating a specific Tung Yüan painting. The scroll is in Taipei.[3] How far he was at this time from a truly inventive and mature realization of this manner can be shown when we contrast *Playing the Ch'in* to an exact, stable landscape painted in 1555 after "Tung-Chü," recently exhibited in a Hongkong exhibition.[4]

Historically, the strongest case can be made for the execution of this undated scroll somewhere in the late twenties or early thirties. Its closeness in design to *Cascading Falls* (fig. 10), which was painted over a period of years—1527 to 1531—seems generally to anchor the time. The feeling for surface and restless design is a quality that particularly marks Wen's art during the 1530s. He was, of course, in the twenties closest to important officials. The demands for this kind of commission would have been the greatest during and shortly after his stay at the capital. The purposes of the painting fit closely the huge hanging scrolls of calligraphy (nos. XIX, XX) whose subjects can only relate to Peking.

Paradoxically, playing the great scholarly instrument, the *ch'in,* refers to withdrawal, to the privacy of nature and to those special remote notes of tree and stream through which nature reveals her uniquely enduring harmonies. If here the tune is a little over-strident for either nature or this subtle instrument, that is the price for public display of a private world.

NOTES:
1. *Ku-kung shu-hua lu* (1965), ch. 5/p. 380.
2. March, *Some Technical Terms* (1935), p. 35, no. 221.
3. *Ku-kung shu-hua lu* (1965), ch. 5/p. 385.
4. *Exhibition of Paintings of the Ming and Ch'ing Periods* (1970), no. 9.

INSCRIPTION BY THE ARTIST:
The pine shadows' swaying green covers the level bank;
I sit and play my lute to quiet the clamor of the world.
Most at song's end, the world is still
Clear of evening clouds, the green mountain stands tall.

Cheng-ming
(based on tr. Elizabeth Bennett)

SEALS OF THE ARTIST:
Wen Cheng-ming yin   [painting: II/1]
Heng-shan   [painting: II/2]

10. Wen Cheng-ming, *Cascading Falls in the Pine Ravine,* 1527–1531. National Palace Museum, Taipei

XXI, detail

Return to Art
1528–1539

XXII. TEN POEMS BY FRIENDS AND FAMILY OF WEN CHENG-MING

No date
Folding fan, ink on gold paper, 5½" high and 20²³/₃₂" wide
  (14.0 x 52.6 cm.)
Signatures and seals of the artists
Mr. and Mrs. Richard Edwards, Ann Arbor, Michigan

When Wen returned from Peking in the spring of 1527, that unhappy experience was behind him. Ambition for official success had been blunted. For him it was an impossible course. He wrapped himself in the mantle of the scholar-artist and never relinquished it. He was on the edge of his sixtieth birthday, which was in 1529. This is always a landmark in Chinese life. When one moves into the next year, the same cyclical characters that mark the date of one's birth return in the sixty-year rhythm of the Chinese calendar. For Wen, these were *keng-yin* (1470 and 1530), and it must have been near this time that he adopted them on a seal: *Wei keng-yin wu i chiang* 'on *keng-yin* I passed from the womb' (the seal placed on no. IX). The seal legend is a direct quotation from the *Li Sao* ("On Encountering Sorrow") by Ch'ü Yüan, the nobleman poet of the kingdom of Ch'u from the late fourth and early third century B.C.

This great classic poem, part of the anthology *Ch'u-tz'u (Songs of Ch'u)*, came from a region of China to which Wen traced special importance. His ancestors had moved to Heng-shan, the present Heng-yang, in the early years of the Sung dynasty. North of Heng-yang, in the valley of the same Hsiang River, is Ch'ang-sha, center of the Ch'u state. Wen had adopted Heng-shan as one of his names *(hao)*. That a scholar steeped in tradition should call attention to having been born at the same "time" as the region's greatest poet can hardly be incidental. One cannot escape the thought that there are also other parallels:

Ch'ü Yüan was a man of undeviating righteousness who devoted all his loyalty and all his knowledge to the service of his prince; yet he was traduced by false witness. Well might he be called "afflicted." He was faithful, yet he was disbelieved; loyal, and yet calumniated. Is it any wonder that he should have felt wronged? It was the sense of wrong that inspired Ch'ü Yüan's composition of the *Li Sao*.[1]

If the authenticity of the scroll is to be believed, the earliest extant use of the *Li Sao* seal appears to be on a brief sketch of 1526 described by Wen himself as a "small poem and an awkward painting." *Brewing Tea Under Stately Trees* (fig 11).[2]

It is a seal, then, that we can relate not only to his approaching the sixty-first year but also to his own "sorrows" about politics. Ch'ü Yüan ". . . withdrew from the muck and mire. He sloughed off the impurities of life to soar away out of reach of the dust and turmoil."[3] Unlike the great Ch'u poet, however, Wen Cheng-ming did not throw himself into the Yangtze River "clasping a stone to his bosom." Rather he used his retirement to embrace the sympathetic cultural environment of Suchou. He had come home and in the more temperate south was secure among family and friends.

Wen Cheng-ming lived in his father's house, which was northwest of Te-ch'ing ch'iao. Within it was the T'ing-yün kuan, a name which so often occurs on Wen's inscriptions and seals. It was in three parts with a large *t'ung* tree (pawlonia) in front as well as a hill, Pi-shan (apparently in shape or plan like the ancient circular disc, *pi*). Behind were over a hundred stalks of bamboo. To the east of T'ing-yün kuan was another retreat, Wu-yen shih, which was itself made up of other pavilions: the Yü-lan t'ang (magnolia hall), the Yü-ch'ing shan-fang (jade-chime mountain house) and the Ko-ssu lou. It is clear that Wen lived in the pavilion-garden environment he so often painted.

In Suchou he had already enjoyed this kind of milieu, but now his position must have changed. His close artistic associates were often younger than he. He was the master.[4]

One of the most interesting indications of his association with like-minded friends at this time can be seen in his connection with the Yüan family. Chiang Chao-shen has written about this in exploring various scrolls involving the lute master Yang Chi-ching (d. 1530). Yang had been one of a close group of friends associated with the Wen-te Studio, which took its name from a nearby bridge in Suchou and was connected with the Yüan family. There were six brothers and cousins: Kun, Ch'iu, Piao, Chiung, Pao, and Chih. We have already met Yüan Chih since his colophon followed the landscape of 1502 (no. IX). The "studio friends" included Wen Cheng-ming.[5] Although Wen's own calligraphy is not included, this calligraphy fan has three members of the Yüan family: Yüan Chiung, Yüan Kun and Yüan Ch'iu. These and other writers show it to be a kind of symbol of the closeness of Wen's friends and family. Despite its small format, poems—many in the tight, crisp calligraphy of standard script; most in the same rhyme scheme—have been written by the ten scholars listed below. The first, at the right, is by P'eng Nien and indicates the collective theme:

A thousand peaks and the colors of trees
  hold the clouds' damp;
A hundred paths with the sounds of springs
  carry the rain's flight.

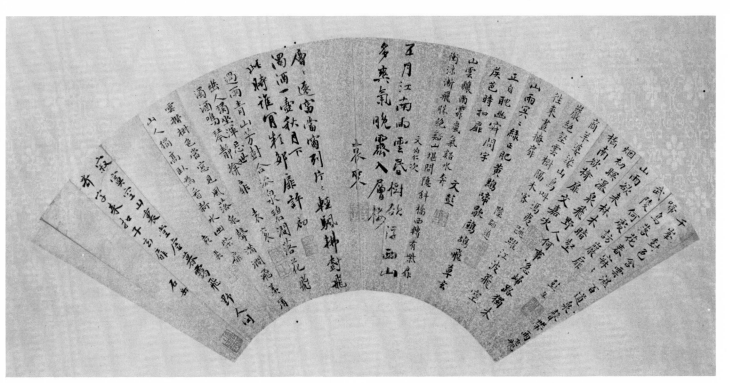

XXII

Birds' songs, falling petals,
    spring's quiet reaches—
Where then at Wu-ling is found
    the cliff's door?[6]

The poems are centered on an idea—the cascading of spring freshets in the shape of high mountain waterfalls—that on more than one occasion was used as a painting theme by Wen and his followers. Indeed, the claim has been made that, drawn from the poetry of the T'ang dynasty, it was invented as a painting theme by Wen. Thus it is found painted on an unpublished fan of 1536, now in the Palace Museum in Taipei, recalling the lines of Wang Wei:

A night of rain in the mountains
And the tips of the branches become hundreds of waterfalls.

Tu Fu also had written:

The distant blue water pours down from a thousand crevices,
The twin peaks of Jade Mountain, lofty and cold.

Wen had, by 1531, also incorporated the idea into the upper section of *Cascading Falls in the Pine Ravine* (fig. 10). Much later, in 1576, Wen's son Wen Chia was to exactly illustrate it.[7] But Wen Cheng-ming may well have been the originator, at least in the high mountains. Late in his life, Shen Chou had created a low-level version in a river-grotto.[8]

NOTES:
1. Ssü-ma Ch'ien's biography as translated by Hawkes, *Ch'u Tz'u* (1962), p. 12.
2. *Ku-kung shu-hua lu* (1965), ch. 8/p. 80.
3. Hawkes, *Ch'u Tz'u* (1962), p. 12 (again Ssü-ma Ch'ien's account).
4. For Wen's house see *Wen shih tsu-p'u* (1929), p. 25. When

Wen is sixty-one *sui*, his friends and artist contemporaries all seem to be of another generation. Running down the list: Ch'iu Ying, thirty-seven; Wang Ch'ung, thirty-seven; Lu Chih, thirty-five; Wang Ku-hsiang, thirty; Ch'ien Ku, twenty-three; Chou T'ien-ch'iu, seventeen; Lu Shih-tao, fourteen. They are his sons' generation or younger. Sons Wen P'eng, thirty-four, and Wen Chia, thirty; nephew Wen Po-jen, twenty-nine. Hsieh Shih-ch'en, forty-four, and Ch'en Shun, forty-nine, come only a little closer to Wen's age. See Chiang, "Life" (1971–1972), pp. 51–53.
5. Chiang, "Yang Chi-ching" (1973), p. 11.
6. The last line refers to the fisherman from Wu-ling who in the well-known *Peach Blossom Spring* found an opening in the mountains that led to an ideal land (see no XXXVIII).
7. An album leaf in the Palace Museum, Taipei. Reproduced in Cahill, *Chinese Painting* (1960), p. 135. Information about the fan comes from Chiang Chao-shen's recent exhibition of Wu School painting at the National Palace Museum, Taipei.
8. *Liao-ning* (1962), II, pl. 23.

THE ARTISTS AND THEIR SEALS:
P'eng Nien (1505–1566)
    P'eng K'ung-chia yin   [calligraphy: I/1]
Wen Chia (1501–1583), second son of Wen Cheng-ming
    Wen Chia Hsiu-ch'eng   [calligraphy: II/1]
Lu Shih-tao (1517–after 1570), calligrapher and painter
    Lu Shih-tao   [calligraphy: III/1]
    Tzu-ch'uan fu   [calligraphy: III/2]
Wen P'eng (1498–1573), first son of Wen Cheng-ming
    Wen Shou-ch'eng shih   [calligraphy: IV/1]
Wen Po-jen (1502–1575), nephew of Wen Cheng-ming
    No seal
Yüan Chiung (sixteenth century)
    Yüan Shang-chih shih   [calligraphy: V/1]
Hsü Ch'u (sixteenth century), seal carver and calligrapher
    Yüan-fu   [calligraphy: VI/1]
Yüan Kun (1538 *chin-shih*)
    Pu-chih   [calligraphy: VII/1]
Yüan Ch'iu (sixteenth century)
    Shao-chih   [calligraphy: VIII/1]
Shih Yüeh (sixteenth century)
    Min-wang fu   [calligraphy: IX/1]

OTHER SEALS:
Wu Chün-ch'ing (T. Ch'ang-shih, 1844-1927), painter, calligrapher
    Ts'ang-shih tao-jen chen-pi   [calligraphy: X/1]

BIBLIOGRAPHY:
The Grand Tradition (1975), no. 11.

XXIII. TASTING TEA IN THE PURE SHADE

(Ch'ing-yin shih-ming t'u)
Dated 1528, third month, sixteenth day
Folding fan, ink on gold paper, 6⅞" high and 19" wide (17.3 x 48.2 cm.)
Inscription and seal of the artist
Vannotti Collection, Muzzano, Switzerland

The importance of being with friends is to enjoy their company. There is also, inevitably, parting. This fact was built into China's social patterns, for members of the scholar class were called to serve the state in seemingly endless official posts, and often then had to leave for distant parts of a vast country. And we must remember that for modern mechanized sensibilities these distances are inevitably increased, for they were traversed floating on rivers or lakes, and overland by foot or, as summed up in Shen Chou's poem (no. II E), ". . . having left his carriage wheel for a horse's hoof." What a journey meant has been clearly recorded in Wen Cheng-ming's letters (no. XVIII). He traveled 3,600 li to reach Peking. Across distance, there was, however, memory—and art which with a poem or a painting could seal that memory. This in Wen's Suchou was what gave importance to the painting of the scholarly meeting. It held the essence of the good life. Such truth must endure.

In painting it Wen often does so with great simplicity. This is because, while one is describing a fact, a momentary experience, one is also presenting an idea. Lofty minds are uncluttered. Here is no place for the confusion of dust-filled detail. Further, dealing only with basic forms, the artist drives right to the heart of things. He presents precisely what can endure. Thus, closely allied to the theme is the stylistic notion of archaism. The art of the distant past is by definition something which has not changed. It will inevitably say the right things about this theme. To revive an ancient style is the surest way of joining a moment of time to what in Chinese culture had, in standing the test of time, become timeless.

The idea of the scholar, the famous man, seated by a single tree was a well-established device, certainly by the fifth century. A little later, T'ang artists presented their figures in isolation except for the inclusion of a rock or a tree which stood for a garden and as a garden suggested the wider reaches of nature.

The organization of this fan, Tasting Tea in the Pure Shade, must be thought of against such a background. Trees have grown to a small grove, but they are carefully selected and placed: a pine tree, four deciduous trees, a cypress. Rocks are likewise exactly defined, associated with each tree or tree-grouping and with the flat rock a convenient plateau for the seating of scholars. Land itself is only symbolically rendered as dotted horizontal lines that extend like brief fixed shadows from the resting place of each rock or tree.

The arrangement of these objects creates a distinct sense of space. Forms are clearly behind other forms. Tea-brewing is half hidden. Before we meet the scholars we have the central grouping of three trees and rocks. As we have pointed out in connection with Shen Chou (no. IV), figures are unmistakably in the "landscape." The only tree behind a figure is the old cypress, as often in Wen Cheng-ming associated with scholarly converse (cf. nos. XV, LVII). Thus the symbolic brevities of archaism are allied to a mature, exact sense of space. Historically, such spatial clarity did not develop until the Sung. It could be added that the figures themselves are related to similar historical complexities, for in them, too, is the dichotomy between fixed, archaic, even puppet-like poses and the "advanced" fact of their formation by an easy-flowing expressive line—now thick, now thin—which again we know of most exactly in the late Sung.

But as so often with this artist, there is a clear sense of pattern. In keeping both with antiquity and Wen's own style, space, exact as it is, reveals only a stage—the pattern of tree leaves and limbs spreads out across the pure gold ground above the land and leads us through the arc of the fan to the flat square of regular calligraphy, where poetry and historical recording further seal the experience.

INSCRIPTION BY THE ARTIST:
> Jug on the ground, facing each other, talk was easy;
> Cleansing a sand pot we boiled mountain water.
> Meeting unexpectedly this lofty man from Yang-hsien,
> We stayed long into the night over very fine tea.
> Toughest on the mind is the search for a poem;
> Groggy eyes roll pitifully and sleep comes late.
> No match for the mountain priest who truly knows,
> Before the lamp another sip, humbled to be his friend.

At Hsiang-ch'eng I met with Wang Te-chao from I-hsing, and we boiled Yang-hsien tea. I painted this Tasting Tea in the Pure Shade together with an eight-line poem. Inscribed by Cheng-ming, 1528, third month, sixteenth day.

(tr. Stephen Goldberg)

SEAL OF THE ARTIST:
Cheng-ming   [painting: I/1]

REMARKS:
Yang-hsien is the ancient name for I-hsing, a district not far from Suchou.
Hsiang-ch'eng is east of the city of Suchou. It is where Shen Chou lived.
Wang Te-chao, unidentified.

BIBLIOGRAPHY:
Dubosc, Wen Cheng-ming (1961), pp. 16–17.

XXIII

XXIV. SCHOLARS MEETING: THE STUDY BY OLD TREES

(Ku-mu shu-shih)
Dated by inscription before 1534
Hanging scroll, ink on paper, 20⅝" high and 12⁵/₁₆" wide (52.4 x 31.3 cm.)
Inscriptions and seals of the artist
Hwa's Hou Chen Shang Chai

This small unassuming scroll is little more than a precise personal symbol of Wen's scholarly life. It fits exactly with the kind of social-artistic phenomenon that we are now examining in Wen's career. It is completely unpretentious. Flat grey ink, blunt outlines, and limited shapes all are so much a product of what scholar-artists often persistently sought and described as *cho* 'unskilled' that it is a painting easy to overlook. This ideal was an exact one within the scholarly stereotype because it emphasized the fact that one was not supposed to present an outward show. "Skilled," *ch'iao*, might lead to brilliant display, but such painting carried with it a personal pretension—perhaps even individual pride —which by definition must reflect a superficial view of life. It certainly was something not to be actively sought. Truth never resides in surfaces. *Cho* is, thus, really a positive idea closely related to the whole concept of necessary withdrawal, whether it be from superficial art or superficial statecraft that was in many ways the ultimate human right and often a necessary goal within the long history of Chinese society. Certainly it was an acceptable view in Ming Suchou, as has already been shown in Shen Chou's *Pine and Hibiscus* (no. V). And Wen's own struggles both with the examination system and with actual government service were to lead his life on the path of withdrawal. This rejection indeed took place close to the time when this painting was painted.

The unpretentious look of the scroll is an accurate reflection of the circumstances surrounding it. Wen had previously written a poem which he had given Wang Ku-hsiang (1501–1568):

That was on the eighth day of the sixth month in 1528. Now it is seven years later. He (Wang) has returned from other duties and searching in his effects found it, brought it over, and we looked at it together. I had forgotten it. And so taking a small painting I had previously done I wrote (the poem) on it.

In a word, now in the year 1534, he is piecing together old experience; the calligraphy is of this year. The poem is of 1528; and the painting? We can well imagine Wen hunting around among an old pile of sketches, unmounted and uninscribed, to find a scene that would fit the immediate situation, something like the poem, a little forgotten, inevitably personal, but properly from about the time he wrote the poem, which was soon after his return from Peking.

The small scroll in Taipei, *Brewing Tea Under Stately Trees* (fig. 11), likewise unpretentious, with an informal inscription (almost like a letter), bears the date of 1526. As such it appears to be a rare example of a painting surviving from Wen's Peking period. Already noted (no. XXII) is the fact that on it is an important seal—*Wei keng-yin wu i chiang*. In the inscription Wen specifically refers to it as being *cho*. This is a matter of modesty, but it is also an accurate description of the sketch. To reject such a painting as not meeting standards of expected brilliance is to reject the often very personal nature of Wen's art, now especially at a time when he was far from being "into" his craft. Its closeness in style to *The Study by Old Trees* helps affirm that style's validity for this time. One notes particularly the grey-dark rocks, their blunt "cut-out" shapes and their thick outlines, and the leaf-designs against white trunks. Patterning of grasses replaces moss-dots on the ground, but the tree-seated scholar is a close cousin of one of the rock-seated scholars in *Tasting Tea in the Pure Shade* (no. XXIII).

As with that fan, in *The Study by Old Trees* rather exact archaic conventions have been subtly infused with contemporary style and personal meaning so that the painting has, withal, curious and yet appealing inconsistencies. Of such is the tiny scale of the figures drawn with simple line so that they are like far-off puppets in the vast empty rooms of an austere grass-roofed architecture. The architecture, for which a ruled line seems to have been used, is placed in what for Wen was a characteristic exact overlap. The dark cliff suggests a huge, even threatening mass of rock whose real purpose, however, as artistic convention seems apparent when one contemplates the flat patterns of the rock-layers and the tree grove that clings, or is placed against, their upper edge. It has little physical substance. The extended bare-twig pattern is a typical convention for Wen (cf. nos. X, XIII, XIV) and might here be considered a natural pattern to contrast with the man-made pattern of the woven fence toward which it angles at the lower right edge. Finally, the over-thin, over-sparse pine is much a Wen Cheng-ming convention and almost an absolute necessity in the subject of the garden retreat.

INSCRIPTIONS BY THE ARTIST:
Recently I have been sick and deep in melancholy; for ten days I have not combed my hair.
Avoiding the wind, I could not even roll up the window curtain.
From a distant place there drifts the fragrance of an ancient *ting*.

重陰繚樹霞
茅堂卹索遺
編苓榷商量
子烹茶承妨
煖相投水乳
正言長
庚辰仲秋
湘髮

近來無柰病淹愁十日巖梳頭
遊風簾幕何堪憁然處慶古嚣香
浮興主間書柴几目来時霞茶
甌新凍如水篁紋流六月顙清
秋盡替坊裡人如玉空相揁相見
無由最是詩成酒醒月明明徐度南
樓右調風入松病中有悰
王君祿之偁州奉時戊子歲六月八
日也越今七年啟歸自耀曹檢蕉得之
特卆相示而起之矣丑以蕉作小面俾錄
於上而余日益蒙老無復當時情致書
罨為之怏然嘉靖甲午四月十曾微明記

With delight comes leisurely writing on the yew table;
When tired I pour a frequent cup of tea.
Fresh cool like water is in the mat's flowing texture.
The sixth month feels like the clear autumn.
Neighbors gathering together—like jade;
Now is empty longing—
We cannot meet.
Most when the poem is finished, and waking from wine,
The bright moon slips past the southern pavilion.

> Written following the rhyme "Wind through the Pines," during an illness.

I rhymed this thinking of Wang Lu-chih (Wang Ku-hsiang) and sent it to him. That was on the eighth day of the sixth month in 1528. Now it is seven years later. He (Wang) has returned from other duties and searching in his effects found it, brought it over, and we looked at it together. I had forgotten it. And so taking a small painting I had previously done I wrote (the poem) on it. With the passing days I sink into old age—no longer to return is the spirit of those days. In writing this are feelings of sadness. The fourteenth day of the fourteenth month, recorded by Cheng-ming.

SEALS OF THE ARTIST:

Cheng-ming	[painting: IV/1]
Wen Cheng-ming yin	[painting: IV/2]
Cheng-chung	[painting: IV/3]

COLOPHONS AND SEALS:
Ch'ien-lung emperor (r. 1736–1795)

San-hsi t'ang ching-chien hsi	[painting: I/1]
I tzu-sun	[painting: I/2]
Shih-ch'ü pao-chi	[painting: I/3]
Ch'ien-lung yü-lan chih pao	[painting: II/1]
Ch'ien-lung chien-shang	[painting: III/1]
Chi-hsia i-ch'ing	[colophon]
Te-chia ch'ü	[colophon]

Unidentified

Lan-hui t'ang ts'ang	[painting: I/4]
Pao-i chü-shih chien-ts'ang	[mounting]

REMARKS:
Poem is recorded, with minor differences, in *Wen Cheng-ming hui-kao* (1929) ch. 1/p. 37a.

Wang Ku-hsiang (1501–1568), a painter and calligrapher from Suchou. For a discussion see Wilson and Wong, *Friends* (1974), pp. 113–115.

There is what appears to be a copy version of this painting—with different calligraphy above—in the Mu-fei collection, Cambridge, England.

BIBLIOGRAPHY:
Shih-ch'ü san (1969 ed.), vol. 7, p. 3112.
Hao-ku t'ang (1969), p. 90.

11. Wen Cheng-ming, *Brewing Tea Under Stately Trees,* 1526. National Palace Museum, Taipei

XXV. THE RED CLIFF

(Ch'ih-pi t'u)
No date
Handscroll, ink and light color on silk, 7¼" high and 33⅜"
  long (18.5 x 85.0 cm.)
Inscription, signature, and seals of the artist
Mr. and Mrs. Wan-go H. C. Weng, New York

Of the paintings on the traditional theme of the
Red Cliff that are included in the exhibition this
short undated handscroll on silk gives every indication of being the earliest. The others are to
be assigned to the last decade of Wen's life. In
addition, the Freer Gallery owns a beautiful
handscroll in ink and light colors on paper (fig.
12)—one of the finest extant versions of this
theme by Wen—and that too, is to be dated late,
in 1552.

Wen seems to have written out on countless
occasions Su Shih's famous "First Prose Poem on
the Red Cliff" of 1082 (see no. LXII), which is
the basis for this painting. Attached here, however, is a transcription of the ode by Wen's pupil
and younger friend Chou T'ien-ch'iu, who in 1556
saw a handscroll of The Red Cliff by Wen and
wrote out the ode to append to the painting. Unfortunately there is only noncommittal praise by
Chou which offers no exact assurance that this is,
in fact, the painting he saw.

It is most helpful to compare this scroll with
the Freer version. In doing so we anticipate
qualities in Wen's work which will be even more
apparent as we look at paintings from late in
Wen's life. The Freer *Red Cliff* is a scroll that
shows confidence in broad, serene spaces along
with a free and open touch of the brush that can
only reflect a complete maturity. Some of the
differences in the exhibited scroll result from the
fact that it is painted on silk. This helps create
a tighter, flatter, less rich effect both in individual
brushstrokes and on textural surfaces. But there
is much more than that.

To begin with, however, the view of the scene
is essentially the same: the introduction of broad
spaces on which floats the modest skiff; and the
cliff, an important mass at the left cut by the top
of the scroll, slanting down to more or less fill
the scroll's end. Within this there is a major
angling of cliff forms that directs one toward the
upper left border. The boat is the same boat, and
similar too is the placement of the trio of friends,
with Su Shih in the bow and the tiny boatman
huddled in the stern.

Here similarities end. Although rock or land
may present analogous shapes, in the Freer painting the "flow" is far easier. Outlines are broader
(even showing "flying white") and less angular.
But most striking is the all-over effect so that in
the Freer painting one is not carried to a rather
blunt flat ending—the single focus of the few
trees and a narrow gorge; instead there is a clear
reverse movement that carries one back from left
to right, back into the hanging spaces of the upper
edge, to the moon and to distant promontories.
Rather obliquely presented, it is such qualities
that distinguish the Freer masterpiece. In contrast, the Weng scroll is arranged simply. We
move to the left without interruption. We accept
the juxtaposition of the rather flat shapes as,
placed in front or behind, they create the illusion
of a tight shallow recession. Along the upper
edge, distance never truly materializes. There is
no real sky, no real gap of pure space, no moon.
Dark lines in the "distance" help bring it back to
the surface and relate it to the flat calligraphy of
Wen's poem with which the painting fittingly
begins.

In this rather blunt approach to formal arrangement—a basically static, limited view—the undated *Red Cliff* bears rather striking similarities
to the scholars' gathering that we have just considered: flat rocks, sparingly textured, with often
pointed contour-lines, and fringed with a similar
random scattering of pepper-dots; the fixed flat
trunks of trees with an occasional isolated brush-
stroke within, stubby skeletons for the ink leaves
that surround them; an isolated flat pattern of
bare twigs bending from left to right; on occasion
the long bare trunk of a pine, and similar pine-
needles. (In the Freer painting there is no pine,
only a cypress.)

In suggesting this comparison we cannot
escape the fact that *The Red Cliff* is, too, a
scholarly gathering—Su Shih and friends endure
to remind Wen and his friends that what they
both did was part of China's certain tradition.
These affirmations of the just life, *The Red Cliff*
and *The Study by Old Trees,* must have occurred
at a similar time close to the late twenties.

INSCRIPTION BY THE ARTIST:
  Beyond heaven, green mountains
    half there, half not.
  The river flows ten thousand *li*—
    bright solitary moon.
  In the deep night, then,
    sensing traces of Ts'ao Man,
  I am moved
    to do the picture.

Cheng-ming
(tr. Steven D. Owyoung)

SEALS OF THE ARTIST:
  Cheng-ming   [painting: I/1]
  Wu-yen shih yin   [painting: I/2]

COLOPHONS AND SEALS:
Chou T'ien-ch'iu (1514–1595), student of Wen, orchid and bird
and flower painter from Suchou:
["First Prose Poem on the Red Cliff" in standard script, for
translation see no. LXII; followed by:]
In 1556, ninth month, ninth day, I passed by (Wang Chih-
teng's home) the Tsun-sheng chai and was able to see Heng-
shan's Red Cliff handscroll. The trees were luxuriant and the

XXV

rocks rough, capturing heaven's flavor. I could not bear to release it from my hands; thus I wrote the First Poem to append after it. Chou T'ien-ch'iu.

(tr. James Robinson)

Chou   [colophon: I/1]
T'ien-ch'iu   [colophon: I/2]

Weng T'ung-ho (1830–1904); dated 1900, tenth month, eighteenth day

Sung-ch'an lao-jen   [colophon: I/1]
T'ung-ho   [colophon: I/2]

REMARKS:

Ts'ao Man, another name for Ts'ao Ts'ao (died 220 A.D.), ruler of the Wei dynasty, Three Kingdoms period. He was in a famous naval battle at this site.

The poem is recorded in *Wen Cheng-ming hui-kao* (1929), ch. 7/p. 75b.

12. Wen Cheng-ming, *The Red Cliff,* 1552. Freer Gallery of Art, Washington

月明孤枕深　偶蔵曹暁蹟者
彼倣人画作図　徴明

XXVI. FAREWELL AT T'ING-YÜN

(T'ing-yün kuan yen-pieh)
Dated 1531, fifth month, tenth day
Hanging scroll, ink and color on paper, 20½″ high and 10″ wide
(52.0 x 25.2 cm.)
Inscriptions and seals of the artist
Vannotti Collection, Muzzano, Switzerland

Of all the paintings of this time on the theme of scholarly friendship this is the most perfect. The now-familiar subject shows two scholars in close converse supplemented by an equally brief, pure but appropriate setting—strong old trees, friendly rocks, enough suggestion of land so that they may sit or walk, two servants to supply their needs. The picture faithfully transposes onto a small hanging scroll the fan design of 1528 (no. XXIII): tall pine, the three deciduous trees, even the old cypress beside conversing scholars. Artists clearly had designs either before them or in the mind which they could repeat. The difference here rests in placement to fit a changed format and in a far stricter attention to archaism—a finer line, a precise jewel-like handling. As such it is a completely "new" creation.

Anne Clapp has pointed out the immediate source of this archaism as resting in Chao Meng-fu and cites for comparison a painting of Chao's now owned by Mr. C. C. Wang, *Scholars Playing the Ch'in in the Woods*. She further tells how Wen has carried the idea far beyond that of Chao to show a very special sense of refined purity:

Everything is treated as part of a single graphic image: fine, clear, dry, and fastidious and so sparingly touched with color as to resemble an etching more than a painting.[1]

Possibly this extra care is because it was for a special friend, Wang Ch'ung, who until his death just two years after this scroll was painted was so often involved with Wen's artistic enterprises. All the more poignant, then, this living-on of friendship.

These etched forms, including the chaste block of thin standard script in the upper left, convey a delicacy that might be linked to the often miniature care of the earlier work. But is is here presented with a maturity that combines light detail with strong feeling for total form—and even beyond that to a kind of "play" of those forms. Thus the thin borders of tree trunks fuse into modeling tones of rather exact three-dimensionality, and these in turn become a play of shapes—knots, twisting surfaces, darks and lights that are both a pattern and affirmations of vibrant living form. The same is carved into arrangements of branch and leaf. Leaves in curved clusters or fixed star-like fronds are both foliage and tense pattern. No natural single-direction wind moves the needles in the lofty pine. They are as though pressed by some mysterious centrifugal force always facing outward; but the spokes of this flat-topped wheel are like weaving dragons. Behind the right-hand rock there is no further distance—only emptiness, or paper. The line between nature and art is thin.

NOTE:
1. Clapp, *Wen Cheng-ming* (1975), p. 50.

INSCRIPTION BY THE ARTIST:
Spring comes and day after day rain is with the wind;
As the rain passes, the spring returns, the green more lush.
This white head has now no dreams of "early market."
The green moss often holds an old friend's footprints;
My thought of joy is the bird before the wine-jar.
Heaven's heavy-browed ends are mountains beyond the suburbs.
Certainly parting can cause suffering,
Yet still forebearing, this "old eye" sees off the soaring bird.
Lü-jen (Wang Ch'ung) was going to proceed to Nan-yung (Nanking) and passed by T'ing-yün kuan to say farewell; thus I presented this with my respects. Tenth day of the fifth month of 1531. Cheng-ming.
(tr. James Robinson)

SEALS OF THE ARTIST:
T'ing-yün	[painting: I/1]
Cheng-chung	[painting: I/2]
Cheng-ming	[painting: II/1]

REMARKS:
Wang Ch'ung (1494–1533), famous Suchou scholar and calligrapher. For a discussion see Wilson and Wong, *Friends* (1974), pp. 98–99.

A close version of this same design is in the National Palace Museum, Taipei with the title *Pure Conversation in Green Shade* (*Ku-kung shu-hua-lu*, 1965, ch. 5/p. 378). The poem refers to the capital and the dust there, and thus has been dated to ca. 1523. However, the quality of execution is so inferior to the Vannotti scroll that it may not even be admissible for the artistically barren Peking years.

BIBLIOGRAPHY:
Dubosc, *Mostra d'arte* (1954), no. 803.
Arts of the Ming (1958), no. 8.
Giuganino, *La pittura* (1959), II, p. 335.
Clapp, *Wen Cheng-ming* (1975), fig. 14.

XXVII. BREWING TEA ON A SPRING EVENING

(Chien ch'a)
No date
Hanging scroll, ink and light color on silk, 36″ high and 18¼″ wide
  (91.5 x 46.5 cm.)
Inscription, signature, and seals of the artist
Mr. and Mrs. Jackson Burke, New York

XXVII

The Vannotti scroll was painted for Wen's intimate friend Wang Ch'ung at Wen's T'ing-yün kuan. He had apparently already painted a similarly intimate scene for Wang Ch'ung's elder brother, Wang Shou. The poem for that scene, which is the poem repeated on this scroll, is recorded in Wen's collected works. There it is noted as having been done for Wang Shou, a fact omitted from this painting's inscription. Poems in this collection are generally placed in chronological order, and the position in the anthology indicates that it was originally written ten or fifteen years earlier than the Vannotti scroll.

The Burke painting is on silk rather than paper and thus inevitably has a crispness, even hardness, of execution that is not a part of the softer touch of the *Farewell.* The subject of the Burke painting is tea-tasting, but the same two friends are there—only now, if we follow the original poem, it is Wen Cheng-ming and Wang Shou. Since names are omitted we cannot know exactly for whom this particular painting was done. As in the Vannotti painting there is no depth. A short stream suddenly appears on the paper. No space exists beyond the silhouetted edge of the curved rock forms.

There is, however, a major difference between the two scrolls. It has to do with the all-over unity of the scene. With *Brewing Tea* there is no break in a continuous movement from lower left to upper right (including the calligraphy). Tree and bridge carry one across the stream where one slips easily into the pocket of space that holds the scholars, around and above whom are the interlocking shapes of tree, branch, and foliage. There is even a conscious action being performed in the making of the tea. It is tensely animated, as moving, varied shapes attest; but it is at base a "scene."

One may relate the difference to tradition. *Farewell* is conceived in terms consistent with the quiet static balance of T'ang forms. This tea-tasting, with its angled approach to a directly revealed scene, is of the late Sung. They are linked, however, in that both paintings are tense formal patterns only reluctantly accepting hints of ordinary space and time. Wen's art has made his own world. Rather quietly in *Farewell.* In *Brewing Tea,* the angled tensions are more overt. There is little rest anywhere. The two scholars seem themselves to symbolize this. Front and back the figures face each other in an almost mirror sequence—at the left a ramrod back, to the right the front view of this form with arm and hand so impossibly frail as to have nothing to do with natural support or action.

XXVII, detail

The essence of mirrored tension is in the lower hem of their robes—one flowing to a sharp dark point at the right, the other countering it to the left.

This undated scroll, apparently repeating an earlier experience, shows elements of conscious restless pattern that will become increasingly familiar as the art of the 1530s unfolds.

INSCRIPTION BY THE ARTIST:
Fresh water waiting to boil,
The proud new tea swelling like green banners.
Chiang-nan's "grain rains": the festival is near.
Under Mount Hui's springs, a skiff returns,
Gauze cap and mountain man at "the place of the halter."

The meditation mat, wind-borne flowers, the flying, swirling beard;
The blocked-up wine guest wakes from a dream of dust,
Reclines, and watches the spring sun sink through the pine door.

SEALS OF THE ARTIST:
Wen Cheng-ming yin	[painting: II/1]
T'ing-yün kuan	[painting: II/2]

SEALS:
Hsiang Yüan-pien (1525–1590), important collector
Hsiang Yüan-pien yin	[painting: I/1]
Tzu-ching	[painting: III/1]
Mo-lin pi-wan	[painting: III/2]
Hsiang Tzu-ching chia chen-ts'ang	[painting: III/3]
Hsiang Mo-lin fu pi-chi chih yin	[painting: I/2]

Unidentified
Tseng ts'ang ——— Li ——— ———	[painting: I/3]
Undeciphered	[painting: IV/1]

REMARKS:
The poem by Wen is recorded in both *Wen shih* (1934–1935), ch. 6/pp. 28a–28b, and *Fu t'ien* (1968 ed.), ch. 6/p. 9a (p. 203). The latter entry implies a date of 1516 for the poem.

Grain rains: the grain-producing rains of mid-spring.

The meaning of "the place of the halter" *(lung-t'ou ch'u)* is not clear.

BIBLIOGRAPHY:
500 Years (1962).

XXVIII. OLD TREES BY A COLD WATERFALL

(Ku-mu han-ch'üan)
Dated 1531, seventh month, twenty-fourth day
Hanging scroll, ink and color on paper, 21⅜" high and 9⅝" wide
(54.5 x 24.5 cm.)
Inscription and seals of the artist
Los Angeles County Museum of Art, The Ernest Larsen Blanck
Memorial Collection

With a title made famous in Wen's late years, this archaistic landscape, to follow its inscription, was done in solitude in 1531 to be paired with a scroll of "Pine Ravine" *(sung-ho)*.[1] The painting itself is of considerable beauty, the deep greys of the rocks marking out a sparse structure for the play of equally selective warm and cool tones of tree and foliage and the two doll-like low-waisted scholars. Solid shapes are enlivened by the careful linear play of water, the random scattering of black moss-dots *(tien)*.

Is this acceptable as yet another variant of the now so familiar theme? It certainly abandons both the tensions of *Brewing Tea* (no. XXVII) and the jewel-like quality of *Farewell at T'ing-yün* (no. XXVI). Yet with the latter there is an analogous selection and placing of archaizing forms, now around the notion of water and distance, rather than the garden close-up. Curiously, into the archaic form intrudes something of the notion of *cho,* the unskilled, so that shapes (particularly the rocks) seem to fall somewhere between the tight archaism of *Farewell* and the blunt handling of *The Study by Old Trees* (no. XXIV). For example in the latter the massing of grey cliff with its flat tree-grove at the crest might be compared with the archaic cliff and clinging tree-grove at the back of *Old Trees by a Cold Waterfall.* Certainly within the range of Wen's work fall such ideas as the cypress with conversing scholars, dancing ink-splashed water (no. XV), the lack of deep receding space so that form appears from nowhere so much as the flat paper, and the far ink-curtains of distant mountain peaks.

As is often true of such reduced landscapes, they can become a kind of play on numbers—here "two," occasionally modified by a third accent: two men, two rocks, two trees, two masses of cliffs, two far peaks. However, what is here can also be described as an almost excessive archaism—figures are dolls; a face, a mask; mountains, garden rocks, which are both dwarfed and ancient beyond belief. As though to make them more tangible within this cut-out world, the far ridge of mountain is outlined.

Further, despite its timeless art, the landscape has its touches of the disquieting moment. The black outline that defines the plateau edge in the lower left is brushed rather over-harshly on a thin, blue line beneath it. The lines of water below the upper falls tangle with the tip of the central restless tree.

Throughout, despite the static framework, there is a personal inexact touch that is not firmly integrated with the precision of the basic idea—the loose pools of dark ink that are rockholes and crevices, ink that flows over outline, outline itself now rather dark, now light, now powdery, now wet. The brush feels out the wrinkled textures of the old trees.

XXVIII

Positively, this is the typical scholarly approach—for Wen, hallowed by Chao Meng-fu—personal exploration within the certainty of the antique idea, archaism linked to *cho*.

The closest claim for the validity of Wen's experimenting with such expression in 1531 comes from a folding fan of the same year in the National Palace Museum of Taipei, *Leaning on a Rock* (fig. 13). While one might make allowances for working on the smooth golden surface of such a format, one finds, as with the Los Angeles scroll, similar dark grey shades of rock pocketed by deeper spots of wash, outlined (rather more thickly) plateaus, the wrinkled textures of rounded tree-trunks, lines of water and dancing foam, sparse ink-dots (to which a touch of pigment has been added). And always, particularly with the rayed lines of the fan, one is aware of the paper, a surface on and behind which the rock, rounded tree and tipped plateau never really are permitted an easy recession into space.

NOTE:
1. While it is difficult to claim that it should be properly joined with

the Palace Museum masterpiece *Cascading Falls in the Pine Ravine* (fig. 10; in size the Los Angeles scroll is half the height), the dates support the idea.

INSCRIPTION BY THE ARTIST:
By my rainy window without visitors, in a quiet and lonely mood, I took the brush and painted *Old Trees by a Cold Waterfall* to pair with the *Pine Ravine*. Twenty-fourth day of the seventh month of 1531, recorded by Cheng-ming.

SEALS OF THE ARTIST:
Wen Cheng-ming yin	[painting: I/1]
Cheng-ming	[painting: III/6]

SEALS:
Ch'ien-lung emperor (r. 1736–1795)
San-hsi t'ang ching-chien hsi	[painting: I/2]
I tz'u-sun	[painting: I/3]
Ch'ien-lung yü-lan chih pao	[painting: II/1]
Ch'ien-lung chien-shang	[painting: III/1]
Shih-ch'ü pao-chi	[painting: III/2]

Unidentified
Pai-na pao-chi	[painting: III/3]
Pai-na chai-jen	[painting: III/4]
Lu-ho Chang I yen-mou so ts'ang	[painting: III/5]

BIBLIOGRAPHY:
Dubosc, *Mostra di pittura* (1950), fig. 10.
"Oriental Art Recently Acquired," 1956, p. 71, fig. 15.
Lee, *Chinese Landscape* (1962), no. 55.

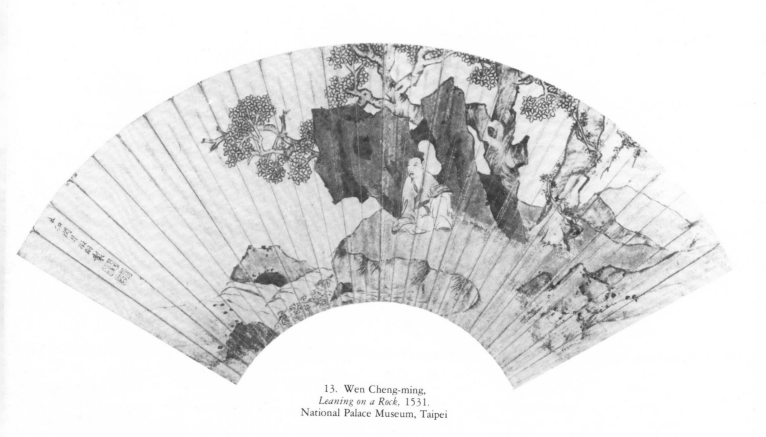

13. Wen Cheng-ming,
Leaning on a Rock, 1531.
National Palace Museum, Taipei

XXIX. WATCHING THE WATERFALL

Dated 1532, fifth month
Folding fan, ink and color on gold paper, 7¹⁵/₁₆″ high and 22″ wide
   (20.1 x 56.0 cm.)
Inscription and seal of the artist
Vannotti Collection, Muzzano, Switzerland

By now and at this time the scholar's meeting both as style and subject has been so well-established that the viewer will clearly recognize this fan as a familiar variant. Here, however, the scene is removed to a plateau at the foot of a dramatic fall of water, a high place somewhere in a mountain world.

Otherwise expected motifs are found: the tall spare-branched pine, the cypress tree, the two scholars, the selected deciduous tree, the rather flat shapes of rocks with their thick outlines, white extended tree trunks clinging impossibly to the high edge of a cliff, patterns of grass, scattering of moss-dots.

What particularly distinguishes this arc of mountain scenery, however, is an infusion of dramatic content. This is even true of the texture-strokes on the rocks. One notes especially, however, the restless pattern of the washes of the far peaks as they play against the dance of foreground trees and land.

The beginnings of such tensions help us to understand the extraordinary "dance" in the following scroll, created in the same summer of 1532.

INSCRIPTION BY THE ARTIST:
Painted in 1532, fifth month. Cheng-ming.

SEAL OF THE ARTIST:
   Cheng-ming   [painting: I/1]

SEAL:
Unidentified
   Li Tzu-yün shen-ting chang   [painting: II/1]

BIBLIOGRAPHY:
Arts of the Ming (1958), no. 10.
Dubosc, *Les Quatre* (1966), pl. 11.

XXIX

XXX. THE SEVEN JUNIPERS OF CH'ANG-SHU

(Yü-shan ch'i hsing)
Dated 1532, summer
Handscroll, ink on paper, 11¼" high and 142½" long (28.8 x 362.0 cm.)
Inscriptions and seals of the artist
Honolulu Academy of Arts, gift of Mrs. Carter Galt, 1952

These Junipers were presented by Wen Cheng-ming to an as-yet unidentified friend, Mr. Wang Shih-men. We know of this from colophons added to the scroll by Wen and by Ch'en Shun, Wen's student. Wen's own brief inscription on the painting itself simply declares that he was rather exactly copying *(mo)* Chao Meng-fu. Ch'en Shun affirms that his master has, indeed, captured the essence *(san-mei, samādhi)* of that much-admired Yüan master.

Wen's own teacher, Shen Chou, had himself on a trip to Ch'ang-shu previously painted the three oldest of the seven. Originally planted in 500 A.D., four had died and were replaced around 1044. Here is the essence of Wen—a subject hallowed by history, made famous pictorially by Wen's own master, and by Wen reinterpreted in the style of his favorite model from the past: Chao Meng-fu.

As translated by Tseng Yu-ho, the *fu* itself stresses the wonder of the scene—and we learn from it something of why such trees become *the* great subject for Wen Cheng-ming. Marvelously enduring, they are statements of vital immortality and may be likened to all auspicious revelations in worlds of mortals and immortals: martial as spears, like the arms of gibbons, the necks of cranes, branches sweeping the lonely night like brooms, creaking ropes, split horns, blunted claws, dragon wrestling with tiger, whales rolling, giant birds swooping; like ghosts they vanish, reappear, continuously entangled forms.

One is, thus, urged to draw on an almost limitless variety of metaphor, and Wen's tense vision demands it. A glance at Shen Chou's version (fig. 14) only serves to reinforce Wen Cheng-ming's uniqueness. The essential difference is similar to what we have already noted in examples of Shen's painting shown in this exhibition (nos. IV, VII). Shen saw his subject directly. His selection of three trees is its own subtle commentary. Age must come from the trees themselves. For Wen all seven were equally valid, even necessary, as a basis for his own expression. In contrast to Wen's interlocking forms, Shen's trees are each a separately growing form surrounded by its own implied space. Cutting at the top and bottom is only a device to bring the tree closer to us. We know that it grows beyond what

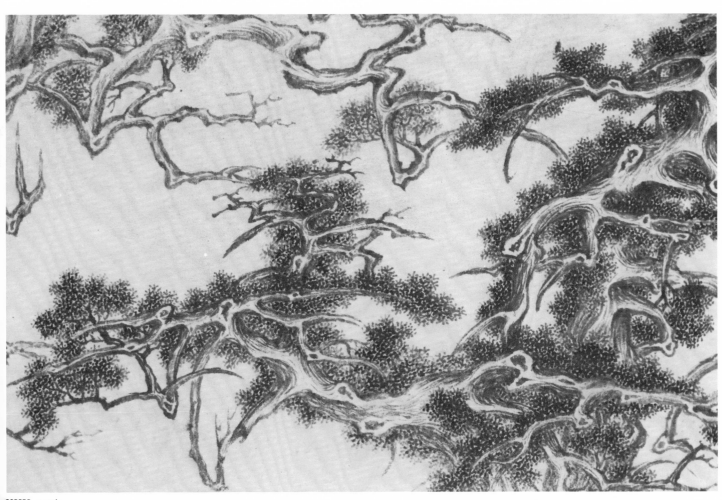

XXX, section

XXX

we see. Wen's view is distinctively different. As described by Marsha Weidner, Wen's conscious *making* of the picture is paramount:

Thus, as Wen Cheng-ming pushed and pulled his forms around, he forced them to interact not only with one another, but also with such abstract and non-representational forces as negative space and the boundaries of the picture plane.[1]

It is all art. We are immediately aware of movement, variety, the urge to endless metaphor. But what takes the painting beyond the ordinary is its intensification through formal restraint. Thus curve and countercurve, "arm" and "wave," "spear" and "rope" and "claw," the wrestling of primeval spirits are, like the clenched fist, the uncoiled spring, never completely released; their strength is present always. Power contained is true and enduring power. It is power never dissipated.

In terms of historical traditions the *Seven Junipers* has a composition of the T'ang. In connection with painting, Wen's writing after the scroll does refer to the T'ang painters Pi Hung and Wei Yen. The vertical trunk halfway through is like a central column or middle motif in a T'ang scroll. Two broad arcs of shape lead to it; four smaller ones lead away. There is a pause of space at beginning and end. But the strictest limitation is the paper itself. Forms are continually stopped and held in check by its edge. Unlike Shen Chou's version this occurs so often that it is impossible to imagine what goes on beyond. We have no earth, we have no sky. It is in the truest sense abstracted vision. It is paper, brushstroke, ink, pattern, dark and light, solid and void. Lifted out of immediate nature it is, thus, nature transformed. Again, in a single word, it is art.

Why is it like Chao Meng-fu? Broadly and fundamentally because it abstracts an ancient form and subtly transforms it into the immediacy of personal expression. Specifically because Wen makes so much of an understated grey brush, an expressiveness of unspectacular ink—related, for example, to Chao's mastery that led him to such strokes as his "flying white" (where in the movement of brush itself, ink and paper were subtly related) and Chao's dictum: "rocks like flying white, trees like seal script."[2]

But of course, it is Wen.

Specifically this can be detailed: the tight,

120

ordered patterns of ink dots, now light, now dark, contrasting with twisted wrinkled forms; the sharp-pointed twig, the blunt-eyed knot; light or dark suggesting recession or advance, but only for a moment. There is no settled space. Always on the paper there is, to use seventeenth-century terminology, "rising and falling," "opening and closing." Controlled repetitive detail, tight structure, limited space and extraordinary technical finesse are clear marks of Wen's style in the 1530s.

These qualities are found as well in at least three contemporary masterpieces, unavailable for this exhibition, that are now in the National Palace Museum in Taipei—*Cascading Falls in the Pine Ravine* (fig. 10), a hanging scroll finished in 1531 and related to experiences with his friend Wang Ch'ung, to whom he had said "farewell" the year before (no. XXVI); *Snow on the Mountain Passes,* a handscroll which was finished in 1532 likewise for Wang Ch'ung (fig. 15); and the towering tight mountainscape in the style of Wang Meng of 1535 (fig. 16). This last is the 1530s version of what we have seen earlier in the Michigan landscape (no. XV). It presents in vertical form many of the

horizontal intensities seen in the Honolulu scroll: rocks and land-contours, stream-arms, and leaf-dots, the wrinkled twisting cliffs like the ancient tree trunks of the *Junipers.* Like the *Junipers,* there is no deep space. Forms crowd the narrow format. Depth is only present in hesitant pockets. That the structure of a landscape is so basically close to the structure of a "treescape" tells us much about Wen's essential aims in the early years of the 1530s.

NOTES:
1. Marsha Weidner, "The Paintings of Wen Cheng-ming: 1527–1539," (seminar paper, University of Michigan, 1974), p. 3.
2. Tseng, "The Seven Junipers" (1954), p. 23.

INSCRIPTION BY THE ARTIST:
Behold, memorials of days gone by, the Seven Junipers of Ch'inch'üan, celestial as the constellation of the Seven Stars, divinely planted in the time of Liang! They stand immune to Sui-jên's flaming fire. Forms superb, flawless idols, spirits infinite—their shadows, cast on jade, still guard the ancient halls, hallowing the Palace of the Stars, attending Heaven's majesty. Up float their arms, their hair hangs clustered. Mysterious forces, chaste and taut! Unheard poems are deepest. Ten thousand oxen will not pull out the spreading roots, anchored in primeval soil. They wedded the weird in thunder and darkest *Yin.* Dry lichen binds their bone knots. Now the boughs trail and now they soar, swirling in a gyre or suddenly drooping. Now martial as spears, now supine and flat. Now the boughs writhe

like the arms of apes, grasping at some shifting prize. Now, like the necks of haughty cranes, they bend as if to preen themselves. Wrinkles crack as though struck by axes. The russet bark bursts asunder, pierced through by tiny leaves. The branches sweep the lonely night like brooms. By day a sound of roaring waves echoes in the hollows of the trunks. Like creaking ropes the junipers dance to the wail of the wind, conjuring up a thousand images: split horns and blunted claws, the wrestling of the dragon with the tiger, great whales rolling in the deep, and giant birds who swoop down on their prey. And now, like ghosts, they vanish, now reappear, vast entangled forms.

To further their perfection, the sky bestows its blessing, the elixir of sweet dew. They are visited by gods and fairies who play upon them as though on twanging instruments. They feed upon the color of the dawn; they drink a heavenly wine. Like the jade trees on the Fairy Isle, disdainful of the uproar of the world, they stand before the towering blue hills. They are indifferent to war and peace, not caring if the bronze camels be hidden in the weeds, while the Sun

14. Shen Chou (or close copy), *The Three Junipers*, 1484, detail. Nanking Museum

15. Wen Cheng-ming, *Snow on the Mountain Passes*, 1528–1532, section. National Palace Museum, Taipei

and Moon pursue their fixed course in the firmament.

The Cedar of Szech'uan was once deemed worthy to be a symbol of Han, the T'ai Shan Pine of a gentleman of Ch'in. Lao-tze's Blue Cow vanished far away, and the Confucian Cypress dwindled and collapsed. Still stand the Seven Junipers, magic witnesses of days done by. Who knows what is to come hereafter? Pi Hung, Wei Yen died long ago, Shen Chou, the old master, painted these trees. Admiring antiquity I compose this *fu*. My words are not like those of Su Shih or Han Yü. My portrait of these junipers is like the admiration of a northerner for an orange tree. And yet, may I attain, inscribed in granite, a touch of immortality!

In the summer of the year 1532, Cheng-ming painted and wrote this for Wang Shih-men.

(tr. Tseng Yu-ho)

SEALS OF THE ARTIST:

Wen Cheng-ming yin	[frontispiece: I/1]
Heng-shan	[frontispiece: I/2]
Heng-shan?	[painting: I/3]
Cheng-ming	[painting: II/1]
Wu-yen shih yin	[painting: II/2]
	[colophon: I/2]
Wen Cheng-ming yin	[colophon: I/1]

COLOPHONS AND SEALS:

Ch'en Tao-fu (Ch'en Shun, 1483–1544), a painter from Suchou and pupil of Wen Cheng-ming; undated:

In the spring of 1532, Mr. Wang (of) Shih-men came from Hai-yü (that is Ch'ang-shu where the ancient junipers were standing), he visited me at the lake, stayed over night and left. In the autumn, 1538, Mr. Wang again visited me. He showed me the scroll with the Seven Junipers of my teacher, Master Heng-shan (*i.e.,* Wen Cheng-ming). He told me that after he had seen me last time, he visited Master Heng and begged him to let him have the scroll. And now he wants from me a few words of comment. I carefully studied the scroll and could not relinquish it. This is indeed my teacher's masterpiece. In his lines and washes, delicate and lush, he attained the essence of Chao Meng-fu's genius. Such a painting is not easily given away. Mr. Wang was certainly not afraid to ask and was lucky to get it. If it had not been for Mr. Wang's appearance and his personal culture, so appealing to the Master's taste, how could the latter have given it to him? So much the more should Shih-men treasure it!—Tao-fu.

(tr. Tseng Yu-ho)

Fu-fu shih	[colophon: I/1]
Ch'en Tao-fu shih	[colophon: I/2]
Unidentified	
Ni shih Hsien-sun chia-ts'ang	[painting: I/1]
Pai-hsien shan-jen	[painting: I/2]

REMARKS: Tseng Yu-ho tells us that the poem written by Wen Cheng-ming is published in *T'u-shu chi-ch'eng,* attributed to Huang Yün (active late fifteenth–early sixteenth century), from K'un-shan (cf. no. XI, colophon). Wen, however, states that he composed (*fu*) the poem himself. She explains some of the names:

Ch'in-ch'üan is an ancient name of the seven rivers crossing the Ch'ang-shu region.

The *Seven Stars* are in the Great Bear.

Sui-jen is a legendary figure said to have invented fire in China.

Bronze camels in the weeds refer to bronze camels once adorning the gates of the imperial palace of the Ch'in dynasty. So Chin was a diviner who, forseeing war, pointed at these camels and exclaimed: "I shall see you soon amongst the weeds."

Lao-tze's *Blue Cow* is the famous animal on which this philosopher is said to have ridden during his lifetime.

Pi Hung and *Wei Yen,* active in about the eighth century, were known for their tree and rock paintings.

BIBLIOGRAPHY:
Tseng, "The Seven Junipers" (1954), pp. 22–30.
Sirén, *Chinese Painting* (1956–1958), VI, pl. 210.
Lee, *Chinese Landscape* (1962), no. 56.
Ecke, *Chinese Painting* (1965), III, pl. LV.
Clapp, *Wen Cheng-ming* (1975), fig. 32.

16. Wen Cheng-ming, *Landscape After Wang Meng,* 1535. National Palace Museum, Taipei

XXX, detail. Signature following painting

XXX, detail. Signature following poem

XXXI. SAGES OF MOUNT LU

(Lien-she t'u)
Dated 1532, autumn, eighth month, eleventh day
Pair of fans: painting in ink and color on gold paper; calligraphy in ink on gold paper; each 7″ high and 21½″ wide (17.5 x 54.2 cm.)
Inscription, signature, and seals of the artist
Jean-Pierre Dubosc, Paris and Tokyo

Here is Wen Cheng-ming completely involved with matters of tradition. These two fans, presumably once mounted back to back, affirm Wen's connections to the scholarly ideals of the Sung. We have already seen the importance to him of Mi Fu and Su Shih, or, in calligraphy, Huang T'ing-chien. Now we must add another paragon of excellence in that important Sung group—Li Kung-lin (1049–1106). As with Su Shih's *Red Cliff*, this gathering lent itself both to pictorial representation and literary composition. Also its importance for Wen rested in its affirmation of history and ideas which gave important foundation to his own existence.

Locked in tradition, these two fans are more closely allied to matters of preserving a record than to personal expression. Thus, the calligraphy is in tight standard script. The painting, while generally acceptable within Wen's oeuvre, is not stylistically individual. We can attribute this to his attention to the model. Wen tells what he did:

Li Kung-lin's painting of "The Eighteen Sages of Mt. Lu" was completed in more than a month. I, starting and stopping (on my copy) for nearly half a month, am unable to resemble his (work) by one ten-thousandth. How shameful. (I) also recorded the *chi* at the end. Whether beautiful or ugly, skillful or awkward *(cho)*, viewers, I trust, will not laugh at it. Written in the Yü-lan t'ang on the eleventh day of the eighth month, 1532. Heng-chün. Wen Cheng-ming.

(tr. Ellen Johnston Laing)

The only aspect of style that is clearly at harmony with the artist's during the 1530s is a compositional one. He has crowded many forms into a small space. The result is that denial of depth, a conscious feel for surface that is a constantly recurring factor in Wen's art at this time. At best, there are tipped-up pockets of space on which the great heroes of the past are somewhat precariously placed.

As befits the subject a major interest in the fan rests with the event itself. Ellen Laing from her long-standing research into literary gatherings has kindly supplied this catalogue with just such an account:

"The Lotus Society," according to tradition, refers to an informal organization of eighteen secular and clerical followers of the monk Hui-yüan (334–417), who established a monastery on Mt. Lu. The earliest representation of these worthies was done by the Northern Sung artist Li Kung-lin in 1080, for his cousin Li Chung-yüan (T. Yüan-chung). Wen Cheng-ming's delineation of this subject is presumably based upon this now-lost work by Li Kung-lin. On the calligraphy face of the fan, Wen has inscribed the *Record (chi)* composed by Li Chung-yüan in 1081 describing members of the society and Li Kung-lin's pictorialization of it.

Frequently interwoven with factual information about men of substantial reputation and prestige are hearsay, myth, and legend. Today, scholars recognize as spurious many amusing tales and purportedly historical anecdotes centering on Hui-yüan's relationships with his gentry and ecclesiastical associates. One of the now discredited traditions, "The Eighteen Sages of the Lotus Society" is believed to be a fabrication of the late T'ang period, even though many of the individuals on its roster indeed were colleagues of Hui-yüan and some actually participated in his famous assembly before an image of Amitābha to vow to strive for rebirth in the Western Regions.[1]

Beginning in the eleventh century, however, both "The Eighteen Sages of the Lotus Society" (at times called "The White Lotus Society" or "The Eighteen Sages of Mt. Lu") and the *chi* by Li Chung-yüan became moderately popular subjects for painting and calligraphy (Wen's name is found in conjunction with these more than once),[2] but only a few illustrations of the theme survive. With the exception of a handscroll now in the Freer Gallery of Art, Washington, D. C., supposedly by Li Kung-lin but unrelated to Li Chung-yüan's *Record* and stylistically probably a late sixteenth-century work, the known depictions, closely linked by their adherence to a single general iconographic program, surely derive from a common model. Since all manners of minor liberties are taken, however, no two are absolutely identical. Wen Cheng-ming's fan is an abbreviation of this "standard" scheme.

At the upper right, the two men standing on a cliff-side path refer to an apocryphal incident: having sworn never to cross Tiger Stream, which marked the boundary of his monastic establishment, Hui-yüan, engrossed in conversation with the Taoist Lu Hsiu-ching while seeing him off, suddenly discovered he had inadvertently broken his self-imposed restriction. At the lower right, the poet Hsieh Ling-yün (385–433), who does not number among the eighteen sages but is included in all representations of them, arrives on horseback. Tradition has it that he assiduously sought acceptance into Hui-yüan's community but the latter considered Hsieh's mind to be too confused and denied him entry. Undaunted, Hsieh persisted in visiting the Mt. Lu retreat and ordered the construction there of lotus ponds (one is seen near the center of the painting). Hsieh's situation contrasts with that of another well-known versifier, T'ao Ch'ien (365–427), who also is not listed among the eighteen worthies proper, but is always present in "Lotus Society" portrayals. Although Hui-yüan repeatedly endeavored to detain him, T'ao refused to join the society and departed in his basket sedan-chair, used because he was afflicted with a disabling foot ailment.

Above T'ao, the Buddhist doctrine is expounded to four lay and monk auditors displaying varying degrees of interest and to a totally bored servant. Further to the right, three worshippers gather in front of a sculpture of Mañjuśrī, the Bodhisattva of Wisdom. The presence

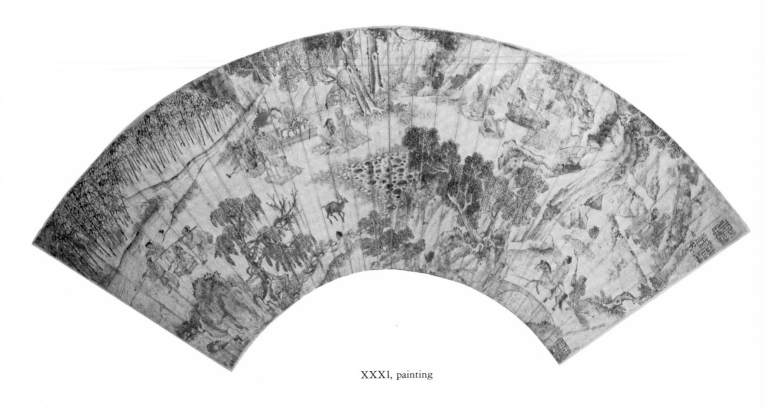

XXXI, painting

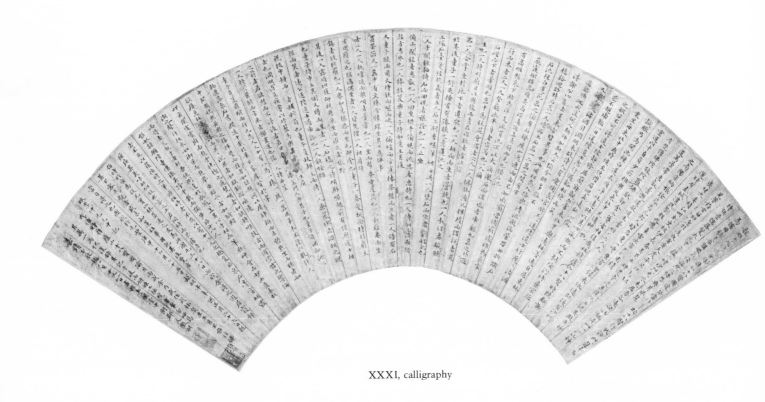

XXXI, calligraphy

of Mañjuśrī, where one might expect Amitābha, is explained by a somewhat fictionalized account of Hui-yüan's life wherein it is related he miraculously recovered a lost Asokan image of this Bodhisattva.[3]

The buck strolling near the stream and the monkey swinging in the branches serve to suggest not only the wilderness environment of Mt. Lu, but also the harmony existing there, in a religious context, between nature and man. But on the level of Buddhist symbolism, these two beasts have opposing connotations. Deer are associated with the Buddha's First Sermon, given at the Deer Park in Sarnath, and here perhaps this docile creature signifies the religiously disciplined spirit of man. The reverse of this is conveyed by the Buddhist simile: "The Sage has not the human mind which leaps from object to object like the ape in the tree."[4]

In the companion piece, the text of the *chi* by Li Chung-yüan, the author recounts a few of the supernatural events attending Hui-yüan's arrival on Mt. Lu and presents some brief sketches concerning the sages and the two "outsiders." He next turns to the painting itself, beginning with a description of the landscape passages and then identifying each person by name and how he is shown. Altogether, he says, there are thirty-eight figures. Near the end of the essay is an encomium of Li Kung-lin's art, and it is pointed out that he completed the picture in thirty-eight days.[5]

NOTES:

1. For a full account of Hui-yüan's achievements, see E. Zürcher, *The Buddhist Conquest of China* (Leiden: E. J. Brill, 1959), pp. 204-253; for an analysis of the data and arguments for the later invention of "The Eighteen Sages of the Lotus Society" as well as several other popular stories concerning Hui-yüan, see T'ang Yung-t'ung, *Han Wei Liang-Chin Nan-pei ch'ao fo-chiao shih,* 1938 (reprint ed., Taipei: The Commercial Press, 1962), I, pp. 266–270.

2. For example, (a) Wen inscribed Li's *Chi* on a "Lotus Society" hanging scroll by Li Kung-lin: Kao Shih-ch'i, *Chiang-ts'un hsiao-hsia lu* (n.p., 1693), ch. 1/pp. 22a–22b; Wu Sheng, *Ta-kuan lu* (Wu-chin, 1920), ch. 12/pp. 25a–27b. (b) Wen copied Li Kung-lin's painting: Chang Chou: ʿCh'ing-ho shu-hua fang, n.p., ch. 8/p. 56a (under Li Kung-lin); Ku Fu, *P'ing-sheng chuang-kuan* (Shanghai: Jen-min mei-shu, 1962), ch. 10/p. 84. (c) Wen collaborated with other artists on this theme: Pien Yung-yü, *Shih-ku t'ang shu-hua hui-k'ao* (Shanghai: Chien-ku shu-she, 1921), ch. 30/p. 43a; Chang Chao, et. al., *Pi-tien chu-lin,* 1744 (reprint ed., Taipei: National Palace Museum, 1971), 12/p. 140 (under Ch'iu Ying); Wang Chieh et al., *Pi-tien chu-lin hsü-pien,* 1793 (reprint ed., Taipei: National Palace Museum, 1971), 6/p. 263, done with Ch'iu Ying, also in *Ku-kung shu-hua lu* (1965), ch. 8/p. 134.

3. See Zürcher, *Buddhist Conquest,* p. 243 and note 41 and Alexander C. Soper, *Literary Evidence for Early Buddhist Art in China,* Artibus Asiae Supplementum XIX (Ascona, 1959), p. 31.

4. Walter Liebenthal, *The Book of Chao,* Monumenta Serica Monograph XIII (Peking: The Catholic University of Peking, 1948), p. 82, n. 316.

5. A second *chi* relating to Li Kung-lin's "Lotus Society" painting was written by his contemporary, Ch'ao Pu-chih (*Chi-lei chi,* Ssu-pu ts'ung-k'an ed., ch. 30/pp. 8b–10b).

INSCRIPTION OF THE ARTIST: translated above in text

SEALS OF THE ARTIST:

T'ing-yün sheng	[painting: I/1]
Wen Cheng-ming yin	[painting: I/2]
Cheng-ming	[calligraphy: I/1]

SEALS:

K'ung Kuang-t'ao (nineteenth century), T. Hsiao-t'ang, from Nan-hai Kuangtung, collector

Kuang-t'ao	[painting: I/3]
Shao-t'ang mo-yüan	[calligraphy: I/2]

XXXII. SCHOLAR FISHING

No date
Folding fan, ink on gold paper, 7¾" high and 21¹⁵/₁₆" wide
    (19.5 x 55.7 cm.)
Signature and seal of the artist
Jean-Pierre Dubosc, Paris and Tokyo

This fan presents a striking composition that is brushed with authority both in its use of ink and the once-strong addition of color against shining gold: the anchoring of the design at one end, the clear space of the gold paper at the other, and the direct view of a selected part of nature are all ultimately related to the late Sung, when the so-called "one-corner" composition was a favorite device. However, motifs and brushwork are completely Wen Cheng-ming. His signature and seal float on the gold space like some reassuring sun for the two conversing scholars below.

For centuries, now, the rustic fisherman had been a symbol for withdrawal, for the life of contemplation, for something of real importance as opposed to the show of a dust-filled world. As Wen wrote of a garden angler (no. LI, EE):

You must know that he who stretches his line
Is not one who desires fish.

Fishing thus becomes yet another scholarly "activity." The purpose was not fish. That view is maintained here where the two figures are marvelously indifferent to what is happening at the end of a pole, but completely absorbed in each other beneath the benediction of an old cypress. Two lofty pines and one deciduous tree help complete the limited forest. Scholarly removal is accentuated by an intervening stream; the strong layers of rock at the right firmly anchor the scene. In a rather exact reversal of normal expectation, the further one goes (right to left) from solid forms, the closer one gets to importance, the thin, unsubstantial end —that incidental gesture of pole and line—which is the meaning.

Wen's simple signature seals it. Again, it is very personal art. As with the seven junipers, here is a beautiful screen of form within which the play of solid and void are major components of a tense excellence. Despite the absence of an inscribed date, there is assurance that aesthetic purposes are consistent with this decade.

SEAL OF THE ARTIST:
    Cheng-ming   [painting: I/1]

SEALS:
Ho Kuan-wu (twentieth century Hong Kong collector)
    Man ——— hsin-shang   [painting: II/1]
    Kuan-wu chen-ts'ang   [painting: II/2]
    T'ien-ch'i shu-wu   [painting: II/3]
    P'an-yü Ho shih Ling-pi shan-fang ts'ang   [painting: II/4]

BIBLIOGRAPHY:
Dubosc, *Les quatre* (1966), no. 10.

XXXII
See frontispiece for detail

XXXIII. LISTENING TO THE BAMBOO

(T'ing chu t'u)
No date
Hanging scroll, ink on Sung sutra paper, 38″ high and 12″ long
(94.5 x 30.5 cm.)
Inscription and seals of the artist
Jean-Pierre Dubosc, Paris and Tokyo

Here is the great traditional "abstract" theme of Chinese painting—ink bamboo. It at once reveals the purity and strength of brush-and-ink itself, yet at the same time is a theme which in the very crispness of its art parallels exactly the brittle enduring green that nature itself gives to this extraordinary grass.

The abstractions of Wen's brilliant *Listening to the Bamboo* might be emphasized by suggesting that it may be viewed with satisfaction from any edge of its format. That the artist's way is as presently hung —rather than upside down or sideways—is affirmed by the placing of his two seals, which can only be read correctly in this position. The bamboo, with its main thrust to the left, turns back to partially enfold or point in their direction along the lower right edge. Other seals, with the exception of the faint sutra-paper seal in the upper center, must be mentally erased in order to grasp the painting's original fresh precision.

Beginning at the lower right, somewhat lost in the tangle of forms, two main stems cross each other. Both end abruptly, one early, the other extending through most of the leaves and thus becoming the painting's central core. Leaves, however, do not hang exactly from a stem but rather are joined by implication. It is a tense, sometimes explosive grouping. We may read this as natural growth, but it is exactly the artist's own rhythmic arrangement. Ink is generally lighter at the base where the moist, varied quality of its placement is clearly visible. Often semi-transparent, we can follow the overlap of strokes, the building of structure. From these paler beginnings we move to increasingly tense spears of black. Always, however,. because of the way the moist ink has reacted to the heavily sized paper, there is a spontaneously varied texture to each leaf. The composition moves to a heightened intensity. In the end is the sharp exactness of selected dark thrusts of ink flashing across pure paper to final thin clean points—rare as the pure and noble sound described in the poem above.

Like the twisted shapes of *The Seven Junipers* (no. XXX), this bamboo lives in an airless world. Although there is the notion of thrust and counter-thrust, the stem does not bend but rather shifts direction at a joint. There is no easy flowing wind to return us directly and comfortably to nature. As with the junipers, Wen has made his own world. It is his art.

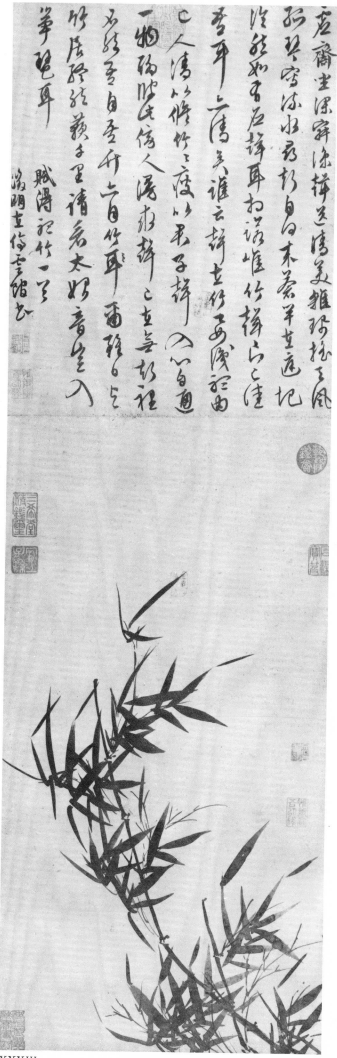

XXXIII

This overriding sense of the artist's skill and craft is a major aspect of Wen Cheng-ming's painting in the 1530s. As we have already done with *The Seven Junipers,* it is well to compare *Listening to the Bamboo* with still other paintings at this time, particularly those close to this subject in the National Palace Museum in Taiwan. *Mallow* of 1533 (fig. 17) shares with *Listening to the Bamboo* not only the fact of working in subtle values of ink alone, but also the almost abstract arrangement of tense pointed shapes placed like cutouts on space-less ground beneath a full block of calligraphy. It, too, is a composition which builds in intensity and importance as one "grows" into the upper part of the painting, an effect which also may be noted in

the *Rock and Chrysanthemums* (no. XXXV) in this exhibition. In 1534 Wen painted a tall thin bamboo in red ink on blue paper (fig. 18). While format and color create a far different effect, here is the same sense of a conscious placing of selected leaves, the play of outward pointing shapes; and in the thick and thin of their strokes one can find close parallels to *Listening to the Bamboo.* Also the strokes that create the stems are clearly analogous. Finally there is a bamboo album of 1538. Its leaves move with rich freedom through a whole range of historical modes. The detail of one leaf might be cited (fig. 19) as showing the same dark strength and stroke form in a thin stem and a similar—although subtly less exact—brushing of the leaves themselves.

Wen's calligraphy, which writes out a prose-poem about bamboo, is on a piece of the same sutra paper as the painting, and the undated signature is followed by the same two seals as on the painting. They seem, thus, to belong together—a fact which is strengthened by the rather special character of the calligraphy. The calligraphy clearly harmonizes with the brilliance of the bamboo below. One could almost say "dances" in harmony with it. There is a special elegance in the sharp black's quick shifts from thick to thin on the smooth paper, as can be seen especially in some of the long tensile curving or angled strokes. Often one can isolate a stroke and realize its relation to some of the thinner, more consciously "calligraphic" leaves or stems of the bamboo. Broadly speaking, the calligraphy seems not inconsistent with such writing as can be found from the period of the letters of the 1520s (no. XVIII) well into the 1530s and as late, let us say, as the inscription on the bamboo paintings of 1538. The seal, *Wei keng-yin wu i chiang,* is a seal that we can find with confidence only from the late twenties on (see no. XXII). To relate this sprig of bamboo to the conscious artistic elegance of the 1530s becomes thus all the more a justified historical appraisal.

INSCRIPTION BY THE ARTIST:
 In the empty studio sitting in deep loneliness;
 A cool sound sending pure beauty.
 The mixed pendants swing in the wind;
 The solitary *ch'in* like running water.
 Where is that sound from?
 The green poles in the courtyard.
 Clear and light like an echo,
 The sound and ears in tune.
 The sound of bamboo now very beautiful;
 My ears are also clear.
 Who says the sound is in the bamboo?
 To know it depends on oneself.
 A pure person is like a tall bamboo;
 A thin bamboo is like the noble man.
 When the sound enters, the mind is clear;
 A thing is just that and this.
 A bystander carelessly searching for sound
 Is already within no sound.
 On the contrary, I am still I,
 Bamboo is still bamboo.
 Although each day living with bamboo,
 Still the music is a thousand miles away.

17. Wen Cheng-ming, *Mallow,* 1533. National Palace Museum, Taipei

Look at sound's most ancient source:
Did it enter a zither or a lute?
Composing a poem on *Listening to the Bamboo*. Cheng-ming wrote it at T'ing-yün kuan.

(tr. Ling-yün Shih Liu)

SEALS OF THE ARTIST:
  Wen Cheng-ming yin   [painting: II/1]
                                    [calligraphy: II/1]
  Wei keng-yin wu i chiang   [painting: II/2]
                                      [calligraphy: II/2]

SEALS:
Ch'ien-lung emperor (r. 1736–1795)
  Ch'ien-lung chien-shang   [painting: I/1]
  Shih-ch'ü pao-chi   [painting: I/2]
  Ch'ien-lung yü-lan chih pao   [calligraphy: I/1]
  San-hsi t'ang ching-chien hsi   [painting: III/1]
  I tzu-sun   [painting: III/2]
Unidentified
  Lu-ho Chang I ts'ang shu-hua chi   [painting: III/3]
  Wen Ch'i chen-wan   [mounting: I/1]

REMARKS: The poem is recorded in *Wen Shih* (1934–35 ed.), ch. 3/pp. 5b–6a and in *Wen Cheng-ming hui-kao* (1929), ch. 7/p. 85b.

19. Wen Cheng-ming, *Bamboo and Rock*, detail. Fifth leaf from the album *Bamboo Paintings*, 1538. National Palace Museum, Taipei

18. Wen Cheng-ming, *Bamboo*, 1534. National Palace Museum, Taipei

XXXIV. BAMBOO, ORCHIDS, ROCK, AND CALLIGRAPHY

Running script
No date
Handscroll, ink on paper, 11¹/₁₆″ high and 47″ long (28.5 x 119.5 cm.)
Signature and seals of the artist
Worcester Art Museum, Charlotte E. W. Buffington Fund

A direct reading of Wen Cheng-ming's inscription after this painting tells us that this scroll began, not with its painting, but with its calligraphy:

I wrote for Shih Chu several poems that I had previously composed. When the calligraphy was finished, I saw that there was ink left in the ink-stone and so I also sketched this.

In his colophon toward the end of the scroll, the modern Shanghai painter and critic Wu Hu-fan points out that there is no way of telling when calligraphy and painting were cut to make two, but from the appearance of the paper there seems to be no question of their belonging together.

The poems that Wen writes are, with some variations, recorded in Wen's collected writings. While none is dated, they are assembled in a general chronological sequence and the latest of the poems are found shortly after 1527. The calligraphy is, indeed, brilliant, and although less flamboyant than that over *Listening to the Bamboo* (no. XXXIII), it has much of the same swift varied sureness. The

same characters in each display a similar touch.

The painting itself is of a style consistent with the period of the 1530s. About it there is an inescapable sense of precision that rides with each exact stroke as it helps weave a close net of bending patterns. One cannot avoid comparing it to the well-known hanging scroll *Orchid and Bamboo* in the National Palace Museum (fig. 20), likewise undated. The latter is on the same highly sized sutra paper as was *Listening to the Bamboo,* and hence the ink quality differs from this handscroll. *Orchid and Bamboo* is also subtly freer in execution and in this respect comes closer to the album of 1538, which has already been cited (fig. 19). But throughout, forms closely parallel the Worcester handscroll in all major elements: orchid blossoms and leaves, bamboo stems, bamboo leaves, grasses, ground plants, rocks, and earth texture-strokes. Compositionally it presents the same shallow space so that much is made of the surface of the paper. Within the shallow stage, the orchid is behind bamboo and grasses as is appropriate for this plant of hidden fragrance and discrete withdrawal, traditional symbol of rare friendship.

Symbolic of something intensely personal, it is a theme to reflect the person of the artist. Here Wen's art is consistent with the outward brilliance of the thirties. It is also exactly tied to the art of Chao Meng-fu, not only in such strokes as the "flying white" that defines rock and land, but also in the subject itself, the "still life" within nature that was so important to Chao and his time.

XXXIV

CALLIGRAPHY OF THE ARTIST: Nine poems for Shih Chu (see remarks); following the poems is a brief notation:
Several poems I had previously done sent to Mr. Shih Chu. Please instruct. Cheng-ming bowing his head, again offers.

INSCRIPTION OF THE ARTIST (on painting): translated in text.

SEALS OF THE ARTIST:
Wen Cheng-ming yin	[calligraphy: II/1]
Cheng-chung	[calligraphy: II/2]

COLOPHONS AND SEALS:
Wu Hu-fan (1894?–1969); dated 1931
Ch'ou-i ch'ang-nien	[colophon: I/1]
Wu shih t'u-shu chi	[painting: IV/1]
Hu-fan shen-ting	[painting: IV/2]

Wu Hua-yüan (twentieth century); colophons dated 1942 (two), 1947 (one) No seal
Hsü Ch'uan-cheng (twentieth century)
Po-mei so ts'ang	[painting: I/1]
Te-ch'ing Hsü Ch'uan-cheng Po-mei fu	[painting: II/2]
Ts'eng-tsai Hsü shih Po-mei shih	[painting: IV/3]
Po-mei pi-wan	[calligraphy seam: I/1]
	[calligraphy seam: II/1]
Te-ch'ing Hsü Ch'uan-cheng chen-ts'ang yin	[calligraphy: III/2]
Hsü Hsi-tao t'ang t'u-shu	[calligraphy: III/1]

Wang Chi-ch'ien (twentieth century)
Wang shih Chi-ch'ien ts'eng-kuan	[painting: II/1]

P'eng Kung (twentieth century)
Kung fu pi-chi	[painting: III/1]

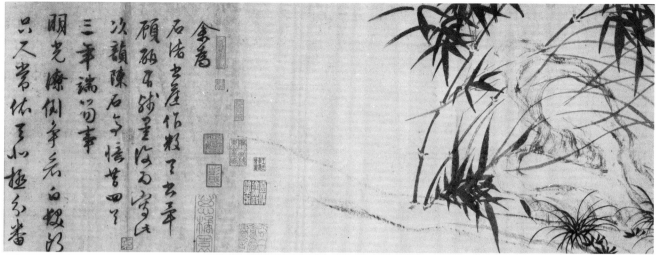

XXXIV, detail. Inscription and beginning of poems

P'eng Lang [painting: IV/4]
P'eng Kung-fu [calligraphy seam: III/1]

Unidentified
Hsüan-pai chai t'u-shu chi [painting: II/3]
[calligraphy: I/1]
[calligraphy: III/4]

Wan-chü yüan [painting: IV/5]
Lung-hsi Huai-tung lu ts'ang [painting: III/2]
Ku Kuo-wan yin [calligraphy: III/3]
Ch'en-hsi [calligraphy seam: I/2]

REMARKS: The nine poems were all composed earlier on different

occasions. The first four are recorded in *Fu-t'ien* (1968 ed.), ch. 12/2b–3a (pp. 306–307); just before them is a date, 1527. The poems follow the rhymes of his friend, Ch'en Lu-nan, with whom he visited the Western Gardens (see no. XX). They are related to Wen's Peking experience and imperial splendor. The fifth and sixth poems are recorded in ch. 3/8b (p. 144). They tell respectively of a sleepless night and the first cold of winter. They date from about 1511. The last three poems are recorded in ch. 7/5a-b (pp. 217–218); a few pages before these is a date 1517. One is related to the year's end; the other two are entitled "Southern Pavilion."

BIBLIOGRAPHY:
"Oriental Art Recently Acquired" (1961), p. 46, fig. 38.
Worcester Art Museum, *News Bulletin* (1962), XXVII, no. 5.

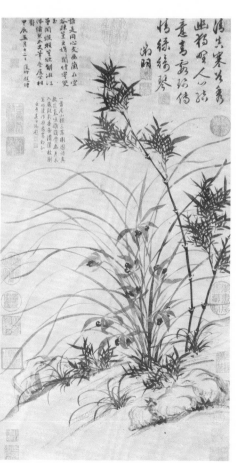

20. Wen Cheng-ming, *Orchid and Bamboo.*
National Palace·Museum, Taipei

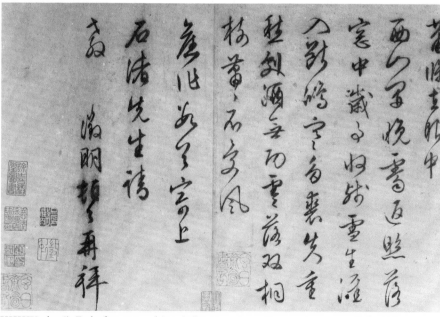

XXXIV, detail. End of poems and inscription

133

XXXV. ROCK AND CHRYSANTHEMUMS

(Tui chü t'u)
Dated 1535 by accompanying colophon
Hanging scroll, ink on paper, 18⅞" high and 10⁷/₁₆" wide (60.5 x 25.0 cm.)
Signature and seals of the artist
The Arthur M. Sackler Foundation

From the poetry at the top of the scroll by Wen's friend Hsü Chin, we can be assured that these chrysanthemums are another way of expressing friendship. The flowers, blooming late and in their own time with rare and aloof fragrance, stand for the uniqueness of a special relationship. They are also joined to the familiar pastime of drinking tea.

They have been carefully published by Marilyn and Shen Fu. Further, we have already referred to the scroll in discussing the painting of Shen Chou (no. VII) and the early work of Wen himself (no. XII). Here it would be redundant to further labor what has been said, but the flowers should be specifically viewed in the context of Wen's painting during the 1530s.

21. Wen Cheng-ming, *Plaintain and Rock.* Seventh leaf from the album *Flowers,* 1533. National Palace Museum, Taipei

It now, perhaps, becomes all the more apparent how significant at this time is the notion of art itself. Thus the treatment of a tree grove, a line of cypress branches, a screen of trees in a fishing scene, the pattern of bamboo, even, as we shall see, a limited garden retreat, have in common the factor of conscious creation that delights in taut arrangements on a surface and the skillful display of a well-learned craft. Subtly, this is not a relaxed nature but a nature which is revealed in the tense spontaneity of an artist's personal inspiration. Wen

expressed this verbally in painting other flowers for Hsü Chin just two years before (fig. 21), when flowers were physically before him, but, as translated by Anne Clapp, "At the moment I took up the brush I was only aware of the force of inspiration."[1]

In the sure patterns of such paintings as this modest scroll one has visible proof of that inspiration's result.

NOTE:
1. Clapp, *Wen Cheng-ming* (1975), p. 32. The colophon is printed in *Ku-kung shu-hua lu* (1965), ch. 6/pp. 46–47.

SEALS OF THE ARTIST:
Wen Cheng-ming yin	[painting: III/1]
Heng-shan	[painting: III/2]

COLOPHON AND SEALS:
Hsü Chin (fifteenth–sixteenth century), friend of Wen Cheng-ming; dated 1535:

> Open shutters reveal the fading dusk
> Solemnly around the courtyard settles chilling frost.
> A gentle wind sways the slender bamboo
> And rustles vines near the room.
>
> Together we sat in the studio
> Leisurely viewing the chrysanthemums blooming in profusion.
> Their flowering late makes them all the more aloof and appealing,
> Leaving a fragrance to charm only the secluded ones.
>
> I tilt the teapot to pour *Lu-ya* ("dew-sprout") tea.
> We picked it on the south side of the hill and brought it
>   to the foot of the mountain.
> There was the essence of bubbling spring and stones;
> Stalks and leaves were cut for their autumn fragrance.
> The clay brazier brings the water to the boil
> And with one sip—a feeling refreshing as a shower!

Written in autumn of the year *i-wei* (1535) with Mr. Wen as we sat in the Yin-pai studio enjoying chrysanthemums and tasting tea. Hsü Chin.

(tr. Marilyn and Shen Fu)

Chia-hui	[painting: II/1]

Feng Ch'ao-jan (twentieth century), Shanghai collector
Ch'ao-jan hsin-shang	[painting: I/2]

Ma Chi-tso (twentieth century), Hong Kong collector
Chi-tso	[painting: IV/1]

Wu Hu-fan (1894?–1969), Shanghai collector
Mei-ching shu-wu pi-chi	[painting: IV/2]

Unidentified
Ching-chai hsin-shang	[painting: I/3]
Po-yüan shen-ting	[painting: I/1]

REMARKS:
Hsü Chin (T. Tzu-jung, 1498 *chü-jen,* 1505 *chin-shih*) was a close friend of Wen Cheng-ming. The two traveled together *(Wen shih,* ch. 6/p. 38b); Wen wrote poems relating to Hsü as well as a sacrificial writing for him (see *Fu-t'ien,* ch. 11/pp. 5b–6a, pp. 294–295; ch. 24/pp. 8a–8b, pp. 561–562). Hsü's collection contained works that Wen greatly admired such as Chao Po-chü's *Later Red Cliff* and Chao Meng-fu's *Hun-fan* calligraphy, which have Wen's colophons of 1546 and 1535 respectively. Both are now in Taipei's National Palace Museum.

Yin-pai studio, mentioned in Hsü's poem, possibly belonged to Hsü Chin.

BIBLIOGRAPHY:
Fu, *Studies* (1974), no. 2, pp. 82–85.

采隐原夕靡庭宇薦
霜蕭瘦竹入踈風颯
颯響蘿屋軒中一
歷地摺迂敧襄菊
開晚更淒斷為芳媚
幽榻傾壺出霧芽摘
米防挹蕉中有泉后
精打葉剪秋馥玉斝
擊漱濤一斟蘇絪沐
乙未秋與文君生蔭白軒
對菊試若賦此 徐緒

XXXVI. BOATMAN BY A CLIFF: RETURNING FROM WEST MOUNTAIN

(Hsi-shan kuei-chou)
Dated 1536
Hanging scroll, ink on paper, 23¹³/₁₆″ high and 9¹³/₁₆″ wide (60.5 x 25.0 cm.)
Inscription, signature, and seals of the artist
Charles A. Drenowatz, Zurich

This hanging scroll is not exactly to be matched by the major portion of Wen's existing work. But if it is accepted in the category of a swift and freely executed sketch, the relationship to Wen becomes plausible and for the exact understanding of a wide-ranging scholar-painter even necessary.

Certainly it is difficult to fault the calligraphy which tells of the circumstances.

On a summer day in 1536 I was returning from West Mountain. The breeze was light and the water almost waveless. The boat stable as a room. Suddenly feeling a great desire to paint, I playfully did this picture of what I saw on the way. This was on the third day of the fourth month.

If, as we saw in discussing the last painting, the notion of spontaneous creation is a key to the ideals of Wen's art, it is here, and to a degree where the freedom is outwardly visible. This is a painting essentially unrelated to the accepted strictures of Yüan style or even to the pressure for a kind of orthodoxy related to involvement with a friend. The brush plays easily. No one was looking over Wen's shoulder. He was simply recording an impression of what he saw: a fisherman, a few straight reeds, a bridge, a cliff from which extends the brush-play of some "trees."

If this was a general time when Wen displayed a certain virtuoso surface design, that, too, is here: the dramatic rise of the cliff, curve of the boat, and the fisherman with his split poles answered by the counter-curve of the bridge and the forked shape of its supports; the play of tree-trunk, twig, and vine, the spiky grass, the swift free ink-dot.

Chu-tsing Li has written a careful analysis of the painting and within the freedom of the scroll he points out certain special manners of the brush: axe strokes, flying white—adding that such matters as composition and atmospheric effect help suggest a close relation to Wen's contemporaries in the so-called Che School. As such it can be compared to Chang Lu's *Fisherman* (fig. 22). Chang Lu died two years after Wen's scroll was painted. That it was typical to be atypical is one of the marks of Wen Cheng-ming's great range. Personally free in a very Ming sense, this work is a painting which has its real historical base in the late Sung and the immediate view of a particular scene, an aesthetic which lay at the heart of so much painting at that time. Distinct, however, from Sung-inspired works that we have noted earlier (nos. II F, XVI, XXVII) is the virtuoso message of the brush itself—a clear revelation of technique which is consistent with both Wen's approach to painting at this time and, incidentally, the aims of the Che School.

INSCRIPTION BY THE ARTIST: translated above in text

SEALS OF THE ARTIST:
Cheng-ming	[painting: II/1]
Heng-shan	[painting: II/2]

SEALS:
Cantonese collector (twentieth century)
Huang shih Huai-hsüan t'ang ts'ang	[painting: III/1]

Unidentified (a Ma family in Su-chou)
Pao-sung lou chen-ts'ang	[painting: I/1]
Ma Erh-liang chen-shang	[painting: IV/1]
San-fu chien-ting Ch'ui-yü hou k'un	[painting: IV/2]
Ch'ang-chou Ma Yü-ch'ui tzu Ting-san hao T'ing ——— chien-ts'ang shu-hua	[painting: IV/3]

BIBLIOGRAPHY:
Li, *A Thousand Peaks* (1974), I, pp. 58–61, II, fig. 8.

22. Chang Lu (ca. 1464–ca. 1538), *Fisherman.* Gokoku-ji, Tokyo

XXXVII. THE CASSIA GROVE STUDIO

(*Ts'ung-kuei chai t'u*)
No date
Handscroll, ink and color on paper, 12½″ high and 22″ long (31.3 x 56.0 cm.)
Inscription, signature, and seal of the artist
Jean-Pierre Dubosc, Paris and Tokyo

Similar to two other brief handscroll paintings in this exhibition (nos. V, XLVIII), the gem-like *Cassia Grove Studio* is the painting of an auspicious idea for a friend and fellow scholar. More than likely, it is also the depiction of a specific garden. But that has yet to be identified. The late Ming connoisseur Chang Ch'ou has recorded the painting, indicating a long list of early colophon writers, most from K'un-shan. On the present scroll only one survives: the first, that of Ku Ting-ch'en (1473–1540). Chang quotes only one of the poems. From what we have it is clear that the poems, directed to a Mr. Cheng, are quite literally flowery metaphors for official examination success. Plucking the cassia indicated that success. Specifically, since it is a fall flower, it related to the provincial examinations which were traditionally held in the autumn. As the red vine leaves indicate, this painting is an autumnal scene.

Somewhat unexpectedly the scroll, undated, comes into focus within the range of Wen's work when we compare it to the free sketch of 1536. The introductory cliff at the right is a kind of horizontal version of the similar but sketchier and more dramatic cliff that towers over the boatman on that vertical scroll. Among other paintings recently discussed, the same kind of introduction is found in the fan, *Watching the Waterfall* of 1532 (no. XXIX).[1]

This motif is distinguished not alone by overlapping layers of piled-up rock (edged by accents of grasses) and cliff-faces that begin a little back from the lower border and extend to reach or fade into the top edge, but by a marked overhang and the device of crossed horizontal trees that cling precariously to the vertical or undercut cliff.

Comparing closely the brushwork on *The Cassia Grove Studio* rocks with that on the *Boatman* cliff, there is in the former a subtly greater sense of precision—as befits the subject. But there are also axe-strokes and flying-white. There is, too, the occasional use of a long vertical stroke. The interplay between paper and ink, between light and dark, creates a vibrant, even shimmering effect of surface.

Apparently, however, we must place the scroll in time a little earlier than the 1536 date of the *Boatman* sketch. Chang Ch'ou's recording lists among other writers Wen's friend, Huang Yün, whom we have met rather early (cf. no. XI). But more important is the name Ku Ch'ien, for Ku

Ch'ien died in 1534. Clearly, *The Cassia Grove Studio* must antedate the *Boatman*.

As with the *Boatman,* however, the handscroll is a specific view, and in keeping with this period it is a rather shallow view. We are very much aware of the play of rock surfaces, the patterns of tree leaves and even the calligraphy upon the paper's surface. But still it is a view—the view of a gentleman's garden. It shows us the retreat of simple overlapping blocks of architecture within that garden, the gentleman himself and his servant. It is not incidental riverside genre, but "serious" painting reflecting the heart of the life most prized by Wen Cheng-ming and his class. The other retreat seen so far in this exhibition, *The Study by Old Trees* (no. XXIV), was merely an "awkward" personal symbol. Here Wen is painting for a patron who wants a portrait, really no less than a personal portrait, for the garden is but an extension of the man. Indeed, we scarcely see the man at all. His form is cut by the wall of the house. He makes no effort to look at us. But everywhere we are to read his presence, of course, in rocks and trees and grasses—but nature for this society was not wilderness. What was important was the conscious placing of the self in nature and by that placing making man and nature one.

Thus this painted view tells us about the man because it tells us what in nature he has marked out for himself. He is withdrawn. Our entrance is blocked by the mass of rock already discussed, in which are suggestions of hidden mountain paths. This "mountain" partly enfolds the architecture. The architecture and the fence clearly define the limits of the place the man has set. There is learning. The ends of scrolls peek out from beneath the rock and within the open window of the house. Even the servant helps reveal importance—the nobility of the man. Standing as a kind of guardian protecting his master's presence, by the very fact of his lesser though more clearly revealed form he exalts the more hidden "majesty" within. Insofar as we see—as opposed to sense—the major figure, his gaze is directed toward the tall and noble vine-wrapped pine which compositionally balances the opening rock-cliff. Only cliff and pine are tall enough to be cut by the top of the painting.

Judging by the name of the studio, the other trees must be cassia trees, a green-leafed tree which when in fall bloom has tiny flowers of great fragrance. Since an awareness of the scent precedes a visual awareness of the flowers, they are thought of in terms of hidden fragrance. Here, while there is no attempt physically to reveal the blossoms, there is, indeed, fragrance in color. Subdued cool and warm tones increase the sense of idyllic perfection. The red of the scholar's gown and the autumnal red of the vine leaves on the pine help accent the painting and strengthen its seasonal and psychic focus.

XXXVII

Wen's brief calligraphy helps to emphasize the completeness of the painting by giving it an even surer beginning and a more exact end. At the right in ancient clerical script he gives us the title. At the left is Wen's own signature and seal with the name Tzu-ch'ung, whose portrait we have seen. As already mentioned, colophons contemporary with the painting that once were placed after it referred to a Mr. Cheng. As yet we do not know exactly who was Cheng Tzu-ch'ung. We only know how at one time his compatriots saw him.

NOTE:
1. The motif, however, is not unique to this period. It is found on a large scroll, *Scholar's Leisure at Valley's End,* dated 1519, in the Palace Museum, Taipei (*Ku-kung shu-hua lu* [1965], ch. 5/p. 380).

INSCRIPTION BY THE ARTIST:
Cheng-ming painted (this) for Tzu-ch'ung.

SEAL OF THE ARTIST:
T'ing-yün sheng   [painting: II/1]

COLOPHONS AND SEALS:
Ku Ting-ch'en (1473–1540), T. Chiu-ho, from K'un-shan, Kiangsu; undated
Wen Ting (1766–1852), from Hsiu-shui, Chekiang; dated 1846, third month
  Wen Ting   [colophon: I/1]
  Ch'ien-lung ping-hsü sheng   [colophon: I/2]
T'ang I-fen (1778–1853), T. Yü-sheng, from Wu-chin, Kiangsu; dated 1832, seventh month, seventeenth day
  I-fen   [colophon: I/1]
  Yü-sheng   [colophon: I/2]
Yü Yo (nineteenth century), T. Tzu-chün, from Wu-chin, Kiangsu; dated 1838, autumn, seventh month
  Li-che Ou-yin   [colophon: I/1]
  Tzu-chün   [colophon: II/1]
  Kuei lu   [colophon: II/2]

Wu Yung-kuang (1773–1843), T. Shih-yün shan-jen, from Nan-hai, Kuangtung; dated 1840, seventh month
  Wu Yung-kuang yin   [colophon: I/1]
  Shih-yün   [colophon: I/2]
Chang Chien (1768–1850), T. Ch'iu-shui, from Wu-hsing, Chekiang; dated 1842, autumn
  Chang Chien chih yin   [colophon: I/1]
Chiang Pao-ling (ca. 1821–ca. 1850), T. Ch'in-tung i-shih, from Ch'ang-shu, Kiangsu; dated 1829
  Ch'in-tung   [colophon: I/1]
  Ch'en Pao-ling yin   [colophon: II/1]
  Tzu-yen   [colophon: II/2]
Ts'ao Chung; dated 1836
Yang Hsieh (1781–1850), T. Lung-shih, from Wu-chiang, Kiangsu; dated 1841, fourth month
  Hsieh   [colophon: I/1]
  Hsin-ch'ou jen-feng hsin-ch'ou nien   [colophon: I/2]
Yin Shu-po (1769–1847), T. Yün-lou, from Chia-hsing, Chekiang; dated 1842, first lunar month, fourteenth day
  Yin Shu-po yin   [colophon: I/1]
  Man-ch'ing   [colophon: I/2]
Shen T'ao; dated 1847
  Pao-weng   [colophon: I/1]
  Hsiao-fu shan-kuan   [colophon: I/2]
Weng Lo (1790–1849), T. Mu-chung, from Wu-chiang, Kiangsu; dated 1842, spring, second month
  Weng Lo yin   [colophon: I/1]
  Mu-chung   [colophon: I/2]
Chang P'ei-tun (ca. 1821–ca. 1850), T. Yen-ch'iao, from Wu-hsien, Kiangsu; dated 1843
  —— *shan ju hua*   [colophon: I/1]
  P'ei-tun   [colophon: II/1]
  Yen-ch'iao   [colophon: II/2]
Unidentified
  Wang ——   [painting: I/1]
  Shou-ts'ang   [painting: I/2]
  Shou-yang Chang shih shu-hua chi   [painting: I/3]
  Wu Mei-yin chia-ts'ang yin   [painting: II/2]
  Chien   [painting: II/3]
  Chien   [T'ang I-fen's colophon: I/3]

BIBLIOGRAPHY:
Chang Ch'ou (fl. 1616), *Chen-chi* (1918 ed.), I, pp. 55b–56a.

Late Maturity
1540–1549

XXXVIII. PEACH BLOSSOM SPRING

(*T'ao-hua yüan chi t'u*)
Dated 1542, spring, third month, sixth day
Folding fan, ink and blue-green color on paper with gold ground,
   8³/₁₆" high and 21⅝" wide (20.6 x 54.2 cm.)
Inscription, signature, and seal of the artist
Jean-Pierre Dubosc, Paris and Tokyo

To see Wen's mature art moving with the rhythm of decades is perhaps somewhat misleading since living is a continuous process. But at the very least, it is convenient. History to have meaning must be seen in patterns. After all, Wen's life started at the beginning of one decade. It ended at the close of another. To leave the 1530s for the 1540s does take us to subtly differing styles. Two of his best-known masterpieces, from the National Palace Museum in Taiwan, come from this decade: the incomparable still and lovely *Spring in Kiang-nan* of 1547 and the tense, vigorous *Old Trees by a Cold Waterfall* of 1549. Both were exhibited in this country during the early sixties.[1]

With the mention of such masterpieces we can expect this decade to reveal a rather special excellence. Wen is in his seventies. There is no longer any question of youth. The revival of his skills in the 1530s often brought a new kind of technical brilliance. Now that can be more easily allied to traditional views of nature. Generally, Wen's painting becomes more spacious.

This confident fan of the spring of 1542 is in its strong spare lines rather beautifully selective. For the complex story of its subject it is amazingly uncluttered. There is a clear sense of placement, a beautiful counterbalance between the tight black screen of calligraphy on the right and the angled landscape on the left—the "weight" of two kinds of form. But perhaps of special importance is the somewhat contrary revelation of depth, so that despite the pull of surface, right and left, there is an even, believable recession across water to far exact mountains which anchors us deeply in the center. The importance of the calligraphy is, of course, in its literary meaning, but visually it adds compositional complexity. Without it space would extend to the right and the whole would be a straightforward single-corner composition like *Scholar Fishing* (no. XXXII).

The surface of the fan is somewhat damaged. Color on what is essentially a so-called blue-green landscape has lost its pristine quality. More than on most fans, one detects exactly the darkened surfaces of the slots where once the pointed bamboo spokes of the frame fitted into the folding fan. The gold surface is a little abraded. But through

this antique wear the basic sureness of the original conception holds.

The subject is drawn from antiquity. It is T'ao Ch'ien's (365–427) story—translated in full below—of the fisherman of Wu-ling who, following the peach blossoms, came to a mysterious opening in a cliff which led to an ideal land. When he returned to tell about it and again searched with others for it, the entrance no longer could be found (cf. the first poem on no. XXII). It was no less than the quest for an enduring world which was, after all, the real goal of the scholar-painter's life. Elusiveness did not destroy it, but confirmed the nature of its reality. The popularity of the theme in Suchou at this time is suggested by paintings of it from the hand of Wen's contemporary, Ch'iu Ying. Two such handscrolls exist in this country, one in The Art Institute of Chicago and the other in Boston's Museum of Fine Arts.

There as here the subject is clothed in the basically ancient style of the blue-green landscape. Wen's calligraphy as well relates to similar antiquity. The model for this particular standard script goes back to Wang Hsi-chih (321–379). In this fan, however, the painting style must be thought of as coming from antiquity through Chao Meng-fu. Without finding an exact surviving parallel, archaic brevities seen here can, however, be attributed to him and, incidentally, are not far from those in Chao's elder contemporary teacher and friend, Ch'ien Hsüan. We know that the two could be linked together in Wen's mind. In Wen's copy of a Chao Meng-fu figure painting he speaks not only of following Chao but also, in respect to color, the art of Ch'ien Hsüan.[2] In this fan, aside from spatial parallels, a particular Ch'ien Hsüan–derived feature as we know it in existing landscapes is the use of deliberately placed extended moist ink lines for the edges of rock and mountain shapes, embellished by selected ink-dots to which pigment may be added at the center.[3]

With the inclusion of the entire literary composition, Wen is able to reduce the story's visual aspects to a moment—the oar-shouldering fisherman about to enter, or to leave, his Shangri-la. The contrasting angles of the sharp-twigged peach trees, the diagonal sweep of rock capping the curving shape of the vine-hung cave-entrance create a subtly tense, even dramatic, setting around the "eye" that opens to reveal the main character. His *contrapposto* form is beautifully delineated in a free sensitive line which, as with the basic composition, owes much to the late Sung. Faintly, one can see at points where the line was partly reinforced with white. There are discreet brilliant accents of mineral blue on hat and cloak. The gold that usually accompanies this style is allowed to shine through from the paper to play against the basic tones of blue that embellish the rocks.

NOTES:
1. *Chinese Art Treasures* (1961), nos. 97, 98.
2. Sickman, ed., *Chinese Calligraphy and Painting* (1962), p. 135.
3. Cf. the detail of Ch'ien's *Wang Hsi-chih Gazing at the Geese* reproduced in Cahill, *Chinese Painting* (1960), p. 102.

INSCRIPTION BY THE ARTIST: [writing of T'ao Ch'ien's "Peach Blossom Spring":]

During the reign-period T'ai yuan (326–97) of the Chin dynasty there lived in Wu-ling a certain fisherman. One day, as he followed the course of a stream, he became unconscious of the distance he had traveled. All at once he came upon a grove of blossoming peach trees which lined either bank for hundreds of paces. No tree of any other kind stood amongst them, but there were fragrant flowers, delicate and lovely to the eye, and the air was filled with drifting peachbloom.

The fisherman, marveling, passed on to discover where the grove would end. It ended at a spring; and then there came a hill. In the side of the hill was a small opening which seemed to promise a gleam of light. The fisherman left his boat and entered the opening. It was almost too cramped at first to afford him passage; but when he had taken a few dozen steps he emerged into the open light of day. He faced a spread of level land. Imposing buildings stood among rich fields and pleasant ponds all set with mulberry and willow. Linking paths led everywhere, and the fowls and dogs of one farm could be heard from the next. People were coming and going and working in the fields. Both the men and the women dressed in exactly the same manner as people outside; white-haired elders and tufted children alike were cheerful and contented.

Some, noticing the fisherman, started in great surprise and asked him where he had come from. He told them his story. They then invited him to their home, where they set out wine and killed chickens for a feast. When news of his coming spread through the village everyone came in to question him. For their part they told him how their forefathers, fleeing from the troubles of the age of Ch'in, had come with their wives and neighbors to this isolated place, never to leave it. From that time on they had been cut off from the outside world. They asked what age was this: they had never even heard of the Han, let alone its successors the Wei and the Chin. The fisherman answered each of their questions in full, and they sighed and wondered at what he had to tell. The rest all invited him to their homes in turn, and in each house food and wine were set before him. It was only after a stay of several days that he took his leave.

"Do not speak of us to the people outside," they said. But when he had regained his boat and was retracing his original route, he marked it at point after point; and on reaching the prefecture he sought audience of the prefect and told him all of these things. The prefect immediately dispatched officers to go back with the fisherman. He hunted for the marks he had made, but grew confused and never found his way again.

The learned and virtuous hermit Liu Tzu-chi heard the story and went off elated to find the place. But he had no success, and died at length of a sickness. Since that time there have been no further "seekers of the ford."

tr. Cyril Birch *(Anthology of Chinese Literature* [1965], pp. 167–168)

To the right is the "Peach Blossom Spring." 1542, spring, third month, sixth day. Written by Cheng-ming at the age of 73.

SEAL OF THE ARTIST:
Cheng-ming [painting: II/1]

SEALS:
Unidentified
Lang-huan hsien-kuan ts'ang shan [painting: I/1]
Illegible [painting: III/1]

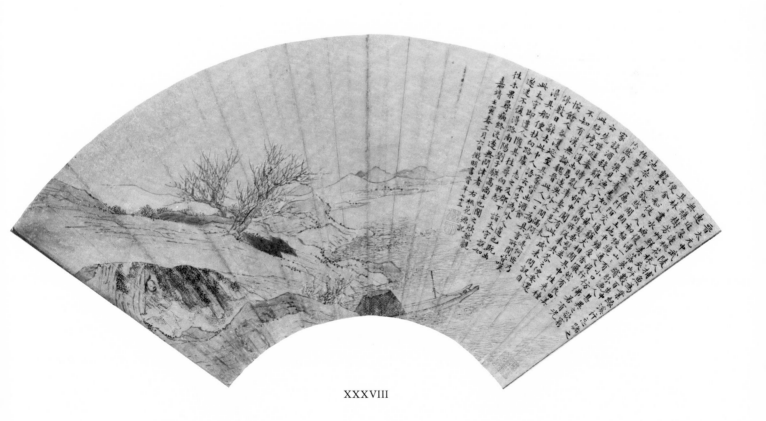

XXXVIII

XXXIX. THE HEART SUTRA: CALLIGRAPHY

(*Mo-k'o-pan-jo-po-lo-mi-to hsin-ching* [*Prajñāpāramitā-hṛdaya-sūtra*])
Standard script
On Ch'iu Ying's painting, *Chao Meng-fu Writing the* Heart Sutra *in Exchange for Tea*
Dated 1542, ninth month, twenty-first day
Handscroll; painting, ink and color on paper; calligraphy, ink on paper, 8½″ high and 30⅝″ long (21.1 x 77.2 cm.)
Inscription and signature of the artist
Cleveland Museum of Art; purchase, John L. Severance Fund

Six months later, Wen is using exactly the same type of calligraphy to write out a Buddhist sutra. Interestingly, as with the fan of *Peach Blossom Spring,* this calligraphy embellishes ideas of Chao Meng-fu. As the former relates to a Chao style of painting, this is connected with his calligraphy. The patron, Chou Feng-lai, owned Chao's poem on this subject. He then asked for Wen's writing of the sutra and subsequently requested a painting on the theme from Ch'iu Ying. Thus, Wen's exact script is appended to Ch'iu's impeccable painting. Wen visited temples, wrote calligraphy, drank tea with friends in sheltered groves—all of the experience painted here by Ch'iu Ying was also Wen's experience. We have seen how Wen treated the theme—or variations of it. Ch'iu Ying's accuracy, his unfaltering attention to detail, his visual exactness, his color, are aspects of painting that Wen, too, embraced; but the essential variants, the sense of personal feeling, the range of antique style, the changing brush, imbue Wen's art with a vitality that Ch'iu Ying's precision could not afford.

There is little evidence that Wen was a friend of Ch'iu Ying. The two seem, as here, to have been brought together by patrons rather than by their own artistic communication. Since, in the finest sense, Ch'iu was the great illustrator, Ch'iu was called upon to paint famous scenes. Wen, constantly writing out great compositions, was the obvious learned calligrapher. It is such a combination, drawn together by a collector, that accounts for another scroll in this exhibition (no. LXI). The Ch'iu Ying handscroll in Chicago of the *Peach Blossom Spring,* mentioned above (no. XXXVIII),

is followed by Wen's writing of the story in a similar combination.

As Sherman Lee points out (see bibliography), the *Heart Sutra* was an important Mahāyāna text involving total denial of the reality of the phenomenal world. Although Buddhist it fits the literati's affirmation of that which is significant as residing elsewhere than in the "dust-filled" world. Thus, in a meaningful way, the *Heart Sutra* parallels the elusive realities affirmed in *Peach Blossom Spring.* More to the point from a personal viewpoint is the fact that Wen's wife had died one month before his writing of this text.[1]

The precise calligraphy style used to brush these compositions is so exactly alike in both the fan and the scroll that there can be little doubt of the same hand. This is true of both the direction of the strokes and the sensitive pressures of the brush that subtly vary this seemingly rigid style. The handscroll with its clean paper, with its refined printed border has inevitably, however, a special purity that is not to be found in the golden illustration of the fan.

As mentioned in the discussion of the fan, the writing follows closely the fourth century calligrapher, Wang Hsi-chih. Here, to prove the point, it can be compared to a rubbing of Wang's writing (or early copy) of the Taoist classic, *Huang-t'ing ching* (fig. 23). Wen's characters, extremely close, are sharper, more varied, and more subtly elegant than the purer, more basic archaism of the model. The uniqueness of Wen's manner can also be affirmed by a comparison with the standard script of some of his family and friends (no. XXII).

NOTE:
1. On the twenty-first of the eighth month, at the age of 72 years (73 *sui*). Wen Chia in his biography of Wen Cheng-ming, in *Fu-t'ien chi,* ch. 36/pp. 4a-4b (pp. 899–900).

INSCRIPTION BY THE ARTIST:
1542, ninth month, the twenty-first day. Written on a boat at K'un-shan. Cheng-ming.

COLOPHONS AND SEALS:
Wen P'eng (1498–1573) painter, calligrapher, first son of Wen Cheng-ming; dated summer, 1543

Wen P'eng	[colophon: II/1]
Wen Shou-ch'eng shih	[colophon: II/2]

XXXIX, painting before calligraphy: Ch'iu Ying, *Chao Meng-fu Writing the* Heart Sutra *in Exchange for Tea*

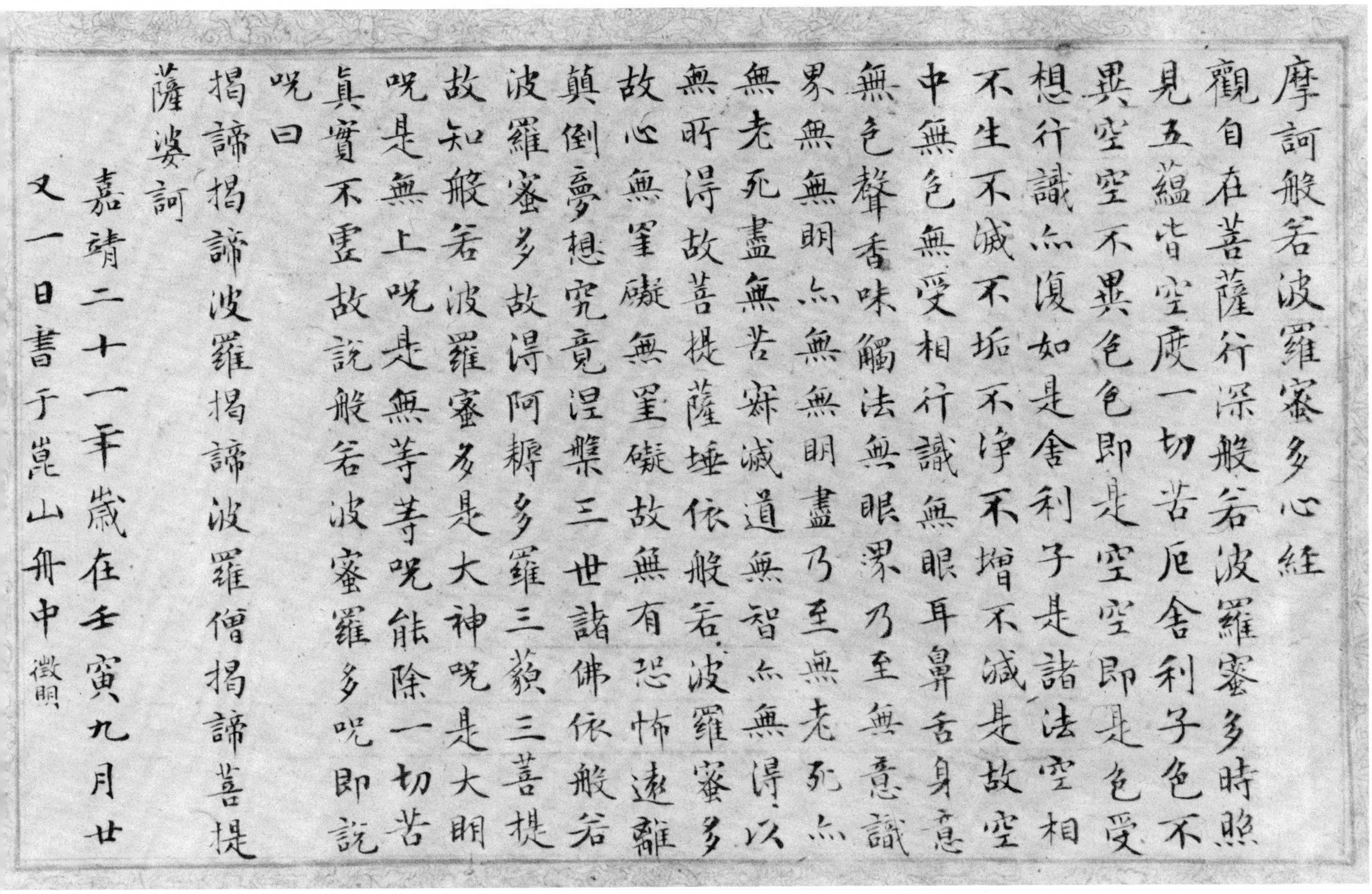

摩訶般若波羅蜜多心經

觀自在菩薩行深般若波羅蜜多時照
見五蘊皆空度一切苦厄舍利子色不
異空空不異色色即是空空即是色受
想行識亦復如是舍利子是諸法空相
不生不滅不垢不淨不增不減是故空
中無色無受想行識無眼耳鼻舌身意
無色聲香味觸法無眼界乃至無意識
界無無明亦無無明盡乃至無老死亦
無老死盡無苦集滅道無智亦無得以
無所得故菩提薩埵依般若波羅蜜多
故心無罣礙無罣礙故無有恐怖遠離
顛倒夢想究竟涅槃三世諸佛依般若
波羅蜜多故得阿耨多羅三藐三菩提
故知般若波羅蜜多是大神咒是大明
咒是無上咒是無等等咒能除一切苦
真實不虛故說般若波羅蜜多咒即說
咒曰
揭諦揭諦波羅揭諦波羅僧揭諦菩提
薩婆訶

嘉靖二十一年歲在壬寅九月廿
又一日書于崑山舟中 徵明

| 葡骨血脉盛忱慢 | 不見過清靈恬惔無欲遂 | 得生還於七門飲大淵道我玄廬過清靈問 | 我仙道與奇方頤載白素距丹田沐浴華池生 | 靈根被髮行之可長存三奇相得開命門五味 | 皆至開善氣還常能行之可長生 | 永和十二季五月廿四日五山陰縣寫 |

23. Wang Hsi-chih, the Taoist text *Huang T'ing-ching*, rubbing of a section

Wen Chia (1501–1583), painter, calligrapher, second son of Wen Cheng-ming; dated August, 1543

Wen Hsiu-ch'eng shih	[colophon: III/1]
Wen Chia	[colophon: III/2]

Wang Shih-mou (1536–1588), T. Ching-mei, brother of Wang Shih-chen; dated 1584

Wang Ching-mei shih	[colophon: IV/1]
Ch'iang-tung chü-shih	[colophon: IV/2]

Sung Lo (1643–1713), collector

Wei-hsiao ts'ao-t'ang hua-chi	[front mounting: I/1]
Sung Lo shen-ting	[painting: IV/1]

Chou Feng-lai (sixteenth century)

Chou Yü-shun shih	[painting: I/3]

Weng Wan-ko (twentieth century), collector

Weng Wan-ko chien-shang	[colophon: V/1]
Wan-ko chen-shang	[painting: I/2]
	[colophon: I/1]

Ch'ien-lung emperor (r. 1736–1795)

Shih-ch'ü pao-chi	[painting seam: I/1]
Ch'ien-lung yü-lan chih pao	[painting: II/1]
San-hsi t'ang ching-chien hsi	[painting: III/1]
I tzu-sun	[painting: III/2]
Ch'ien-lung chien-shang	[painting seam: II/1]

Unidentified:

half of double seal	[painting seam: I/2]
Lung-hsi Chung-tzu chen-ts'ang	[painting: I/1]
double seal fragments	[painting: V/1]

REMARKS:

Chou Feng-lai (died age 33), t. Yü-shun, younger brother of Chou Feng-ming (1498–1550), from K'un-shan, Kiangsu.

Wen P'eng's colophon tells us that Chou Yü-shun owned a poem by Chao Meng-fu. The poem dealt with Chao's writing the *Heart Sutra* in exchange for tea from Priest Kung. Chou also asked Wen Cheng-ming to write the *Heart Sutra* to match the poem.

Wen Chia's colophon repeats the details of the story behind the calligraphy but also informs us that Chou asked Ch'iu Ying to paint a painting in the style of Li Kung-lin illustrating the exchange between Chao Meng-fu and Priest Kung.

Wang Shih-mou's colophon tells first the same story as Wen Chia, then writes that he got this scroll (containing Chao's poem, Ch'iu's painting and Wen's sutra with colophons by P'eng and Chia) from Chou Yü-shun. Wang mentions that his father treasured a *Heart Sutra* written by Chao for another priest Li (Li Shang-jen). He thought that Chao's poem matched perfectly the sutra (written by Chao), so he separated the poem from the handscroll and mounted it with the sutra.

The *Prajñāpāramitā-hrdaya-sūtra* is translated as "The 'Heart of Perfect Wisdom,' short form," in Edward Conze, *The Short Prajñāpāramitā Texts* (London, 1974), pp. 142–143.

BIBLIOGRAPHY:

Lee, "Literati and Professionals" (1966), pp. 23–25, fig. 17.

XL. AFTER LI CH'ENG'S WINTER WOODS

(Fang Li Ying-ch'iu Han-lin)
Dated 1542, twelfth month
Hanging scroll, ink and color on paper, 23¾" high and 9¹³/₁₆" wide
   (60.5 x 25 cm.)
Inscription, signature and seals of the artist
British Museum

The year 1542 is well represented. A few days before its close, the artist's expressive skill reaches a high point in this lonely grey winter painting. At first glance it seems to be a somewhat indiscriminately jumbled thicket of old trees. But as Richard Barnhart points out, there is a focus:

The forest and the composition are dominated by the single tall pine rising from the center, unchanged symbol of strength and enduring virtue, as if directly reflecting Confucius: "Only when the year grows cold do we see that the pine and cypress do not fade." The tree was never a more appropriate emblem of its painter, who at seventy-two was gathering strength and approaching his greatest work.[1]

We have already mentioned the possibility of what can only be a relatively early work, *Magpies and Junipers* (no. XVI), being a direct interpretation of the Ming dynasty idea of Li Ch'eng. As Barnhart further points out in quoting Chiang Shao-yü,

Li Ch'eng painted level plains and wintry forests such as had never been painted before. His painting was alive with unconstricted inspiration and his scenes of misty woods embraced unsullied reaches.[2]

It is such "unsullied reaches," within the context of a close-up of trees, that seem to be indicated in Wen's wintry forest. The elements of conscious design—repeated rocks, landspits, tree trunks, knots, forked twigs—continue the sense of pattern that gave a unique quality to many of his masterpieces of the 1530s. However, here they are arranged to compel a direct recession *into* the picture. The tiny trees at the edge of the land (about a third of the way up the picture and to the left), because of their juxtaposition to large tree trunks in front of them, seem to be a long way off. We are given something close to an eye-level view, only slightly raised, through the aged, empty forest.

The importance of receding space, as has been suggested before, is a notion clearly related to Wen's perception of the Sung. We noted it, for example, in *Magpies and Junipers*. Another feature that *Winter Woods* shares with that earlier picture is an interest in fine and delicate forms. This is particularly true as we reach up into the feathery sprays of tree tips and outer branches, the soft

XL

147

touch of a wash that suggests lingering leaves and the light, dry, sometimes stippled textures of the tree trunks. This love for physical detail is, too, a Sung referent although here it is screened through a vision that has learned to accept it only through the sensitively varied interpretation of brush and ink so valued in the Yüan and early Ming.

Three years later, 1545, a painting in the Palace Museum in Taiwan (fig. 24) shows Wen expanding the theme. We look into a similar grove of trees along an angled path of space. But now a scholar, bluntly archaic (recalling one of the two figures in the Los Angeles painting, no. XXVIII), leans on his staff and fondles his beard. He is the "subject" which Wen, himself, titled *Searching for Poetry in the Empty Forest*. Behind the trees rise sharp cliffs whose summit is a tumble of rock plateau and scrubby growth (motifs noted as early as the Michigan mountainscape, no. XV). In the decade of the forties, earlier ideas reach a confident maturity.

From the inscription we know the length of time it took to complete this painting—ten hours. We know, too, that the landscape is related to feelings about the loss of his wife and a friend's visit of consolation. But now Wen claims better spirits. Still its wintry mood is in harmony with that time and season—a traditional mode that fits the "hard and shadowed seasons of life."[3]

NOTES:
1. Barnhart, *Wintry Forests* (1972), p. 27.
2. Ibid., p. 15, tr. John Hay.
3. Ibid., p. 16.

INSCRIPTION BY THE ARTIST:
Li Tzu-ch'eng of Wu-yüan, in learning that I was in mourning for my wife, did not consider it far to come several hundred *li* to console (me) at Wu-men. Because we talked about the marvels of Li Ying-ch'iu's (Ch'eng) winter woods, I proceeded to make this (painting) for him. Although it is now the year's end, the weather is mild and warm, and my spirit is rather good. Under the basket light I began to scribble, and before I realized it, the paper was filled. In completing this, ten hours (forty *k'o*) had slipped by! Dated on the twenty-first day of the last month in 1542 and signed Cheng-ming, now seventy-three years old.

(tr. James Robinson)

SEALS OF THE ARTIST:
Cheng-ming	[painting: V/1]
T'ing-yün	[painting: V/2]
Wen Cheng-ming yin	[painting: I/6]

COLOPHONS AND SEALS:
Chang Hsiao-ssu (late 16th–early 17th century), from Chen-chiang, Kiangsu
Chang Hsiao-ssu shang-chien yin	[painting: I/3]
Chang Tse-chih	[painting: I/4]

Pien Yung-yü (1645–1702), Ch'ing dynasty collector
Pien Ling-chih chien-ting	[painting: I/1]
Hsien-k'o	[painting: I/2]
Shih-ku t'ang shu-hua	[painting: V/5]

Ch'ien-lung emperor (r. 1736–95); dated 1746
Ch'ien-lung chien-shang	[painting: I/5]
Shih-ch'ü pao-chi	[painting: II/1]
Ch'ien-lung yü-lan chih pao	[painting: III/1]
Chi-hsia lin ch'ih	[painting: IV/1]
San-hsi t'ang ching-chien hsi	[painting: V/3]
I tzu-sun	[painting: V/4]

REMARKS:
The recorded description varies from the present painting. In *Shih-ku t'ang* (ch. 28/p. 33) the arrangement of seals does not coincide with the painting. It notes a *Cheng-ming* double seal at the inscription's top left corner, and at the painting's bottom right corner, the square *T'ing-yün* and *Wen Cheng-ming yin* seals.

The closeness of Mr. Li's name to that of Li Ch'eng must have had some importance in the conversation that led to the painting connected with that artist.

BIBLIOGRAPHY:
Pien, *Shih-ku t'ang* (1921 ed.), IV, p. 492.
Barnhart, *Wintry Forests* (1972), p. 26.

24. Wen Cheng-ming, *Searching for Poetry in the Empty Forest*, 1545. National Palace Museum, Taipei

XLI. MASTER LIU'S GARDEN

(Lou-chü t'u)
Dated 1543, autumn, seventh month, sixteenth day
Hanging scroll, ink and color on paper, 37½" high and 18" wide
    (95.2 x 45.7 cm).
Inscription, signature, and seals of the artist
Mr. and Mrs. David Spelman, Great Neck, New York

Master Liu's Garden is firmly dated in the early autumn of 1543. It takes us to the always important Suchou theme of the retreat. Its conception, however, is ideal rather than "real." Master Liu, Liu Lin, four years younger than Wen and now 70 *sui,* had retired from government service but had not yet built the house suitable for his new life. Wen writes a poem and paints the scene in anticipation of its realization. Still, ideal or physically real, Wen would not have to look farther than the gardens and retreats in and near Suchou which he and his friends knew so well. We have already had confirmation of the interchangeability of idea and physical reality that can focus on the subject of the garden retreat (no. XXXVII).

The iconography is exact: water which separates from the ordinary world; the simplest of plank bridges; the mud-plaster wall with its patterned rock foundation and its top thatched against the rain; the thatched gate, plank door ajar; the pavilion likewise with roof of thatch, its two stories soaring into the free air over the trees, obviously suitable for the lofty minds conversing within. This takes us to the purity of the upper reaches of the painting and the thin uncluttered washes of the hills. Soft colors help preserve the scene's idyllic mood.

Yet the view is a tamed version of what Wen had painted the year before as a wilderness of *Winter Woods* (no. XL). We look similarly down and through the receding trunks—only now the trees are garden trees. They are carefully placed on the smooth ground and arranged in only slightly irregular columns as a "V" that draws us exactly to a hidden pavilion entrance. In the foreground the arms of two crossed willows reach out to both frame and screen the thatched, walled gate. Wen is comfortable in this precise and carefully limited spatial ambient.

Here is a perfect expression of the retreat into nature's garden. It is wild: thick foliage, flowing water, lofty mountains. Ordered, it is completely civilized. And if one contemplates its thin strong line, its subtly varied tones of ink, its ephemeral touches of color, *Master Liu's Garden* partakes not a little of a lasting magic.

INSCRIPTION BY THE ARTIST:
    Immortals have always delighted in pavilion-living:
    Windows open on eight sides—eyebrows smiling,
    Overhead towers and halls welling up,
    Down below "cloud and thunder" halls dimly viewed.
    Reclining on a dais, a glimpse of Japan;
    Leaning on a balustrade, the sight of Manchuria.
    While worldly affairs shift and change
    The lofty man is centered and at peace.
                            (tr. Ling-yün Shih Liu)
    Mr. Liu Nan-t'an (Liu Lin) retired from the government, and upon his return home, he planned to build a dwelling—so you will know his noble character. Although the building is not yet completed, in anticipation of it I have composed a poem and sketched its concept. Another day he can hang it at his right hand to enrich that pavilion-living.
    Inscribed by Cheng-ming on the sixteenth day of the seventh month in the autumn of 1543.

SEALS OF THE ARTIST:
Heng-shan	[painting: I/1]
Yü-lan t'ang yin	[painting: I/2]
Wen Cheng-ming yin	[painting: II/1]
Cheng-chung	[painting: II/2]

SEALS:
Chao Sung (1464–after 1543), 1493 *chin-shih,* an official from Shanghai
    Hung-ch'i Chao Sung chien-ts'ang shu-hua yin [painting: II/5]
Unidentified
    Chao? sheng   [painting: II/3]
    T'ieh-yen ying ——— *p'ing sheng chen-shang* [painting: II/4]

REMARKS:
    Liu Lin (1474–1561) from An-jen (Kiangsi) is known as one of the "Five Hunan recluses," and with Ku Lin and Hsü Chen-ch'ing—both acquaintances of Wen Cheng-ming—known as the "Three Talents east of the River." Once, being unable to realize his own home, he suspended a bamboo sedan chair from a beam; and reclining on it, called it the "spirit pavilion" *(shen-lou).* It is also recorded in the official history of the Ming Dynasty that Wen Cheng-ming did a painting to bequeath to Mr. Liu *(Ming Shih,* ch. 194/p. 226a).
    "Cloud and thunder" halls is a reference to a special palanquin made for the Han emperor Ch'eng-ti. When sped along on this he thought he heard the sound of wind and thunder.

XLII. BEAUTY IN A PAVILION

(Hung-hsiu kao-lou)
No date
Hanging scroll in ink and color on paper, 49½" high and 19" wide
(126 x 48.5 cm.)
Inscription, signature and seals of the artist
Nan-ping Wong, Hong Kong

Beauty in a Pavilion is essentially an extension of *Master Liu's Garden.* Here the scene leaves crowded groves and we are brought to the openness of river and lake. With a slightly altered brush we sense a similar precision in forms, the same exact limiting of space. The definition is a little sharper, the format narrower; cloud and far peak, some of the latter outlined in "flying white," become more positive distant elements. It is a painting more concerned with distance.

That this landscape was basically an accepted Suchou composition is attested by an impeccable painting, *Lady in a Pavilion,* now in the Museum of Fine Arts, Boston, by Wen's contemporary, Ch'iu Ying (fig. 25). The elements are the same: space (water) at the bottom edge; plateau, tree groves, wall, and pavilion crowded in the middle distance right; empty stretches of water; the far land with its distant trees; and the firm, far hills on which rests an exact belt of cloud. Both settings are for a beautiful girl. The degree of difference is also apparent. The colored precision of Wen's execution is idyllic enough, yet it is emotionally expressive in contrast to Ch'iu Ying's cool, impeccable detail. Wen uses certain visual manipulations which lend force and direction; Ch'iu's jewel-like evenness does not permit this. One notes particularly Wen's short-cuts in architectural detail—the way in which the twin pines are raised to dominate the center of the composition—and we are forced to look through them to the distance beyond. (There are several paintings at this time that stress the importance of the pine; cf. no. XL and fig. 24.) The horizon line is lower. Thus the sense of retreating space is more compact and exact. In the distance, the motif of the firm, dark-ink tree-grove beyond which are cloud and far mountain is an echo (in reverse) of the foreground "repoussoir" of willow, pale platform, and high-rising tree grove. In contrast to Ch'iu Ying, Wen's harmonies are bolder and more forceful.

One need not labor further to emphasize the closeness of *Beauty in a Pavilion* to *Master Liu's Garden.* The foreground tree, the architectural detail, leaf-dot and tree-branch patterns, the rich, flat, dark far hills—all are similar. Even the two seals after the inscription are the same—a rare instance of such identity in Wen's work. If the "touch" now is a little sharper, it helps us look forward to the shift in 1548 (no. XLV), to an even more brittle expression. To re-emphasize identities, in *Master Liu's Garden* it is the deciduous foreground trees that seem cut from the same mold as those in *Beauty in a Pavilion.*

INSCRIPTION BY THE ARTIST:
The water surface at Nan-ling is wide and far,
A tight wind and light clouds wish autumn's beauty;
Just when the traveler's heart is turned to loneliness,
To what family belongs that beauty leaning in the high pavilion?
Cheng-ming
(tr. Ling-yün Shih Liu)

SEALS OF THE ARTIST:
Wen Cheng-ming yin	[painting: II/1]
Cheng-chung	[painting: II/2]
Wei keng-yin wu i chiang	[painting: III/2]
T'ing-yün	[painting: III/3]

SEALS:
Nan-p'ing Wong (twentieth century, Hong Kong)
Nan-p'ing chen-ts'ang	[painting: I/1]

Unidentified
Yü-chai	[painting: III/1]
Man-nung ou te	[painting: I/2]

BIBLIOGRAPHY:
Chung-kuo Ming-hua (1926), 26.
Chung-kuo Ming-hua-chi (1923–1929), I, no. 98.
Exhibition of Paintings of The Ming and Ching Periods (1970), no. 8.

25. Ch'iu Ying, *Lady in a Pavilion.* Courtesy, Museum of Fine Arts, Boston, Chinese and Japanese Special Fund

XLII

XLIII. *THE ART OF LETTERS* BY LU CHI: CALLIGRAPHY

(*Lu Chi Wen-fu*)
Standard script
Dated by inscription: begun in 1544 and completed in 1547
Handscroll, ink on paper, 9⅛″ x 46¼″ (23.2 x 117.5 cm.)
Signature and seals of the artist
John M. Crawford, Jr., New York

> I am hewing an axe-handle
> With an axe-handle in my hand.[1]

This part of a couplet, one from a total of 131 such parallel lines that comprise Lu Chi's *Wen-fu*, might well be taken as a theme for Wen's own total artistic task, and in particular for the very calligraphy with which he wrote this text. The axe-handle in hand was no less than the hallowed script of Wang Hsi-chih. Art is made from art.

Wen-fu is the great treatise on literature by an early native of the Suchou area, Lu Chi (261–303). If anyone doubts the high sophistication of Chinese attitudes toward art at an early age, he can do no better than search out the imaginative and pithy translation by Achilles Fang. But here our concern is with its having been written by another great man of Wu more than twelve hundred years later.

Having already looked at two important examples of the script in this decade its form will be familiar. The style is consistent with the period of the original composition since as we have seen it goes back to Wang Hsi-chih, who was born only four years after Lu Chi's death.

If refinement is one of the special qualities in Wen's art in this decade, certainly this standard script is above all an affirmation of it. Seemingly caught in the commonplace of repeating an exact stereotype, Wen's subtle variations are revealed by careful viewing. These have been characterized by Marc Wilson and Kwan S. Wong, whose thorough publication of the scroll is the basis for this discussion. They speak of its "full-bodied" quality, of the "thinning and thickening" of the strokes, of "sharp triangular heads found on many strokes." They point to the use of "only the tiny cohesive tip of a brush," a tribute to the "steady, controlled variation of pressure."

Thus rhythms, a little staccato, are marvelously coherent. Control and order are not inconsistent with life. Apparently an understanding of variations can be carried to the thin point of ultimate recognition. The calligraphy was begun in 1544 and only finished three years later in 1547. Wilson and Wong are able to detect the break that divides these two separate writings. It is found in the "thirty-first column from the right—counting the two characters of the title." This is the last line of the 1544 writing. To their sharp eyes, the first part reveals under magnification a richer quality of ink.

The scroll was written for Wen's good friend in Wu-hsi, Hua Yün (1488–1560, cf. no. XLVII), when he was visiting there in 1544. Hua Yün was a great contemporary collector. He had studied with Shao Pao,[2] a personality we have previously met (cf. colophon, no. XIV). Wen's connections with Hua Yün and his relative, Hua Hsia, only help reinforce Wen's importance in the art-world of his time, and the special admiration accorded this particular kind of writing can be found in Lu Shih-tao's colophon that follows it. As translated by Wilson and Wong:

> The smaller Master Heng-shan's (Wen Cheng-ming) small standard script gets, the more marvelous it becomes, while his big writing becomes even more striking, the bigger it grows. This may be called the ability to combine what

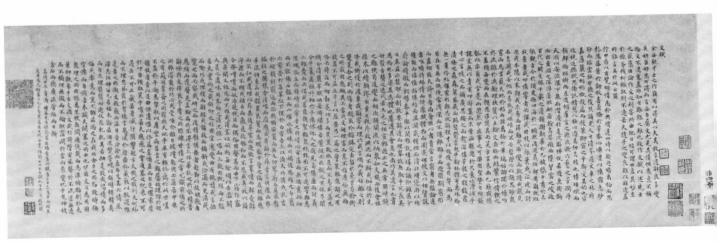

XLIII

Ts'ai Hsiang (1012–1062) and Shih Yen-nien (994–1041) could not. Furthermore, *The Art of Letters* comprises a thousand and several hundred words, and though he was approaching 80 (*sui*) years old, he wrote it out from memory without resort to looking it up. In this respect *Fan P'ang's* (A.D. 137–169) *Biography* as written out by Huang T'ing-chien occupies an inferior position. Who says contemporaries cannot compare with the ancients?

NOTES:
1. Fang, "Rhymeprose" (1951), p. 530.
2. Wilson and Wong, *Friends* (1974), p. 90.

INSCRIPTION BY THE ARTIST:
In the third month of the *chia-ch'en* year (1544) of the *Chia-ching* reign, I went to Mr. Pu-an's (Hua Yün) Green Bamboo Thicket. He took out a piece of paper and asked me to write out this prose-poem. I returned home having written for three days without reaching the mid-point. Now I have returned to finish it up. Three years have come and gone, day by day I have become a befuddled old man, whose fingers are too weak to be skillful. This is not worth looking at.
Inscribed by Cheng-ming in the second month of the *ting-wei* year (1547).

(tr. Wilson and Wong)

SEALS OF THE ARTIST:
Cheng-ming   [calligraphy: V/2]
Cheng-chung   [calligraphy: V/3]

COLOPHONS AND SEALS:
Lu Shih-tao (active ca. 1522–1566, 1538 *chin-shih*), painter, calligrapher; undated
Lu Tzu-ch'uan   [colophon: I/1]
Wang Shu (1668–1743), calligrapher, scholar; dated 1727
Shu   [colophon: II/1]
      [calligraphy: IV/2]
Hsü-chou   [colophon: II/2]
      [calligraphy: IV/1]
Chiang Heng (1672–1743); undated
——— *shan-jen*   [colophon: III/1]
Ch'en Tsun (fl. ca. late eighteenth–early nineteenth century)
Ch'en Tsun ssu-yin   [calligraphy: I/1]
Chung-tsun   [calligraphy: I/2]
Chung-tsun k'ao-ting   [colophon: VI/2]
Liang Chang-chü (1775–1849)
Chang-chü   [colophon: VI/1]
Jean-Pierre Dubosc (twentieth century)
Tu Jang   [front damask: I/3]
John M. Crawford, Jr. (twentieth century)
Ku Lo-fu   [calligraphy: III/1]
Han-kuang-ko   [calligraphy: III/2]
Han-kuang-ko chu Ku Lo-fu chien-ts'ang
Chung-kuo ku-tai shu-hua chih chang   [calligraphy: V/1]
Unidentified
I-pai-hsüan   [front damask: I/1]
Hsing-wu so hao   [front damask: I/2]
T'ieh-ch'in   [calligraphy: II/1]
Kung-chin so ts'ang   [calligraphy: II/2]
Hsi-yün pi-chi   [colophon: VI/3]
Hang-chou Wu shih Sun-ch'in Mi yen?
chen-ts'ang yin   [colophon: VII/1]

REMARKS: *Lu Chi* (261–303), a descendant of the distinguished house of Wu during the struggles of the Three Kingdoms. He held a high military command and was a noted poet and literary commentator.

BIBLIOGRAPHY:
Wilson and Wong, *Friends* (1974), no. 14, pp. 84–87.

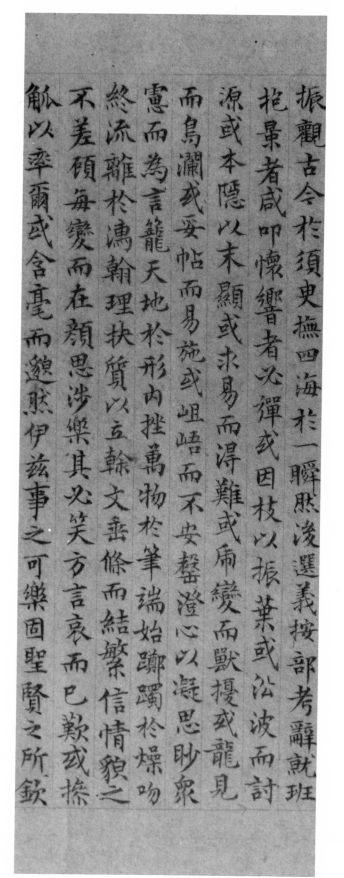

XLIII, detail

XLIV. AWAITING SNOW IN WINTER

(Han-lin tai-hsüeh)
Dated 1547
Hanging scroll in ink and very light color on paper, 39⅝" high and
    10⅝" wide (101 x 27 cm.)
Inscription, signature, and seals of the artist
Mr. and Mrs. Wan-go H.C. Weng, New York

With *Awaiting Snow in Winter* we are now late
in the decade. Five years from the British Museum
scroll (no. XL), Wen here seems to be carrying
the implications of the Li Ch'eng mode to a conclu-
sion of ultimate refinement. Again, the inscription
specifically cites the early Sung master, but
pictorially this painting of 1547 is far more
ambitious. The same essential tree-grove continues.
The stream is broader. There is a boat, and two
figures are in close converse. But the foreground
is the same direct, close-to-eye-level point-of-view
as in the *Winter Woods* of 1542 (no. XL). We look
through the trees to the same kind of distant small
growth; only here instead of a final statement of
empty paper, a misty void transforms itself into the
towering shapes of contending cliffs, bouldery
rocks, jagged plateaus, and the pale fixed arcs of
mountain waterfalls.

The painting is a statement of ambiguity. Of
Wen's Li Ch'eng–inspired work it is the most
ephemeral. Definition is the ultimate in delicate
touch: tiny accents of ink, powdery textures, almost
invisible washes, the slightest addition of pale
color on a smooth-surfaced warm tan paper. One
has to look close to see the sensitive brush-strokes
as they mold the form. In this respect it is not
unlike the earlier detail on the Michigan mountainscape (no. XV), and here the mountainscape and
the narrow format are not unaffected by the same
stereotype of Wang Meng. But what is clearly
different, and seemingly contradictory, is the
precision of total effect: exact spatial recession, mist
interweaving with tips of trees, light-surfaced but
precise hard-edged mountain forms, the certain
waterfalls; calligraphy is hair-thin, as though not to
interfere with non-calligraphic shapes. Although it
creates it, the power of brush and ink is sublimated
in the view. The world, as it was in the glories of
the Sung, is once again directly and surely before
us. It is, perhaps, the "heart transmission" that
Shen Chou valued. It is Wen, and it is Li Ch'eng,
where "misty woods embraced unsullied reaches."

INSCRIPTION BY THE ARTIST:
In 1547 the winter was dry. In my small pavilion I waited for the
snows, and used the brush ideas of Li Ying-ch'iu (Ch'eng) to sketch
this *Awaiting Snow in Winter*. Cheng-ming (now seventy-eight *sui*).
(tr. James Robinson)

XLIV

SEALS OF THE ARTIST:

Cheng-ming [painting: I/1]
T'ing-yün [painting: II/1]
Wen Cheng-ming yin [painting: II/2]

REMARKS: This is one of the few paintings specifically inscribed by Wen as being after Li Ch'eng (see also no. XL). There is damage to the inscription so that the words "Awaiting" and "now seventy-eight *sui*" are interpretations.

BIBLIOGRAPHY:
Chiang, "Life" (1971–1972), V, p. 95.

XLIV, detail

XLV. PLAYING THE CH'IN IN A SECLUDED VALLEY

(Yu-ho ming-ch'in)
Dated 1548, summer, fourth month
Hanging scroll, ink and light color on paper, 52″ high and 19⅞″ wide
　(132 x 50.5 cm.)
Inscription, signature, and seals of the artist
The Cleveland Museum of Art; purchase, John L. Severance Fund

To view the Cleveland Museum's *Playing the Ch'in in a Secluded Valley* is seemingly to move into another world. Yet in time we have only moved to the summer of 1548.

The softness of subdued tonal understatement has left the landscape. Instead we have sharp lines (almost like a wood-block), firm black moss-dots, bright color; shaded areas in the rock-cliffs often have a deliberate sharpness that relates to a type of brush-stroke which has in Chinese terminology been called with descriptive accuracy an "axe-stroke." The rocks are literally "hewn," an effect that is reinforced by the sharp, angular, and seemingly brittle shapes of their outlines. Wen's general practice of seldom admitting a far, deep distance is here, at the top of the picture, exaggerated; and the rocks float against the sky like cut-outs on the unyielding paper. They prepare us for the tiny cluster of calligraphy at the upper left which is like a sign "carved," in both seal and standard script, the latter already familiar to us from several examples in this decade.

The fact that the title is in the ancient seal script is a clue to the archaizing intent of the whole picture. The lack of softness, the "artificiality" of color, and the rather harsh awkwardness of contending shapes take us away from a soft and easy "natural" world. Once again, as in the 1530s, the delicate *art* of Wen Cheng-ming has made its own landscape. The importance of shape and line and color and paper is constantly before us. Because we can only know the world of the past through art and not through direct experience, "art" is readily equated with archaism. Because the world of the past is not the same as the world of the present, just as art is different from ordinary experience, our vision is not ordinary, but extraordinary—magical, if you will, and inevitably timeless. The mood is sharper, even brittle. Its qualities must be related to the tautly plucked private tones and rhythms of the *ch'in.* Its music is the announced subject.

That style of shape may bear a direct relation to style of sound—specifically the *ch'in*—is indicated by a text contemporary with Wen Cheng-ming (ca. 1500), *T'ai-yin ta-ch'üan.* There is illustrated for example, a gibbon climbing a rather brittle, old tree with the specific intent of suggesting how to execute a prolonged vibrato with the thumb of the left hand.[1] The sound of the *ch'in* is also to be

XLIV, detail

thought of as harmonizing with the sound of falling water—tensely strong lines of shape so important to the heart of the mountain gully.

The painting is certainly different from others at this time. However, comparison of its upper section with the upper section of *Awaiting Snow in Winter* (no. XLIV) shows amazing similarities—so much so that we seem clearly to have two different renditions of the same basic view of formal organization. One is immediately struck by the same bright arcs of falling water in both paintings, and then one begins to see more—the plateau with its sharply undercut profile; the deliberate silhouetting of rock against the upper area of paper (with faint, far

peaks); the small standard-script calligraphy; not only the interest in what have already been described as contending rock forms, but the very nature of that form itself, which is created by a concentration of dark in the fold on one rock that is juxtaposed to the deliberate edge of the next. That line in turn is the boundary of a contrasting area of light unshadowed surface.

Closely linked to an underlying similarity of form is the significance of a consistent view-point, something that can be summed up in the word "space." In discussing Wen's adaptation of the Sung style we have seen an effort to recapture a Sung idea of space. *Playing the Ch'in* is not a painting one

XLV, detail

automatically associates with the Sung. (Art-historically it might be placed before the Sung, as tenth-century archaism.) The sharp, tense wall of rock is a negation of the openness of developed Sung vision. But within this the point-of-view, the treatment of space, is like that in the Li Ch'eng–style paintings. We look a little down on the scholars and their grassy plateau. We go past the trees to the waterfall beyond. Indeed, despite a mountain theme calling for verticality, there is a contending horizontality. The format is not the narrow one of the deliberate mountainscape, and at least in its lower reaches we have a direct view that takes us into the tight ravine. Both this and the earlier *Awaiting Snow in Winter* (no. XLIV) thus show an interest in dealing with three-dimensional form: one delicate, quiet, idyllic; the other, harsh, tense, brittle. In a word, granting an obvious intent in the painting of 1548 to move toward a special scholarly music, the total vision suggests a consistency that we can associate with the decade of the 1540s.

Known only through a photograph is another Wen Cheng-ming painting which preserves the same essential design.[2] This bears an inscription dated 1538 (fig. 26). It is of particular interest that

26. Wen Ch'eng-ming, *Playing the Ch'in,* 1538. Present whereabouts unknown

a comparison between the two paintings reveals exactly the contrast we have been indicating as existing between Wen's vision in the thirties and his interests in the forties. In *Playing the Ch'in* of 1538, beginning in the lower left (not unlike the Burke painting, no. XXVII), the forms tend to climb up the surface of the picture and meet the flat ribbons of falling water, and so on up to mountain cliffs and clouds. Ten years later, in varying the same basic design, Wen's interest in both solidity of form and depth of space causes him to conceal much, particularly the passage of the waterfall, cavern-like, within the mountain cliff; and higher up he eliminates a pattern of the cloud.

Those familiar with the great paintings from the Palace Museum in Taiwan mentioned when we began to discuss this decade—*Spring at Chiang-nan* of 1547 and *Old Trees by a Cold Waterfall* of 1549 —will realize how Wen's art at this time can fluctuate between sure, quiet harmonies and the struggles of contending shapes. The brittle tensions of the Cleveland picture are thus to be expected among paintings that are more often concerned with calm serenity.

In sum, a careful analysis of the Cleveland picture shows that—despite superficial contrasts with its own time, and superficial similarities with an earlier decade—it is firmly anchored in Wen's vision during the 1540s.

NOTES:
1. Van Gulik, *The Gibbon in China* (1967), p. 39.
2. In the photographic archives of Princeton University. The same archives has another painting of the same general design dated to 1537. Insofar as one can judge from an imperfect photograph, this latter appears rather inconsistently confused.

INSCRIPTION BY THE ARTIST:
Ten thousand layered lofty mountains reveal the Buddha-truth;
A thousand-foot cascading falls cleanses the dusty heart.
Relying on plucking a song, my red-stringed tune
Is a small reply to the pine wind's ancient notes.

(tr. James Robinson)

SEALS OF THE ARTIST:

Wu-yen shih yin	[painting: I/1]
Heng-shan	[painting: I/2]
Cheng-ming	[painting: II/1]
Cheng-chung fu yin	[painting: II/2]

SEALS:

Unidentified	[painting: III/1]
	[painting: III/2]

REMARKS:
A painting with the same title and similar poem is recorded to have been in the imperial collection (*Shih-ch'ü, ch'u pien* ch. 8/p. 37b–38a). It cannot be the same painting as the present one because there are no imperial seals on this one, and the sizes as well as the dates are different. The recorded painting was dated to the fifteenth day of the fourth month, 1537. As noted above, two other paintings of comparable composition, though neither with the same poem inscribed, were executed in mid-summer of 1537 and the fifth month of 1538 (present location unknown).

"My red-stringed tune" in Wen's inscription refers to the strings of the *ch'in.*

BIBLIOGRAPHY:
Lu, *Jang-li* (1891), ch. 17/p. 13.
Cleveland Museum of Art Bulletin, Jan., 1970, p. 50, fig. 209.
"Oriental Art Recently Acquired" (1970–71), p. 87, fig. 5.

XLVI. LANDSCAPE WITH CYPRESS AND WATERFALL

No date
Folding fan in ink and color on gold paper, 7″ high and 20⅛″ wide
(17.8 x 51.1 cm.)
Inscription, signature and seal of the artist
Honolulu Academy of Arts; gift of Mrs. Carter Galt, 1957

Again we return to the fan format. We also are faced with an undated painting. Although in a "natural" style as opposed to a frankly archaic one, its composition is reminiscent of the *Peach Blossom Spring* of 1542 (no. XXXVIII). There is the same placing of major land-forms in the left, with a grotto area (here with a waterfall) and a major motif of selected leaning trees. There is a recession to rather deep space in the center leading us to the same repeated pattern of far hills beneath which are distant fingers of landspits—their outlines gently rising and falling. The right is, of course, different, for instead of calligraphy are further blocks of land and paths of water.

There are familiar Wen ideas. Again the cypress, here offering a full-shaded cover for the two tiny hut-seated scholars. Rocks with rather sharp, flat texture-strokes are also a recognized aspect of Wen's vocabulary. As a motif, the shallow twin arcs of the waterfall might have been lifted from the last two scrolls. And the way it emerges from a gap high in the cliff is like that in the farthest fall in both of those paintings.

While brushwork is generally freer than in the dry, powdery *Awaiting Snow in Winter* or the crisp, tight lines of *Playing the Ch'in,* the painting shares with those scrolls an interest in fine detail. Thus the cypress is seen as a particularly tight packing of tiny dots to silhouette exactly the dragon-like forms of the branches (forms analogous to tree-branches in the Cleveland picture).

INSCRIPTION OF THE ARTIST:
Cheng-ming did this for Hsiao-yeh.

SEAL OF THE ARTIST:
Cheng-ming   [painting: I/1]

REMARK: *Hsiao-yeh* is unidentified.

BIBLIOGRAPHY:
Ecke, *Chinese Paintings* (1965), I, pl. III, top.
Ecke, "Wen Cheng-ming," (1967), pl. 410.

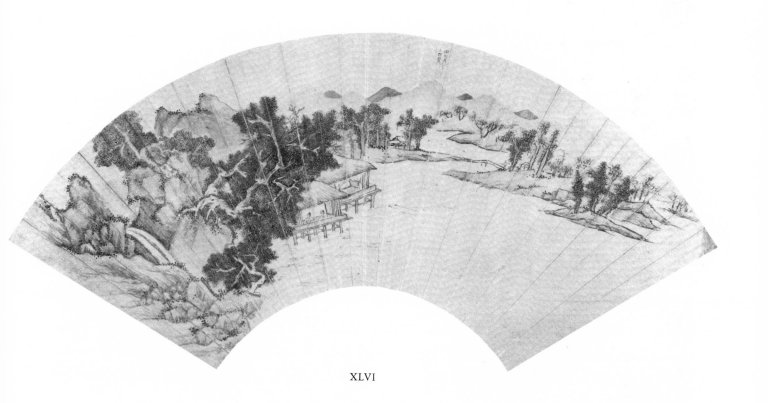

XLVI

XLVII. MAGNOLIA

(Yü-lan)
Dated 1549, second month
Handscroll in color on paper, 11″ high and 52¼″ long (28 x 132.5 cm.)
Inscription, signature, and seals of the artist
John M. Crawford, Jr., New York

Even though the outward subject differs, colored paintings ranging in the 1540s from calm exactly stated views to tensely expressive creations are an acceptable setting for the final painting of the decade shown in this exhibition—a handscroll of magnolia of 1549. By Chinese count, Wen Cheng-ming was eighty.

The painting is a kind of thank-you note for Hua Yün (1488–1560), that important collector-connoisseur of near-by Wu-hsi, for whom five years before Wen had begun the writing of Lu Chi's *Wen-fu* (no. XLIII). It is a return for hospitality. We learn of this in the letter-inscription that follows the painting. This also gives us a close personal touch, which is never far from Wen's paintings: he complains of ill-health (specifically boils); he is to do a stone tablet for Hua and needs further clarification; as he sends the *Magnolia* he adds a postscript to remember him to Hua's sons—the same concern for the younger generation that he showed for his own sons in his letters from Peking (no. XVIII).

These are informal, somewhat disconnected ideas; and with them as background, we are not surprised at the nature of the painting—the sketch lines that are just visible beneath the finished design indicate both care in the original idea and a shifting flexible approach to its final realization. Thus Wen's "feeling" his way helps us realize how much these flowers combine personal sensibilities with direct observation of nature. With all Wen's commitment to style, here for once is proof of nature itself. His inscription tells us they are flowers in his courtyard. Nor, as with Shen Chou's flower we examined earlier (no. V) is there important symbolic meaning. As from the inscription we further learn that the magnolia was "testing" its blossoms, so Wen's inquiring brush seems in complete empathy with this beauty, whose tentative nature is its very heart.

Certain elements of the technique have been carefully described by Marc Wilson and Kwon S. Wong: the unusual smooth, heavily sized tan paper; the preliminary sketch of either charcoal or very light ink; the direct and free brushwork, combining "long loose strokes and short stubby dabs."[1] These only confirm the varied quality of the whole, an expressiveness—both of texture and shape— that we have learned to expect from the mature Wen Cheng-ming.

It is art that grows on one, and as I have written elsewhere,[2] it is a painting that can be viewed positively both as a flower and as man's experience of that flower:

The total result is to give the whole a kind of varied staccato dancing quality. And the broken shapes of the stems are beautifully augmented by the curving, weaving outlines of the petals and the Chinese white that defines their purity. This white would originally have been more intense, for some of the pigment (often made of ground-up shells) has crumbled off during the passage of time. No flower form ever really repeats itself. Even the relatively simple buds are studies in variety. Color tells subtly of spring: tender new leaves of apple green, leaves of blue-green, thin lines of red on stamens, brown of sepals, the whole design placed against the warm buff of the paper. Colors are applied in a "boneless" manner (without ink outline) and thus are all the more reminders of the ephemeral delicacy of the season.

In the end, the painting of a flowering branch which at first seems over-simple in basic design and slightly hesitant in its technical realization emerges, rather as the eighty-year-old artist implies in his brief inscription, as his wonderfully direct experience of the nature of an early flower.

It is an exact, narrow window into Wen's world.

NOTES:
1. Wilson and Wong, *Friends* (1974), p. 88.
2. Sickman, ed., *Chinese Calligraphy and Painting* (1962), no. 61.

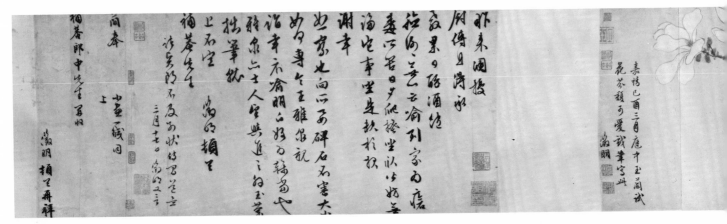

XLVII

XLVII, detail

INSCRIPTION BY THE ARTIST:
In the third month of 1549 the magnolia in the courtyard was just testing its flowers—fragrant and lovely—and for the fun of it I brushed this. Cheng-ming

SEALS OF THE ARTIST:
Wen Cheng-ming yin [painting: IV/5]
Wu-yen shih yin [painting: IV/6]

LETTER OF THE ARTIST: [Wen Cheng-ming's letter to Hua Yün with envelope attached at left follows the painting on a separate sheet of ordinary paper:]
On my last visit I troubled you for the hospitality of your kitchen, and, moreover, had the privilege of receiving your good instruction all day long. What a gracious plenty of wine, for which I thank you. There is no way really to express my gratitude. Since returning home I have been afflicted by malignant boils. Scratching

all the time, day and night, I was disturbed when sitting or lying down, not to mention other matters. Because of this I failed to thank you for your kindness until today. Please kindly pardon me. I do not know how big the stone tablet you formerly asked me to do should be. Now I expressly send you Mr. Wang Ya-ch'üan personally for the matter. Ya-ch'üan is a scholarly man, and I hope you might be able to help him out. Apart from all this, I am sending you my awkward picture of magnolias.

Cheng-ming, with head bowed.

Postscript of the third month, seventeenth day: I cannot write another letter to your sons. Please remember me to them when they attend you.

(tr. Wilson and Wong)

COLOPHONS AND SEALS:

Hua Hsia (sixteenth century), relative of Hua Yün, from Wu-hsi; collector

Chen-shang chai t'u-shu chi	[painting: I/2]

Wang Shih-chen (1526–1590), important late sixteenth century connoisseur; see no. XI

Yüan-mei	[painting: I/5]

Chu I-tsun (1629–1709), calligrapher-painter from Chia-hsing, Chekiang

Chu-t'o shen-ting	[painting: I/4]

Ho Kuan-wu (twentieth century), Hong Kong collector; dated 1957

Kuan-wu chen-ts'ang	[painting: II/1]
T'ien-ch'i shu-wu	[painting: II/2]
San-shui Ho shih T'ien-ch'i shu-wu chien-ts'ang shu-hua	[colophon: I/1]
Kuan-wu shen-ting	[colophon: III/2]
T'ien-ch'i shu-wu chien-ts'ang	[colophon: III/3]
Kuan-wu han-mo	[colophon: IV/1]

John M. Crawford, Jr. (present owner)

Han-kuang ko chu Ku Lo-fu chien-ts'ang Chung-kuo ku-tai shu-hua chih chang	[painting: III/1]
Ku Lo-fu	[colophon: II/3]
Han-kuang ko	[colophon: II/4]

Unidentified:

Ch'ing-hsiang kuan	[painting: I/1] [colophon: III/1]
Lan-tsao chai	[painting: I/3]
Ch'ing-shih	[painting: I/6]
Li-ch'eng Hsü-shih chia-ts'ang	[painting: I/7]
Feng Hung-yeh yin	[painting: II/3] [colophon: III/4]
Mao-yüan	[painting: II/4]
Ch'un-lei ko ts'ang	[painting: IV/1]
T'u-yü	[painting: IV/2]
Ping-t'u	[painting: IV/3] [colophon: II/1]
T'ao-shih	[painting: IV/4] [colophon: II/2]
Ch'ing-ying kuan yin	[colophon: I/2]
Yin-lü hsüan shu-hua yin	[colophon: II/5]

REMARKS:

Hua Yün (1488–1560), one of the leading collectors of the time in this part of China, was friend of many Suchou painters. Painters such as T'ang Yin, Ch'iu Ying, Ch'ien Ku, and Wen Cheng-ming are all recorded as having painted paintings for him from 1510 to 1552 (Chiang, "Life" [1971–1972], entries under various years). At least four hanging scrolls of magnolias and rock are attributed to Wen and dated in 1551 as having been painted for Hua while visiting him and inspired by the magnolias in Hua's courtyard. See also no. XLIII. Hua Yün was sent the appended letter (and hence the painting) by Wen; a *chin-shih* graduate in 1541, he built the Chen-hsiu yüan and is recorded as having had many art treasures.

In autumn of 1549, the same year as the Crawford magnolia painting, Wen painted the Chen-shang chai, or studio of Hua Hsia. Wilson and Wong (*Friends,* p. 90) say the two Huas (Yün and Hsia) were contemporary relatives.

Wilson and Wong (*Friends,* p. 91n.) acknowledge dependence on the translation of Wen's letter by Shujiro Shimada (Sickman, ed., *Chinese Calligraphy and Painting* [1962], p. 136).

BIBLIOGRAPHY:

Sickman, ed., *Chinese Calligraphy and Painting* (1962), no. 61, pl. 38.
Wilson and Wong, *Friends* (1974), no. 15, pp. 88–91.

The Final Decade
1550–1559

XLVIII. CYPRESS AND OLD ROCK

(Ku-po t'u)
No date (datable to 1550 by P'eng Nien's colophon)
Handscroll in ink on mulberry bark paper, 10¼" high and 19¼"
    long (26 x 49 cm.)
Inscription, signature, and seals of the artist
Nelson-Atkins Gallery, Kansas City, Missouri (Nelson Fund)

Westerners have so often described and rightly praised the great masterpiece of *Cypress and Old Rock* in Kansas City that one wonders what more there is to say. Laurence Sickman, speaking of the theme in general tells us: "These ancient shattered trunks and limbs cling to the soil with dragon-claw roots in bleak and stony landscapes . . . ."[1] Sherman Lee: "In many ways it is his masterpiece in this country and one of his most perfect works."[2] Richard Barnhart: "All battles with form and technique have long since been won. Each stroke of the brush is touched with the immutable impress of individuality, no longer to be sought."[3] Sirén: The rock is likened to "an antediluvian animal head . . . . Stone and tree seem joined in a death struggle— still undecided, though it has been going on for centuries."[4]

The purpose of this small masterpiece and its accompanying calligraphy was to offer an auspicious wish—a high-level get-well card—from Wen and his friends to the young scholar-poet Chang Feng-i, then only twenty-three. Chang was ill in a Buddhist temple at near-by Stone Lake. This kind of joint scholarly undertaking in the form of a handscroll of painting and calligraphy was common in Suchou and, as we have seen, is proof of the solidarity of the scholarly artistic community. Shen Chou's *Pine and Hibiscus* (no. V) is exactly the same kind of scroll—on that occasion, consolation for examination failure. So too, in hope of examination success, appears to have been *The Cassia Grove Studio* (no. XXXVII).

Whether or not it is proof of the psychosomatic nature of disease, one can note the effectiveness of *Cypress and Old Rock;* Chang Feng-i recovered to live out a span of eighty-six years and add his own grateful commentary to the scroll sixty-three years later. The list of calligraphers appended to the painting brings together many of the names we saw closely associated with Wen in the 1530s. Friends and family who were together on the calligraphy fan (no. XXII) are reassembled here: Lu Shih-tao, Yüan Chiung, Wen P'eng, Wen Chia, P'eng Nien. Of the others, Wang Ku-hsiang and Chou T'ien-ch'iu are the best known long-standing friends of Wen.

These friends affirm the continuity of a consistent pattern in Wen's life from the time of his return from Peking. The subject and style of the painting do likewise. It is the theme that he treated so dramatically in the *Seven Junipers* of 1532. In the first of those trees, with its basically V-like shape (a minor branch to the right, a major branch to the left), is the essential design of the tree painted in 1550. As the former painting was consciously after Chao Meng-fu, so inevitably, although unstated, is the mode and mood of *Cypress and Old Rock.* Now a rock has been added and so the painting, technically, becomes an exact illustration of Chao's verse, the stylistic manifesto:

Rocks like flying white
Trees like large seal script.[5]

But there is more tradition. Friends' inscriptions are written on a piece of old sutra paper. Wen's poetry after the painting recalls lines of Tu Fu, one of the T'ang immortals:

Crushed by snow, oppressed by frost,
    as the years and months pass,
Branches twisted, habit bent down—
    its strength is still majestic![6]

This brings us to the present, for old-age is Wen's own old age. Tu Fu's lines are in Wen's own poem. Chao Meng-fu's style is now Wen's style. Again we see that in Wen's China tradition was a compelling force behind continuing life. And make no mistake, the painting is about the present. In a terse statement Steven Owyoung catches its quality:

Revealed in sure, unfaltering brushwork and augmented by an accomplished design, the constrained tension—an ancient strength—of the cypress's tortured growth and the rock's corrupted surface symbolizes and affirms the strong character of the artist.[7]

It is the way Wen saw the world in 1550. The single-mindedness of 1532 (no. XXX), when all Wen's skill was directed to the brilliant action of an outward drama, is now stilled in a quieter wisdom. What was thrust forward, tensely compressed in narrow borders has now quietly receded onto a shallow stage. There is no contention with the limits of the format. It is a statement of acceptance. And within that, certainly the beauties of design, the range of ink-tone, the variations of the brush, a feeling for the paper. But somehow it is always more. "Flying white" records the rock. This is a technique affirming that the rock has no precise limitations, nor does the line of the land. There is no exact outline, and within what is defined there is no sure substance. The white of the paper—emptiness—is as important as the hard fact of limiting ink—matter. When is the paper the shaped highlight of the rock? When is it the emptiness that surrounds, erodes into rock's very heart? In contrast, large "seal script" line is round, full and exact. It defines with precision the ancient, even holy script. This exactness is not absent from the Old Tree—the curve and counter-curve of its lower section, the sweep to left and

雪壓霜凌歲月更枝
乳蓋偃勢崢嶸老夫記
待杜陵倔語夫露文童世
己鶯 徵明寫寄
伯起徵才

XLVIII

right of the upper "V," the reciprocal angles of the branches that bend downward to the left, the cross-hatchings of black leafless twigs. These "bones" are made the clearer by the dark leaf-dot clusters that do not intrude upon their pale, or at their tips, dark certainty.

That which is mineral, inert, once smooth and easy, erodes into a thing alive with movement reaching out and enfolding what it originally was not. (It may even reveal living ghost-like forms —an old idea about painting rocks and hills in China). That which started in the early flexibility of moving growth hardens to what is tough, crusty, and deliberately enduring. In age all living things reflect the pattern of a life. There is no concealment.

Still, each fits the other. Rock leans, tree leans; a hole for one is a knot in the other. Shape echoes shape. Harmonies are assured. The ultimate good is affirmed. Old age survives. How much more surely, then, will youth.

NOTES:
1. Sickman and Soper, *Art and Architecture of China* (1968), p. 178.
2. Lee, *Chinese Landscape Painting* (Cleveland, 1962), p. 77.
3. *Wintry Forests* (1973), p. 27.
4. Sirén, *Chinese Painting*, IV, p. 184.
5. Adapted from Bush, *Chinese Literati* (1971), p. 139. From Ts'ao Chao, *Ko-ku Yao Lun* (1387), in *I-men kuang tu* (1597), ch. 6/p. 12b.
6. Barnhart, *Wintry Forests* (1973), p. 54.
7. Steven D. Owyoung, "The Painting of Wen Cheng-ming: Last Period, 1550–59" (seminar paper, University of Michigan, 1974).

INSCRIPTION BY THE ARTIST:
Crushed by snow, oppressed by frost, as the years and months pass,
Branches twisted, habit bent down—its strength is still majestic!
An old man remembers Tu-ling's words,
Which startled the world even before they were expressed in literature.
Cheng-ming sketched this to send to the many talented Po-ch'i (Chang Feng-i).

(tr. Richard Barnhart)

SEALS OF THE ARTIST:
Cheng-ming   [painting: II/1]

COLOPHONS AND THEIR SEALS:
Wang Ku-hsiang (1501–1568); cf. no. XXIV
  Ku-hsiang   [colophon: I/1]
Chou T'ien-ch'iu (1514–1595); cf. nos. I, XXV
  Chiang-tso Chou-lang   [colophon: II/1]
Lu Shih-tao (active ca. 1522–1566); cf. no. XLIII
  Shih-tao   [colophon: III/1]
Yüan Tsun-ni (1523–1574), son of Yüan Chih; on this family see no. XXII
  Lu-wang   [colophon: IV/1]
Huang Chi-shui (1509–1574), T. Shun-fu, from Suchou
Yüan Chiung (sixteenth century); cf. no. XXII
  Shang chih   [colophon: V/1]
Lu An-tao, brother of Lu Shih-tao
  Lu shih Tzu-hsing   [colophon: VI/1]
Wen P'eng (1498–1593), first son of Wen Cheng-ming; cf. no. XXII
  Wen Shou-ch'eng shih   [colophon: VII/1]
  Wen P'eng yin   [colophon: VII/2]
Wen Chia (1501–1566), second son of Wen Cheng-ming; cf. no. XXII
  Wen shih Hsiu-ch'eng   [colophon: VIII/1]
P'eng Nien (1505–1556); cf. no. XXII; dated 1550
  P'eng Nien   [colophon: IX/1]
  K'ung-chia   [colophon: IX/2]
Chang Feng-i (1527–1613), T. Po-ch'i; dated 1612
  Chang Feng-i yin   [colophon: X/1]
  Chang Po-ch'i   [colophon: X/2]

SEALS OF COLLECTORS:
Liu Shu (1759–1816), T. Jung-feng, from Suchou
  Han-pi chu-jen   [frontispiece: I/2]
  Hua-pu Liu shih chia-ts'ang   [frontispiece: I/3]
  Liu shih Han-pi chuang yin   [painting: I/1]

Jung-feng chien-shang	[painting: II/3]
	[colophon: IX/3]
Wu-i Liu Shu shen-ting	[painting: II/4]

Ch'ien Tu (1763–1844) well-known painter, followed style of Wen
Cheng-ming

Hu-kung	[painting: I/2]
Hu-chung mo-yüan	[painting: II/2]

Ku Wen-pin (1811–1889)

Ku Tzu-shan pi-ch'ieh yin	[painting: I/3]

Unidentified

K'o-ch'ing kuan pi-ch'ieh yin	[frontispiece: I/1]

REMARKS: *Tu-ling,* site of a Han imperial burial, was fifty *li* south of Chang-an (Sian), Shensi. It was the residence of the T'ang poet Tu Fu (712–770), who used the place in his sobriquet.

BIBLIOGRAPHY:
Dubosc, *Great Chinese Painters* (1949), no. 32.
———, "A New Approach to Chinese Painting" (1950), p. 52.
Ecke, *"The Seven Junipers"* (1954), p. 25.
Lee, *Chinese Landscape Painting* (1962), pl. 57.
Chinese Art (Smith, 1962), no. 7.
Loehr, *Chinese Art* (Wellesley, 1967), no. 32.
Sickman and Soper, *Art and Architecture of China* (1968), pl. 136.
Barnhart, *Wintry Forests,* (1972), pp. 53-54, pl. 15.

XLIX. GATHERING MULBERRY LEAVES

(Ts'ai-sang t'u)
Dated 1551, third month, eleventh day
Hanging scroll in ink and color on paper, 30¼" high and 13" wide
   (77 x 33 cm.)
Inscription, signature, and seals of the artist
T.Y. Chao, Hong Kong

This gentle scene is as close as Wen ever gets to what we might call "genre." It reminds us of how far earlier Shen Chou had painted a scene of *Gardeners* (no. II A). It looks forward to the refined views of a famous Suchou garden Wen will paint a few months later (no. LI). The gathering of mulberry leaves for the making of silk has long been in China the traditional task of women. Giving us here high-waisted dress and full form not inappropriate for the T'ang dynasty and using a seemingly elegant table as a "ladder," Wen has preserved in his figures a clear traditional flavor of aristocratic elegance.

Much as women are the only figures—as for example they were often the sole subjects in T'ang dynasty court scenes—they are essentially substitutes for the more common scholarly male in a garden setting capped by the rising of mountain peaks. Unusual is the presence of a dog. Wen is not a painter of animals. But the hunched basket-carrying figure in the lower left corner is like the thin hunched bridge-crossing recluse that one can often find in Wen's (or Shen Chou's) scholarly landscapes.

There are few examples of Wen's painting women or, perhaps more exactly, placing women in his compositions and as a consequence subtly altering the setting. Surviving are isolated scrolls from different periods. There is in Peking an archaic example of 1517, without setting, that by Wen's inscription is associated with both Chao Meng-fu and, in color, Ch'ien Hsüan.[1] Further is his stated reinterpretation in 1539 of another Chao Meng-fu, *Lady in the Shade of the Plantain,* now in Taipei (fig. 27). Whereas the former is clearly pre-T'ang in origins, the latter depends broadly on an early T'ang style. In this exhibition, *Beauty in a Pavilion* (no. XLII), which though undated seems as we have seen to be unquestionably a painting of the 1540s, offers within a large landscape another such figure: high-waisted, in profile, and with her face an extended featureless curve, she is like the profile figures in the mulberry scene. Only in the latter the forms are heavier and seem to be drawn rather freely from eighth-century T'ang figures. In such matters as economy of line and treatment of folds, there are close parallels with the Taipei picture, which incidentally is on silk. Color is a necessary component in all these scenes. Although rarely painted, when Wen turns to the theme he is characteristically consistent, presenting a subtle

variety of style and a sense of antiquity often shaped by his admiration for Chao Meng-fu.

With *Gathering Mulberry Leaves* the figures are placed centrally within what for Wen was a contemporary Suchou setting, something directly viewed, a softly colored vignette with moss-dotted piles of rocks in the foreground below and the more dramatic clusters of the same forms above in the

XLIX

upper mountains. These rocks are defined firmly but minutely with delicate curving texture-strokes. Tiny grasses and tiny moss-dots clustered along the rock edges articulate tightly knit shapes that otherwise appear light and cloud-like. Behind them is the ghostly blue of far peaks. Without imitating, the mountain rocks recall the fine expressive treatment of such forms in *Awaiting Snow in Winter* (no. XLIV). They frame but also, in their firm fantasy, harmonize with the idyllic central scene.

In that scene any assertive structure is minimized by soft touches of the brush. Ink tones are subdued so that fragile color can carry the scene and confirm its dream-like truth—clusters of blue foliage, the pale cool wall, warm tree-trunks and thatched roofs, a touch of green for a sleeve, warm for a skirt. The empty, flat land where the mulberries grow and the fading mists above their branches assure the visionary serenity of this exact yet ideal grove.

By comparison the contending rocks seem to return us to a kind of earthy reality. Wen's poem is a verse, possibly for a painting, composed years before: judging by its place in his collected works, some time around 1515. He falters a little in the later writing. He leaves out the last character at the end of the first line, the character for *women*. In his old age he is bringing back memories. But even initially the poem dealt with what was lost:

XLIX, detail

Anxious since below the wall mulberry leaves are
    few,
They do not know above the wall the flower's
    reckless flight.
The bitterness of spring is theirs alone.
In a hundred years how many fine silks can one
    wear?

It is as though Wen here had restored in lasting form
the beauty of those lost springs.

NOTE:
1. Yonezawa, *Chūgoku bijitsu* (1965), III, p. 121, pl. 47 and frontispiece. The poses are analogous to those in *Gathering Mulberry Leaves:*
a figure in profile and a figure turning back to her in three-quarter view.

INSCRIPTION BY THE ARTIST:
    In red skirts and green sleeves, who are these women
    Meeting at the east wall to pick mulberry leaves?
    They gather leaves till the day's end and fear returning late
    For in the room the worm-basket is cold; the silkworms bitterly
        hungry.
    Anxious since below the wall mulberry leaves are few,
    They do not know above the wall the flowers' reckless flight.
    But the bitterness of spring is theirs alone.
    In a hundred years how many fine silks can one wear?
1551, third month, eleventh day. Cheng-ming.

(tr. James Robinson)

SEALS OF THE ARTIST:
    Cheng-ming   [painting: II/1]

SEALS:
T'ung Yü? (1721–1782), painter, calligrapher, and seal carver
    Erh-shu? chien-ts'ang   [painting: I/1]
Wang Chi-ch'ien (twentieth century)
    Wang shih Chi-ch'ien ts'eng-kuan   [painting: III/1]
Ch'eng Ch'i (twentieth century)
    Ch'eng Po-fen chen-ts'ang yin   [mounting: I/1]
    Shuang-sung lou   [mounting: II/1]
    K'o-an chen-pi   [mounting: II/2]

REMARKS: The poem is found in *Fu-t'ien chi* (1968 ed.), I, ch.
6/10a–11b (pp. 206–7), in *Wen Shih,* ch. 4/pp. 14a–b; and in *Wen
Cheng-ming hui-kao,* ch. 7/p. 70b. The translation is based on the
printed version.

BIBLIOGRAPHY:
Hsüan-hui t'ang (1972), painting volume, p. 74.

27. Wen Cheng-ming, *Lady in the Shade of the Plantain,*
1539. National Palace Museum, Taipei

L. OLD TREES BY A WINTRY BROOK

(Ku-mu han-ch'üan)
Dated 1551, fifth month, fifteenth day
Hanging scroll in ink and slight color on paper, 28⅛″ high and 10⁹⁄₁₆″
  wide (71.5 x 27.5 cm.)
Inscription, signature, and seals of the artist
Mrs. A. Dean Perry, Cleveland

Now, three months later, Wen is returning to the mode of Li Ch'eng. *Old Trees by a Wintry Brook* is the loneliest of landscapes. These trees offer no shelter for conversing scholars. They are their own dialogue. Only a few ink-dots suggest that they are alive. Only the thin curving lines of water defy the desert of the land. Fresh growth is nature's ornament. When all ornament has been stripped away, structure alone is left.

This is what the painting is about. This is also the meaning of winter. Here, therefore, although brushed in summer, is a portrait of that season. Wen suggests this in his title, but above all he paints it. In winter, structure is the way one learns of the powerful persistence of life. In a curious fashion, however, it is not a cold winter. It was painted in summer. The barren world is warmed by Wen's devoted touch—as it is also by ever so delicate a suggestion of color. Structure is marvelously transparent, so that one can follow exactly how it is formed—the feel of a wet-dry brush building from uneven ink a tree, a rock, a stream. But such sensitive personal statments are not allowed to disrupt the demands of objective nature. They do, however, create ambiguities, subtle tensions which in turn lie at the heart of the life of the painting. These tensions form the very matrix of the linking of art and nature. One sees this in individual shapes, but particularly it is within the composition as a whole—especially the treatment of space.

There is a great deal of pushing and pulling. Recession is not easy. Dark values, introduced in the foreground, are picked up again further back. There is no far distance. The tree is broken off, the rough land stops. Still, as a whole, the lower part recedes from us, as does a view in nature—but only for a while. This concession to nature's ambient ends abruptly a mere quarter of the way up the paper. And the rest? The empty flat paper, that ultimate restraint—nothing to interfere with the contending shapes of the upper tree. Roots precariously planted in the real nature-space of the barren land, limbs are an abstraction. Still further above, the dark-moist brittle angled strokes of calligraphy and the artist's two seals pick up again the mood of Wen's brush, of Wen's art, and can only re-emphasize the flat pure paper on which the entire painting is created.

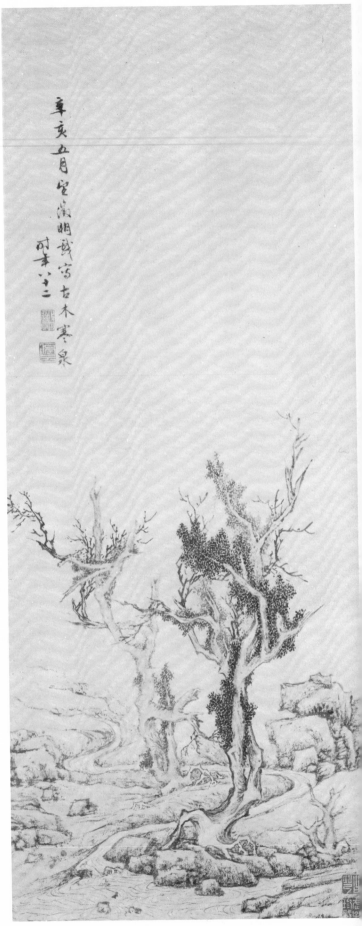

L

We know the date. This is so much Wen's art there is no need to question it with flawed comparisons.

INSCRIPTION BY THE ARTIST:
In the year 1551, fifth month, fifteenth day, Cheng-ming playfully sketched this old tree by a cold stream, aged 82 *sui.*

SEALS OF THE ARTIST:
Cheng-ming	[painting: II/1]
T'ing-yün	[painting: II/2]

SEALS:
Hsü Shu-p'i (1596–1683)
Wu-tzu chen-ts'ang	[painting: I/2]

Unidentified
Yüeh-ch'iung	[painting: I/1]

REMARKS: *Hsü Shu-p'i* (T. Wu-tzu) was noted for his calligraphy. In repeated attempts, he was unsuccessful at the official examinations, and at the end of the Ming dynasty (1644) he went into seclusion, dying at the age of 88. He married the eldest daughter of Yao Hsi-meng (1579–1636), through whom one can draw connections with Wen Cheng-ming. Yao was a nephew of Wen Cheng-heng (1585–1645), the grandson of Wen P'eng and hence the great-grandson of Wen Cheng-ming. See *Su-chou fu-chih,* ch. 88/p. 7a (Taipei reprint vol. 4, p. 2117); for Yao see Charles O. Hucker, "Suchou and the Agents of Wei Chung-hsien," *Silver Jubilee Volume of Zinbun-kagaku-kenkyusyo* (Kyoto, 1954), p. 228, n. 6. For all this information I am indebted to Ellen Johnston Laing.

BIBLIOGRAPHY:
Min shitaika (1924), p. 50.
Sirén, *Chinese Painting* (1956–58), VI, pl. 211 B.
Ecke, "Wen Cheng-ming" (1967), pl. 408.
Masterpieces of Asian Art (1970), pl. 42.
Clapp, *Wen Cheng-ming* (1975), fig. 46.

LI. GARDEN OF THE UNSUCCESSFUL POLITICIAN

(Cho-cheng yüan t'u)
Dated 1551, autumn, ninth month, twentieth day
Eight painted album leaves with facing pages inscribed with poems in
ink on paper, 10½" high and 10¾" wide (26.6 x 27.3 cm.)
Inscription, signature and seals of the artist
Mr. and Mrs. Earl Morse, New York

The Cho-cheng Yüan is a large rambling garden still preserved in Suchou. It was established by Wen's contemporary, the censor Wang Hsien-ch'en. Wen himself was given a studio there, and so the painting of this ablum comes from intimate understanding. Roderick Whitfield has thoroughly published the work, and he points out that these eight leaves are a kind of selective repeat of a much more complete painting (thirty-one leaves) Wen had done in 1535. Each leaf is accompanied by descriptive poems that help explain the particular view.

Gardens change, and there is little left now that could be stretched to show exact parallels to what Wen has painted. However, it is evident in the first place that these leaves combine a sense of the real with the idea. The art of the garden would, of course, itself do just that, but here ideas are further refined by the style of Wen's brush.

Both Wen's sensitivity in the handling of ink and his ability to paint exact and unfaltering detail even now in his eighties are general attributes which have been shown in the two other paintings we have already seen from this same year. Here, as befits a series of specific views, Wen makes use of a delicate and unfaltering precision. There are a good many marks of this style: the close dotting of leaves; the dark silhouette of bare twigs; pointed grasses; moss-dots; simply outlined figures in subtly varied poses and shapes; open, rule-lined architecture; pure, flat plateaus. Here there are no mountains. The views are essentially close-ups that do not need far spaces.

Within these necessary limitations, there is, however, considerable variety in the treatment of the scenes and their spatial arrangements. It reminds us again—as, let us say, with Wen's standard script—how a seemingly unpromising mode can be enlivened with subtle variety. Leaf A, the *Bank of Many Fragrances,* is presented in tight archaic fashion. It is a formal open pavilion placed on a square island surrounded by a fixed band of water. Such an arrangement goes back to the T'ang dynasty, where in often rather map-like landscapes such space-cells helped to articulate the scene and offer a clear area in which to place necessary selected objects. The pavilion has been further formalized by a balanced perspective wherein lines converge from front to rear toward an implied central axis. We are thus drawn to a fixed position.

The horizontal rows of bamboo, trees, fence, bank help reinforce what is ultimately a kind of grid. This formal approach was used in Chinese painting during the T'ang dynasty, where it is found in Buddhist paradises. Its use here certainly connects this Ming garden with the T'ang retreat and most certainly with that patriarch of retired scholars, the poet-painter Wang Wei (699–759), whose Wang-ch'uan villa can be considered a model for all great garden-retreats.

On the other hand, even though we still look somewhat down upon the scene, leaf B, the *Lesser Ts'ang-lang Pavilion,* is one of direct close-up presented with angled informality. Like a modern photograph the edge of the form may be cut anywhere by the picture-edge. There is a little of this and a little of that; the edge of a house, an antique bronze, the corner of a fence, the base of a tree, the edge of a plateau, a touch of swirling water. Certain as is each part, it is a momentary world over which the quiet staff-bearing scholar, framed by the arch of his gate, stands guard. Turning again to history, this is a late Sung view of how we are to approach a corner of man's praise of himself and nature.

So we move, with understated greys, through a rather beautiful compositional variety, entering the scene at left or right, controlled by diagonal or horizontal, calling on spare, curving shapes or, perhaps, a tightly textured mat of crowded tree-leaves. It is as though in our garden wandering the path were continually taking us around a new bend, exposing a hitherto hidden prospect. Implicit in garden design, this is particularly true of such a large garden as the Cho-cheng yüan. Each view—except for the first where formalism is a clear enough witness of the hand of man—has a human figure, either a scholar or a servant. A garden is to be enjoyed. The last scene, leaf H, the *Locust Pavilion,* returns to a frankly archaistic T'ang "space-cell."

The calligraphy in this album, facing each painting, takes a place of equal importance with the garden scenes. It is instructive to compare the final leaf (HH), which bears the date, with the dated inscription to *Gathering Mulberry Leaves* of six months earlier (no. XLIX, inscription). Superficially there are differences, but the essential style is typical of Wen's late calligraphy. It tends toward a marked staccato form, more often than not with a sharp ending which only very rarely carries smoothly to the next character. This sharpness is on many strokes. Technically, it is characterized by the term "exposing the tip" (of the brush, *lou-feng*). It is accentuated by the angle at which the brush is held. Within this general approach the album calligraphy is written rather richly and smoothly. The scroll inscription is less so, and it shows marked variations—from the very moist "blurred" first character to, at times, extremely thin ephemeral strokes. This is partly a matter of scale. Larger characters in this style tend to flow more smoothly in their form. But it is also a matter of brush, paper, ink, and the writer's intent. A worn brush lends itself to a more "broken" form. (The same brush seems to have been used for the dark texturing on the mountains.) Wen has deliberately written some characters a little differently from those in the garden poems. It is instructive to compare identical cyclical date-characters: the third and fourth characters in the next-to-last line in no. LI HH; the third and fourth characters in the last line in no. XLIX, inscription. Perhaps these are most helpful in understanding how a consistent structure can change in its outward appearance.

Just as styles in painting vary in the three works shown here from a single year, so we must expect the calligrapher to have options in what he chooses for his brush to reveal.

INSCRIPTIONS BY THE ARTIST:
[AA, *Bank of Many Fragrances (Fan-hsiang-wu):*]
> Various kinds of flowers are planted next to the thatched house:
> Purple luxuriance and red beauty in random array.
> The spring radiance and brilliance embroiders them with a thousand artifices;
> In the good air and scented mist a hundred fragrances mix.
> I love the odors that fill my bosom and sleeves,
> I do not heed the wind and dew that wets my clothes.
> My high thoughts are already beyond the noisy world.
> Aloof, I watch the bees flying up and down.

The Fan-hsiang-wu (bank of many fragrances) is in front of the Jo-shu-t'ang. It is planted with a mixture of various kinds of peonies, begonias, wisteria and other flowers. Meng Tsung-hsien (act. ca. 1161–1190) said in a poem: "Beside your small house is a bank of many fragrances" (i.e. the name is taken from this poem). Cheng-ming.

[BB, *Lesser Ts'ang-lang Pavilion (Hsiao Ts'ang-lang):*]
> Once a small pavilion was built by the Ts'ang-lang (pond),
> The green water still surrounds its empty railings.
> Here there are always wind and moon to offer to the fisherman,
> And boys, too, singing "Wash your hat tassels!"
> Rivers and lakes fill the whole land, enough for my enjoyment,
> For a hundred years the fish and birds have forgotten walls.
> Shun-ch'in is dead, Tu Ling (Tu Fu, 712–770) far away
> As a paragon of hermits who will compete with me?

The garden has several *mu* of water reservoirs, like Su Tzu-mei's (Su Shun-ch'in of the Sung Dynasty, who had a Ts'ang-lang pavilion at

LI A, *Bank of Many Fragrances*

Suchou) Ts'ang-lang ponds. So a pavilion was built amongst them, and called the Lesser Ts'ang-lang. Formerly Tzu-mei returned from the capital, Pien. Our lord from Wu (i.e. the owner of the garden, Wang Hsien-ch'en, *chin-shih* in the Hung-chih reign, 1488–1505) also came back from the northern capital. The name is taken from this coincidence of their travels.

[CC, *Hsiang River Bamboo Bank (Hsiang-yun-wu):*]
    Bamboos are planted around the low mound
    Forming a bank of bamboo around the edge.
    In full summer it already seems to be autumn,
    So deep is the wood, one cannot tell when it is noon.
    In its midst is one who has abandoned the world,
    Enjoying himself with a *ch'in* and a goblet.
    When a wind stirs he wakes too from drunkenness
    To sit and listen to the rain on the bamboo leaves.
The Hsiang-yün Bank is south of the Peach-blossom rill and north of the Huai-yü pavilion. It is planted all around with bamboos and is especially quiet and secluded. Cheng-ming.

[DD, *Banana Enclosure (Pa-chiao hsien):*]
    The new banana is more than ten feet tall;
    After rain it is clean as though washed.
    It does not dislike the high whitened wall,
    It elegantly matches the curved balustrade.
    Autumn sounds come into the cool pillow,
    Morning colors divide the green window.
    Let no one tell the heedless shears to take it,
    Leave it until the shade reaches the house.

LI C, *Hsiang River Bamboo Bank*

LI B, *Lesser Ts'ang-lang Pavilion*

[GG, *Jade Spring (Yü-ch'üan)*:]

Once I ladled water from Hsiang-shan
Cool as a stream of jade.
Would you know that as far as Yao (seventh star of the Dipper) is
    from the Milky Way
There is another clear jade spring?
Preparing a rope, I draw water with the clouds,
In an earthen jar, I boil it with moonlight.
What need of Lu Hung-chien (Lu Yü, a tea-master in the T'ang)?
At the first sip you will yourself decide.

At Hsiang-shan in the capital there is a Jade spring, where the Master
often ladled the water and made tea, and called himself Yü-ch'üan
shan-jen (Hermit of the Jade spring) after it. When he struck a spring in
the south-east corner of the garden, and the jar kept (its water) cold and
suitable for tea, no less than that of the Jade Spring, he gave it this name,
to show that he would not forget. Cheng-ming.

[HH, *Locust Pavilion (Huai-wo)*:]

Below the pavilion a tall locust tree falls over the wall,
Mist on the cold leaves wets my clothes.
The scattered flowers are sparse but their scent travels far,
The cool shade falls all around, of lasting benefit to the world,
The literary contests of the eighth moon recall past doings,
When the honors of the three ministers were entrusted to the
    candidates.
Since I became old I have not dreamt of Nan-k'o (of receiving high
    office),
Alone I move my bed to lie in the cool of the evening.

LI G, *Jade Spring*

LI E, *Fishing Stone*

The Banana Enclosure is to the left of the Huai-yü-t'ing. Later, palms were planted, to make a suitable shade for the summer months. Cheng-ming.

[EE, *Fishing Stone (Tiao-pi):*]

The white stone is clean and dustless;

Flat, it overhangs the stream of wild water.

I sit and watch the line rolling,

I take quiet pleasure in the jade-like turning (of the water).

I enjoy rivers and lakes, far off,

I forget cares, and terns and egrets become tame.

You must know that he who stretches his line,

Is not one who desires (to catch) fish.

The Fishing Stone is below the I-yüan-t'ai (Pavilion of Distant Thoughts). At the time of spring brightness, the shade of the willows and the falling flowers make one sit so absorbed as to forget to return. Cheng-ming.

[FF, *Garden to Attract Birds (Lai-ch'in-yu):*]

Here in summer a cool shade spreads over ten *mu*.

That is when the fruits begin to ripen in the long orchard.

At the place where the precious heavy baskets are divided and given away,

In a small window, I have got a rubbing of Yu-chün's (Wang Hsi-chih's) calligraphy.

The Lai-ch'in-yu (Garden to Attract Birds) consists of several hundred apple trees (*lin-ch'in*, literally "wood-birds") planted on both sides of the Ts'ang-lang pond.

LI D, *Banana Enclosure*

LI E, *Fishing Stone*

[GG, *Jade Spring (Yü-ch'üan):*]

Once I ladled water from Hsiang-shan
Cool as a stream of jade.
Would you know that as far as Yao (seventh star of the Dipper) is
  from the Milky Way
There is another clear jade spring?
Preparing a rope, I draw water with the clouds,
In an earthen jar, I boil it with moonlight.
What need of Lu Hung-chien (Lu Yü, a tea-master in the T'ang)?
At the first sip you will yourself decide.

At Hsiang-shan in the capital there is a Jade spring, where the Master
often ladled the water and made tea, and called himself Yü-ch'üan
shan-jen (Hermit of the Jade spring) after it. When he struck a spring in
the south-east corner of the garden, and the jar kept (its water) cold and
suitable for tea, no less than that of the Jade Spring, he gave it this name,
to show that he would not forget. Cheng-ming.

[HH, *Locust Pavilion (Huai-wo):*]

Below the pavilion a tall locust tree falls over the wall,
Mist on the cold leaves wets my clothes.
The scattered flowers are sparse but their scent travels far,
The cool shade falls all around, of lasting benefit to the world,
The literary contests of the eighth moon recall past doings,
When the honors of the three ministers were entrusted to the
  candidates.
Since I became old I have not dreamt of Nan-k'o (of receiving high
  office),
Alone I move my bed to lie in the cool of the evening.

LI G, *Jade Spring*

LI F, *Garden to Attract Birds*

The Locust Pavilion, the year *hsin-hai* (1551), autumn, the ninth month, the twentieth day. Wen Cheng-ming wrote.

(tr. Roderick Whitfield)

SEALS OF THE ARTIST:

 Wen Cheng-ming yin   [painting, leaf H: III/1]

 Yü-lan t'ang   [painting, leaf H: III/3]

 Wen Cheng-ming yin   [inscription, all leaves: I/1]

 Heng-shan   [inscription, all leaves: I/2]

COLOPHONS AND SEALS:

Chang Hsiao-ssu (early seventeenth century)

 Chang Tse-chih   [painting, leaf A: I/1]

Chou Tso-hsin (1637 *chin-shih*), T. Yu-hsin, bamboo painter from Kuei-chou

 Chou Tso-hsin yin   [inscription, leaf HH: III/6]

 Mo-nung   [inscription, leaf HH: III/7]

An Ch'i (1683–1742)

 I-chou chen-ts'ang

  [painting, leaf A: II/1]   [painting, leaf E: I/1]
  [painting, leaf B: I/1]   [painting, leaf F: I/1]
  [painting, leaf C: I/1]   [painting, leaf G: I/1]
  [painting, leaf D: I/1]   [painting, leaf H: II/1]

LI H, *Locust Pavilion*

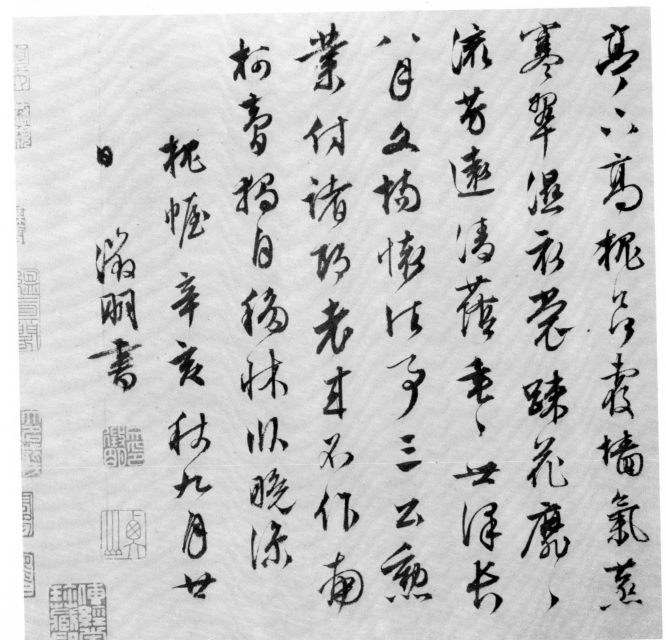

LI HH, 1551, ninth month

Chang T'ing-yü (1672–1755)
  Ch'uan-ching t'ang chen-ts'ang yin [inscription, leaf HH: II/1]

Chang Jo-ai (1713–1746), T. Ching-ts'ai, son of Chang T'ing-yü
  Lien-hsüeh chien-ting [inscription, leaf HH: III/3]

  Yün-chen-ko t'u-shu chi [inscription, leaf HH: III/4]

Yung Jung (1743–1790), sixth son of Ch'ien-lung emperor
  Huang liu-tzu [inscription, leaf HH: III/1]

  Kung ch'in-wang [inscription, leaf HH: III/2]

Yung Hsing (1752–1823), eleventh son of the Ch'ien-lung emperor;
colophon dated 1801

  I-chin chai [colophon]

Ying Ho (1771–1840), calligrapher-painter from Manchuria: label
Pao Hsi (late nineteenth century)
  Shen An p'ing-sheng chen-shang [inscription, leaf HH]
  Pao Hsi ch'ang-shou [inscription, leaf HH]
Naito Konan (1866–1934); colophon dated 1930
  Pao-ma an
Unidentified:
  Ta-ming Ch'eng shih Wei-an shang-chien
    t'u-shuCh'en [inscription, leaf HH: III/5]

BIBLIOGRAPHY:
Toan-zo (1928), IV, pl. 24/1–24/10.
Whitfield, *In Pursuit* (1969), pp. 66–75, cat. no. 3.

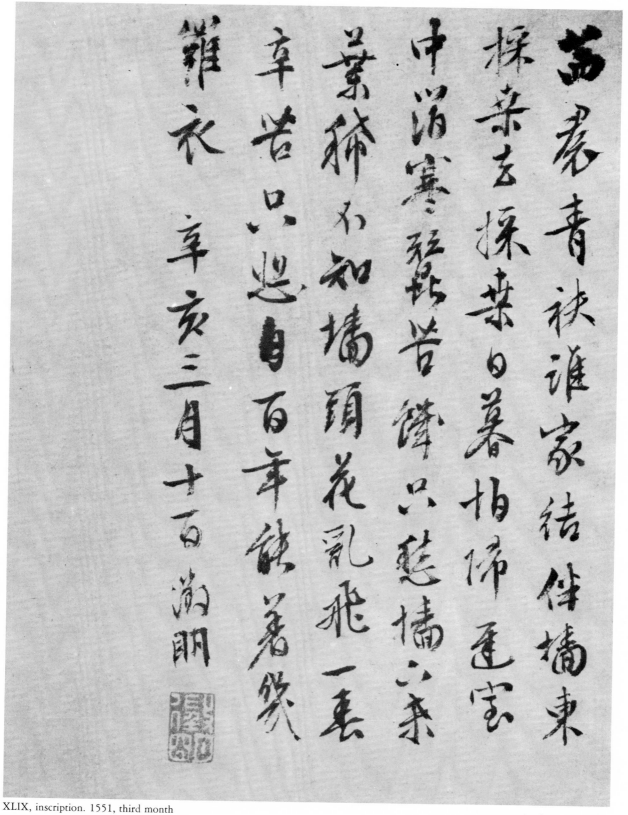

XLIX, inscription. 1551, third month

LII. THE RED CLIFF

(Ch'ih-pi t'u)
Dated 1552
Folding fan in ink and color on gold ground, 6⁵⁄₁₆″ high and 19⁵⁄₁₆″ wide
  (17.5 x 49.0 cm.)
Inscription, signature, and seals of the artist
Jean-Pierre Dubosc, Paris and Tokyo

This fan is of particular interest because it shows us yet another version of the Red Cliff theme (cf. nos. XXV, LVIII, LXII). The boat is rather different in that it is covered. The artist's touch is very light; the regular calligraphy is small, and the fan as a whole has a delicate dream-like quality.

There are also unfortunately key points of damage which affect the perfection of the composition as a whole. The right edge up to the calligraphy is repaired, and the damage extends into the next two segments at the lower edge so that the introductory tree-motif is badly cut. Upper parts of the cliff are similarly affected, but apparently not so significantly since definition must have originally faded at these points. More serious are certain areas of the calligraphy (there seems to have been water damage when the fan was folded). There has been rewriting in the area of the date, and half of the seals has been lost. Still, this cannot be an early work, and so one remains with the date as written.

Even admitting damage, structure is generally looser, the touch more ephemeral than what we have so far encountered. There is, for example, a rather unique double, or split, line that can be picked up in the trees or the bottom of the cliff.

But generally Wen characteristics are much in evidence: the introductory passage in the lower right above and beyond which we look directly into the scene; the tall, thin pine, rising above other trees; the "hanging cliff" at the left from which flows a stream and on which have been placed expected groves of trees, including the suggestion of dark twigs; the rather long, delicate rock texture-strokes; the "floating" smaller rocks.

It is important to see this beside other paintings in determining the exact qualities of Wen's late work. Where does this kind of fragile sensitive performance "fit" in relation to other versions of this theme? As to calligraphy, viewers will have to judge for themselves whether or not the tiny standard script conforms to Lu Shih-tao's assertions (cf. no. XLIII):

> The smaller Master Heng-shan's (Wen Cheng-ming's) small standard script gets, the more marvelous it becomes. . . ."

INSCRIPTION BY THE ARTIST: [Su Shih's "First Prose Poem on the Red Cliff" (translated in no. LXII); followed by]
1552, ——— month. Written by Cheng-ming.

SEALS OF THE ARTIST:
  Cheng-ming   [painting: I/1]
  Heng-shan   [painting: I/2]

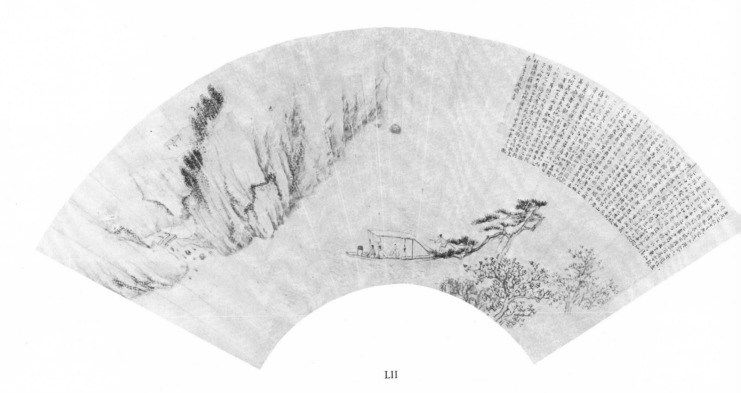

LII

LIII. LANDSCAPES AND PLANTS

Dated 1552, summer
Album of ten leaves in ink and color on gold-flecked paper and silk,
   8¼″ high and 12⁷/₁₆″ wide (21 x 31.5 cm.)
Inscription, signature, and seals of the artist
Mr. and Mrs. Wan-go H. C. Weng, New York

This album, showing on gold-flecked paper or silk either close-ups of small parts of nature or rather free sketches of wider views, appears to be a collection for a certain Yüeh-shan. The dates mentioned on the inscription that explains the general circum-

stances begin with 1543, when Yüeh-shan comes to Suchou asking for an album, and ends with the writing and painting in the summer of 1552. Because of the press of affairs during this interval and also because of Yüeh-shan's further travels, Wen never really got around to it for ten seasons, and then in a moment of inspiration got down to it, painting a leaf a day. Now, he adds, when Yüeh-shan returns in the winter he will have done his duty.

Certainly the whole reflects a good deal of haste; and the sketch-like manner seems consistent throughout. It was also painted from necessity rather than personal delight. The paintings make persistent use of a rather flat application of ink

LIII A

LIII B

that is often found in the brushwork of Wen Cheng-ming and that comes particularly close to the manner of the great Yüan artist Wu Chen—a mode which we will see becomes increasingly important in the last decade of Wen's life. But there are also other manners involved. Thus the ink-daub manner of Mi Fu (leaf G) as well as more Sung-like spatial recessions are evident in a landscape with a solitary fisherman. Here painting is on silk, and touches of free color are added as well. In another leaf the characteristic spare trees, lonely pavilion, and horizontal ink-dots are clear marks of Ni Tsan (leaf I).

As with the last fan, the general Wen manner is evident throughout. The haste or swiftness of execution, combined with the element of compulsion mentioned in the inscription, adds a dimension we have not yet so clearly encountered, and viewers will want to compare carefully the rather appealing informalities seen here with other paintings done at this general time to determine the work's validity within the style-history of this artist of many modes.

INSCRIPTIONS BY THE ARTIST:
In the autumn of 1543, Yüeh-shan, with his records, passed through Suchou. He brought me an old album, and asked me (to paint on it); but because I was too busy with ordinary affairs, I could not do it. Later, he often passed by here. But I was always busy with my brush

LIII C

LIII D

doing other things, or Yüeh-shan was in a hurry, so this album was left with me for almost ten years. During the early summer of this year, after a long rain, the sky cleared; the shade of the *huai* trees was full. Suddenly I was inspired. So I painted a leaf a day. I expect that Yüeh-shan will again pass by here this winter; then I will not have broken a former promise.

1552, summer, Cheng-ming inscribed.

[Leaf J:]

Feng-mu t'u ("wind-blown tree"). Cheng-ming.

SEALS OF THE ARTIST:

Wen Cheng-ming yin	[painting, leaves A–H: I/1]
Wen Cheng-ming yin	[painting, leaves I–J: I/1]
	[inscription: II/1]
Yü-ch'ing shan-fang	[inscription: II/2]

Yü-lan t'ang yin	[inscription: II/3]
T'ing-yün	[inscription: I/1]

COLOPHONS AND SEALS:

Weng T'ung-ho (1830–1904); see no. III

Weng T'ung-ho yin	[colophon: I/1]
Tzu-chih pai-kuei chih shih	[colophon: I/2]

Weng Wan-ko (present owner)

Weng Wan-ko	[inscription: III/1]

BIBLIOGRAPHY:

One Thousand Years (1968), nos. 30 and 31.

REMARKS:

"*With his records*" (artist's inscription) may be an inversion of an official title *chi-hsieh*.

"*Wind-blown tree*" (artist's inscription) is an obscure reference to the idea of the loss of one's parents.

LIII E

LIII F

LIII G

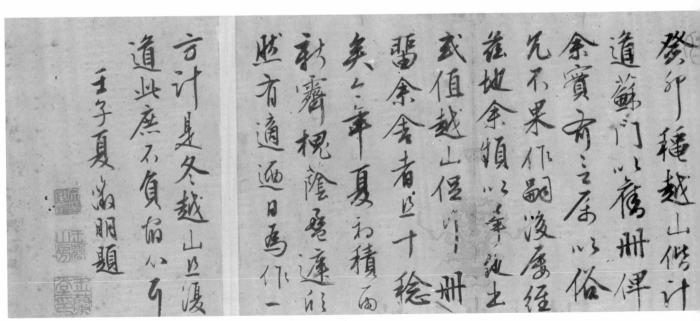

LIII, inscription

LIII H

LIII I

LIII J

LIV. VILLAGE IN THE RAIN

(*Chi-yü lien ts'un t'u*)
No date
Hanging scroll in ink on paper, 34⅝" high and 11⁷/₁₆" wide
 (87.9 x 29.1 cm.)
Inscription, signature, and seals of the artist
Museum of Fine Arts, Boston

This well-known, undated scroll firmly establishes us in Wen's Wu Chen manner, which can be characterized by the flat, bland use of ink. Ink and ink-tones, whether in rather thick lines or in washes, are the essential vehicles that carry the painting's structure. Because Shen Chou was fond of this manner, *Village in the Rain* is sometimes said to follow Shen Chou. The Wu Chen manner is a mode often associated with the later periods of an artist's work, as is true in the case of Shen Chou. Actually, both Shen and Wen used the manner early in life as well. But the claim for the Wu Chen manner as being most important in old age has a good deal of validity. The manner lends itself to this time in a man's life. Its brevities are appropriate for the time when the details of existence lie behind one; when what is important is more a matter of subtraction than addition; when one has said a great deal, and what is left to say can only be in praise of simplicity.

Wu Chen was the most deliberately understated of all Yüan artists.

In the painting of Wen Cheng-ming the work that with its date of 1555 clearly anchors the Wu Chen manner in the last decade of Wen's life is the handscroll on silk in Taipei, *Lofty Recluses in Streams and Mountains* (fig. 28). Keeping in mind that the latter is on silk as opposed to paper, its opening passage of land, rocks, trees, and plateau show Wen to be depending on the same introductory motif and style as in *Village in the Rain*. Two scholars, two huts, and even the fainter tree behind the second hut carry parallels even further. We can add here, too, similarity in the structuring of the far peaks. Closer they are heavily dotted and have accents of flat texture strokes. In the distance they are calm silhouettes.

As we have previously noted, however, one Yüan master may often suggest aspects of another. Thus, *Village in the Rain* is compositionally not too far removed from notions of Huang Kung-wang. The painting of a central receding valley marked by headlands alternating from side to side—hut in the lower right, bridge across the river, and rustic village beyond—is found in the composition we saw very early when Wen was copying Huang Kung-wang's *Leisurely Living at the Stream Pavilion* (no. VIII). In discussing that painting, it will be remembered, we pointed out certain overtones of

28. Wen Cheng-ming, *Lofty Recluses in Streams and Mountains*, 1555, opening section. National Palace Museum, Taipei

Wu Chen. It is also possible to detect on one of the top mountain rocks in *Village in the Rain* that free Y-shaped convention which is the mark of Huang's three-sided rock.

In general, however, it is the simple, flat manner of Wu Chen that dominates the landscape and helps to add its moist textures to the mood of rain. The surface is perhaps a little over-washed so that there is an extra lightness to some of the passages, but the painting is filled with Wen Cheng-ming touches —such matters as the thin, lofty vine-wrapped pine, the white skeletons of the tree forms against the thick, free matting of leaves, dark twig forms in a grove of wet-leaved deciduous trees, a distant waterfall seemingly just there without apparent origin in depth.

If flat ink-forms, consistent with those found in the dated painting of 1555, help assure a late date for this undated scroll, the feeling for receding space may be added as another characteristic that is generally a part of Wen's art at this time. Here this is complex rather than simple. His painting like his late calligraphy does not readily flow easily together. More exactly, there are two levels of distance. Thus in the foreground and middle distance there is a recession across wet-ink shoals in which is centered the net-carrying, rain-coated fisherman as he crosses the bridge. Just beyond the left-hand village, the water seems to recede sharply and directly back. This second plane has a skiff-seated figure as its main human motif.

Village in the Rain is a scroll at once fresh, unfettered in execution, and spacious in effect which helps us understand one of the important late modes of the artist. We will see other paintings in these last years that reveal the same Wu Chen manner.

INSCRIPTION BY THE ARTIST:
> Steady rain veils all the villages.
> Where has the mountain retreat gone?
> The autumn glory is fit to paint.
> (A man in) a straw coat and bamboo hat has come crossing the
> bridge.

Cheng-ming
(tr. Tomita and Tseng)

SEALS OF THE ARTIST:
Cheng-chung fu yin	[painting: I/1]
Wu-yen shih yin	[painting: I/2]

SEALS:
Yeh Meng-lung (1775–1832)
Chieh-ch'en chen-ts'and	[painting: III/1]
Yeh shih Meng-lung	[painting: III/2]

Yeh Yen-lan (1823–1897)
Lan-chi shih ling-sun so ts'ang	[painting: III/3]

Wu Ching-ch'üan (twentieth century)
Wu shih Ching-ch'üan chen-ts'ang chih yin	[painting: II/1]
Pao-hou chen-ts'ang	[painting: II/2]

BIBLIOGRAPHY:
Dubosc, *Great Chinese Painters* (1949), no. 14.
Tomita and Tseng, *Portfolio* (1961), pp. 10–11, pl. 52.
Sickman and Soper, *Art and Architecture of China* (1971), pl. 219.

LV. LANDSCAPE IN RAIN

No date
Fan in ink on gold paper, 5¹³/₁₆″ high and 16⁹/₁₆″ wide (14.7 x 41.7 cm.)
Inscription, signature, and seals of the artist
Jean-Pierre Dubosc, Paris and Tokyo

This modest fan is once again the painting of a landscape in the rain. The Wu Chen manner is inescapable. In the center there is unfortunately important damage. A narrow band running from top to bottom just to the right of the signature has had to be repaired and retouched; while in turn to its right the four final characters of a seven-character-line couplet have worn away, although illegible traces of the brush are still just visible. It is possible, judging from faint spots of ink, that there was once further writing to the left of the couplet and before the signature. The small size of the landscape has been made smaller by trimming across the top where the edge is too close to the hair-like calligraphy; the slots for the bamboo frame, which normally would end a short distance from the top, actually run into the present edge. Otherwise the fan's extant twenty-one segments seem to be all Wen.

It is a slight, informal landscape, and the theme is set by the poetry, broken as it is:

> The river's clouds, thick at evening—
>   ranks of spring trees.
> The fine rain blurs. . . .

For the empty, quiet mood of rains the forms are familiar. The major motif is the flat, white-trunked, richly dotted tree, leaning to offer a kind of sheltering "cave" for the seated fisherman-scholar. Similarly a tree shelters the bridge-crossing fisherman in *Village in the Rain* (no. LIV).

Here, too, is a broad sense of space, with the expected two layers of mountains in the distance. Moist horizontal fingers of shoal help to reinforce the firm horizontal that cuts the bending shape of the fan. The painting is certainly in the Wu Chen manner of Wen's last years. The use of fine hair-like calligraphy seems also consistent with Wen's later art and helps, although the work is slight, to confirm the validity of what we see.

INSCRIPTION BY THE ARTIST: [translated in text; signed:] Cheng-ming

SEAL OF THE ARTIST:
Cheng-ming   [painting: I/1]

REMARKS: see Dubosc, *Les Quatre* (1966), no. 13 for a fan painting of similar style and subject.

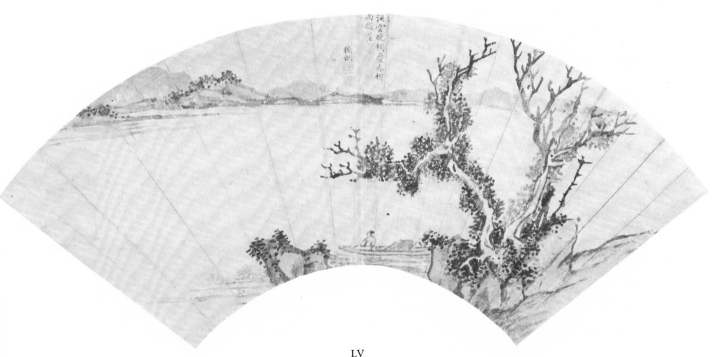

LV

191

LVI. LANDSCAPE IN THE STYLE OF WU CHEN

Dated 1556, third month, sixteenth day
Fan in ink on gold-flecked paper, 6⅝" high and 20¹³/₁₆" wide
  (17 x 53 cm.)
Inscription, signature, and seals of the artist
Hwa's Hou Chen Shang Chai

After two undated paintings in the Wu Chen manner, we have in a third example of the same style the historical assurance of a firm date: 1556. Familiar motifs are evident in what is a different and a much more compact composition: the introductory curve of land at the left; the tall, thin spare-branched pine, a grass hut, foreground patterns of white-trunked deciduous trees, moist ink leaves, the variation of bare-twigged branches, a tree leaning over to "protect" the human figure; then the moss-dotted hills, moist horizontal shoals, the far mountain washes, repeated verticals and shadowy leafage of the exact rows of mid-distance trees. Even the Y-shaped convention on a rock is visible in the foreground.

Motif-wise the style is secure. The skiff-seated fisherman by a bank is another direct Wu Chen idea. The prominent reed-forms in the foreground are, for us, a new feature but a typical Yüan device, again employed by Wu Chen. The compact nature of the composition does not destroy those notions of space we have found so important in this late style. Quite the contrary. The pattern of rocks and trees in the foreground, following in their shifting angles the rayed lines of the fan segments, creates a screen *through* which we look directly into the distance. The surface of the fan itself adds its own texture in that it is of speckled gold. It is not a solid surface and thus contains its own "depth." Brushed with a moist freedom, we are to consider this landscape, as with the last two in the manner, a quiet rain-filled view, reflecting the springtime in which it was painted.

INSCRIPTION BY THE ARTIST:
1556, third month, sixteenth day, written at the Yü-lan Pavilion. Cheng-ming.

SEAL OF THE ARTIST:
  Cheng-ming   [painting: I/1]

SEAL:
Unidentified
  Shen Wu shen-ting   [painting: II/1]

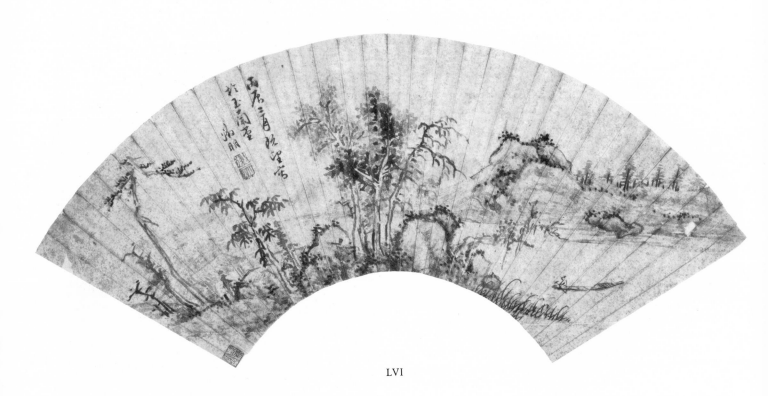

LVI

192

LVII. TWO SCHOLARS, OLD CYPRESS, AND WATERFALL

Dated 1556, fifth month, eighth day
Hanging scroll in ink on paper, 23″ high and 10⁷/₁₆″ wide (58.5 x 26.5 cm.)
Inscription, signature, and seals of the artist
Ernest Erickson, New York

Again, now in the closing years of his life, Wen Cheng-ming returns to the theme of the old cypress. If we contrast the version of the 1530s (no. XXX), we are made aware of how the artist has matured. But the theme in the decade of the fifties shows its own variant interpretations.

The *Cypress and Old Rock* of 1550 (no. XLVIII) is a kind of garden arrangement, something consciously abstracted out of the winter scene of nature for the particular purposes of the artist; it is a manipulated nature-still-life. As such, the theme inevitably holds special personal meaning. An artist-made subject, it speaks of the wider world only insofar as the intensity of personal concentration in interpreting accepted metaphor is able to reveal it.

It is clear, however, from *Old Trees by a Wintry Brook* (no. L), that the tree-portrait could be seen as part of a legitimate landscape. Now, finally, five years later, in *Two Scholars, Old Cypress, and Waterfall* the theme is integrated into a complete setting. Nature quite literally enfolds it. Man and tree, tree and mountain, mountain and water are in tune. There is even the inclusion of music, as the single silent figure of the boy with the *ch'in* suggests— harmony with the notes of nature. This reminds us of a traditional attitude toward figure-painting in China. Figures could be shown isolated against the untouched silk or paper. Then, perhaps to the very same figures could be added a setting of trees, architecture, and land. Wen doubtless knew that in the past more ancient scholars had, in paintings, also leaned on trees. At least one famous composition showing such a figure survives, and it may well go back to the tenth century.[1]

There is, thus, no escape from the fact that the theme continues to be a traditional one and that it is essentially the old tree. A little looser, a little softer, more moist to fit a summer setting—if we can judge both from the appearance of the relaxed scholars and of the foliage and from the time it was painted; the trees, however, are cut from the same mold as in the winter scene of 1551 (no. L). Structure is similar, especially in the main cypress where a major vertical trunk with the richest leafage is countered by a second that forks behind it and to the left. Dots, bark, twigs, broken limb-ends are all analogous. Consistent with the richer scene there are slight embellishments. A dark vine entwines the foreground trunk, hangs from its

upper branches; and a horizontal tree-trunk extends from behind the hill at the right, convenient for the leaning of idling scholars whose poses in turn echo the stance of trees, and one of whose sleeves blends precisely with the spiraled texture of a trunk.

Not only is the setting more complete, it is less harsh. Rocks and landforms are rounded, texture-strokes run parallel. Outlines, no longer stark, are enriched with the ink-dots of low growth. In water

LVII

there is movement, but it also flows to a quiet empty pool.

Space, such an important factor at the time, has similarly lost much of its ambiguity. Scholars are behind the foreground land. We go into the scene which surrounds the whole tree complex. Back of the tree is a mountain, not paper (just as we looked *through* trees in the last fan). And even the cliff recedes to allow a pocket for the fall of water. Only at the very top are we subtly aware of a kind of surface return with darker dots, the presence of the paper and thin calligraphy. But this is at best only in the upper quarter of the picture, not in the upper three-quarters.

The theme as a whole is inevitably one of poignant struggle. To my knowledge western artists have never so justly linked the battle of age, its insistence on survival, its ultimate nobility, to nature's even stronger endurance. Rembrandt saw it directly in the worn and moving patterns of an exact face, and the modern poet cries, even shouts, his personal defiance:

> Do not go gentle into that good night,
> Old age should burn and rave at close of day;
> Rage, rage against the dying of the light.[2]

With Wen Cheng-ming, quieter but no less real, is a very "Chinese" sense that the fight against destruction is not a theme for human isolation. Man's sleeve, man's body, the tilt of a head, even an irregular facial profile find parallel shapes and lines in trees whose selected broken branches offer brittle benediction to the constant life and friend-ship below.

NOTES:
1. Sirén, *Chinese Painting* (1956–58), III, pl. 102. The painting is of *Four Scholars in a Garden Collating Old Writings,* now in the Palace Museum, Peking. There is a copy of this design in the Freer Gallery.
2. Daniel Jones, ed., *Dylan Thomas: The Poems,* London, 1971, p. 207.

INSCRIPTION BY THE ARTIST:
Painted in 1556, fifth month, eighth day. Cheng-ming.

SEAL OF THE ARTIST:
Cheng-ming   [painting: II/1]

SEALS:
Ma Chi-tso (twentieth century)
Ma Chi-tso yin   [painting: III/1]
Chi-tso shen-ting   [mounting: II/1]
Ma shih shu-hua   [mounting: II/2]
Li (unidentified)
Ho-fei Li shih Hsiao-hua-ch'an shih chen-ts'ang [mounting: I/1]
Wang-yün ts'ao-t'ang chen-ts'ang   [painting: I/2]
Shih ch'an sheng-ting chen-chi   [mounting: II/1]
Hsiao-hua-ch'an shih   [mounting: II/3]
Ho-fei Li shih Wang-yün ts'ao-t'ang chen-ts'ang
  chin-shih shu-hua chih chang   [mounting: II/4]
Unidentified
Ting-hou shen-ting   [painting: I/1]
Shuai chiu chia yu Yüan T'an kung i i tzu——chou?
  tsai tzu Ts'ang-feng chien-shang chih chang [painting: III/2]

BIBLIOGRAPHY:
Sirén, *Chinese Painting* (1956–58), VI, pl. 212.
Gyllensvärd, "Some Chinese Paintings" (1964), pls. 11 and 12.

LVIII. THE RED CLIFF

(Ch'ih-pi t'u)
No date (appended calligraphy dated 1556, autumn)
Handscroll, ink and light color on paper, 12″ high and 59″ long
    (30.5 x 150 cm.)
Seals and calligraphy of the artist
Hellen and Joe Darion, New York

This beautiful idyllic rendering of what is by now a familiar theme offers still further variations. The same basic iconography is present: introductory land (in this case dominated by four pine-trees), the angle of water, the necessary boat (here covered and with a red rail), a tiny moon over a far line of hills, and then the left-hand block of land with its overhanging cliffs and falling water.

It differs in important respects from other handscrolls of the theme that we have considered: the early undated version from the Weng collection (no. XXV) and the 1552 painting in the Freer Gallery (fig. 12). Now the taut diagonal of the composition is considerably relaxed. The vertical stance of tree, or cliff, or waterfall is more pronounced. Thus we have rather stable blocks of land both at beginning and end. Similarly, the space between recedes more exactly, directly back. It is a rather certain recession into distance which is helped by patterns of water and exact clumps of reeds. The far mountains, over which hovers the tiny moon, present no real ambiguities as to the nature of their distance.

Some of the "looseness" that we noted in the brief fan of 1552 (no. LII) is also here, but it is treated with far greater assurance and imagination. Certainly by now we have enough familiarity with the motifs of Wen Cheng-ming so that in all important aspects they will be recognized as present here—trees, rock-forms and textures, dotting, the wash of far hills. But what marks their presence here is a sense of freedom which leads to a kind of unfettered pouring out of these forms—their fullness, the constantly shifting broken outlines so that shapes are not exact, the varied dancing touches of texture, the looseness of the dotting, the flow of many streams, the delight in free touches of wash. There is a very special flavor to this rendering of a traditional scholarly theme.

Thus, along with a more stable composition and more exact sense of space—possibly as a consequence of that structural order—we find a free delight. Expressiveness is above all sealed by its color. Color is traditional and like that in other Suchou painting of the time restricted to a limited palette of warm and cool tones. But its application is consistent with the kind of freedom we have already described. More often than not, it spills over edges of form. It covers leaf-areas, a rock, or even a figure with a veil of transparent tone, a light ephemeral cloud that has its own independent existence which yet reinforces form and gives to that form a special vibrant, magical existence. Because this color spills over edges, forms are not confined. They are constantly interacting and even extending out into the surrounding space.

The painting itself is identified as the work of Wen Cheng-ming only by seals, but following the painting is the writing of Su Shih's ode in beautiful running script, inscribed with the date of the mid-

LVIII

autumn of 1556. The original ode also told of an autumnal experience. The calligraphy is written on carefully ruled paper and thus, despite the freedom of its form, takes on a special formal elegance. Earlier we spoke of Wen's late calligraphy as having a rather unique sharp staccato quality (no. LI) with a marked range of thick and thin in its strokes and above all a sense of the separateness of each individual character. The exposed tip at the end of a stroke had special importance. All this holds here, although partly because of the larger scale, partly because of the more elegant formal lay-out, Wen is much smoother in his execution. It comes closer to the "flow" found in the calligraphy of Wen's artistic model, Chao Meng-fu.[1] Insofar as this is the direct result of a slightly larger scale it fits Lu Shih-tao's praise (cf. no. XLIII) ". . . his big writing becomes even more striking the bigger it grows."

NOTE:
1. Cf. my brief essay on a late Wen Cheng-ming calligraphy scroll in *The Grand Tradition* (1975), where Wen's writing is compared to Chao Meng-fu.

CALLIGRAPHY BY THE ARTIST: [writing of the "First Prose Poem on the Red Cliff" (*Ch'ien Ch'ih-pi fu*) by Sung poet Su Shih (1036–1102), for translation see no. LXII; signed]
1556, mid-autumn (*chung-ch'iu*, i. e., eighth month, fifteenth day), written in the T'ing-yün Pavilion. Cheng-ming.

SEALS OF THE ARTIST:

T'ing-yün	[painting: I/1]
	[calligraphy: I/1]
Wen Cheng-ming yin	[painting: III/1]
	[calligraphy: III/1]
Heng-shan	[painting: III/2]
	[calligraphy: III/2]

COLOPHONS AND SEALS:
Wang Ku-hsiang (1501–1568)

Chien-pai chai	[painting: I/5]
Hsiang Yüan-pien (1525–1590)	
Mo-lin shan-jen	[painting: I/7]
Tzu-ching fu yin	[painting: I/8]
Hsiang Shu-tzu	[painting: I/9]
Fang Kuan-ch'eng (1698–1768), T. I-t'ien, Wen-t'ing from T'ung-ch'eng, Anhui	
I-t'ien	[painting: I/6]
K'ung Kuang-t'ao (nineteenth century), T. Hsiao-t'ang, from Nan-hai, Kuangtung; dated 1800	
Kuang-t'ao	[colophon: I/1]
K'ung	[frontispiece: I/1]
Shao-t'ang shen-ting	[frontispiece: I/2]
	[painting: II/3]
Yüeh-hsüeh lou	[painting: I/3]
Nan-hai K'ung shih shih-chia pao-wan	[painting: I/4]
	[calligraphy: VI/1]
Chih-sheng ch'i-shih shih sun Kuang-t'ao yin	[calligraphy: I/2]
K'ung shih Yüeh-hsüeh lou shou-ts'ang shu-hua yin	
K'ung	[calligraphy: I/3]
K'ung-shih chien-ting	[calligraphy: II/1]
Hou-ch'ang fu hsin-shang	[calligraphy: IV/1]
Shao-t'ang han-mo	[calligraphy: IV/2]
Yüeh-hsüeh lou chien-ts'ang chin-shih shu-hua t'u-chi chih chang	[calligraphy: IV/3]
	[calligraphy: VI/2]
Chung Han? (probably nineteenth century or before)	
Lung-shan Chung Han? hoa Chi-an chih chang	[frontispiece: III/1]
Liu-i chü-shih	[frontispiece: III/2]
Mo-liang	[frontispiece: II/1]
Chang Ching (first half of the nineteenth century)	
Chang Ching chih yin	[calligraphy: IV/4]
Keng-pai so ts'ang	[calligraphy: IV/5]
Huang Wen (twentieth century), Cantonese collector	
Huang shih Huai-hsüan t'ang ts'ang	[painting: II/1]
Joe Darion (present owner)	
Tai Li-an ts'ang	[calligraphy: V/1]
Weng Wan-ko (twentieth century); dated 1971	
Weng Wan-ko chien-shang	[painting: I/2]
	[calligraphy: IV/6]
Weng Wan-ko	[colophon: I/1]
Unidentified	[painting: II/2]

BIBLIOGRAPHY:
K'ung, *Yüeh-hsüeh lou shu-hua lu* (1907), IV, p. 11.
Chinese Painting, Chang Erh-shih (1971), pp. 36–37.

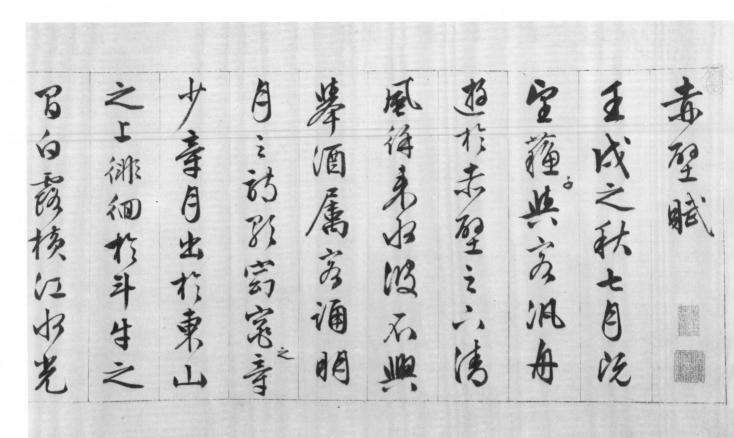

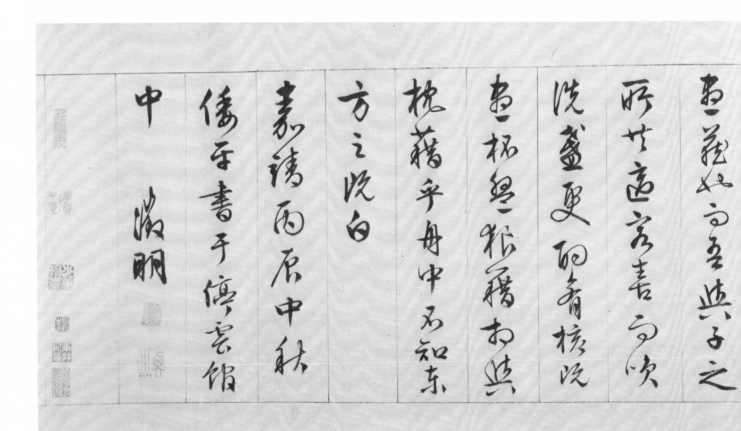

198

LIX. ALBUM OF PAINTING AND CALLIGRAPHY

A, *Narcissus;* B, *Geese and Reeds;* C, *Plum Blossoms;* D, *Crows and Old Tree;* E, *Magnolia*
Dated 1558, spring
Ten album leaves mounted as handscroll (five paintings with following leaves inscribed with poems); painting in ink on plain paper, calligraphy (running script) in ink on gold-flecked paper; 12″ high and 254″ long (30.7 x 645 cm.)
Inscriptions, signature, and seals of the artist
Anonymous loan

Now we have reached all but the final year of Wen's life. He is eighty-eight (by Chinese count, eighty-nine). His calligraphy remains strong and, as we shall see, capable of unfaltering stylistic variants. His painting is itself not far from calligraphy. It is pictorially rather simple, depending a great deal on how brush reacts with a surface, playing with pattern, but where space is called for very much aware of its importance. This album sums up these qualities.

There are three flowers and two abbreviated landscapes. The flowers are close-ups. Their forms are cut by the edge of the picture. This has the effect of thrusting them forward. They are shapes on or just beneath the surface of the paper. With *Narcissus* (leaf A), flat long strokes define a bending screen of leaves against which play the briefer curving shapes of blossoms. Seen through this light

pure form, is the darker shape of a rock for whose borders Wen still calls on the old convention of "flying-white." There are characteristic brief texture-strokes. It is a direct view. Form is the result of calculated simplicities, but form—and space—are very much present in the twisted curve of a leaf, the varied poses of a blossom, and the placing of something in front and something behind.

With *Plum Blossoms* (C) a similar touch is found. Flat, independent strokes are called on to create the sharpness of bare twigs. Again brief blossoms in varied poses enliven this brittle frame. Lines showing a split brush and textures moist and dry are reserved for the tree-trunk, which is somewhat withdrawn behind the most forward branches. It is not without meaning that in its sharp taut form, in its sense of a partially glimpsed view of something seen in nature, it recalls a similar plum-blossom study by Shen Chou.[1] Wen's study is marked by a special light purity of tone. *Magnolia* (E) brings back the same approach to this flower that we saw in an earlier *Magnolia* (no. XLVII). Here, however, there is no color, and to bring out the white a light cloud of ink-wash is brushed around the blossoms. Beyond matters of color and evidence of under-drawing that marked the painting of 1549, there is no essential change in this later flower. The blossoms are more fragile, a little looser, a little freer, but stem and branch are built up by the same moist overlays of touches of the brush.

If pattern that does not destroy a respect for

LIX A

LIX B

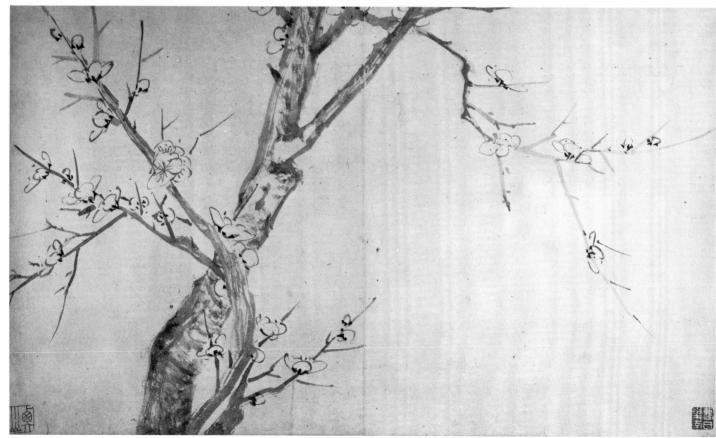

LIX C

three-dimensional form is a key to the understanding of the flowers, the brief landscapes are pattern that respects a sense of space. *Geese and Reeds* (B) combines an introductory slant of land, textured by both wet and dry strokes, with precisely placed islands of moist horizontal shoals and vertical sharp-leafed reeds that retreat directly into the distance where again we pick up a pattern in the spotted bent-winged Vs of birds. In *Crows and Old Tree* (D) the tree is reduced to such a defoliated sketched symbol that its species is not easily definable; but its leaning textured trunk, its fan of twig shapes, its "decor" of birds and spare moss-dots are placed against a low receding backdrop of water. Rocks help further to articulate exactly this shallow fading space.

In sum, what is found here is a limited number of forms—brushstrokes, if you will—whose visual and structural purposes are clear. Certainly all outward show of brilliance is stilled. Pattern, surface, materials, technique—the things of conscious art—are subdued in their simplicity, in their understatement. A sense of quiet unassuming space—never strong or deep—attests to the continuing reality of our experience of the physical world. But surely these are statements of acceptance. The *Magnolia* shows little real change from nine years before. *Plum Blossoms* is not far from Shen Chou. Space and ink-touches in the brief landscapes are often close to his Wu Chen manner. What is known

can be said again with the "play" of the brush. It is possible that it is said with greater purity, or with greater assurance through lesser means. But invention is for youth.

Nor does Wen write new poetry. The poems of youth are brought back again (cf. no. XLIX). Although only one can be found in Wen's collected works, where it is in an early sequence, his inscription makes no effort to distinguish it from the others. All appear to be "former works." They are written, sometimes in characters so personal that they are difficult to read, in a carefully framed space on gold-flecked paper. The style is a running style that on occasion flows briefly but more often reveals a sharp brittleness—points, abrupt change from thick to thin, the separateness of each form—that is often a mark of Wen's late calligraphy.

NOTE:
1. Edwards, *The Field of Stones* (1962), pl. 48 D.

INSCRIPTION BY THE ARTIST: [a poem is written after each of the five leaves; the fifth reads as follows:]
>The green *t'ung* tree is already bare;
>In the iced valley, the rushing flow—
>Alone I walk through formless spaces.
>Dogs bark away all trace of men,
>The dawn sun dresses the trees in the woods;
>Blue mist suddenly is gone.
>For a while I watch the temple-cliff wind
>Blow snow from the tops of pines.
>   (based on tr. by Elizabeth Bennett)
In the spring of 1558, I happened to come across several leaves

LIX D

LIX E

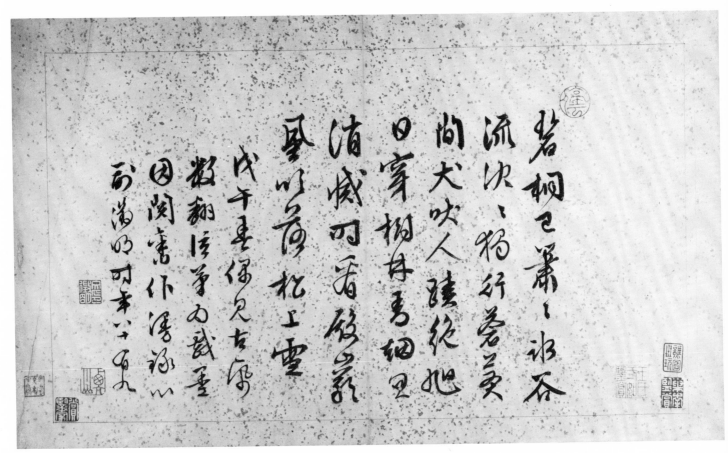

LIX, calligraphy, leaf E

of old paper and rather swiftly made ink-plays. Since I had been looking over some old works (poems), I leisurely wrote down a group of them.

SEALS OF THE ARTIST:
T'ing-yün
[calligraphy, leaf A': II/1]
[calligraphy, leaf B': I/1]
[calligraphy, leaf C': II/1]
[calligraphy, leaf D': II/1]
[calligraphy, leaf E': III/1]

Wen Cheng-ming yin
[painting, leaf A: I/1]
[calligraphy, leaf A': III/1]
[calligraphy, leaf B': II/1]
[painting, leaf E: II/1]
[calligraphy, leaf E': IV/1]

Wen Chung-tzu
[painting, leaf B: I/1]
[calligraphy, leaf A': III/2]
[calligraphy, leaf C': III/1]
[calligraphy, leaf D': III/1]

Heng-shan
[calligraphy, leaf B': II/2]
[painting, leaf C: II/1]
[calligraphy, leaf C': III/2]
[calligraphy, leaf D': III/2]
[calligraphy, leaf E': IV/2]

COLOPHONS AND SEALS:
Lo Chen-yü (1866–1940), scholar; dated 1914
Lo Chen-yü yin   [colophon: I/1]
Naito Tora (1886–1934), Japanese scholar and collector; dated 1915
Ch'en Hu   [colophon: II/1]
Pao-tso an-chu   [colophon: II/2]
Nagao Ko (nineteenth–twentieth century), Japanese; dated 1915
Yü-shan   [colophon: III/1]
Ts'ao Ch'ao-nan (unidentified)
Ts'ao shih Ch'ao-nan
[painting, leaf A: II/1]
[calligraphy, leaf A': IV/1]
[painting, leaf B: II/2]
[calligraphy, leaf B': III/1]
[painting, leaf C: I/1]
[calligraphy, leaf C': IV/1]
[painting, leaf D: I/1]
[calligraphy, leaf D': IV/1]
[painting, leaf E: I/2]
Tzu-sun pao t'zu
[painting, leaf B: II/1]
[painting, leaf E: I/1]

Ch'iao-kuo shih wan
[calligraphy, leaf E': I/1]

Ch'ao-nan chien-shang
[calligraphy, leaf E': I/2]

Shang-chien chia
[calligraphy, leaf E': V/1]

Wang Erh-ju (unidentified)
Wang shih Ehr-ju chien-shang
[calligraphy, leaf A': I/1]
[calligraphy, leaf B': I/2]
[calligraphy, leaf C': I/1]
[calligraphy, leaf D': I/1]
[calligraphy, leaf E': II/1]

Unidentified
Yen-chou t'ai-shou
[calligraphy, leaf C': V/2]

Shang-hai Wang Ch'ing-hsün chia ts'ang kuo
[calligraphy, leaf C': V/1]
[calligraphy, leaf E': VI/1]

Shu-i k'an kuo
[calligraphy, leaf D': V/1]

REMARKS: Of the five poems by Wen Cheng-ming, only one (calligraphy, leaf E') is recorded in *Fu-t'ien-chi,* ch. 2/p. 3b. (p. 108). This poem, which has nothing to do with spring or the *Magnolia* it follows, indicates either that the mounting is wrong or that Wen was not concerned with such relationships.

LX. TAOIST SCRIPTURE: CALLIGRAPHY

(Huang-t'ing ching)
Seal script
Dated 1558, sixth month, fifteenth day
Handscroll, ink on paper, 9⅛″ high and 31″ long (23.2 x 78.7 cm.)
Inscription, signature, and seals of the artist
Mr. and Mrs. Wan-go H. C. Weng, New York

Wen's versatility in reasserting the validity of established forms now at the very close of his life was never more clear than in his writing of this complex ancient style. The text is the same text mentioned earlier (no. XXXIX) in comparing Wen's standard script to the writing of the Taoist scripture *Huang-t'ing ching,* dealing with the nourishment of the human body. The old classics return again and again and take on new life, not just because of their content but because the form through which that content is expressed clothes it in proper antiquity. That antiquity lives because a modern man has remade it. Wen dates the scripture itself to 356, which is the inscribed date of Wang Hsi-chih's writing. He also copies down the place of the original writing, Shan-yin hsien (cf. fig. 23), and even Wang's mistaken writing of the character for "five" *(wu)* that precedes it. Wen's recreation, transforming the original standard script into seal script, comes twelve-hundred and two years later. Again it is appropriate to recall Lu Shih-tao's praise of Wen's calligraphy, "Who says contemporaries cannot compare with the ancients?" (see no. XLIII).

Here, by writing not the standard script of the fourth century but the seal script of the much earlier Chou dynasty, a Ming scholar is giving the text even more of an antique look—not inappropriate for the ancient wisdom of Taoism and suitable for scholarly notions of archaism. But more important from an artist's view is that we are therefore taken to a different medium, that of calligraphy cast in ancient bronze or carved on antique stone. To the purist this is perhaps stretching the brush too far, for in imitating the permanence of stone and bronze it has no real chance to show inherent qualities of flexibility and expressiveness. However, Wen is an artist who in fact is not afraid to transcend his medium —or at least stretch it to its furthest limits. We have seen him using a brittle, almost "carved" line in a landscape (no. XLV). His interest in the craftsman-like blue-green colored scene (no. XXXVIII) or his "illustrations" of scholarly gatherings and retreats bring him closer to such craftsmen as Ch'iu Ying (no. XXXIX) than might always seem proper for the pure scholar-painter. At any rate, Wen is not to be confined to bland variations in learned tones of ink. We have often mentioned the brittle, staccato quality of much of his callig-raphy. Thus, within the range of his art, these seemingly impeccable wire-like forms are completely in keeping with what Anne Clapp has described above as a "premeditated formalism, which takes precedence over literary and illustrative meaning and defies natural subject matter."

It must be admitted, however, that Wen's seal script is rare. Nor did it receive excessive praise. Wang Shih-chen (1526–1590), in lauding Wen's regular script, maintained that he had little confidence in his seal writing, that it was only "competent" or "adequate."[1] All the more remarkable, that at eighty-eight he should still be writing it and with such obvious strength and care.

Another important example of the style may be found in the National Palace Museum in Taiwan when Wen was writing out the *Thousand Character Classic* in four different scripts, among them, in 1536, a seal-script version. Here, then, is a precedent for taking a text in one script and transforming it into another. Individual characters differ from the 1536 writing, but as with his painting in this twilight year, one cannot escape the feeling that Wen is continuing to reveal what a long life has already established.

Here, despite a closeness to ancient writing, there is a difference. Later writers in this archaic style inevitably create changes. As opposed to staunch archaic strength, there tends to be a manipulation of shape, perhaps an elongation of form, a thinner and more flexible line.[2] Certainly Wen here presents a sharp elegance, a movement in a not quite tightly even brush, and a variety of shapes that affirm his consistent expression. The guise of antiquity does not conceal it.

NOTES:
1. Ecke, *Chinese Calligraphy* (1972), no. 50.
2. See an analysis of an eighteenth century writer in this style in Ledderose, "An Approach" (1972), pp. 3–6.

INSCRIPTION BY THE ARTIST:
1558, sixth month, fifteenth day, Heng-shan Cheng-ming, seal-script.

SEALS OF THE ARTIST:

Wen Cheng-ming yin	[calligraphy: II/1]
Heng-shan	[calligraphy: II/2]

COLOPHONS AND SEALS:
Wang Ku-hsiang (1501–1568), painter from Suchou

Yu-shih	[calligraphy: V/1]
Lu-chih	[calligraphy: V/2]

Chu Chih-ch'ih (sixteenth century), collector

Hsiu-ning Chu Chih-ch'ih chen-ts'ang t'u-shu	[calligraphy: III/2]
Liu-keng t'ang yin	[calligraphy: III/3]
Chu Chih-ch'ih chien-shang	[calligraphy: I/1]
Tzu-sun pao-chih	[calligraphy: I/2]

Ts'ai Fang-ping (b. 1626), calligrapher; dated 1704

Pu-sui shih	[colophon: I/1]
Ts'ai Fang-ping yin fu	[colophon: II/1]
Ch'ien-shou	[colophon: II/2]
Ch'en pen pu-i	[colophon: II/3]

Li Hung-shih (1786 *chin-shih*), calligrapher

Jung-p'u kuo-yen	[calligraphy: V/5]

Wen Ting (1766–1852), painter, calligrapher from Hsiu-shui, Chekiang

Wen Ting	[front damask: I/1]
Wen Ting	[colophon: III/1]
Ch'ien-lung ping-hsü sheng	[front damask: I/2]

Hsüeh-k'uang fu yin	[calligraphy: IV/2]
Wen T'ing pao-chih	[calligraphy: IV/3]
T'ing-yün	[colophon: I/2]

Chang T'ing-chi (1768–1848), calligrapher; dated 1835

Shu-wei	[colophon: IV/1]
Chang T'ing-chi yin	[colophon: IV/2]

Yin Shu-po (1769–1847), painter from Chia-hsing, Chekiang; dated 1837

Shu-po yin	[colophon: V/1]
Man-ch'ing	[colophon: V/2]
Chi-ch'ou wu-ch'en chi-ch'ou wu-ch'en	[colophon: VI/1]

Ta-shou (b. 1791), monk; dated 1838

Ta-shou chih yin	[colophon: VII/1]
Liu-chou	[colophon: VII/2]

Ch'ien T'ien-shu (Ch'ing dynasty), calligrapher

Ch'ien T'ien-shu yin	[calligraphy: III/4]
	[colophon: III/2]

Chang Nan-i (Ch'ing dynasty)

Nan-i	[calligraphy: III/1]

Weng Wan-go (present owner)

Weng Wan-ko ts'ang	[calligraphy: IV/1]

Unidentified (probably sixteenth century)

Mao shih Chiu-shou	[calligraphy: V/3]
T'ien-ch'ih shih-pi	[calligraphy: V/4]
Heng-yen ko shu-hua yin	[calligraphy: I/3]

BIBLIOGRAPHY:
Ecke, *Chinese Calligraphy* (1971), no. 50.

LX

LXI. RECORD OF THE GARDEN FOR SOLITARY ENJOYMENT: CALLIGRAPHY

(Tu-lo yüan chi)
Running script
On the painting *The Garden for Solitary Enjoyment,* by Ch'iu Ying
Dated 1558, second month, fifteenth day, and 1558, intercalary seventh month, thirteenth day

Handscroll; painting in ink and color on silk, calligraphy in ink on paper; 11″ high and 150″ long (28 x 381 cm.)
Inscription, signature, and seals of the artist
Mr. and Mrs. Wan-go H. C. Weng, New York

Wen Cheng-ming's contribution to this impressive scroll is his calligraphy. Again he is writing out one of the classics—a theme from the past that helps reinforce the ideals of Wen's existence. Ch'iu Ying's painting illustrates it.

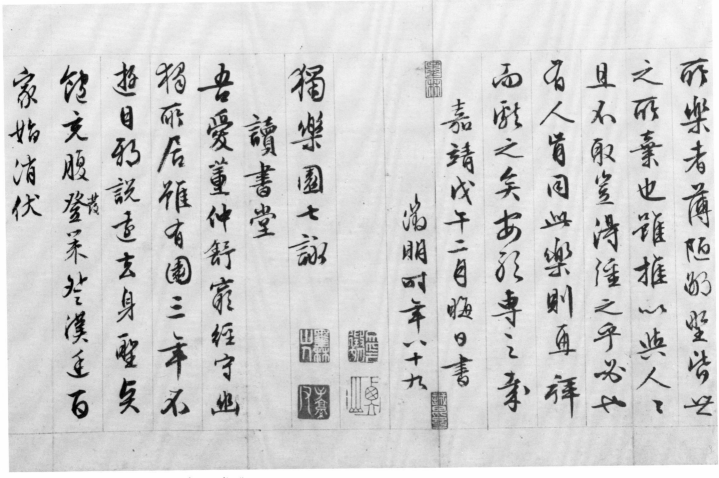

LXI, *Record,* end, and the poem "Hall for Reading"

LXI, painting before calligraphy: Ch'iu Ying, *The Garden for Solitary Enjoyment,* section showing, from right, Hall for Reading,

The calligraphy comprises the text of Ssu-ma Kuang's (1019–1086) *Tu-lo yüan chi (Record of the Garden for Solitary Enjoyment)* of 1073, which Wen wrote out in the second month of 1558. Seven poems, all by Ssu-ma Kuang, and then a final poem in praise of the garden by the slightly younger Su Shih, the poet who has figured most prominently in this exhibition as the originator of the Red Cliff theme, were added by Wen in the autumn. Ssu-ma Kuang was the great statesman-

historian of his time. In 1071 he moved to Loyang in Honan province, where he bought twenty acres of land to the north of Tsun-hsien fang in 1073 and built his Garden for Solitary Enjoyment.

Here again is that special combination of artistic excellence in sixteenth-century Suchou—the calligraphy of the great scholar artist, Wen Cheng-ming, and the picture by the great illustrator-painter, Ch'iu Ying (cf. no. XXXIX). Again there is no evidence of contemporary collaboration. They were

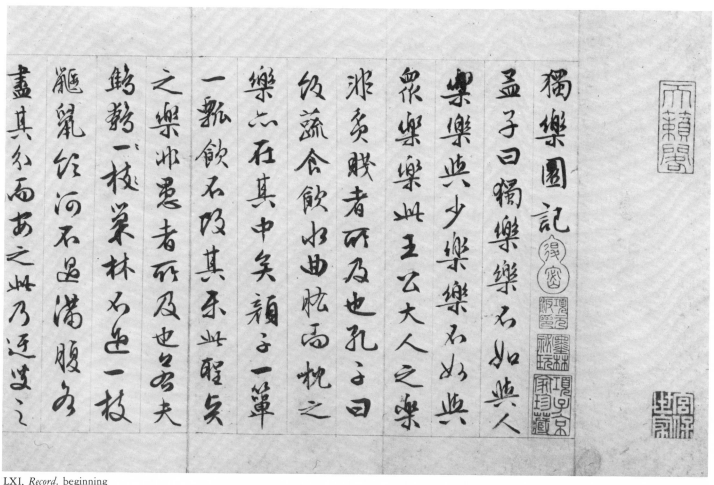

LXI, *Record*, beginning

Retreat for Fishing, Hut for Planting Bamboo

assembled in the present scroll in the seventeenth century. However, the collector who put them together, Hsiang Yü-k'uei, was the grandson of Hsiang Yüan-pien (1525–1590), the patron of Ch'iu Ying. Since the seals of that famous sixteenth-century collector are on both the painting and calligraphy in proliferation, the two works were at least in the same collection at an early date. The grandson inherited the painting. He found and bought back the calligraphy which he recognized, of course, from the seals if not personal knowledge, as having formerly been owned by his grandfather.

This garden is an imaginary garden relying on verbal records and drawing on Ch'iu Ying's ideas of Sung painting. In this respect it differs from Wen's views of the specific Suchou garden he knew so well, the Cho-cheng yüan, the Garden of the Unsuccessful Politician (no. LI). But Ssu-ma Kuang's garden was also his retreat for retirement. Poems and painting isolate, as well, separate focal points in the garden so that the experience of a Sung man predicts the experience of the Ming. Thus Wen's calligraphy of Ssu-ma's poems progresses from point to point: Hall for Reading, Retreat for Fishing, Plot for Picking Herbs, Terrace for Viewing Mountains, Pavilion for Playing with Water, Hut for Planting Bamboo, Pavilion for Watering Flowers. In the painting, Ssu-ma Kuang is shown in six of these seven points. Only in the Terrace for Viewing Mountains is he missing, although it is not difficult to sense his presence hidden within the architecture. The order of Wen's writing the poems does not follow the order of appearance in the scroll, perhaps further testimony that calligraphy and painting could not have been a close collaborative effort.

The uniqueness of Ssu-ma Kuang's garden rests in its association with a person. The Cho-cheng yüan is seen by Wen as a series of places. In *The Garden for Solitary Enjoyment* each place involves the "action" of the single individual. Focal points become alive because the same person is in each. The garden is not just a garden but the portrait of the man. In much more condensed fashion this is exactly what Wen had accomplished in his *Cassia Grove Studio* (no. XXXVII). As Wango Weng has written, "'Nothing to beseech from others; nothing to expect from without'—so Ssu-ma Kuang exulted in his feeling of independence in solitary enjoyment. For him, a garden was not merely for pleasure, but more for peace of mind."

Wen's calligraphy is very close to that of *The Red Cliff* of two years earlier (no. LVIII). It is the same kind of running script. It is similarly brushed on carefully ruled paper. There are like pressures of the brush that seem consistent with all Wen's late writing in this mode: the exposed tip, the brush often held at an angle, an interest in the slanting stroke, often an abrupt shifting from thick to thin lines. And as we have noted before, despite the running style there is an unmistakable staccato rhythm. The flow of running calligraphy is somehow broken. There is a special quality of life, of tension still in this late art. The conscious craftsman does not relinquish his touch. And there is one more painting. . . .

INSCRIPTIONS BY THE ARTIST:
[Following the *Tu-lo yüan chi*:]
Brushed in 1558, second month, fifteenth day. Cheng-ming at the age of eighty-nine.
[Following the "*Tu-lo yüan*: seven poems":]
Brushed in 1558, intercalary seventh month, thirteenth day. Cheng-ming.

SEALS OF THE ARTIST:
Wen Cheng-ming yin	[calligraphy: IV/1]
	[calligraphy: IX/1]
Heng-shan	[calligraphy: IV/2]
	[calligraphy: IX/2]

COLOPHONS AND SEALS:
Hsiang Yü-k'uei (sixteenth–seventeenth century), third grandson of Hsiang Yüan-pien; dated 1644
Ho-hsiang?	[colophon: I/1]
Wu-shan hsiu-shui chung-jen	[colophon: I/2]
Ch'en Yü-k'uei	[colophon: II/1]
Tzu-p'i fu	[colophon: II/2]
Shan-chu ch'i-feng	[colophon: II/3]
Hsiang Tzu-p'i chen-shang chai	[calligraphy: XII/2]
Tung-yeh t'ang t'u-shu chi	[calligraphy: XII/3]

Hsiang Yüan-pien (1525–1590), collector
Eleven seals appear at the beginning of the painting and thirteen at the end. Twenty-seven seals appear at the beginning, middle, and end of the calligraphy.

Weng T'ung-ho (1830–1904), scholar, collector, high government official, tutor and advisor to the emperor (cf. no. III). A colophon dated 1880 indicates that six people saw this scroll at Weng T'ung-ho's home.
Shu-p'ing hua-chien	[damask after painting: I/1]
Ch'iu-hu ko chu	[damask after painting: I/2]

Han Ch'ung (nineteenth century)
Han Ch'ung kuo-yen	[colophon: III/2]

Ch'eng Chen-i (nineteenth century)
Ch'eng Chen-i kuan	[colophon: III/3]

Weng Wan-go (present owner)
Wan-ko chen-shang	[damask after painting: II/1]
	[colophon: III/1]

Unidentified
Hsi-yen chai	[calligraphy: VI/1]
Chien-chai shih	[calligraphy: XII/1]

REMARKS: In the National Palace Museum in Taipei, there is a handscroll by Wen Cheng-ming dated the seventh month of 1558. The calligraphy and the subject matter of the painting is also the Tu-lo yüan. The painting, however, is in the style of Wang Meng (1308–1385). See *Ku-kung shu-hua lu* (1965), ch. 4/p. 195 (MH 29).

BIBLIOGRAPHY:
Weng, *Gardens in Chinese Art* (1968), pp. 10–11.

LXII. THE RED CLIFF

(Ch'ih-pi t'u)
Dated 1558, a winter's day
Hanging scroll, ink on paper, 55⅜" high and 13" wide (141.3 x 33.0 cm.)
Inscription, signature, and seals of the artist
James Freeman, Kyoto

For this final painting from the last months of 1558, Wen returns to the theme of the Red Cliff. The elements for its illustration are immediately familiar. Working from bottom to top: the introductory land, the wide expanse of space with its boat a key central point, the overhanging cliffs, the suggestions of far land, the disc of the moon, and the complete writing of the ode.

All this is layered on the thin, tall format of the hanging scroll, almost a turning-on-end of the paper whose proportions might equally have permitted it to be treated as a handscroll. This format is, of course, found early in Wen's career. We have seen it in the teens (no. XV). It allows, indeed even forces, a progressive view as one moves up the scroll from section to section.

The mode is that of the Yüan artist Wu Chen. The nature of the manner is now too familiar to repeat. It can be checked against other landscapes in this decade (nos. LIV, LV, LVI). If the format was established early, if the brush and ink are most characteristic of Wen's last decade, then treatment of space finds its surest parallels beginning with the 1540s. In such vertical scrolls there are two main levels of space. Beginning at the bottom with a stable introductory angle of land and a thin vertical line of trees one moves up the painting, receding only at a rather steep angle. In this lower part of the painting the sense of surface counteracts the inevitable tendency to retreat into the distance. Then, possibly a third of the way up the scroll, there is a marked change created by the presence of middle-distance forms. At this point the angle of recession shifts, and there is a sharp retreat directly into the distance. In this exhibition we pick up something of such a spatial organization in *Beauty in a Pavilion* (no. XLII). It is most beautifully painted in the great masterpiece, *Spring in Chiang-nan* in Taipei.[1] That it is a conscious organization appropriate only to certain hanging scrolls is clear when we compare it to others. Thus both *After Li Ch'eng's "Winter Woods"* (no. XL), and *Awaiting Snow in Winter* (no. XLIV) show, in contrast, a consistent direct recession throughout. This is because they are modeled on Li Ch'eng and recreate an exact Sung idea of space. In turn the "two-level" spatial recession depends on the Yüan. This tells us how clearly art-historical was Wen's vision. Wen's *Spring in Chiang-nan* is related to the Yüan artist Ni Tsan, just as this late *Red Cliff*

LXII, detail

is related to the Yüan artist Wu Chen. Further, we have already seen the same double space in the other late Wu Chen–style hanging scroll in this exhibition, *Village in the Rain* (no. LIV).

Returning to the year 1558, the lower part of *The Red Cliff* is certainly close enough to the brief landscapes in the album of the spring of this year (no. LIX) to affirm a consistent brush: trees with a similar touch in the thick free lines that define them; the articulation of rocks; the marked treatment of moss-dots that are loose but in convincing clumps and repeated often enough to be an insistent aspect of the design; finally the sense of space behind the foreground plane given partial definition by islands of reeds. The boat is like the boat in the Freer *Red Cliff* of 1552 (fig. 12). The figures are, however, more spare and vertical, with the added feature of the heating of wine. We last saw the slanting overhanging vertical cliff in the brief sketch of 1536 (no. XXXVI). Now a strong, rising stability reinforced by pale vertical texture-strokes is somehow allied to still-lingering angled tensions—the shape of a tree, the projecting facet of a rock. The strong pattern of dotting for the tree-leaves is closely allied to similar handling in the 1555 *Landscape after Tung Yüan and Chü-jan,* now in Hong Kong.[2] The far hills number among those distances that have been increasingly possible from the 1540s on. The calligraphy is typically late, filled with that staccato character which we have seen to be so much a part of Wen's writing in the fifties. Its position here, after the space below, brings us back to the surface. And if we linger on that surface and absorb its practiced distinct hand, its repeated wisdom points to those final things that gave "grace" to the life of the artist scholar, Wen Cheng-ming:

"Do you know how it is with the water and the moon? 'The water flows on and on like this,' but somehow it never flows away. The moon waxes and wanes, and yet in the end it's the same moon. If we look at things through the eyes of change, then there's not an instant of stillness in all creation. But if we observe the changelessness of things, then we and all beings alike have no end. . . .

". . . Only the clear breeze over the river, or the bright moon between the hills, which our ears hear as music, our eyes see beauty in—these we may take without prohibition, these we may make free with and they will never be used up. These are the endless treasures of the Creator, here for you and me to enjoy together!"

My friend was pleased and, laughing, washed the wine cups and filled them up again.

(tr. Burton Watson)

The importance of surface—most purely a matter for calligraphy—and the necessity for spatial recession—only to be realized in a landscape—are both in this latest of paintings. One cannot escape its conscious sense of design, its cool open serenity, its reduction to essentials. It is as though the calligraphy were a bamboo curtain raised in our window on a still autumn night—just a little above the moon. We once again look out upon the tradition of the gathering of selected noble men. Above all it is the affirmation of age that the heritage of times past must always be visible and real for the time that is now.

NOTE:
1. *Chinese Art Treasures* (1961), no. 97.
2. *Exhibition,* Hong Kong (1970), no. 9.

INSCRIPTION BY THE ARTIST:
[Su Shih's "First Prose Poem on the Red Cliff":]

In the autumn of the year *jen-hsü,* the seventh month, when the moon had just passed its prime, a friend and I went out in a small boat to amuse ourselves at the foot of the Red Cliff. A fresh breeze blew softy across the water, leaving the waves unruffled. As I picked up the wine jar and poured a drink for my friend, I hummed a poem to the moon and sang a phrase on its strange beauty.

In a little while, the moon rose from the eastern hills and wandered across the sky between the Archer and the Goat. White dew settled over the river, and its shining surface reached to the sky. Letting the boat go where it pleased, we drifted over the immeasurable fields of water. I felt a boundless exhilaration, as though I were sailing on the void or riding the wind and didn't know where to stop. I was filled with a lightness, as though I had left the world and were standing alone, or had sprouted wings and were flying up to join the immortals. As I drank the wine, my delight increased and, thumping the edge of the boat, I composed a song that went:

With cassia sweep and
Oars of orchid wood,
Strike the empty moon,
Row through its drifting light.
Thoughts fly far away—
I long for my loved one
In a corner of the sky.

My friend began to play on an open flute, following my song and harmonizing with it. The flute made a wailing sound, as though the player were filled with resentment or longing, or were lamenting or protesting. Long notes trailed through the night like endless threads of silk, a sound to make dragons dance in hidden caves, or to set the widow weeping in her lonely boat.

Saddened by his playing, I straightened my robe, bowed and asked, "What makes you play this way?"

He replied,

"'The moon is bright, stars grow few,
Crows and magpies fly to the south.'

That's how Ts'ao's Ts'ao's poem goes, doesn't it? There you can see Hsia-k'ou to the west, Wu-ch'ang to the east. A dense tangle of dark green, bounded by mountains and river—this is the very spot where the young Chou Yü swooped down on Ts'ao Ts'ao, isn't it? After Ts'ao Ts'ao had conquered Ching and taken Chiang-ling, he sailed down the Yangtze to the east. The stems and sterns of his ships touched for a thousand miles, and his flags and pennants blocked out the sky. He drank wine overlooking the river, laid his lance across the saddle, and wrote his poems. Surely he was the greatest hero of his time—yet where is he now?

"What then of you and me? Fishermen and wood gatherers by the banks of streams, companions to fish and crayfish, friends of deer and elk, riding this leaf of a boat, dipping gourds into the wine jar and pouring for each other—we are no more than summer flies between heaven and earth, a grain of millet on the waste of the sea! It grieves me that life is so short, and I envy the long river that never stops. If we could only link arms with the flying immortals and wander where we please, embrace the moon and grow old with it. . . . But I know that such hopes cannot quickly be fulfilled, and so I confide these lingering notes to the sad air."

I asked, "Do you know how it is with the water and the moon? 'The water flows on and on like this,' but somehow it never flows away. The moon waxes and wanes, and yet in the end it's the same moon. If we look at things through the eyes of change, then there's not an instant of stillness in all creation. But if we observe the changelessness of things, then we and all beings alike have no end. What is there to be envious about?

"Moreover, everything in the world has its owner, and if a thing doesn't belong to us, we don't dare take a hair of it. Only the clear breeze over the river, or the bright moon between the hills, which our ears hear as music, our eyes see beauty in—these we may take without prohibition, these we may make free with and they will never be used up. These are the endless treasures of the Creator, here for you and me to enjoy together!"

My friend was pleased and, laughing, washed the wine cups and filled them up again. But the fruit and other things we had brought to eat were all gone and so, among the litter of cups and bowls, we lay down in a heap in the bottom of the boat, unaware that the east was already growing light.

(tr. Burton Watson [*Su Tung-p'o* (1965), pp. 87–90])

[Signed:]
1558, on a winter's day, Cheng-ming painted and wrote this at the age of 89 *(sui)*.

SEALS OF THE ARTIST:

T'ing-yün	[painting: I/1]
Wen Cheng-ming yin	[painting: II/1]
	[painting: I/3]
Cheng-chung	[painting: I/4]

SEALS:
Chou Mo-nan (twentieth century)

Chou shih Ku-ch'in ko	[painting: I/2]

Unidentified (twentieth century?)

Ming-ts'un	[painting: III/1]
Hsiao ———	[painting: III/2]

Seals of Wen Cheng-ming

by Stephen D. Owyoung

Nearly all of the more than four hundred paintings attributed to Wen Cheng-ming bear one or more of the artist's seals. To encompass all these works is a task beyond the intent and scope of this survey. Aside from the seals which appear on paintings catalogued herein, a group of seals on works not included in this exhibition is presented, however. The selection of a greater part of these seals is based on the quality and renown of the paintings on which they are impressed; still other works are included in an effort to round out any single seal's chronology.

The occurrence of identical seals on the works of the artist, though not rare, is infrequent enough to pose a problem in many instances of formulating a distinct pattern in usage and dates. It became evident early on in this study that Wen used only twenty-three legends but many seal types. Within a single type there might be as many as eight different seals or more, all superficially resembling one another but in fact bearing subtle variations in carving. The artist's son, Wen P'eng, was a seal carver who undoubtedly created many of his father's seals on request. The fortune of having a seal carver in the family seems to have allowed Wen an uninhibited yet not indiscriminate use of a great number of seals.

The impression made by a seal is a product subject to several variables: the age of the seal, newly carved or worn with use; the inking, thin and even or thick and heavy; the amount of pressure used to stamp it; the surface on which it is pressed, whether paper or silk; and the surface beneath the painting. All affect the imprint. The most consistent feature of any seal lies in its linear configurations; any two lines will vary in appearance because of inking, stamping, pressure and receiving surface, but they will always remain in a constant and clearly recognizable structural relationship to one another and to lines surrounding them. It is this underlying structure of the seal characters which is significant in determining the similarities and differences in any comparison of seals within a seal type.

Below, seal types are arranged alphabetically. Each seal is reproduced in approximate size. Chinese characters accompany each seal type and duplicate the order in which the legend is read. In cases where the legend and reading order are the same, but the carving differs, several examples usually are given to demonstrate the wide variety of seals in a type. These seals are identified with their respective paintings either by year, collection, catalogue entry number, or in the case of undated works (n.d.), by a raised Arabic number. Matching lower-case letters appearing before paintings indicate identical seals. Paintings with asterisks are not in the exhibition; such paintings are followed by a bibliographical reference or the name of the

collection. "NPM" refers to the National Palace Museum, Taipei; letters and numbers following refer to the Photographic Archives cataloguing system. Under each type, paintings in the present exhibition and other major dated works of the artist are placed in chronological order. In some cases these dates, though far from comprehensive, suggest and help determine the longevity of a seal or type.

1547

Cheng-chung   *intaglio, rectangle*

	1535–36	*Thousand Character Essay in Four Scripts* (NPM, MH 18)
	1547	*The Art of Letters* (XLIII)
	n.d.[1]	*Mist in the Trees in the Spring Mountain* (NPM, MV 144)

1528   1541   1558 (Freer)   n.d.[4]

Cheng-chung   *relief, square*

	1502	*Landscape* (IX)
	1510	*Stone Lake* (Dubosc, *Wen Tcheng-ming*, pp. 42 and 43)
a	1520	*Orchid Album* (Dubosc, *Wen Tcheng-ming*, p. 48)
	1528	*Scholars Meeting: The Study by Old Trees* (XXIV)
c	1531	*Farewell at T'ing-yün* (XXVI)
c	1534	*Chung K'uei in Winter Woods* (NPM, MV 127)
a	1538	*Bamboo Album* (NPM, MA 13j)
d	1541	*colophon on Chrysanthemum, Rocks, and Pine* (Freer Gallery of Art)
c	1545	*Searching for Inspiration in the Empty Woods* (NPM, MV 163)
a	1543	*Master Liu's Garden* (XLI)
	1552	*The Red Cliff* (Freer Gallery of Art)
b	1555	*colophon on the Odes of Pin* (Freer Gallery of Art)
b	1558	*colophon on Cloudy Mountains* by Chen Shun (Freer Gallery of Art)
	1558	*The Red Cliff* (LXII)
a	n.d.[1]	*Beauty in a Pavilion* (XLII)
d	n.d.[2]	*Bamboo, Orchids, Rock, and Calligraphy* (XXXIV)
b	n.d.[3]	*Homeward Bound in the Snow* (NPM, MV 167)
a	n.d.[4]	*Landscape* (Private Collection, Hong Kong)
	n.d.[5]	*Huang Kung-wang's Leisurely Living at the Stream Pavilion* (VIII)

1517

1547 (XLIII)

1547 (XLIV)

n.d.³

n.d.⁴

Cheng-chung fu   *relief, square*

a	1517	*Deep Snow over Streams and Mountains* (NPM, MV 165)
a	1531	*Cascading Falls in the Pine Ravine* (fig. 10) (NPM, MV 154)
a	1535	*Thousand Character Essay in Four Scripts* (NPM, MCH 18)

1552 (Freer)

n.d.²

Cheng-chung fu yin   *intaglio, square*

b	1528–32	*Snow on a Mountain Pass* (NPM, MH 23)
b	1532	*Snow Landscape* (NPM, MV 168)
a	1548	*The Red Cliff* (NPM, MH 27)
b	1548	*Playing the Ch'in in a Secluded Valley* (XLV)
a	1552	*The Red Cliff* (Freer Gallery of Art)
	1555	*Red Bamboo* (NPM, MV 181)
a	n.d.¹	*Huang Kung-wang's Leisurely Living at the Stream Pavilion* (VIII)
b	n.d.²	*Village in the Rain* (LIV)
b	n.d.³	*Conversations in the Stream Pavilion* (NPM)

Cheng-ming   *relief, rectangle composed of two small seals*

	1508	*Traveling to T'ien-p'ing Mountain* (X)
	1528	*Tasting Tea in the Pure Shade* (XXIII)
	1528	*Scholars Meeting: the Study by Old Trees* (XXIV)
	1531	*Farewell at T'ing-yün* (XXVI)
	1531	*Old Trees by a Cold Waterfall* (XXVIII)
a	1532	*Watching the Waterfall* (XXIX)
	1532	*Sages of Mount Lu* (XXXI)
	1534	*Preparing Tea* (NPM, MV 175)
d	1535	*Snow Ride Through Mount Hu* (C.C. Wang)
c	1535–36	*Thousand Character Essay in Four Scripts* (NPM, MCH 18)
b	1536	*Lake T'ai* (Dubosc, *Wen Tcheng-ming*, p. 19)
	1542	*Peach Blossom Spring* (XXXVIII)
d	1542	*After Li Ch'eng's Winter Woods* (XL)
c	1547	*The Art of Letters* (XLIII)
b	1547	*Awaiting Snow in Winter* (XLIV)
	1552	*The Red Cliff* (LII)
a	1556	*Landscape in the style of Wu Chen* (LVI)
	1556	*Two Scholars, Old Cypress, and Waterfall* (LVII)
	1558	*Tu-lo Yüan* (NPM, MH 29)
	n.d.¹	*Landscape in Rain* (LV)
	n.d.²	*Landscape with Cypress and Waterfall* (XLVI)
d	n.d.³	*Listening to a Spring after a Good Rain* (NPM, MV 156)
	n.d.⁴	*Landscape in the Style of Wang Meng* (Crawford collection)

1548

1551 (XLIX)

1541

Cheng-ming   *intaglio, rectangle*

	1528–32	*Snow on a Mountain Pass* (NPM, MH 23)
b	1535	*Snow Ride through Mount Hu* (C.C. Wang)
b	1541	*Chrysanthemum, Rock, and Pine* (Freer Gallery of Art)
c	1546	*Winter Landscape* (Burke collection)
	1547	*Spring in Chiang-nan* (NPM, MV 142)
c	1548	*Playing the Ch'in in a Secluded Valley* (XLV)
	1548	*The Red Cliff* (NPM, MH 27)
a	1550	*Cypress and Old Rock* (XLVIII)
a	1551	*Old Trees by a Wintry Brook* (L)
a	1551	*Gathering Mulberry Leaves* (XLIX)
b	n.d.¹	*The Red Cliff* (XXV)
a	n.d.²	*Scholar Fishing* (XXXII)
a	n.d.³	*Autumn Pavilion after Rain* (NPM, VA 28e)
	n.d.⁴	*Huang Kung-wang's Leisurely Living at the Stream Pavilion* (VIII)
	n.d.⁵	*Conversations in the Stream Pavilion* (NPM, MV 158)

1536

Cheng-ming   *intaglio, square*

1508	*Cloudy Mountains* (XI)
1532	*The Seven Junipers of Ch'ang-shu* (XXX)
1533	*Calligraphy and Painting with Lu Chih* (NPM, MH 68)
1536	*Boatman by a Cliff* (XXXVI)
1544	*Springtime Wandering* (NPM, MH 25)
n.d.	*Orchid and Bamboo* (NPM, MV 180)

1520

1555

n.d.³

Heng-shan   *relief, square*

	1502	*Landscape* (IX)
b	1504	*colophon on *Two Letters* by Chao Meng-fu (NPM, YC 9)
	before	
a	1504	*Storm over the River* (II F)
c	1512	*Summer Retreat in the Eastern Grove* (XIII)
a	1520	**Orchid Album* (Dubosc, *Wen Tcheng-ming,* p. 46)
	1532	*Seven Junipers of Ch'ang-shu* (XXX)
	1535	*Rock and Chrysanthemums* (XXXV)
	1536	*Boatman by a Cliff* (XXXVI)
	1538	**Album of *Bamboo* (NPM, MA 13 h)
	1542	**Verdant Pines and Clear Springs* (NPM, MV 155)
	1543	*Master Liu's Garden* (XLI)
	1544	*Springtime Wandering* (NPM, MH 25)
	1548	*Playing the Ch'in in a Secluded Valley* (XLV)
	1551	**Scholar's Retreat* (Cheng Ch'i, Tokyo)
	1551	*Garden of the Unsuccessful Politician* (LI)
c	1552	**The Red Cliff* (Freer Gallery of Art)
	1555	**Landscape after Tung Yüan and Chü-jan (Exhibition of Paintings of the Ming and Ch'ing Periods,* p. 9)
	1556?	*The Red Cliff* (LVIII)
	1558	*Album of Painting and Calligraphy* (LIX)
b	1558	*Record of the Garden for Solitary Enjoyment:* Calligraphy (LXI)
	1558	**Tu-lo Yüan* (NPM, MH 29)
	1558	*Taoist Scripture* (LX)
	1558	*Blue-green Landscape* (Royal Ontario Museum)
	n.d.¹	*Magpies and Junipers* (XVI)
	n.d.²	*Old Pine Tree* (XVII)
c	n.d.³	*Waiting Upon the Emperor's Return from the Southern Suburbs* (XIX)
	n.d.⁴	*Great Liquid Lake* (XX)
	n.d.⁵	*Playing the Ch'in in the Shade of Pines* (XXI)

533

T'ing-yün   *relief, ellipse*

1508	**Misty Landscape (Tō Sō Gen Min meiga taikan,* II, p. 292)
1512	*Chrysanthemum, Bamboo, and Rock* (XII)
1519	**Orchid, Rock and, Bamboo* (Osaka Municipal Museum of Fine Arts)
1533	**Album of *Flowers* (NPM, MA 14 i A)

1538

1544

1558 (LIX)

1558 (Royal Ontario)

T'ing-yün   *relief, circle*

	1507	**Spring Trees after Rain* (NPM, MV 156)
a	1520	**Orchid Album* (Dubosc, *Wen Tcheng-ming,* pp. 48, 50)
a	1535	**Snowy Mountain Landscape* (NPM, MA 24)
b	1535–36	**Thousand Character Essay in Four Scripts* (NPM, MCH 18)
a	1538	**Album of Bamboo* (NPM, MA 13 e, i)
a	1540	**Landscape after Shen Chou (Chinese Painting,* VI, p. 206)
d	1544	**Springtime Wandering* (NPM, MH 25)
c	1546	**The Book of Filial Piety* with Ch'iu Ying (NPM, MH 67)
	1551	**The Red Cliff* (Princeton)
	1555	**Lofty Recluses in Mountains and Streams* (NPM, MH 22)
c	1556?	*The Red Cliff* (LVIII)
b	1558	*Album of Painting and Calligraphy* (LIX)
	1558	**Cloudy Mountains* by Ch'en Shun (Freer Gallery of Art)
c	1558	**Blue-green Landscape* (Royal Ontario Museum)
d	1558	*The Red Cliff* (LXII)
	n.d.¹	*Waiting Upon the Emperor's Return from the Southern Suburbs* (XIX)
a	n.d.²	*Beauty in a Pavilion* (XLII)

1545

1551

T'ing-yün   *intaglio, square*

a	1531	*Farewell at T'ing-yün* (XXVI)
a	1542	*After Li Ch'eng's Winter Woods* (XL)
a	1545	**Searching for Poetic Inspiration in the Empty Forest* (NPM, MV 163)
b	1547	*Awaiting Snow in Winter* (XLIV)
b	1551	*Old Trees by a Wintry Brook* (L)

1546

n.d.

T'ing-yün kuan   *intaglio, square*

	1546	*Shen Chou/Wen Cheng-ming Joint Handscroll* (III)
	1549	**Old Trees by a Cold Waterfall* (NPM, MV 157)
	n.d.	*Brewing Tea on a Spring Evening* (XXVII)
a	1520	**Orchid Album* (Dubosc, *Wen Tcheng-ming*, p. 52)
	1548	**West Tung-t'ing Mountain* (NPM, MV 164)
	1558	**Blue-green Landscape* (Royal Ontario Museum)
a	n.d.	*Beauty in a Pavilion* (XLII)

n.d.²   n.d.³

T'ing-yün sheng   *intaglio, square*

	1502	*Landscape* (IX)
	before	
a	1504	*Storm over the River* (II F)
	1532	*Sages of Mount Lu* (XXXI)
	1547	**Spring in Chiang-nan* (NPM, MV 142)
a	n.d.¹	**Autumn Mountains* (Dubosc, *Mostra d'arte cinese*, 808)
a	n.d.²	*The Cassia Grove Studio* (XXXVII)
a	n.d.³	**colophon on T'ang Yin's *Journey to Nanking* (Freer Gallery of Art)

1502   1520

Wei keng-yin wu i chiang   *relief, rectangle*

	1502	*Landscape* (IX)
	1519	**Orchid, Rock, and Bamboo* (Osaka Municipal Museum of Fine Arts)
a	1520	**Orchid Album* (Dubosc, *Wen Tcheng-ming*, p. 52)
	1548	**West Tung-t'ing Mountain* (NPM, MV 164)
	1558	**Blue-green Landscape* (Royal Ontario Museum)
a	n.d.	*Beauty in a Pavilion* (XLII)

n.d.

Wen Cheng-ming Chung-fu   *square, intaglio*

	n.d.	*Letters Home from Peking:* Calligraphy (XVIII)

1502   1508   1531   1558

n.d.⁹   n.d.¹⁴   n.d.¹⁵   n.d.¹⁸

Wen Cheng-ming yin   *intaglio, square*

h	1502	*Landscape* (IX)
e	1507	**Spring Trees after Rain* (NPM, MV 146)
b	1508	*Cloudy Mountains* (XI)
d	1510	**Stone Lake* (Dubosc, *Wen Tcheng-ming*, p. 43)
f	1515	*Summer Retreat in the Eastern Grove* (XIII)
d	1520	**Orchid Album* (Dubosc, *Wen Tcheng-ming*, p. 49)
	1528	*Scholars Meeting: The Study by Old Trees* (XXIV)
a	1531	**Cascading Falls in the Pine Ravine* (fig. 10) (NPM, MV 15
a	1531	*Old Trees by a Cold Waterfall* (XXVIII)
g	1532	*Seven Junipers of Ch'ang-shu* (XXX)
	1532	*Sages of Mount Lu* (XXXI)
d	1533	**Album of *Flowers* (NPM, MA 14 i A)
h	1534	**Chung K'uei in Winter Woods* (NPM, MV 177)
	1535	*Rock and Chrysanthemums* (XXXV)
d	1536	**Quiet Fishing by Trees and Streams* (NPM, MV 170)
a	1541	**Chrysanthemums, Rock and Pine* (Freer Gallery of Art)
a	1542	*After Li Ch'eng's Winter Woods* (XL)
d	1542	**Verdant Pines and Clear Springs* (NPM, MV 155)
d	1543	*Master Liu's Garden* (XLI)
g	1545	colophon on *Walking in Spring* by Shen Chou (Fre Gallery of Art)
b	1546	*Shen Chou/Wen Cheng-ming Joint Handscroll* (III)
b	1547	*Awaiting Snow in Winter* (XLIV)
	1549	**Old Tree by a Cold Waterfall* (NPM, MV 157)
	1549	*Magnolia* (XLVII)
	1551	**The Red Cliff* (Princeton)
	1551	*Garden of the Unsuccessful Politician* (LI)
c	1552	**The Red Cliff* (Freer Gallery of Art)
	1552	*Landscapes and Plants* (LIII)
g	1554	**Elegant Pleasures of Groves and Springs* (NPM, MH 30)
b	1555	**Landscape after Tung Yüan and Chü-jan* (*Exhibition Paintings from the Ming and Ch'ing Periods*, p. 9)
	1555	**colophon on the *Odes of Pin* (Freer Gallery of Art)
	1555	**Red Bamboo* (NPM, MV 181)
	1555	**colophon on *Lofty Recluses in Mountains and Strea (NPM, MH 22)
	1556?	*The Red Cliff* (LVIII)
e	1558	*Album of Painting and Calligraphy* (LIX)
	1558	**colophon on *Tu-lo Yüan* (NPM, MH 29)

	1558	*Taoist Scripture* (LX)
b	1558	*Record of the Garden for Solitary Enjoyment* (LXI)
a, g	1558	*The Red Cliff* (LXII)
	1558	**Blue-green Landscape* (Royal Ontario Museum)
	n.d.[1]	*Autumn Mountains* (XIV)
	n.d.[2]	*Mountain Landscape* (XV)
a	n.d.[3]	*Brewing Tea on a Spring Evening* (XXVII)
b	n.d.[4]	*Playing the Ch'in in the Shade of the Pines* (XXI)
d	n.d.[5]	*Beauty in a Pavilion* (XLII)
	n.d.[6]	*Old Pine Tree* (XVII)
	n.d.[7]	*Listening to the Bamboo* (XXXIII)
a	n.d.[8]	*Bamboo, Orchids, Rock, and Calligraphy* (XXXIV)
c	n.d.[9]	*Waiting Upon the Emperor's Return from the Southern Suburbs* (XIX)
	n.d.[10]	*Great Liquid Lake* (XX)
d	n.d.[11]	**Landscape after an Old Master* (NPM, MV 173)
d	n.d.[12]	**I-ch'üan* (NPM, MH 26)
d	n.d.[13]	**Imitating Wu Chen's Landscape* (NPM, MH 28)
f	n.d.[14]	*Autumn Mountains* (XIV)
g	n.d.[15]	**Album of Flowers* (H.C. Weng)
g	n.d.[16]	**Snow Landscape* (NPM, MV 169)
	n.d.[17]	**Winter Forest in Flying Snow* (Indianapolis Museum of Art)
	n.d.[18]	**Landscape* (private collection, Hong Kong)

1508   1558

Wen Cheng-ming yin   *intaglio, square*

a	1499	**colophon on *Autumn Landscape of T'ung-kuan* (Boston)
	before	
	1504	*Storm over the River* (II F)
b	1508	*Cloudy Mountains* (XI)
c	1520	**Orchid Album* (Dubosc, *Wen Tcheng-ming*, p. 47)
a	1558	*Album of Painting and Calligraphy* (LIX)
b	n.d.	**colophon on *Lady Pan Holds the Autumn Fan* by T'ang Yin (NPM, MV 122)
b	n.d.	**Listening to the Spring Beneath Pines* (NPM, MV 465)

1556?   n.d.[2]

Wen Cheng-ming yin   *intaglio, square*

	1551	*Scholar's Retreat* (Cheng Ch'i collection, Tokyo)
	1555	**colophon on the *Odes of Pin* (Freer Gallery of Art)
a	1556?	*The Red Cliff* (LVIII)
a	n.d.[1]	*Playing the Ch'in in the Shade of Pines* (XXI)
a	n.d.[2]	*Old Pine Tree* (XVII)

1507   1552   1558

Wen Chung-tzu   *intaglio, square*

	1507	**Spring Trees after Rain* (NPM, MV 146)
	1546	**The Book of Filial Piety* with Ch'iu Ying (NPM, MH 67)
	1552	**The Red Cliff* (Freer Gallery of Art)
	1558	*Album of Painting and Calligraphy* (LIX)

1502

Wen Pi Cheng-ming   *intaglio, square*

| | 1502 | *Landscape* (IX) |
| | n.d. | **on *Cheng-shou Hall* by T'ang Yin (Contag and Wang, p. 22, no. 34) |

1507   1508 (Osaka)   1508 (XI)

Wen Pi yin   *intaglio, square*

	before	
	1504	*Storm over the River* (II F)
a	1507	**Spring Trees after Rain* (NPM, MV 147)
	1508	**Cloudy Mountains* (Osaka Municipal Museum of Fine Arts)
	1508	*Cloudy Mountains* (XI)
	1512	*Chrysanthemum, Bamboo, and Rock* (XII)
a	n.d.	**colophon on *Journey to Nanking* by T'ang Yin (Freer Gallery of Art)
	n.d.	**colophon on *Lady Pan Holds the Autumn Fan* by T'ang Yin (NPM, MV 122)

1541   1549   n.d.³   1552

Wu-yen shih yin   *intaglio, square*

	1502 before	Landscape (IX)
b	1504	Storm over the River (II F)
	1508	Cloudy Mountains (XI)
a	1512	Chrysanthemum, Bamboo, and Rock (XII)
	1520	*Orchid Album (Dubosc, Wen Tcheng-ming, p. 46)
a	1528–32	*Snow on a Mountain Pass (NPM, MH 23)
c	1532	Seven Junipers of Ch'ang-shu (XXX)
a	1534	*Chung K'uei in Winter Woods (NPM, MV 177)
b	1535–39	*Snowy Mountain Landscape (NPM, MH 24)
a	1535	*Snow Ride through Mount Hu (H.C. Wang)
a	1536	*Thousand Character Essay in Four Scripts (NPM, MCH 18)
b	1540	*Landscape after Shen Chou (Sirén, Chinese Painting, vol. 6, p. 206)
a	1541	*Chrysanthemum, Rock, and Pine (Freer Gallery of Art)
b	1548	Playing the Ch'in in a Secluded Valley (XLV)
c	1549	Magnolia (XLVII)
	n.d.¹	Mountain Landscape (XV)
a	n.d.²	The Red Cliff (XXV)
b	n.d.³	Village in the Rain (LIV)
	n.d.⁴	*Snow Landscape (NPM, MV 168)

n.d.²

Yen-men shih chia   *intaglio, square*

	1527	*Returning in the Rain (NPM, VA 27j)
	n.d.¹	Autumn Landscape (XIV)
	n.d.²	*Calligraphy by Li Tung-yang (NPM)

1533

Yü-ch'ing shan fang   *intaglio, rectangle*

	1533	*Flower Album (NPM, MA 14 i A)
a	1533	*Mallow (NPM, VA 30f)
a	n.d.	*Orchid and Bamboo (NPM, MV 180)

1552

Yü-ch'ing shan fang   *relief, rectangle*
(this seal usually cut in intaglio)

     1552   Landscapes and Plants (LIII)

1551   n.d.²

Yü-lan t'ang   *intaglio, square*

	1508	Traveling to T'ien-p'ing Mountain (X)
	1548	*West Tung-t'ing Mountain (NPM, MV 164)
	1551	Garden of the Unsuccessful Politician (LI)
	n.d.¹	*Landscape Fan (Metropolitan Museum of Art)
	n.d.²	*Album of Flowers, Bamboo, and Rocks (H.C. Weng)

n.d.

Yü-lan t'ang t'u-shu chi   *rectangle, relief*

     n.d.   Letters Home from Peking: Calligraphy (XVIII)

1543   1552   n.d.

Yü-lan t'ang yin   *relief, square*

	1533	*Painting and Calligraphy with Lu Chih (NPM, MH 68)
	1534	*Preparing Tea (NPM, MV 175)
	1543	Master Liu's Garden (XLI)
	1552	Landscapes and Plants (LIII)
	n.d.	Letters Home from Peking: Calligraphy (XVIII)

Bibliography, Maps, and Index

Bibliography

An Ch'i. *Mo-Yüan hui-kuan* (Ink-remains, examined and classified). Peking, 1742. 1908 ed.

The Arts of the Ming Dynasty. Detroit Institute of Art, Detroit, 1952.

The Arts of the Ming Dynasty. The Arts Council of Great Britain, London, 1958.

Barnhart, Richard. *Wintry Forests, Old Trees: Some Landscape Themes in Chinese Painting.* China Institute, New York, 1972.

Birch, Cyril, tr. "T'ao Ch'ien: Peach Blossom Spring." In *Anthology of Chinese Literature from Early Times to the Fourteenth Century.* Edited by Cyril Birch. New York, 1965.

Bush, Susan. *The Chinese Literati on Painting: Su Shih (1037–1101) to Tung Ch'i-ch'ang (1555–1636).* Harvard-Yenching Institute Studies, XXVII. Cambridge, Mass., 1971.

Cahill, James. *Chinese Painting.* Skira, Geneva, 1960.

Chang An-chih. *Wen Cheng-ming.* Shanghai, 1959.

Chang Ch'ou. *Chen-chi jih-lu* (Daily records of authenticity). [Seventeenth century.] 1918 ed.

Chiang Chao-shen. "Wen Cheng-ming nien p'u" (The Life of Wen Cheng-ming). *Ku-kung chi-k'an,* V (1971), no. 4, pp. 39–88; VI (1972), no. 1, pp. 31–80; no. 2, pp. 45–75; no. 3, pp. 49–80; no. 4, pp. 67–109.

————. "Yang Chi-ching and the Wu School of Painters." *The National Palace Museum Bulletin,* VIII (1973), no. 3, pp. 1–13.

Chiao-yü-pu ti-erh-tz'u ch'üan-kuo mei-shu chan-lan-hui chuan chi (A special collection of the Second National Exhibition of Chinese Art under the Auspices of the Ministry of Education). Commercial Press, Shanghai, 1943.

Chinese Art. Smith College Museum, Northampton, 1962.

Chinese Art Treasures [exhibition of art from the National Palace Museum in the United States, 1961–62]. Skira, Geneva, 1961.

Chinese Painting from the Chang Erh-shih Collection. Parke-Bernet, New York, 1971.

Chu Chih-ch'ih. *Chu Wo-an ts'ang shu-hua mu* (List of paintings and calligraphy owned by Chu Wo-an). In *Mei-shu ts'ung-shu,* vol. 62. Shanghai, 1928.

Chūgoku bijutsu gosennen ten, Osaka Municipal Museum of Fine Arts (Exhibition of 5,000 years of Chinese Art). Asahi Shimbunsha, Osaka, 1966.

Chūgoku kaiga mokuroku (Catalogue of Chinese paintings, Abe Collection). Osaka, 1954.

Chūgoku meigashu (Collection of famous Chinese paintings). 8 vols. Ryubundō, Tokyo, 1935.

Chung-kuo hua-chia jen-ming ta tz'u-tien (Biographical dictionary of Chinese painters). Compiled by Sun Ta-kung. Shanghai, 1934.

Chung-kuo jen-ming ta tz'u-tien (Dictionary of Chinese biographical names). Shanghai, 1931.

Chung-kuo li-tai shu-hua chuan-k'o chia tzu-hao so-ying (Index to aliases of Chinese artists in the past generations). Hong Kong, 1968.

Chung-kuo ming-hua (Famous Chinese paintings). 42 vols. Yu-cheng Book Co., Shanghai, 1926.

Chung-kuo ming-hua chi (Famous Chinese paintings collected by the P'ing-teng ko). 2 vols. Yu-cheng Book Co., Shanghai, 1934.

Clapp, Anne De Coursey. *Wen Cheng-ming: The Ming Artist and Antiquity.* Artibus Asiae, Ascona, 1975.

————. "Wen Cheng-ming: the Ming Artist and Antiquity." Vol. 2 (Lists). Harvard University doctoral dissertation, 1971.

Contag, Victoria, and Wang, Chi-ch'ien. *Seals of Chinese Painters and Collectors of the Ming and Ch'ing Periods.* Hong Kong, 1966.

Dubosc, Jean-Pierre. *Great Chinese Painters of the Ming and Ch'ing Dynasties.* Wildenstein, New York, 1949.

————. *Mostra d'arte cinese, Venezia: Settimo centenario di Marco Polo.* Venice, 1954.

————. *Mostra di pittura cinese delle dinastie Ming e Ch'ing.* Instituto Italiano per il medio ed estremo oriente, Rome, 1950.

————. "A New Approach to Chinese Painting." *Oriental Art,* III (1950), pp. 50–57.

————. *Les Quatre grands peintres de la dynastie des Ming, XVe et XVIe siècles.* Collections Baur, Geneva, 1966.

————. *Wen Tcheng-ming et son école.* Maurice Bridel, Lausanne, 1961.

Ecke, Gustav. *Chinese Painting in Hawaii.* 3 vols. Honolulu, 1965.

Ecke, Tseng Yu-ho. *Chinese Calligraphy.* Philadelphia Museum of Art, Philadelphia, 1971.

————. "The Seven Junipers of Wen Cheng-ming." *Archives of the Chinese Art Society of America,* VIII (1954), pp. 22–30.

————. "Wen Cheng-ming." In *Encyclopedia of World Art,* vol. 14. McGraw Hill, New York, 1967.

Edwards, Richard. *The Field of Stones.* Freer Gallery of Art, Washington, D.C., 1962.

————. "Pine, Hibiscus and Examination Failures." *Bulletin,* The University of Michigan Museum of Art, I (1965–66), pp. 15–28.

Exhibition of Paintings of the Ming and Ch'ing Periods. City Museum and Art Gallery, Hong Kong, 1970.

Fang, Achilles, trans. "Rhymeprose on Literature: The *Wen-fu* of Lu Chi (A.D. 261–303)." *Harvard Journal of Asiatic Studies,* XIV (1951), pp. 527–546.

Ferguson, John C. *Li-tai chu-lu hua-mu* (Catalogue of recorded paintings of successive dynasties). Nanking, 1934.

Five Hundred Years of Tradition: Chinese Painting of Fifteenth to Twentieth Century. Mi Chou Gallery, New York, 1962.

Fourcade, François. *Art Treasures of the Peking Museum.* Abrams, New York, n.d.

Fu, Marilyn and Shen. *Studies in Connoisseurship: Chinese Paintings from the Arthur M. Sackler Collection.* Princeton, 1973.

Giuganino, Alberto. *La pittura cinese.* 2 vols. Rome, 1959.

The Grand Tradition: Chinese and Japanese Calligraphy. The University of Michigan Museum of Art, Ann Arbor, 1975.

Gyllensvärd, Bo. "Some Chinese Paintings in the Ernest Erickson Collection." *Bulletin of the Museum of Far Eastern Antiquities,* XXXVI (1964), pp. 159–170.

Hao-ku t'ang chia ts'ang shu-hua chi (Hao-Ku t'ang collection of painting and calligraphy). Taipei, 1969 ed.

Hashimoto Sueyoshi. *Hashimoto shuzo Min Shin ga mokuroku* (Catalogue of Ming and Ch'ing Paintings in the Hashimoto Collection). Kadokawa Shoten, Tokyo, 1972.

Hawkes, David. *Ch'u tz'u: the Songs of the South.* Oxford, 1962.

Hsüan-hui t'ang shu-hua lu (Record of calligraphy and painting in the Hsüan-hui t'ang). 2 vols. Hong Kong, 1972.

Hua-yüan to-ying (Gems). Compiled by Hsü Shen-yü. 3 vols. Shanghai, 1955.

Hummel, Arthur H. *Eminent Chinese of the Ch'ing Period (1644–1912).* Washington, 1943–44. Reprint, Taipei, 1964.

Imaseki Tempo. "Bun Chomei hyoden" (Life of Wen Cheng-ming). *Kokka,* nos. 475 (1930), pp. 168–172; 476 (1930), pp. 197–203.

Ku Wen-pin. *Kuo-yün lou shu-hua chi.* 1882.

Ku-kung shu-hua lu. 4 vols. Taipei, 1965.

K'ung Kuang-t'ao. *Yüeh-hsüeh lou shu-hua lu* (Record of painting and calligraphy from the Yüeh-hsüeh lou). 5 vols. 1907.

Laing, E. J. *Chinese Paintings in Chinese Publications, 1956–1968.* Ann Arbor, 1969.

Ledderose, Lothar. "An Approach to Chinese Calligraphy." *National Palace Museum Bulletin,* VII, no. 1 (1972), pp. 1–13.

Lee, Sherman and Ho, Wai-kam. *Chinese Art under the Mongols: The Yüan Dynasty (1279–1368).* Cleveland, 1968.

Lee, Sherman. *Chinese Landscape Painting.* Cleveland, 1962.

————. *Colors of Ink.* Asia House Gallery, New York, 1973.

————. "Literati and Professionals: Four Ming Painters." *The Bulletin of The Cleveland Museum of Art,* LIII, no. 1 (1966), pp. 2–25.

Li, Chu-tsing. *A Thousand Peaks and Myriad Ravines: Chinese Paintings in the Charles A. Drenowatz Collection.* 2 vols. Artibus Asiae, Ascona, 1974.

Li Lin-ts'an. "Huang Kung-wang's 'Chiu chu feng ts'ui' and 'T'ieh-yai t'u'." *National Palace Museum Bulletin,* VII, no. 6 (1973), pp. 1–9.

———. "Pine and Rock, Wintry Tree, Old Tree and Bamboo and Rock: The Development of a Theme." *National Palace Museum Bulletin,* IV, no. 6 (1970), pp. 1–12.

Liao-ning-sheng po-wu-kuan ts'ang-hua chi (A collection of paintings from the Liao-ning Provincial Museum). Peking, 1962.

Loehr, Max. *Chinese Art: Symbols and Images.* Wellesley, Mass., 1967.

———. "A Landscape Attributed to Wen Cheng-ming." *Artibus Asiae,* XXII (1959), pp. 143–152.

Lu Chün. *Sung Yüan i-lai hua-jen hsing-shih lu* (Record of painters from Sung and Yüan on). 1829.

Lu Hsin-yüan. *Jang-li kuan kuo-yen lu* (Record of what passed before the eyes of the Jang-li kuan). Wu-hsing, 1891.

March, Benjamin. *Some Technical Terms of Chinese Painting.* Baltimore, 1935.

Masterpieces of Asian Art in American Collections II. Asia House Gallery, New York, 1970.

Min Shin no kaiga (Paintings of the Ming and Ch'ing). National Museum, Benrido, Tokyo, 1964.

Min shitaika gafu (Paintings of four great Ming masters). Hakubundō, Osaka, 1924.

Ming-Ch'ing Dynasties A.D. 1368–1644, 1644–1912. The Art Institute of Chicago, 1964.

Ming-jen chuan chi tz'u-liao so-ying (Index of Ming biographies). 2 vols. National Central Library, Taipei, 1965.

Munsterberg, Hugo. *The Landscape Painting of China and Japan.* Rutland, Vermont, 1955.

Na Chih-liang. *Hsi-yin t'ung-shih* (General explanation of seals). Taipei, 1970.

Nakamura Hideo. "Bun Chomei ippa ni tsuite" (Wen Cheng-ming and artists of his school). *Museum,* no. 55 (1955), pp. 5–8.

One Thousand Years of Chinese Painting: T'ang to Ch'ing. Indiana University Art Museum, Bloomington, 1968.

"Oriental Art Recently Acquired by American Museums." *Archives of the Chinese Art Society of America,* various years, 1950–65; *Archives of Asian Art,* 1966–75.

Osaka Exchange Exhibition: Paintings from the Abe Collection and other Masterpieces of Chinese Art. Osaka Municipal Museum of Fine Arts and San Francisco Center of Asian Art and Culture, 1970.

Ostasiatiska Museet. Museum of Far Eastern Antiquities, Stockholm, 1963.

P'an Cheng-wei. *T'ing-fan lou shu-hua chi* (Notes on calligraphy and painting of the T'ing-fan lou). In *Mei-shu ts'ung-shu,* Taipei, 1974 ed., IV/7, pp. 1–666.

P'ei-wen chai shu-hua p'u (Encyclopedia of painting and calligraphy). 1708. Reprinted Taipei, 1969.

Pien Yung-yü (1645–1712), comp. *Shih-ku t'ang shu-hua hui kao* (Classification and examination of painting and calligraphy). Preface 1682. 1921 ed.

Shih-ch'ü pao-chi ch'u pien (Ch'ien-lung collection, part one). 1744. Shanghai, 1918 ed.

Shih-ch'ü pao-chi hsü-pien (Ch'ien-lung collection, continuation). Compiled by Wang Chieh. 1793. 1948 ed.

Shih-ch'ü pao-chi san pien (Ch'ien-lung collection, part three). Taipei, 1969 ed.

Shodo zenshu (Complete collection of Chinese and Japanese calligraphy). Edited by Kanda Kichijiro and Tanaka Takami et al. 25 vols. Heibonsha, Tokyo, 1954–61.

Sickman, Laurence, ed. *Chinese Calligraphy and Painting in the Collection of John M. Crawford, Jr.* New York, 1962.

Sickman, Laurence, and Soper, Alexander. *The Art and Architecture of China.* Baltimore, 1968.

Signatures and Seals on Painting and Calligraphy. Vol. 2. The Arts and Literature Press, Hong Kong, 1964.

Sirén, Osvald. *Chinese Painting: Leading Masters and Principles.* 7 vols. New York, 1956–58.

———. *A History of Later Chinese Painting.* 2 vols. London, 1938.

Sōraikan kinshō (Chinese Paintings in the Collection of Abe Fusajirō). 6 vols. 1930–39.

Su-chou fu-chih (Gazetteer of Suchou). In *Chung-kuo fang-chih ts'ung-shu,* no. 5. 1883. Ch'eng-wen reprint, Taipei.

Sugimura Yuzo. "Bun Chomei to sono kankyo" (Life of Wen Cheng-ming). *Yamato Bunka,* no. 29 (April, 1959), pp. 27–34.

Sullivan, Michael. *An Introduction to Chinese Art.* Berkeley, 1961.

Suzuki Kei, "Bun Chomei to Goha bunjinga" (Wen Cheng-ming and literati paintings of the Wu School). *Museum,* no. 151 (Oct., 1963), pp. 6–10.

1000 Jahre Chinesische Malerei. Haus der Kunst, Munich, 1959.

Tōanzō shogafu (Catalogue of the Saito collection). 4 vols. Compiled by Naitō Torajirō, Osaka, 1928.

Tomita, Kojirō, and Tseng, Hsien-ch'i, *Portfolio of Chinese Paintings in the Museum: Yüan to Ch'ing Periods.* Museum of Fine Arts, Boston, 1961.

Tseng, Hsien-ch'i. *Loan Exhibition of Chinese Paintings.* Royal Ontario Museum of Archaeology, Toronto, 1956.

Van Gulik, R. H. *The Gibbon in China.* Leiden, 1967.

Wang K'o-yü. *Shan-hu-wang hua-lu* (Record of paintings in the Coral Net). Preface 1643.

Wang Shih-chen. *Yen-chou shan-jen ssu-pu-kao.* Preface 1577. Ching-t'ang edition.

Watson, Burton, tr. *Selections from a Sung Dynasty Poet: Su Tung-p'o.* New York, 1966.

Wen Cheng-ming. *Cho-cheng yüan shih-hua ts'e.* 2 vols. Chung-hua album, 1929.

———. *Fu-t'ien-chi* (The writings of Wen Cheng-ming). 36 chüan. Ca. 1574. Central Library facsimile of Ming edition, Taipei, 1968.

Wen Cheng-ming ch'üan-chi (Fu-t'ien chi). Reprinted Shanghai, 1935.

Wen Cheng-ming hui-kao (Compilation of writings by Wen Cheng-ming). 2 vols. Shen-chou kuo-kuang-she, Shanghai, 1929.

Wen Chia. *Ch'ien-shan t'ang shu-hua chi* (Record of calligraphy and painting at the Ch'ien-shan t'ang). 1569. In *Mei-shu ts'ung-shu,* II/6, pp. 39–64.

Wen shih tsu-p'u (Wen family geneology). In *Ch'u-shih ts'ung-shu.* Prefaced by P'eng Ku-sun. Suchou, 1929.

Wen shih wu-chia chi (Collections of five members of the Wen family). Preface 1770. In *Ssu-k'u ch'üan-shu.* Shanghai, 1934–1935 ed.

Weng Fang-kang. *Fu-ch'u chai wen-chi* (Weng Fang-kang's collected writings). In *Chin-t'ai Chung-kuo shih-liao ts'ung-k'an,* vol. 421, nos. 1-3. Taipei, 1966.

Weng, Wango H.C. *Gardens in Chinese Art.* China Institute, New York, 1968.

Whitfield, Roderick *In Pursuit of Antiquity: Chinese Paintings of the Ming and Ch'ing Dynasties from the Collection of Mr. and Mrs. Earl Morse.* Princeton, 1969.

Wilson, Marc, and Wong, Kwan S. *Friends of Wen Cheng-ming: a View from the Crawford Collection.* China Institute, New York, 1974.

Yonezawa Yoshiho. "Autumnal Landscape among the Hills by Shen Chou." *Kokka,* no. 894 (1966), pp. 37–45.

———, ed. *Chugoku bijitsu* (Arts of China). Vol. 3. Kodansha, Tokyo, 1965. English translation: *Arts of China: Paintings in Chinese Museums, New Collections.* Kodansha, Tokyo, 1970.

Yü Feng-ch'ing. *Yü shih shu-hua t'i-pa chi* (Yü family collection of colophons on painting and calligraphy). 1634.

Suchou Environs

Other names for places located on the map: Chih-p'ing Temple (contains Shih-hu ts'ao-t'ang); Leng-ch'ieh shan (Shang-fang shan); Leng-ch'ieh Temple (contains Shih-hu ts'ao-t'ang); Lin-wu shan (West Tung-t'ing shan); Pao shan (West Tung-t'ing shan); Pao-en shan (Chih-hsing shan); Tung-t'ing shan (West Tung-t'ing shan); and West Mountain (West Tung-t'ing shan).

Important contemporaries of Wen Cheng-ming and the places where they at times resided: Ch'en Shun (Ning-ts'ui-lou and Ta-yao-tu); Chou T'ien-ch'iu (Chih-hsing shan); Hsü Chin (West Tung-t'ing shan); Lu Chih (Tien Bridge at Chih-hsing shan and West Tung-t'ing shan); Shen Chou (Hsiang-ch'eng); Ts'ai Yü (West Tung-t'ing shan); Wang Ao (East Tung-t'ing shan); Wang Chih-teng (Chih-hsing shan); Wang Ch'ung (Ning-ts'ui-lou); Wen Cheng-ming (Ning-ts'ui-lou); Yang Hsün-chi (Chih-hsing shan); and Yüan Chih (Heng-t'ang).

A memorial shrine (the Wu-hsien tz'u) for T'ang Chen, T'ang Yin, Wang Ch'ung, Wang Shou, and Wen Cheng-ming is located in the Chih-p'ing Temple.

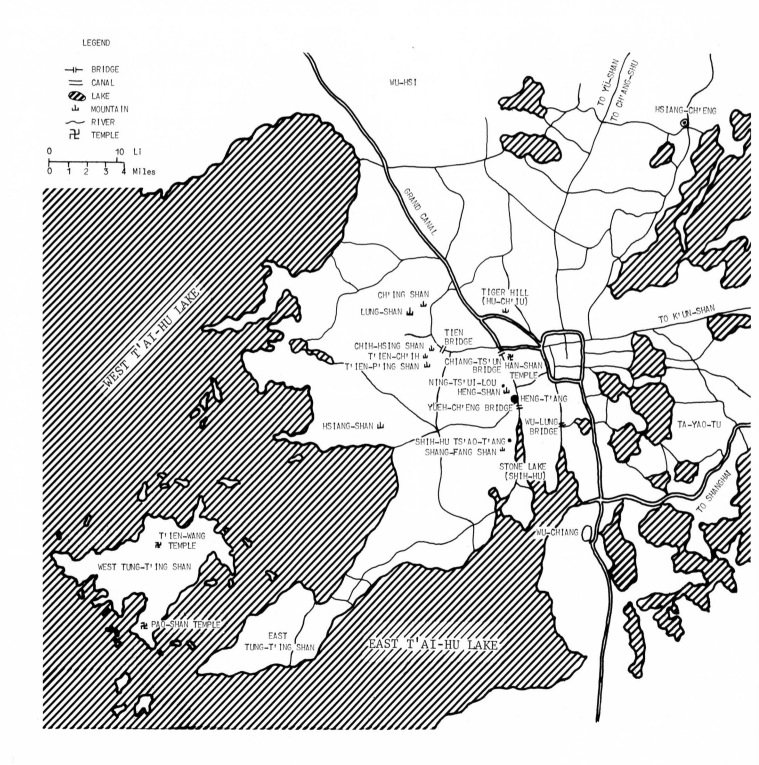

Suchou

The following is a list of famous people and the places marked on the map at or near which they lived: Chou T'ien-ch'iu (Ho-feng-ts'ang); Hsü Chen-ch'ing (Ta-li district); Li Ying-chen (T'ung-kuan district); Liu Chüeh (Ch'i-men); T'ang Yin (T'ao-hua-wu); Tu Ch'iung (Le-p'u, also known as Tung-yüan); Wang Ao (I-lao-yüan); Wang Chih-teng (Tsun-sheng-chai); Wang Ku-hsiang (Ho-tsan district); Wu I (Tung-chuang); Wu K'uan (Shang-shu district and Tung-chuang); Wen Cheng-ming (San-t'iao bridge, a local name for the Te-ch'ing, Lu-t'i-hsing, and Ch'ung-li bridges); Yüan Chih (Pao-lin temple); and Yüan Tsun-ni (Pao-lin temple).

A funerary shrine for Hsü Chin was at the K'ai-yüan temple, and one for Wen Cheng-ming was at the Fu school.

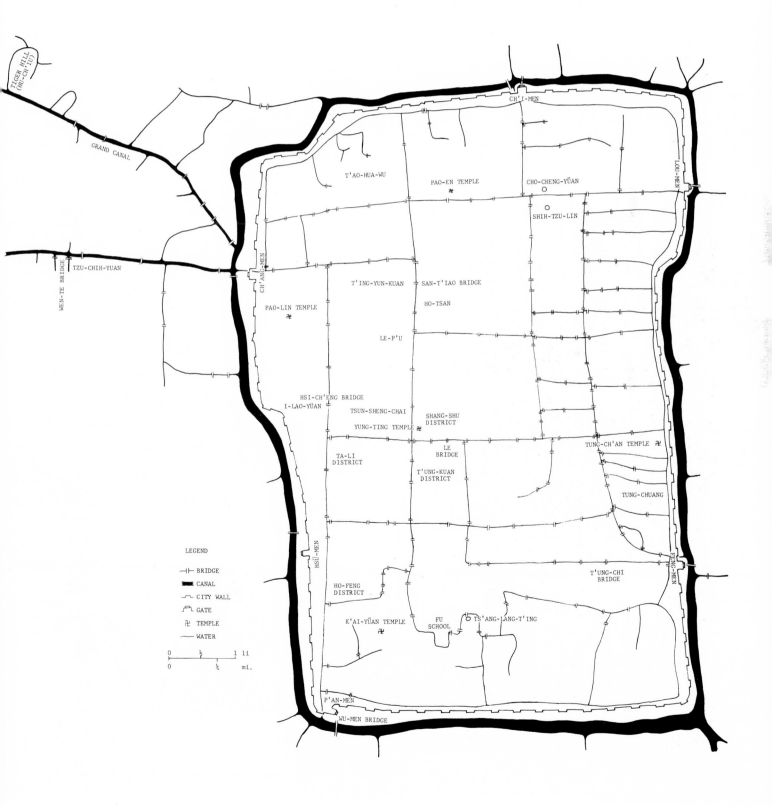

Index

232

Photographs of works in the exhibition have been supplied by the lenders or lending institutions, except for III, details (Richard Edwards), VI (Princeton University), VIII (The University of Michigan Museum of Art), IX (Chozo Yamanouchi), LI (Princeton University). The National Palace Museum, Taipei has kindly granted permission to reproduce the following illustrations of works in its collection: figs. a, b, d, 1, 2, 3, 8, 9, 10, 11, 13, 15, 16, 17, 18, 19, 20, 21, 24, 27, and 28. Sources for the other figures are as follows: c *(Hua-yüan to-ying [Gems]*, II, no. 11); 4 (Edwards, *Field of Stones,* pl. 20B); 5 (Richard Edwards); 6 *(Gems,* I, no. 29); 7 (courtesy of the Musée Guimet, Paris); 14 *(Gems,* II, no. 10); 22 *(Min Shin no kaiga,* pl. 6); 23 *(Shodō Zenshu,* IV, pl. 9); 25 (courtesy Museum of Fine Arts, Boston); 26 (Stephen Addiss, after photographic archives, Princeton University). The maps were produced by James Robinson and the Freer Gallery of Art.